THE GARDEN

SOURCEBOOK

GENERAL EDITOR: Caroline Boisset

THE GARDEN SOURCEBOOK

THE ESSENTIAL GUIDE TO PLANNING AND PLANTING

MITCHELL BEAZLEY

THE GARDEN SOURCEBOOK

Edited and designed by
Mitchell Beazley International Ltd
Michelin House
81 Fulham Road
London SW3 6RB

Editors Emily Wright, Simon Ryder,
   David Joyce, Richard Rosenfeld
Designers Jeremy Roots, Geoff Fennell
Senior Art Editors Larraine Lacey, Mike Brown
Editorial Assistant Jaspal Bhangra
Production Controller Sarah Schuman
Commissioned Photography Sue Atkinson,
   Paul Barker
Commissioned Artwork Tony Graham, Andrew
   Macdonald, Coral Mula, Gillie Newman, Sandra
   Pond, Will Giles
Picture Research Christine Rista

Executive Editor Sarah Polden
Design Director Jacqui Small

The six gardens shown on pages 20-25 were
designed by Alison Coleman and illustrated by
Vivien Monument.

A CIP catalogue record for this book is available
from the British Library

ISBN 1 85732 986 4

The publishers have made every effort to ensure
that all instructions given in this book are accurate
and safe, but they cannot accept liability for any
resulting injury, damage or loss to either person or
property whether direct or consequential and
howsoever arising. The authors and publishers will
be grateful for any information which will assist
them in keeping future editions up to date.

Typeset in Plantin by SX Composing Ltd,
Rayleigh, Essex
Colour reproduction by Mandarin Offset,
Hong Kong
Produced by Mandarin Offset, Hong Kong
Printed and bound in Hong Kong

Please note: for guidance on the hardiness zones
given in **The Plant Selector** see page 7.

Contents

Introduction

This book provides the amateur gardener with a totally new approach to garden design. It avoids any vague aesthetic suggestions and offers hard facts and a wealth of practical solutions. The extensive range of options and ideas gives unmatched assistance to those planning and creating an ideal garden. *The Garden Sourcebook* is the answer for people who require a good deal more than the conventional design book full of imaginary, unattainable schemes.

It is always difficult to define what makes a good garden. Style, a well defined layout, strong axes, elements of surprise, eye-catching ornaments, healthy plants – all are very important; but it is the sum of these factors that ensures the success of a garden design. This book sets out to achieve this sum, step by step, in a logical sequence.

First, an overview of the garden, as it is and how it will be in the future, must be considered. This will ensure that a coherent whole with a distinctive style is achieved. Within this picture, each detail of the garden – whether hard landscaping or plant material – must be carefully thought out so that everything fits into the design and no one element detracts from another or jars with the whole.

The plan of the book is simple and logical. The first section deals in a practical way with the assessment of the plot itself, what it offers and what its potential may be. Every garden, whether a new or an established site, has its own given characteristics in terms of the climate and microclimate, the quality of the soil and the existing plants and structures. Some of these elements must be accepted and the design adapted to accommodate them; others can be improved to suit the gardener's tastes, needs and preferences.

In subsequent sections the focus is narrowed to concentrate on and analyze each component in the garden – structural and architectural features, ornament, and, finally, the plants. This last section is broken down into useful categories of plants that allows the reader to evaluate the qualities of trees, shrubs, perennials and so on, and to appreciate their role in the garden. The extensive directories of plants are divided to identify plants to suit particular situations, seasons and styles, satisfying the gardener's every need and ambition.

Extensive information on the appearance, size and cultivation requirements of every recommended plant is given. A hardiness zone is also included in each instant (denoted by "z" followed by a number). This relates to a range of average annual minimum temperatures and should be used as a guide to the best plants for a particular area. The temperatures are as follows: zone 1: below -45.5°C/-50°F; zone 2: -45.5 to -37°C/-50 to -35°F; zone 3: -37 to -29°C/-35 to -20°F; zone 4: -29 to -23°C/-20 to -10°F; zone 5: -23 to -20.5°C/-10 to -5°F; zone 6: -20.5 to -15°C/-5 to 5°F; zone 7: -15 to -12°C/5 to 10°F; zone 8: -12 to -6.5°C/10 to 20°F; zone 9: -6.5 to -1°C/20 to 30°F; zone 10: -1 to 4.5°C/30 to 40°F. Most plants will succeed in warmer zones than the given zone, and it can pay dividends to grow a more tender plant than the hardiness zone might suggest in a warm microclimate (for example, a sheltered corner of the garden).

The authors, all experienced gardeners, take a lively approach to the text, within the clear-cut concept of the book, making *The Garden Sourcebook* a distinctive, practical and highly original guide to planning a very individual garden.

FIRST
STEPS

FIRST STEPS

Anyone can have a dream garden. No matter where you live, or how undeveloped your horticultural skills, creating the perfect garden is not only feasible, but much easier than you might think. Few are lucky enough to inherit an ideal site but hardly anyone finds a truly hopeless situation. The art of gardening is evaluating what you have got and transforming it into what you want. And above all knowing exactly how to do it. One simply cannot visit enough different, specialist gardens to see the full range of available effects. Investigate the formal Renaissance style, cottage garden informality (or even chaos), Mediterranean courtyards, one-colour borders, water features, and gardens with inventive examples of topiary. On seeing something you like, note down how the effect is achieved. As a vital complement to these records, keep enormous lists of plants.

All good gardeners cheat. The more you borrow ideas the better. If it works recreate it. If you cannot provide exactly the same growing conditions then play around with the idea and reinvent it. Amend it to your own needs. If you like formal gardens then the range of tricks is huge, more or less everything can be whipped into art. Hedges can be given windows onto contrasting areas, with "doors" leading into corridors and alleys. Never settle for the obvious.

You have to be equally imaginative with plants. When you find a particular plant that you like the next step is to visit a national collection. Most countries have them. See if there is a variety with even better colour and/or scent. Also get into the habit of visiting major horticultural shows. Thereafter start visiting small specialist nurseries which invariably sell a wider range of rare plants than garden centres.

While at times one relishes getting carried away, beware of totally overdoing it. Creating a garden is one thing, time-consuming and expensive though it can be. But looking after it year after year is something else. Shrubs are a godsend if only because they tend to require relatively little attention. One of the biggest pitfalls is collecting tender perennials. Because so many are exotic, they need to be kept in pots in a frost-free greenhouse over winter, or indoors. It is easy to run out of space and money for fresh compost and eventually even bigger containers.

But given some basic knowledge, a clear idea of the do's and don'ts, and three key ingredients – time, patience, and the will to make it work, then everything will go according to plan. Your dream garden can become a reality. And sooner rather than later.

ASSESSING THE SITE

Whether the site is brand new or an old established plot, the same principles apply to planning and designing your ideal garden. First, assess what is at your disposal, then decide what kind of garden you want and whether you can provide its requirements. For example, a kitchen garden needs fertile soil and full sun, whereas woodland species need shade; alpine and rock plants need less space than an arboretum, when nothing less than about four acres (1.6 hectares) will do justice to a collection.

For most purposes, one needs reasonably fertile soil and a sunny, sheltered position, but even without these ingredients do not give up. Assess your garden's potential, its strengths and weaknesses, and then decide how to take advantage of the former while minimizing the effects of the latter. It is the surest way to successful garden design.

Dimensions

The first step with a new garden is to familiarize yourself with its dimensions. Size matters, but only in so far as it might limit the number of different areas you can create, and the size and number of plants and features within them. If the garden is on the small side, there are several ways of putting the available space to more efficient use. Vertical surfaces, for instance, offer scope for climbers, wall plants and hanging baskets. The range of plants is enormous. One small area could contain the dark red flowers of *Clematis viticella* growing up through the long catkin-like racemes of *Itea ilicifolia*, with a *Cytisus battandieri* nearby bearing early summer, pineapple-scented yellow flowers. Though the latter is strictly speaking a freestanding tree, it can also be grown against a sunny wall. Raised beds and terraces also extend the growing areas, and containers make maximum use of sterile locations such as paving and window sills. Furthermore, the *illusion* of size is easily achieved. Clever design demonstrates how even the most cramped plots can, with crafty positioning of screens in the form of hedges and trellises, give a spurious impression of size and stature. The secret is to have a surprise around every corner, and to make the visitor think there are more corners than really exist. One of the most sophisticated forms of illusion is *trompe l'oeil* (see page 212). At its most developed, it involves painting a scene on a wall suggesting an extra area beyond, but "receding" trelliswork and the clever use of mirrors can easily give an impression of depth that does not exist.

Incidentally, too large a garden can also cause problems, although they are easily solved by strategic planting, with the emphasis on trees and shrubs underplanted with ground cover. However, since the great majority of gardeners find themselves with limited space rather than too much, this text will concentrate on that extreme rather than coping with extensive acres. By itself smallness is not a problem, what counts is how it is used.

Planning considerations

When planning your garden, once you have accepted the size of the site, begin by considering these four factors: shape, topography, division and ambience.

Shape This influences design considerably. Few plots are symmetrical but that really does not matter. Indeed, an L-shape or a triangle offers more design potential than a rectangle. Perhaps the most difficult shape of all is a square, particularly when it is too small to subdivide, but even this problem has solutions (see pages 22 and 23).

Topography Surprisingly, a level site is less desirable than one with interesting, gradual changes, and the attraction of a slope is that it often provides the possibility of terracing. Since steep slopes are unstable, especially when cultivated, devices such as retaining walls, steps or buttresses are needed.

Division Hedges, walls and fences make ideal screens and can introduce different moods and styles as you walk through the garden. They are also invaluable for screening off unsightly but essential areas like the compost heap and refuse storage areas, but do not just erect screens and forget about them. They ought to be attractive, architectural features. Hedges, for example, in addition to decorative entrances and exits, can be given scalloped or battlemented tops. Alternatively, you could plant a tapestry hedge consisting of hornbeam and *Lonicera nitida*.

A design for an awkward garden shape needs to be carefully thought out. A long thin area, for example, can be divided into contrasting sections (the Mediterranean garden, the black and white garden, the ornamental kitchen garden) by means of barriers across its width, but by leaving a narrow view running through from one end to the other you create an additional vista. Furthermore, by placing an ornamental feature – for example, a statue, seat or urn – at the far end, you gain the full benefit from the site's length while the screens minimize the disadvantages.

Ambience The atmosphere of a potential garden is an important consideration. Even when you are working on a bare site the potential of the space needs to be assessed and compared with the "feel" you want to achieve. Walk around the area, take measurements, and observe natural features such as wet spots, bumps or edges, and any other quirks and oddities because they may well have the potential to become focal points. The emphasis is on making use of your natural resources, and converting the apparently insignificant into eye-catching attractions.

CLIMATE AND MICROCLIMATE
Geographical location
Climate is all-important because it dictates the kinds of plants you can grow and exerts an immense influence on design. If you have moved to a new area it is easy to discover average temperatures and rainfall, but you must always allow for extremes.

Regional climate is influenced by fundamental geographical factors like latitude, altitude, proximity of large land masses and the sea and the influence of major ocean currents. Every district has its own special quirks too, such as the Mistral, a cold wind funnelled down the Rhône Valley in France, the "Fremantle Doctor", a cooling wind that relieves the inhabitants of Perth in Western Australia from heatwaves, and the high altitude of the Alps and Rockies that shortens the growing season.

Then there are microclimates, natural and artificial. For example, in most winters central London is nearly frost-free because of the artificial heat exuded by the city. Consequently many tender plants like certain abutilons can be kept outside while in colder country areas they have to be tucked up in a conservatory over winter. More surprisingly, given the northerly latitude, gardens on the northwest coast of Scotland can grow subtropical plants outdoors with minimal risk of damage because of the moderating effect of the Gulf Stream. In the Pacific Northwest of the United States the climate is made more temperate and wetter than adjacent regions by warm Pacific currents, giving milder winters than are found in the more southerly Kansas.

Though it is wise to learn about your local climate, it is equally important to set about creating your own special microclimate. You cannot do much about the weather but you can do a great deal to minimize its effects, perhaps by erecting a protective windbreak against slicing, icy winds. Often, famous established gardens succeed because their creators have taken great care to improve conditions, enabling them to grow a wider range of delicate and more interesting plants. In cold areas frost and snow do no harm provided you are growing hardy plants and no tender perennials have been left outside. A much bigger problem is wind. It dehydrates soil and stunts growth, while constant buffeting bruises young, emerging plant tissue, impairing growth and development. The first task, therefore, in trying to influence the climate in a new garden is to eliminate or at least reduce the potentially destructive wind.

Creating shelter
If the site is badly exposed, conditions may be too unpleasant for even shelter plants to establish themselves, in which case you will need to erect either temporary or permanent windbreaks. Although it may seem like a good idea to build a solid wall, this does more harm than good. The wind will eddy over the top of the wall and swirl down, creating a whirlwind effect in the garden. The only solution is to create a

filtering windbreak that is approximately 40 percent porous, which reduces wind speed but does not stop it dead. Since the screen should become an attractive garden feature rather than a simply functional object, plants are preferable to fencing, but they do, of course, take longer to develop.

Windbreaks usually protect an area ten times their height, so they will produce an immediate change to the growing conditions within the enclosure. For example, two of them running from east to west on either side of a garden will create a dark, cool side and a warm, well-lit one. The advantage of such a windbreak is that it provides an opportunity for two contrasting garden areas, each with its own range of plants, each with its own character.

The type of screen chosen depends on personal preference. Walls will need to have trees or shrubs planted nearby to minimize the eddying effect of the wind; evergreens or matching shrubs successfully complement such solid structures. Alternatively, consider hedges, whether clipped formally or kept in trim with an annual haircut. For a more natural look, thickly planted shrubs, interspersed with taller trees, create a good shelter belt. The selection of plants should ensure a changing pattern of interest running through the seasons with spring blossom, fresh, ex-

Above: Besides forming boundaries, walls and hedges provide essential shelter, improving the climate within the garden. When choosing hedging or building materials, make sure they harmonize with foreground planting.

citing contrasting foliage in summer, autumn berries and interesting twigs, branches and bark over winter. Pay particular attention to colour, texture and outline. With thoughtful planning you will be able to create an outstanding garden feature which is also functional. This does not have to be formal and symmetrical; a seemingly random planting will blur the garden boundary and give the illusion of space.

Frost

Frost in winter is seldom a problem unless you want to grow bananas outdoors in upstate New York or daturas on the Cotswold hills. Given that there are in excess of 60,000 hardy plants to choose from, even the coldest areas can be planted up to suit most tastes.

Frost at the wrong time of year, on the other hand, is disastrous. It kills tender young growth, destroys spring blossom and, in extreme cases, wipes out whole plants, especially the marginally hardy. The most likely scenario for unseasonal frost is a clear, still night which follows a calm, bright day. Without wind currents to move it, cold air accumulates in low places, like water forming a pool at the lowest level. The problem with erecting shelter is that it increases the danger of untimely frost by damming up cold air. This is particularly likely on a hillside or in a hollow and is known as a frost pocket. A natural frost pocket cannot be eliminated, but you can at least reduce the problem by creating perimeter gaps so that the cold air flows out of the garden and away.

Having said that, though, it is worth stressing that winter frost can be a fantastic advantage. This is particularly true of gardens strong on structure, with topiary or with clipped low hedges roping in different areas. Not only can the form of plants be more clearly appreciated than in summer when they are usually part-hidden by flowers, but such architectural shapes look quite sensational when crested with frost. The same goes for the herbaceous border. Many gardeners cut down the straggly growth in autumn, but this can easily be left until the following spring so that it, too, will give a fine display of mid-winter, frosty outlines.

SOIL TYPES

How inappropriate and demeaning that, in certain parts of the English-speaking world, soil is known as "dirt". First-rate gardens cannot exist without excellent soil. If yours is poor and infertile then it has to be improved. Drastic steps may be necessary, but first, since soils vary hugely in texture, structure and quality, it is vital that you begin by assessing its

Right: In a very informal setting aim for naturalistic planting. This woodland scene includes groups of shade-tolerant plants such as hostas. Spring bulbs and winter flowering species would give excellent year-round interest.

character. The soil in any area is the product of local geology. During the ice ages glaciation transported huge quantities of rock across the globe. Each type of rock responded differently to weathering so that limestone bedrock, for example, broke down to a very different material than volcanic rock. Some areas, such as the Rhine Valley in Germany, benefit from loess, a fine, fertile soil formed by wind erosion. However, the most fertile soils are found in flood plains, being the sediment deposited by rivers.

Soil is a living material. If healthy it contains billions of micro-organisms which live off the organic content which mainly consists of decaying vegetation. Good soil must also contain moisture and oxygen, and usually carries a high proportion of mineral particles. When very fine, the soil resembles clay; when coarse, a sandy loam. On fen- and peatland the topsoil may be composed almost entirely of organic material, the result of millennia of sedges or mosses living and dying, gradually forming a thick layer of fibrous material.

Most gardeners need only know whether their soil is clay-like or sandy. Clay retains moisture, is difficult to work and sticky when wet, and sets very hard with surface cracks in a dry summer. It needs regular breaking up over winter with a soil conditionier (for example, mushroom compost), although it is often very fertile in its own right. Sandy soil is easy to work and dries out quickly, but needs plenty of well-rotted manure or compost to improve moisture retention. Alluvial silt in a flood plain is an exception to the sandy rule; it is easy to work, fertile, and though free-draining, excellent at retaining moisture.

Acidity and Alkalinity

Plants manufacture their own food by converting carbon dioxide in the atmosphere into carbohydrates. Other essential ingredients come from mineral salts dissolved in the water that coats the soil particles. Nitrogen, phosphorus and potassium are needed in fairly large quantities, with minor but vital additions of magnesium, calcium, sulphur, oxygen, iron, manganese, boron, molybdenum, copper and zinc.

Plants differ in their ability to take up these mineral nutrients. Some are only efficient at absorbing iron, for example, in acid soil. Others can obtain everything they need even in the most alkaline conditions. That is why it is essential to know the character of your soil. If it is alkaline you will not be able to grow limehaters such as rhododendrons or camellias. In very acid soils limestone plants such as philadelphus, clematis and dianthus will flounder. You can easily buy cheap pH testing kits which you should apply to different parts of the garden since conditions will vary. (The pH refers to the negative decimal logarithm of hydrogen ion concentration expressed in moles per litre). A pH of 7 is neutral; anything higher, and the scale goes up to 14, is alkaline, and anything lower acid. Generally, most plants thrive at 6.4-7, vegetables preferring 7-7.5. To confirm your readings look around the neighbourhood to see what plants are growing well in other people's gardens. If you want to increase soil alkalinity add lime. But note such a step tends to be irrevocable so think carefully before you act. It is not so easy to increase the acidity. The best way is to create raised beds, or special enclosures, filled with acid soil for ericaceous plants.

Improving the soil

There are a number of ways to improve the quality of the soil; drainage can be made more efficient and the substance and fertility of the soil enhanced.

Drainage The most important consideration on any land that is to be productive is drainage. This fact has been recognized almost as long as gardening has been a practise. The ancient Roman poet Virgil, a keen horticulturist, waxed lyrical about it. While soil must contain water if it is to sustain plant growth, saturation or waterlogging can be as harmful as drying out. This can be fatal. If water fills all the interstices between the soil particles there is no room for air, and so the essential oxygen, and the plant roots begin to rot. Good drainage enables water to pass through the soil and run away to its natural level. In well-drained soils, root development is unimpeded and roots will grow to surprising depths, improving the plant's efficiency at absorbing nutrients and therefore maximizing growth and vigour.

Some soils drain naturally, but not all can be relied upon to do so. In a particularly damp garden it may be worth considering installing a drainage system. The most effective consist of underground pipes laid in trenches at regular intervals and backfilled with gravel, but this is an expensive procedure. Cheaper but less effective methods include digging organic material or sand and gravel into the soil. Such measures may not assist deep drainage, but they do improve soil condition just below the surface. Raising borders slightly to produce a trench along their edges also improves drainage, particularly for shallow-rooted plants. Some species are more tolerant of wet feet than others, but there is still no substitute for truly efficient, beneficial drainage.

Building up the soil Soil that has been well managed will be rich in organic matter and therefore rich in beneficial micro-organisms. If you are lucky enough to inherit a garden in good condition then rejoice, but remember you have got to keep working at it. If the soil is poor do not despair, but start digging in whatever rotted or rotting vegetation you can find – manure, leaf mould, compost, and so on. Thereafter, treat your soil as a hungry beast and feed it with compost or manure every year. After three summers you should notice a considerable difference.

Fertility This is different from soil condition, though often confused with it. To thrive, plants need adequate levels of every essential plant nutrient, but in the act of gardening you automatically remove vital plant material, such as crops and prunings, so these lost minerals need replacing. Furthermore, many garden plants have been bred to grow faster and larger than their wild counterparts and therefore need higher levels of nutrients.

Manure used as a soil conditioner also tackles this problem, but it is not always available. Fortunately plant foods are easy to come by, either organic (such as fish or bone meal) or inorganic (in the form of proprietary products). The concentration of nutrients in inorganic fertilizers varies, the exact ratio sometimes being indicated by the letters NPK. The accompanying numbers, say 10:11:27, indicate 10 percent nitrogen, 11 percent phosphorus, and 27 percent potassium. Nitrogen promotes leaf growth, phosphorus ripens fruit, and potassium produces good fruit and flowers. Generally a balanced, all-in-one fertilizer is adequate, but sometimes a plant needs extra quantities of one nutrient. For example, leafy vegetables such as spinach require heavy nitrogen application.

High fertility, once achieved, needs to be kept at that level. I use dried poultry waste at roughly a double handful per square yard (square metre) once a year on my mixed borders. This works well as a source of nitrogen, phosphorus and potassium. (Occasionally I have missed a year but the garden has not suffered because the general level of fertility in the soil is high.)

Soil structure and damage

Inexperienced gardeners often fail to recognize the fragility of soil structure. While some soils are less stable than others, all are liable to damage. The main problem is compaction. This results from mechanical pressure which forces the particles together, driving out air and spoiling the environment for micro-organisms. In extreme cases roots will be unable to penetrate and water will not drain away. Light, sandy soils may not suffer but heavier soils with a high clay content can be ruined and are particularly prone to compaction if walked on when wet. It is like stepping on, and sinking into, semi-hard concrete, and does plant roots no good whatsoever. The best way to avoid this problem involves creating beds never more than one footstep wide, so there is no need to walk on the soil, with stone paths running between. The ideal is rarely practical in the flower garden, but you can minimize difficulties when undertaking winter projects by laying planks on the soil surface. These reduce the pressure on the ground, distributing weight more evenly, and are more pleasant to tread on than mud.

A hard compacted layer below the surface is known as a "pan". It can be created by the weight of a mechanical cultivator, although you may not be aware of the problem because the surface soil can still look friable or crumbly. One of the worst instances occurs when a garden has previously been used as a building site. The contractors will have churned up the subsoil and afterwards, as a cosmetic exercise, spread a load or two of imported topsoil over the plot, hiding faults and problems. Standing water after rain is a sure sign, but even without it, investigate the state of the soil sooner rather than later.

Once the pan forms it impedes drainage and needs to be broken up. Various tools are available, those particularly worth considering being mechanical cultivators which have an extension at the back designed to crack through the pan as the machine drives forward. Otherwise compaction is best repaired by deep digging and by incorporating bulky material, particularly in heavy soils, to open up the structure and let in oxygen. In cold areas, deep digging can be undertaken in autumn and the ground left rough throughout the winter, allowing the action of frost and thawing to convert clotted land into a more manageable tilth.

To conclude this section, three examples of problem soils are given with suggested treatments.

Heavy, sticky clay The problem with clay is that it does not forgive abuse, being easily damaged and difficult to repair. Any means of making it more porous and getting more air into the mix will improve growing conditions. The prime objective is to build up the humus by digging in bulky compost. As the garden develops, be assiduous in your composting, hoarding every scrap of organic refuse from rose prunings to kitchen waste. Farmyard manure, if you can obtain it, is beneficial, adding humus as well as nutrients. Further additions of coarse grit, shingle and even ash will also open up the texture and give a crumbly, more manageable texture in which plants thrive.

In many respects the plants themselves help to improve heavy soils. The roots penetrate and open the structure while falling foliage increases the organic content so that gradually, over the years, the surface soil becomes easier to work.

To establish new plants in the heaviest soils you must improve conditions around their roots. When digging planting holes incorporate extra quantities of leaf mould enriched with bone meal or a slow release fertilizer at the bottom to ensure rapid establishment. The one huge compensation for having heavy clay is that once the plants have settled they succeed much better than in less fertile ground.

Fine, blowing sand In some areas, particularly near the coast, shifting sands or sandy soil may cause problems. Unlike clay which stays put, sand at its worst can literally blow away, leaving roots exposed, or it can blow in, depositing a desert-like dune over the entire surface of the garden.

The main advantage of sandy soil is that it is easy to work and difficult to damage. The drawback is that water runs straight through it, flushing away dissolved mineral salts, leaving plants dry and undernourished. It may seem contradictory to suggest that organic matter is the best way of adding body when it also lightens heavy clay, but it works. The addition of humus in the form of leaf mould or rotted manure improves moisture retention. In the case of existing beds which need bulking up, it may be necessary to remove all the plants, transferring them to a temporary bed, while the soil is treated. Most sands tend to be acid, so if you want to grow food, mix lime into the soil.

Thin topsoil over chalk or bare rock In such conditions, moisture retention will be impaired since there is very little soil to hold the water (made worse with chalk as it is so porous); as a result, plants are likely to suffer from summer drought. Also, pure chalk or pure rock are poor sources of plant nutrients. As an additional problem, soil over chalk is likely to be strongly alkaline, restricting the choice of plants to the most lime-tolerant.

The solution to these difficulties is simpler than you might think. Wise plant choice is the first consideration. Species which thrive in the wild on chalk downs or rocky outcrops will be natural choices and many have superb garden cultivars. Blossom trees, such as crab apples and hawthorn, do well, and among chalk-loving herbaceous plants are pinks, carnations and many campanulas.

It also makes sense to build up the topsoil as much as possible with imported material. Extra loam will help, as will generous additions of leaf mould and organic matter or manure. As for moisture retention, building up the soil's humus content will enable it to hold more water, and a thick mulch either of compost, tree bark chippings or similar material spread generously over the surface helps reduce the evaporation rate from the ground.

SHADE AND SUN

After soil type, climate and topography, comes the final key consideration, light quality. Sunlight is essential because it is absorbed by chlorophyll in the plant cells and converts moisture absorbed through the roots and carbon dioxide absorbed through the leaves into sugar and water. This vital food-making process is known as photosynthesis. Generally, the sunnier a plant's position the more it reaches its full potential, but there are many notable exceptions. Thousands of plants have adapted to various kinds of shade. You only have to consider the darkness of a jungle floor and the abundance of lush vegetation growing there to realize how successful these plants are. Indeed, far from restricting choice, shade provides plenty of planting options and the chance to create a contrasting area of garden. It makes an excellent foil to bright areas with hot colours, so much so that, in a large, open, sunny garden it is worth planting a small tree simply to create an area of shade.

Types of shade

Before completing a garden design, and certainly before planting, assess what kind of shade you have. The degree varies according to the amount of light received, which itself is dependent on the time of year.

Dappled shade This is thrown by the leaf canopy of trees overhead. It can be quite cool and dense in summer but non-existent in winter. This creates good woodland conditions where spring flowers bloom in full light before the tree foliage emerges, followed by a summer in cool shade.

Partial shade Such shade is created when an area is in shadow for part of the day and receives direct sunlight at other times. A wall or building is the most likely cause. The further the site is from the equator, the lower the sun in winter, so that in London or Oslo, New York or Chicago, such obstacles throw more shadow than in Rome, Madrid or Los Angeles. This makes no difference in mid-winter but has a considerable influence in spring, when even as little as an hour of direct sunshine is sufficient to tempt a crocus or an aconite into bloom.

Full shade Full shade refers to an area which is always in shadow but which, nevertheless, has enough diffused daylight to support a reasonable plant collection. For example, the space between two buildings might be in constant shadow, as would the area of ground directly behind a wall running east to west (this, in turn, produces a cooler microclimate).

Dense shade This type of shade is the most likely to cause problems. There may appear to be too much gloom to grow anything but the dullest evergreen which even then languishes and looks miserable. But even dense shade is plantable.

The most challenging problem is dense, dry shade where surrounding buildings also restrict the amount of rainfall. Although there are plants that will cope with such surroundings, they seldom look as good as when growing in more suitable locations. There are, however, ways of minimizing the disadvantages. Container-grown plants can be moved here for a number of hours each day, provided at other times they get plenty of sun. Another good choice is spring bulbs which have their own food supplies and flower well in their first season even in the densest shade, but they must be replaced each year since they are unlikely to bloom again. Improving the soil to minimize moisture loss and maximize fertility will also help.

Reducing shade

There are three particularly useful ways to minimize the presence of shade. They are garden design, tree selection and tree thinning.

Garden design One of the side effects of creating shelter is that windbreaks may well impede light. This is particularly so if they enclose a long, thin garden running east-west and are approximately 5ft (1.5m) high. The solution involves a compromise be-

tween wind shelter, creating privacy, and letting in daylight. One obvious answer, if the site is large enough, is to enclose part of the garden creating sheltered, private shade, while leaving the remainder more open to ensure higher light levels. Alternatively, use trelliswork above a low white wall.

Tree selection Since evergreens create permanent shade, they frequently make it impossible to grow plants beneath them. Deciduous trees let in winter light, but the choice of species makes an enormous difference. Those which come into leaf late create better lighting conditions beneath their canopies. *Robinia pseudoacacia*, for example, does not begin to

Above: Shade makes for special planting opportunities and effects. Glossy, evergreen foliage is an asset while pale leaf variegations show up better than strong colours, like the magenta flowers of *Geranium psilostemon* here.

sprout until late spring and even then its foliage is frail and lacy, letting in a fair amount of daylight until it is fully developed in mid-summer. Large-leaved trees such as paulownia and catalpa also open late but they produce a dense canopy.

Tree thinning Many trees lend themselves to artistic pruning, which is another means of reducing the effect of dappled shade. With practice it is possible to remove whole branches cleanly instead of crudely lopping off their ends, producing a shapely, balanced tree with a smaller, more open arrangement of limbs. Please note this can be tough, even dangerous work, and you may prefer to employ a professional tree surgeon or a very experienced gardener.

Plant selection

There is a far wider choice of plants for cool, moist, woodland-type shade than for the dense dry kind, but in both cases the same planting principles apply. Since shady areas are usually sheltered from the wind, plants with large, soft leaves can be selected, with special attention to contrasting textures and colours. A light touch is necessary to avoid fussiness. A good example of plant combination features the broad, blue-green foliage of the plantain lily, *Hosta sieboldiana* (which produces violet flowers in late summer), spreading in front of the feathery fronds of the Lady fern, *Athyrium filix-femina*. Place an evergreen shrub at the back, perhaps a camellia, or a *Mahonia japonica* for its fragrant primrose-coloured winter flowers and glossy foliage, and complete the picture with a foreground cover of sweet violets.

Flowers that open in shade are plentiful but try to select pale colours because they show up much better than do dark reds and blues. Subtle suffusions of pink, mauve or cream, lost in full light, are more obvious in darker areas, so use plants whose flowers exhibit gentle contrasts and harmonies of hue rather than stark differences. Furthermore, since the air is often still in shady areas, scent tends to linger. This is the ideal site for a good range of fragrant plants like honeysuckle and lilies in pots which can be moved here from sunnier areas for at least part of the day. Plants for dry shade are few and far between, and in really severe cases there is not much choice. You could train a white *Clematis montana* over the offending wall, or try *Euphorbia amygdaloides robbiae* beneath it, with *Iris foetidissima*. Bulbs are the best idea, particularly beneath deciduous trees, with Solomon's seal, lily-of-the-valley and bluebells well worth trying for a delightful display.

Sun and heat

The diversity of planting possibilities in full light is so vast that it would be impossible to do justice to the subject here. However, it would be useful to point out some of the hundreds of plants that tolerate extremes of heat and drought. The base of a sunny wall, a dry bank, and the "hot" side of a rock garden provide conditions which suit the kinds of plants that grow naturally in the maquis of the Mediterranean and the semi-desert-like conditions in Australia and North America. Such plants, with their toughened, often silvery foliage, easily cope with heat.

Many have beautiful and distinctive flowers, others have stately architectural shapes. The tall, creamy flower spikes of yuccas, for example, make superb living sculptures in a garden and are fully drought-tolerant. Most of the wormwoods (artemisias) have filigree foliage in silvery tones, and gems like the delicate flowered *Convolvulus cneorum* are exquisite with their silver foliage and pinkish white blooms.

Many bulbs and corms thrive in hot, dry conditions too, from Mediterranean anemones and dwarf irises to various green, brown and purple fritillary species. Later in the season, the alliums relish heat, as do autumn-flowering amaryllis and crinum.

The Mediterranean look Gardens with a reliably dry, bright, sloping area are ideal for a wide range of scented Mediterranean shrubs like lavender, myrtle, thyme and rosemary (both the upright forms and the trailing *Rosmarinus officinalis* 'Prostratus'). Many cystus do equally well in such conditions (for example *C. crispus*, which has grey foliage, and *C. albidus*, with leaves verging on white).

Unless you can guarantee frost-free conditions over winter the tender, heat-loving plants will have to be put into containers and brought inside. This is certainly true of *Nerium oleander*, which is never going to be as big in temperate regions as one growing in the Mediterranean or California where it makes a massive flowering hedge; even so it is definitely worth its place on a hot patio.

Some plants, like the prolific, white-flowering *Osteospermum ecklonis*, can be risked outside over winter in most areas except for the very coldest, though it is still best to take cuttings in case the temperatures dip well below freezing and kill the parent plant.

Besides the ornamental plants, also consider fruit bushes like *Citrus limon* 'Meyer'. Discovered in China at the turn of the century it gives good size fruit and is hardy enough to stand outside even in a disappointing summer. In contrast, the European olive tree can be surprisingly hardy, and ought to be grown more widely in unusually warm city centres like London.

HOUSE AND GARDEN

Having assessed the garden's advantages and disadvantages, the next task is to consider your special needs and what you want from the garden as a space and as a reflection of your lifestyle.

Garden designers are now very fond of pointing out that the garden is an extension of the house. The term "extra room" keeps cropping up. But which room? One in which to rest and relax, enjoy a barbecue, grow vegetables, play games, or build up a specialist collection of plants? In a large garden the

problem does not exist – the only concern is how much space to assign to each room, and how to divide the one from the other. But with a smaller area you simply have to be ruthless, limiting yourself to one or two rooms, and be particularly crafty, accepting the need for compromise. The less space there is to play with, the more ingenious the design must be.

The potager is a brilliant example of a dual-purpose room. The word means a decorative or ornamental kitchen garden, and features different colour vegetables (for example the reddish leaves of 'Lollo Rosso' lettuces as well as the traditional green), herbs (basil 'Ruffles Green' and 'Ruffles Purple'), and flowers. Herbaceous penstemons come in a wide range of colours from white (*Penstemon* 'Snowflake') to dark purple (*P.* 'Blackbird') and bloom from mid-summer until late autumn, even early winter in mild seasons. They mix well with vegetables, are usually contained in separate beds, and can be set off with topiary; for example, balls of clipped box in Versailles tubs. The Renaissance garden at Villandry in France has a particularly good, formal potager, and, although it is enormous, it is worth visiting to see how many ideas can be incorporated in a far smaller garden.

The second kind of compromise means beginning with one kind of garden, say predominantly lawn where children and animals can play, later converting it into another when there is no longer risk of damage to plants. Lawn can easily be replaced with paving and flower beds. The one advantage of making such changes is that at least you have time to visit scores of different gardens and work out exactly what kind of look you finally want, and the most appropriate combination of plants that will achieve these ends.

The third compromise involves children. Beware of ponds since a person can drown in even a few inches of water. Instead use a water feature which has no depth: a fountain dribbling into a dish in the wall for instance, or a cascade which disappears into stones.

Planting

In small gardens the most important rule is that each and every plant must earn its keep. Only the best forms should be planted and your choice should be tempered by such questions as: Will this plant give more than one display? Does it repeat flower? What is it like in winter? Are there good seed heads, or fruits as well as spring or summer blossom? What is its autumn foliage like? Does it have good scent?

Good planting and clever design should allure, keeping the visitor's curiosity alive. What goes on behind that screen? Where does this path lead? What is that flash of pink in the shrubbery? As you move around the garden you want to create changing moods and styles. Part of the key is sensitive, imaginative planting, but having learnt the basic rules do not be afraid to play with and even break them. Try introducing a few surprises. For instance, an ivy-leaved pelargonium can easily be turned into topiary. Grow a single stem up a 4ft (1.2m) high cane and then around a circular piece of bamboo attached to the top. Or create a yellow area and finish it off in high style with pots of *Lilium* 'Citronella' which twirl butterfly-like flowers to a height of 4ft (1.2m).

Linking house and garden

From indoors, the view through the windows into the garden is at least as important as the view from any vantage point outside. The garden design must therefore include vistas or scenes which look tempting from inside, from the room where you spend most time. If you are lucky enough to look out over open countryside or a fine cityscape, make sure the garden design blends with the background: for example, in a wild valley a cottage garden is most appropriate.

Looking back to the house from the garden, it should be an integral part of the design and not an alien presence. A conservatory, for instance, can be designed to open on to a terrace or patio so that in summer, when the doors are open, the garden feels as though it is extending into the house and vice versa. Climbers and wall plants can soften the harsh outline of a building and, where pergolas lead to and echo the style and fabric of the house, the link between indoors and outdoors is sealed.

GARDEN DESIGNS: SITE ONE (right and far right) A south-facing garden, 20 × 50ft (6 × 15m), with a slight slope from north to south. Neutral soil

INHERITED FEATURES

In some way it is best to begin with a bare site. You can more or less do what you like with it, providing there are no overwhelming restrictions. Far trickier is reworking an established garden. But before you demolish it, do wait one full season. It really is essential. Even the apparently most hideous layout is likely to have some feature worth preserving, though it may not be immediately obvious. Note down the existing spring bulbs, shrubs for winter colour, colourful autumn seedheads, boggy winter areas, particularly dry hot summer beds and then you can decide which features to keep.

Plants

In the case of an overgrown garden, dig out known weeds and give established plants a chance to show what they can do. In cases of serious neglect this may be difficult because of the urgent need for renovation, but even so it pays to be circumspect.

Overgrown shrubs and trees can be pruned and tidied up without damage – indeed many shrubs respond well to being cut hard back. Furthermore, do not be afraid to impose shape on the apparently shapeless. The Japanese are particularly good at it. For example, *Ceanothus thyrsiflorus* can be converted from shrubbiness to a shapely, weeping tree. Again, *Prunus laurocerasus* 'Magnifolia' can be turned from a floppy specimen into something more statuesque and upright. When it comes to transplanting, mature woody plants can be difficult, but perennials are easy to lift, divide and replant into temporary nursery beds, perhaps while new borders are being laid out. In such cases, it pays to plan a new design carefully, to avoid heaving up plants again.

Large natural features

Objects such as large trees or natural water courses, which make prominent features, could push you on to the horns of a dilemma: how will they look when incorporated into a new design? It is impossible to suggest general solutions, but the basis for your decision should be tempered by the following considerations: is the tree or natural feature particularly fine, rare or special in any other way? Could you reshape your design to work around the feature? Since maturity is lacking in a new garden, and since the established look is going to be the aim, is it possible to keep the feature for the medium term until the garden has mellowed and matured, and then think about replacing it with your ideal specimen tree or sculpture?

INFORMAL GARDEN

This design recaptures the spirit of an old cottage garden, using both traditional and modern plant species, combined with natural materials. The landscaping is of blue-grey stone, slate and gravel; most of the pathways are designed to allow plants to spill over at either side. The east-facing wall includes (top to bottom) *Pittosporum* 'Garnetti', *Polygonatum* × *hybridum*, *Rheum alexandrae*, *Hosta sieboldiana*, *Lupinus* 'Inverewe Red', *Amelanchier lamarckii*, *Papaver bracteatum* 'Goliath' and *Thalictrum delavayi*. An apple tree provides a focal point; underplanting includes *Milium effusum*. *Verbascum olympicum* and *Digitalis purpurea* 'Alba' give height to the bed beyond the terrace which is lined with tubs of fragrant *Lilium regale*. A cold frame, compost container and shed are set apart.

FORMAL GARDEN

A linear, symmetrical form has been given to the space by means of clearly defined surfaces and structures and controlled planting. The terrace is framed by ivy, ferns and containers planted with *Trachycarpus fortunei*; this has an architectural quality. The facing benches lead the eye into the garden. The small parterre is planted with *Buxus sempervirens* which will frame seasonal planting in restricted colours. Bay trees (*Laurus nobilis*) sit at each corner. The central, raised summer house gives a focus to the vista; espalier pears or pleached quince are trained at either side. A well-clipped *Taxus baccata* hedge encloses a seat and hides the compost area and cloches at the end of the garden. *Actinidia kolomikta* plants shroud the greenhouse and shed. The surfaces are yellow-ochre gravel and pink granite.

Structural and ornamental features

Hard landscaping and architectural and ornamental features present less of a problem than natural features because in most cases they can be dismantled and relocated. The advantage of re-using such existing materials – stone walls and troughs, paving slabs, millstones and so on – is that they will be weathered and worn, as compared to the rather sterile appearance of new materials. If you want to dispose of existing features, it is worth looking to auction houses to sell ornaments and the small advertisements in local newspapers for building materials. Many garden details have a surprising value.

TIME AND MONEY

The joy of gardening is that it suits every pocket. Landscaping a small area with choice materials and lavish, mature plants is expensive; by contrast, using inexpensive materials, propagating as many plants as possible, and being prepared to wait is the best way to develop a fine garden on a shoestring.

Interim measures have their uses: beds can be filled with annuals until you can afford more expensive shrubs; an arrangement of pots can provide the focal point until a statue or sculpture has been added. For example, an architectural *Cordyline indivisa* can be set in a tall or raised pot with pots of scented flowering heliotropium, such as the fine 'Chatsworth', 'Princess Marina' or 'White Lady', and the yellow-orange flowers of echeveria around the base.

From the gardening point of view phasing the work has many advantages, but the question is which major structures should you complete first? Clearly the answer depends on your own priorities but it is logical to begin with the basic layout. Lawns, pathways, main borders and the seating area provide the garden skeleton and take priority. Later, when your pocket has recovered, you can add a little more flesh to the bones by adding special features like a pond, conservatory, gazebo and so on. Usually, the biggest cost item is the hard landscaping: structures such as walls, terraces, buildings and paving. There may be earth-moving exercises too, such as digging ponds or creating different levels. These, especially if done by contractors, will be costly but are one-off expenses.

Inexpensive plants

Mature trees are the costliest plants to buy, and the bigger they are, the dearer. In effect you are buying the time taken to grow specimens. If you are prepared to nurture them, most small, immature plants grow

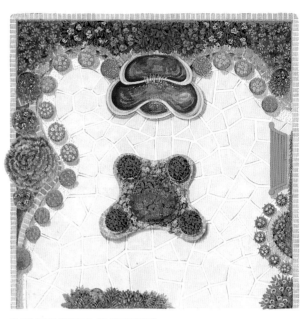

GARDEN DESIGNS: SITE TWO (right and far right) A west-facing walled garden, 20 × 20ft (6 × 6m). Acid soil

very quickly and are much cheaper. The important point to remember is that they will grow just as large as their bigger, more expensive counterparts, and need spacing out according to their potential and not their current size.

The cheapest plants of all are those that you propagate yourself. Shrubs grow surprisingly fast from cuttings and many are easy to root. Space is too limited to cover the subject here but there are dozens of specialist books on propagation, so do have a go. The skill needed to strike cuttings is so basic that anyone can learn it in minutes. Essentially, all that is required is a piece of healthy young stem, a pot of compost, and a warm, moist atmosphere that prevents the shoot wilting. Within a few weeks you should have a new plant.

A clear plastic bag and a windowsill will suffice for small numbers of cuttings, but results are quicker and better with an electrically-heated propagator. The most basic types are widely available in a range of sizes and are easily affordable. The crudest consist of a large open tray with low sides, a plastic cover and a heating pad. If you have a cold frame or a cold greenhouse you can wait for decent summer temperatures around 60°F (15.5°C) and raise cuttings there. Place them in a sheltered, shady position, and remember to close the greenhouse to keep in the heat. A cold frame is not essential when it comes to acclimatizing the young plants to outside conditions but it helps. Alternatively, stand the pots outside for an increasing amount of time during the warmest part of the day; eventually you should be able to leave them out over a mild night – but do not rush the process.

Nor should you be afraid to ask neighbours for cuttings of plants or for seed. You should have a good success rate with both, as with layering (bending a branch down to soil level, pegging it in place, waiting for it to develop its own root system, and then separating this new, young plant from its parent), dividing one plant into several (each with top growth and roots), and stooling (building up soil around the base of a japonica or lilac, for example, which encourages rooting higher up the stem so that ready-rooted pieces can be removed and replanted).

MAINTENANCE

The labour-free garden does not exist, but there are ways in which such chores as weeding and tidying can be kept to a minimum. Clearly, what you get out of a garden is in proportion to what you put in, and it will never be possible to expect a plantsman's paradise to thrive on neglect. Those who want beauty without

CONTAINER GARDEN

Shrub roses, small rhododendrons and foliage plants set off the containers in this grotto-like space. The late spring display shows blue hyacinths and white and pink tulips on a gravel sweep. (In summer impatiens, lilies and fuchsias can be used; in autumn, dahlias.) Pots of *Phygelius aequalis* 'Yellow Trumpet' stand either side of the large *Acer japonicum* 'Aureum'; herbs and ferns are placed beside the house. The central feature has four specimens of the evergreen *Ligustrum japonicum*, with hydrangeas in the middle (bergenias in winter) and gap-filling *Alchemilla mollis*.

effort are being unrealistic, but there is no need to become a slave. Any means of reducing the more troublesome tasks to a minimum is worth pursuing.

Design

Much labour can be saved by thoughtful design. All parts of a border, for example, should be accessible without having to walk on and damage the soil surface. This is achieved by laying stepping stones or pathways along the back as well as in the more visible areas. Paving is easier to maintain than lawn and, in a small garden, flagstones can look better than grass.

Gravel, as a mulching device, is gaining popularity, easing maintenance and providing plants with a friendly environment. Plants growing in gravel or shingle seed freely; to prevent this, lay the mulch over a woven polypropylene sheet; water will still pass through. To plant shrubs or specimens, a crisscross slit is made in the sheet, the plant inserted and the gravel carefully replaced.

The vertical surfaces in a well planned garden will be covered with a wealth of climbing and wall plants. To encourage them to grow up and sideways and not flop over the plants in front of them, tie in all growths to horizontal wires. These should be attached to vine eyes or large nails inserted into the masonry at regular intervals. With this permanent anchorage, it is easy to display wall plants to their best advantage.

MODERN GARDEN

The theme here is cool greens and whites, with scented flowers for evening entertaining. Marbled tiles swirl around a fibreglass table and seat, protected by a parasol (cut away in this view). The planting uses tender species, including *Lonicera splendida*, *Hedera helix* 'Telecurl' and *Wisteria floribunda* 'Alba' around the walls. The central beds have a pleasing symmetry: *Ficus benjamina* with its variegated form grow hydroponically in the raised triangle; *Camellia japonica* 'Commander Mulroy', *Phanerophlebia falcata* and nicotiana are either side of a raised mirror pool.

Planting

Choice of plants, and their arrangement, exert an enormous influence on the amount of time needed for maintenance. The aim, in a carefree garden, is to make the plants themselves do as much of the work as possible. Thus, shrubs which need little pruning are preferable to those like hybrid tea roses which require more attention. Disease- and pest-resistant plants will always be desirable and, unless a species is especially glorious, vigour takes preference over delicacy.

Among herbaceous varieties, those which self-seed freely without becoming invasive are ideal in the low-maintenance garden. Ground cover plants are perfect for filling the spaces between shrubs and give excellent weed control, provided the ground in which they are planted is completely free of perennial weeds. There are so many to choose from that dull planting is inexcusable. It is perfectly possible to arrange a weed-proof ground cover which changes in colour, texture and mood month by month.

STARTING THE DESIGN

Once you know all about your site, exactly what you want from your garden, what inherited features are worth preserving and how much time you want to spend on maintenance, you can begin the design. To do this you will need squared or graph paper and a pencil, but to generate any useful ideas, first stand in the garden – or on the patch of wasteland that is to become your garden – and think. Turn the area into a dream space in your mind's eye. Think not of specific plants but in terms of shapes and colours. As ideas begin to form, you can then explore practicalities and solve problems. Finally, you should measure the plot and trim your dream to fit the area, and your pocket.

Preparing the plan

The practical business of designing – preparing drawings to scale, organizing plant lists, and so on – appears to be far more daunting than it really needs to be. Accuracy is important but it is not that difficult to achieve; if you are methodical and careful, the site can be measured and a true plan drawn. You should include all important details: architectural features, the herb garden, beds and borders, pond, large trees, topiary, key shrubs, and the like. If you find it difficult to visualize designs from lines on a piece of paper, there is really no reason why you should not use the garden itself as your drawing board. The site, if not already clean, will have to be cleared of any rubbish or unwanted objects before you begin. Then, using sticks and lengths of string (preferably strong and very visible baler twine) as markers, it is possible to indicate where everything should go. Keep making adjustments to these markers until you have the layout you want. A length of hosepipe is very useful for marking out curving border fronts. I certainly feel much more comfortable working on the design in the garden itself, juggling my sticks, string and hosepipe until I feel I have laid out all the features and details in the best order and proportions.

Complicated details, like a parterre, may require a more striking outline. This can be achieved with whitewash, brushed over the grass or surface of the proposed location. Eccentric though this may sound, any step between planning and planting is invaluable and saves subsequent heartache. It is also worth visualizing height where this is a vital factor. A step-ladder erected to the height of a mature hedge will give you a good idea of the ultimate effect. If this looks too tall, obscuring a fine view and casting too much shade, select a different hedging plant. Again, if you intend to include a lengthy pergola, you could draw on a clever technique of an earlier era. In the 1920s, wealthy house owners placed cardboard cut-out pillars in various positions until they looked exactly right. Another eccentricity, but useful and potentially great fun if enough people are involved. Improvise in such a manner wherever possible: put a chair in a

GARDEN DESIGNS: SITE THREE (right and far right) An east-facing, irregular garden, between 35ft (10.5m) and 10ft (3m) wide, and 65ft (19.5m) long. Alkaline soil

proposed seating area and try it out. Is this the best place, or will it be ruined by an unpleasant view?

When you have a clearer idea of the arrangement of your site it will be easier to transfer the details onto paper; this will be essential for reference once the heavy work has begun. Before you draw up the plan, leave the markers in place for a week or so to ensure that the idea really is going to be practical. Then, when you are finally happy with the main elements of the design, draw up the plan.

The proposed planting

With the outline in hand, start filling in planting details on the plan – shapes, colours, texture and scent, leaving the choice of most plants until last. Scent is most easily dealt with. Tobacco plants, pots of lilies, *Choisya ternata* and the like, need to be in sheltered positions where the fragrance will hang in still air. Ideally such plants should surround the seating and eating areas where they are really going to be appreciated. A bench or patio can be backed by a semicircular, enclosing trellis threaded with scented climbers. The plants should be chosen so they flower in succession right through the summer and you get a prolonged spell of delightful perfumes, not one overpowering blast for two weeks in August.

The next stage is to ensure that the planting line-up is going to provide colour and interesting shapes right through the year. Use four different coloured pens (signifying winter, spring, summer and autumn) to mark blocks of plants on the plan and, if possible, grow a star plant for every season in each area. (When planting, leave space around the young specimens to accommodate their ultimate spread. Annuals and bedding plants can fill the gaps temporarily.) Many gardeners are drawn to the idea of an all-white garden at some point, but it is important to remember that they generate a lot of extra work as faded blooms present a glaring eyesore.

Foliage

One key point rarely mentioned is that most plants only flower for a relatively short period, which means foliage and shape ought to be rated just as highly as flowering interest. Palm trees are impressive on both counts. They *do* grow in mild areas, with the advantage that their fronds will not turn the frazzled brown seen in hotter climates. Agaves are much hardier than generally realized and make good focal points, having the additional benefit of a dramatic flowering spike something like once every 20 years! Much smaller but

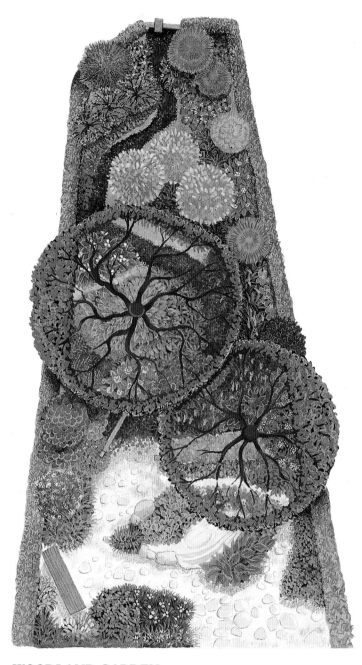

WOODLAND GARDEN

Tranquil woodland gardens come into their own in spring, when bulbs and woodland herbaceous plants provide a riot of colour, as here. The two pin oaks, *Quercus palustris*, are about fifteen years old but will cast only dappled shade even when mature (they are cut away to reveal the underplanting). The right-hand tree stands in front of a hedge of *Prunus spinosa*; a drift of yellow *Primula vulgaris* sweeps up into the garden, past a dark holly. Corsican pines (*Pinus nigra*), three *Betula utilis jacquemontii* and an *Acer saccharum* 'Temples Upright' are surrounded by cyclamen, honesty and bluebells. A stile leads into a wood beyond. On the other side of the path a *Crataegus oxycantha* 'Plena' is grouped with three *Hamamelis* × *intermedia* 'Jelena'. Beneath the second oak is an *Epimedium* × *perralchicum*, surrounded by trillium, bluebells, foxgloves and ferns. Primulas and hazels grow beside the gate. Around the log bench are snowdrops, chamomile and *Rosa rugosa* 'Fru Dagmar Hastrup'. The pond is planted with yellow *Primula florindae*, giant cowslips and *Myosotis scorpioides*.

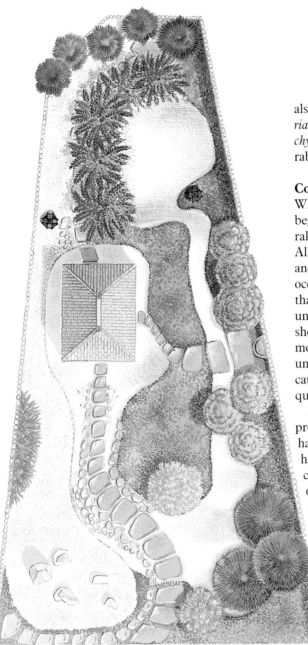

also effective are the white spotted leaves of *Pulmonaria longifolia* and the velvety, light grey foliage of *Stachys byzantina*, appropriately called lamb's tongue or rabbit's ears. Hunt out other, eye-catching examples.

Construction

With your well-considered plan complete, work can begin. Borders can be dug out, areas for lawns dug, raked and rolled and foundations for paving installed. All the time this is going on, keep reviewing the scene and be prepared to make any changes that might occur to you. This is much easier to do at the outset than later when more permanent construction is under way. With regard to heavy equipment, you should always be sure to hire well-maintained, modern and safe machinery. Make sure you fully understand how to use it, taking all necessary precautions, and leave no harmful devices to hand for inquisitive children to discover.

Needless to say, there is always the option of using a professional garden designer and a contractor. If you have ambitious plans, limited time or an aversion to hard physical work, such experts should be seriously considered. Their involvement could raise the cost of a project quite dramatically, but equally costly mistakes could be avoided. You will not have the complete satisfaction of knowing that all you survey is your work, but you might have come that much nearer to achieving your dream garden. It is a matter of weighing up the advantages and disadvantages to both approaches. A good designer will be sensitive to your preferences and tastes as well as to the context: the style of your house and the surrounding view, quite apart from the size, shape and contours of the space.

Perhaps the key point about a garden is that it is never complete. As with a sitting room, owners occasionally get bored with a particular look and rearrange things. Then, a plant that succeeded in its previous place may, for no known reason, fail in the new, apparently more appropriate site. Another plant must be sought, and the colour scheme suddenly leaps from pink to yellow and different, complementary features become desirable. It is a matter of being aware of the alternatives and gauging whether they can be made to work. The six garden designs included on these pages give you some impression of the range of options available. The idea is not to copy them slavishly – some of the design elements are solutions to very specific problems – but to apply similar principles of design to serve your own needs and tastes.

JAPANESE GARDEN

The distinctive flavour of a Japanese garden is achieved by combining a traditional layout with special features, such as lanterns and a washing basin, included here, and sculpture with a Japanese theme – dragons, temples and shrines. This strictly contrived, restful landscape includes the central elements of water and rocks, making a perfect setting for the small tea house which provides a charming focal point. Opposites run through the design, with moving and tranquil water, jagged rocks versus smooth boulders, and gravel against moss. The planting is essentially Japanese, in the selection and groupings. Around the water, from the house front, a *Cryptomeria japonica* 'Vilmoriniana' leads to groups of *Pinus parviflora*, *Acer palmatum* 'Ozakazuki' and *A. p.* 'Senkaki'. Spring-flowering white cherries (*Prunus* 'Tai-Haku') curve around the top of the pool, with a strong accent supplied by the Japanese black pines (*Pinus thunbergii*). Bamboo is used in a tied cane fence and as a planted hedge and curving clump. Japanese gardens can take a long time to mature; they demand patience and careful training.

THE LOOK
OF THE
GARDEN

SHAPES

The use of different shapes is perhaps the single most important element in designing a garden. It is the chief tool with which a gardener defines the spaces and structures of a garden – his working vocabulary. In a really good garden, consideration will have been given to the shape and purpose of every component, from broad issues such as the outline of a path or lawn to the details such as the contrasting shapes of miniature shrubs in a particular stone trough. It is the sum of all these parts, large and small, which gives a garden its character.

The garden's perimeter is the first shape to consider in relation to the site as a whole. The internal structure can complement the shape through a geometrical composition, using straight lines and circles, with the emphasis on hard landscaping (the walls, paths, steps and so on). Alternatively, natural flowing forms with no straight lines may be preferred. Again, a blend of the two approaches might be more suitable. In making this decision, the practical requirements of the garden must be considered: the need to get from one place to another, to create enclosures and the like. All the components of a garden – from lawns, borders, island beds and parterres to paths, topiary, pergolas and water features – can be treated in a geometric or an organic way. There is no right or wrong, only a variety of options with which the imagination can experiment.

Within the layout, the shape of the plants themselves comes into play. All plants fall into one of a number of basic shape categories, the plants in each category fulfilling a similar role in the overall scheme. There is the tall upright shape of fastigiate trees and conifers which leads the eye upwards and commands

Left and right: The first shapes to consider in a garden are those of the ground plan. Here, two perfectly geometric schemes are achieved, one by the formal planting of hedges and lawns, the other largely by the use of hard landscaping. Both gardens show remarkable attention to the detail of shapes. The planting is noteworthy. An orderly yet imaginative series of beds compares with symmetrical but strong forms that soften the modern design.

Below: A woodland garden begins life under mature trees, on organic rather than geometric lines. Unless the shapes of an organic plan are broad and simple, the effect is fussy and appears just as contrived as a formal garden, even though the scheme is non-symmetrical.

Top far left, top left and right: Strong shapes, such as tall upright conifers, make an even greater impact when repeated, and usually strong horizontals and more earthbound shapes are needed to balance the effect. Horizontal lines of great substance are most often gained from hard landscaping, such as walls and paths, reinforced by plants with a naturally tiered, architectural habit, or those that have been trained to form striking, flattened shapes. Notice the clever use of an espalier-trained weeping blue cedar (*top left*). The combination of horizontal and vertical lines will weave a design together, forming unifying connections. This is demonstrated by the strategically placed ornaments – the obelisk and pots – that point up from the flat lines of the retaining walls (*right*).

Bottom left: Shapes repeated often enough provide a large-scale texture, as do these domes of lavender. When shapes are repeated in a straight line, like the mounds beneath the pergola, they are almost more effective than a clean straight line in leading the eye forward. In summer, these bushes would provide a glorious, aromatic display of flowers, giving a very different face to the garden. The cypress arch and the trimmed laurels (either side of the steps) present different but connected forms. The climbing roses have an altogether freer disposition and open effect.

attention, especially when used repeatedly in a group or row. The effect is the same whatever the scale: notice how the *Kochia scoparia tricophylla*, burning bush, dominates in this way when used in a bedding scheme. Low rounded shapes or domes are equally arresting, but in a more earthbound way. They sit heavily upon the ground and fix the eye. Think of clipped spheres of box or chunky potentilla bushes. Fans or fountain shapes offer a softer touch, lifting the eye but in a gentler lighter way than a conifer. Grasses, bamboos and irises all shoot up in a fan, and many then droop over at the top, like a subsiding firework. A more extreme version of this effect is the weeping shape, less visually static than the sphere and less busy than the fountain. Finally, there are the horizontal shapes, found in plants like the architec-

tural *Viburnum plicatum* 'Mariesii', *Cornus controversa* and some of the low junipers, for example *Juniperus horizontalis* and *J.* × *media* 'Pfitzeriana'. They keep the eye peacefully arrested, moving neither up nor down, forwards nor backwards. Obviously there are endless variations within and between these categories, but when planning a layout they are very useful tool.

It is the arrangement of these typical shapes that gives movement, balance and punctuation to a garden design. For example, movement can come from the repeated use of upright shapes which takes the eye away into the distance. The effect will work either in a formal symmetrical context, as in an avenue, or in a more informal zigzag fashion. Balance will help the garden to look restful to the eye. For instance, a dramatic upright shape can be countered by an adjoining

Below: The main contrasting elements here are the fans of iris leaves, the closed shape of a clipped euonymus and the airy form of the variegated *Acer negundo* trees.

Top right: Shape is relevant in every aspect of the garden. It is expressed in the ground plan – lawns, beds, borders, paths, hedges, walls and containers. Also important are the outlines of single plants and groups of plants, and even the shape of flowers. Shape, however, must work hand in glove with texture and colour: none exists in isolation.

Bottom right: Much can be made of the interaction of colour and shape. A sombre walk of tall cypresses is brightened and balanced by a horizontal streak of pebbles.

low mound, and the two held together by some horizontal shapes. Strong shapes can be used to focus and punctuate the different areas within a garden, perhaps by closing an avenue with a tight specimen tree or by flanking a gateway with two strong mounds or sentinels of foliage.

Apart from these structural uses of shape, a garden is kept alive through its detail, by the constant interplay between neighbouring plants. Shape is just as important here as texture or colour. It is the continuous interplay between shape, colour and texture which makes a mixed or herbaceous border so fascinating, and so difficult to achieve over a long period, presenting a challenge to the gardener.

It is often helpful in the planning stages of a garden, or even a border, to make simple sketches that block in the most important shapes and lines (as well as the main colour effects). This will enable you to envisage the composition in advance and allows the main refinements to be made before planting begins. It is also useful for considering the mature aspect of the garden, which should include appropriate spacing of trees and large shrubs. This is an excellent tool for clarifying your ideas; on paper, the imagination can run riot, but once planting begins, changes become much more difficult. A plan can bring you that much closer to your ideal, well balanced garden. (See page 23 for further advice on starting the design.)

CONTOURS

Not everyone is blessed with an easy, level site for a garden, and those who are often long for a more varied terrain. Whatever your preference, there is no doubt that level ground makes gardening easier and that changes of level create a set of problems, both in planting and with access. But however steep the site, so long as you work within its limitations, it is perfectly possible to have an interesting and fulfilling garden. Virtue must be made of necessity.

Steeply sloping gardens lend themselves to different treatments depending upon their aspect. South-facing slopes receive the maximum heat from the sun and are especially suitable for Mediterranean plants or make good scree gardens. Drainage will be fast, which is an advantage to many slightly tender plants. These slopes also offer the possibility of creating streams or waterfalls, which can be made to be as formal or informal as required. Terraces can be constructed across the slope, as in the great villa gardens of Italy, to maximize the potential for planting, using either retaining walls or turf banks.

Cold north-facing slopes make good woodland gardens, but will equally make an ideal site for a terraced alpine garden because they are naturally well drained, fully exposed to light, but without the drying heat found on a south-facing slope.

The approach used on a sloping site also depends on its relationship to the house. A garden that slopes up from the house will be far more dominant than one that slopes away: it will fill the whole view and offer the opportunity for a real *tour de force*, whether formal or informal. It could be perfectly symmetrical with pairs of circular steps or an idealized Japanese mountain waterfall. Sites which slope away from the house are less imposing in themselves and throw the eye outwards into the view beyond. It might be Mount Fuji, a power station or just your neighbour's garden. Whether this view should be incorporated

Left: This change of levels has been made less daunting and more interesting by the use of intermediate levels. A shallow circular podium makes a gentle approach to the lower steps, while a landing halfway up accommodates a seat for restful contemplation, with a view of the garden.

into the garden's design or excluded to produce an enclosed oasis will depend on its merits or demerits. If the view is good, and it can be relied upon to remain so, then make the most of it. If the focus needs to be kept within the garden then try using a formal arrangement of large pots or upright conifers. These may not mask a poor view but they will give details of some substance to attract the eye.

Irregular changes of level within a garden can make it more interesting and offer the chance to create surprise views and features. The move from one level to another does not necessarily have to be negotiated in one go; a flight of steps can be split up and intermediate levels inserted in between. Steps are one of the most significant built features of a garden and deserve to have plenty of attention given to their detail. If the garden contains large mounds or hollows, consider enlarging them to create a major feature, such as a pond or a mount or rockery.

During the planning stage always keep in mind the maintenance implications of the finished garden. Steps are attractive, but they can stop easy access with a wheelbarrow or lawn mower. Terraces are fine, but will there be suitable access to take away prunings? Should the compost heap be positioned at the bottom or the top of the slope? Where access is limited, it is often better to opt for a style of planting that requires little pruning, such as an alpine or heather garden.

Finally, soil erosion can be a problem on banks and can be solved in a variety of ways. Turf banks will hold the soil once they are established, but ruts can soon develop where people constantly walk. Ground cover plants such as *Hypericum calycinum*, which have underground stems to bind the surface soil in a tight mat, can be used to stabilize a bank, but they may take some years to become effective. In extreme cases, terracing and channelled drainage may be essential.

Top right: Changes of level break up a garden. Here a sense of open space is retained by avoiding the use of steps and letting a grass bank link the lower and upper lawns to form one space. The grass flows around the contours.

Centre right: Terraces always present problems of access. Here a grass ramp allows a mower to be driven onto the terrace, but steps also make it visually more satisfying and close the vista.

Bottom right: A long flight of shallow steps is awkward to walk on and is generally not the best solution on a gradual slope. A path with a gentle gradient is usually more satisfactory, although you will need to make provision for water running off fast and hard when it rains. This detail is a fine illustration of a well conceived design. The mixed border has been planned to show every plant to its best advantage. It is backed by an attractive plant-clad wall.

Top left: Steps provide a good opportunity for interesting planting. There is no reason at all why you should not plant into the steps themselves, so long as they remain safe.

Top right: On terraced sites, sprawling evergreen perennials soften the edges of retaining walls, even in winter.

Above: Terrace walls and steps lend themselves easily to a very formal treatment, especially in front of an imposing symmetrical house. A formal planting with evergreens offers greater winter interest than an informal scheme. This clever planting affords very varied textures and shapes.

Opposite, top: Even in a small, flat garden changes of level can be introduced by building raised areas like this circular platform. The seat gives it an added *raison d'être*. Repeated motifs can be used in subtle ways in garden designs. The gentle bend of the steps and wall and the circles of the urns echo the curving theme.

Opposite, bottom: This grass terrace has been introduced as a means of separating the garden from grazed fields without the need for a solid, stock-proof fence. The wall has been built at an angle to help it resist the weight of soil pushing from behind. It presents a pleasing sweep, perfect for strolling along.

MANIPULATING SCALE

It is a rare gardener indeed who wishes to make a garden look smaller than it is, unless he or she is motivated by an underlying passion for bonsai landscapes. Most wish to increase the apparent size; others to make a broad site with little depth appear longer than it is, or to make a long and narrow garden seem less tunnel-like; or the aim may simply be to make a small garden seem less confined. A way to do all these things is through the manipulation of scale.

Making a small garden appear less cramped is often best achieved by avoiding a single unified design; rather, the space can be broken down into even smaller portions, where the attention is focused onto the detail of planting and hard landscaping. These spaces or garden rooms can each be given different characters which are presented as a series of little surprises. There is no golden rule which says a garden must have an open lawn in the middle; if space is really tight it is usually better to go for a fuller, heavier planting. One possibility is to turn the garden into a miniature ornamental jungle, where paths wind in among the plants in such a way as never to reveal the full extent of the site.

Long thin gardens can also be treated this way, so that it is never possible to see down the full length of the long axis. If this is unavoidable, then try to arrest the eye with some major feature in the foreground or middle distance, such as a circular lawn or a specimen tree, or place horizontal features such as low walls, wide steps, paving or hedges across the axis. Tiered plants like *Viburnum plicatum* 'Mariesii' have the same effect. In a less symmetrical garden, features can be placed down the sides, causing the eye to swerve and pause – perhaps a painted seat in a formal arbour or the striking trunks of a multi-stemmed tree. In all of this it is a good idea to begin by making a sketch plan of the garden and drawing in the sight lines to see where the visual emphasis lies.

There are many ways of increasing the sense of depth in a garden. Vistas can be emphasized and

Far left: Clever transitions, from one part to another, increase the feeling of variety and size within a garden. One area can be used like the hall of a house, giving access to different "rooms" that may or may not pick up motifs and materials from the useful linking areas.

Left: Even in informal gardens, vistas can be emphasized by careful planting. A solid screen of shrubs would be much less effective than the golden foliage and the elegant, upright blue cypress that form the focus of this vista.

Right: The lines of tile detail on this rendered wall lead the eye on and succeed in increasing the false perspective through the two arches, making the second seem further away. The glimpses of plants and steps beyond enhance this impression.

Below: The stripes produced by a lawn mower can be used to draw the eye according to the direction of the cut. Here they emphasize the vista, counteracting the cross-banding of the steps and leading the eye to the statue.

"lengthened" by stressing the distant perspective. Eye-catching features can be used to draw the eye away into the distance, and there is no need to rely solely on the contents of your garden to do this. Make use of the landscape outside: let a distant hilltop or church spire become the focus of a garden vista. On the other hand, a door in a garden wall 20ft (6m) away will work in the same way for a smaller garden. It is a matter of degree and using opportunities.

Creating a false perspective is another useful technique. By placing large plants in the foreground and smaller ones of the same shape in the distance, at a glance they all appear to be the same size but receding into the distance. It is possible to do the same with foliage, by planting thin airy foliage close by and denser foliage further away.

Lawn-mower stripes in a lawn can be used to give direction to a view or to pull the eye in a particular direction, lengthening or shortening the perspective. Arches and pergolas will enhance perspective, while fences and trelliswork have a strong linear impact. Trellis can also create *trompe l'oeil* effects, giving the impression of three dimensions where only two exist. Even mirrors have been used in garden doorways to double the length of a vista. *Trompe l'oeil* can be used to highly sophisticated ends, with false scenes and features painted onto flat surfaces. Such tricks can be very restrictive to a whole design so they should be used with care. Simpler devices might be preferable; the reflective surface of a pool of still water offers tranquillity and a vertical dimension (its own depth and the reflection of the sky above).

SEASONAL PLANNING

A garden can never be as colourful in winter as in summer, but there is no reason why it should not be just as interesting but in different ways. This is simply a matter of planning so that there is always something attractive to be seen. Each season needs thinking about in terms of the colour of flowers, foliage and fruit, form, texture, perfume and the uses to which the garden will be put. Even if a grand slam of summer colour is desired, it is still possible to underplant and interplant for other times of the year.

There is almost no season in which bulbs do not flower and most of them are easy and trouble-free to grow. Use dry shade under trees for winter aconites and spring and autumn cyclamen. Plant the early dwarf daffodils and the very late, scented pheasant-eye types as well as the mid-season hybrids. Tulips in all their variety have a long season from March to May. There are spring- and autumn-flowering crocuses, as well as the colchicums (meadow saffron) which flower in September. Lilies and galtonias will fill the middle of the summer. Remember that bulbs do not need to occupy a space solely for themselves; they can be tucked in among other plants, almost as a bonus. Bulbs naturalized in grass are a delight.

Perfume can be present in the garden throughout most of the year. There are headily scented, late winter and early spring shrubs such as *Azara*, *Sarcococca*, *Chimonanthus*, *Viburnum* and *Hamamelis*. Even heather is very sweet on the air in March. Try to make room near to a door for a shrub with good perfume in winter, and have those with summer perfume by windows or sitting-out areas, especially if they produce

Left: Autumn colour should be planned for at all levels of the garden, from the tree canopy down through shrubs (such as the Japanese maple shown here), to herbaceous plants with berries or colourful foliage. It is not just trees and shrubs that colour in autumn. The foliage of herbaceous plants, including bergenias, gillenias and *Euphorbia cyparissias,* can colour just as beautifully as the leaves of the larger plants. The euphorbia, for one, also has delightful spring interest, bearing lime green flowers.

Top: Summer showpiece borders, awash with colour as here, steal all the limelight for a few months, but gardens need to compensate elsewhere to give interest throughout the year. The focus of interest can move round the garden as the year progresses.

Bottom right: In the depths of winter, late berries and flowers, coloured bark, evergreens and even snow itself lend colour to a garden. It would be hard to better these "flowers" of ice. The skeletal forms of plants are central to the winter garden.

Right: Heathers and conifers can be very bright in winter, seen in the selection here. Their evergreen colours are best woven subtly into the entire fabric of the garden.

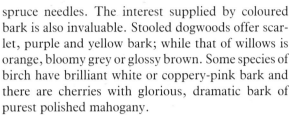

their strongest scent in the evening. There are also plants with scented foliage to consider, such as *Artemisia abrotanum* (ladslove) and *Helichrysum italicum* (the curry plant).

In many places herbaceous perennials can be found in flower for almost 11 months out of the 12, and by planting a good cross section it is possible to get a long season. Hellebores are invaluable in late winter and are soon followed by pulmonarias. Both of these have an unseasonal lushness. Spring and summer are well supplied with colourful perennials, but there are plenty more which flower in the autumn such as *Rudbeckia*, *Persicaria*, *Schizostylis*, michaelmas daisies and dahlias.

In the winter the focus shifts to evergreen foliage, and there is a great variety of textures and colours to choose from including the glossy spiny leaves of holly, the soft gold of some variegated yews, or the blue of spruce needles. The interest supplied by coloured bark is also invaluable. Stooled dogwoods offer scarlet, purple and yellow bark; while that of willows is orange, bloomy grey or glossy brown. Some species of birch have brilliant white or coppery-pink bark and there are cherries with glorious, dramatic bark of purest polished mahogany.

Autumn colour can be found in trees like maples and rowans, but there are vines of equal brilliance and even herbaceous plants such as euphorbia and gillenia. Fruits and berries need not just be an autumn feature. Many roses carry their hips and *Mahonia aquifolium* bears its blue berries in late summer. Later come the reds, yellows and oranges of holly, rowans, cotoneasters and pyracantha. Usually the paler the berry, the later the birds will descend to eat them.

In winter a garden falls back on its structure to make itself interesting, and it is then that the most

benefit is gained from light and shade and the clarity of the design. Think of the long low shadows from an orange winter sun cast by pencil cedars or a castellated hedge; a tremendously satisfying effect.

Other things to consider are the provision of privacy for the summer and of open spaces for children to play. They will need grass for the lively games of summer and a hard surface to avoid mud and damage in the winter. To get the most out of a garden, think of the luxury of a sitting area in a sun-trap, which could be comfortable on a sunny day in early spring or in autumn. Every detail has seasonal significance; if water features are included as part of the seasonal plan, then it is possible to have the sound of running water in the heat of summer and the still mirror-like surface of a pool to reflect scudding clouds in winter.

Far left: Bark like that of this red-stemmed dogwood (*Cornus alba*), can be an important feature of winter gardens. Many other trees and shrubs, especially birches, cherries and pines, have coloured bark that is a great bonus in winter.

Left: Most autumn foliage colours are complementary, as in the case of *Cotinus coggygria* 'Royal Purple' and *Acer palmatum*. There is no need to worry too much about colour schemes in this season, except to take into account possible clashes with highly valuable late season flowers.

Above: Fruits are just as much a part of the autumn scene as coloured leaves, so try to find room for some fruiting plants in your garden, even if it is on a wall. Here the rich tints of a medlar glow with seasonal promise. There is little to match the pleasure of harvesting home-grown fruit.

Right: This yellow border is infiltrated with golden-leafed evergreens, which will maintain colour and substance in the border long after the leaves on other plants have fallen. In summer they play a more discreet role.

COLOUR

As harmony is to a tune, so colour is to a garden: it gives a more precise feeling and mood to the underlying design. Colour alone cannot make a garden, but it can enrich the design and highlight different parts of the scheme at different times. It can attract attention by means of bright harmony or by shocking contrasts; it can produce tranquillity through quiet harmonies or monotones, or create movement within the design by means of flowing harmonies and contrasts (which is perhaps the most ambitious and difficult part of gardening). Edwardian herbaceous borders were so magnificent precisely because of their fine tuning of colour on a grand scale over a long season. Use colour purposefully, to your own ends and tastes, but never underestimate its power. Right and wrong may be in the eye of the beholder, but almost everyone recognizes chaos for what it is. Above all, colour in gardens is a means to an end like any other tool, rather than an end in itself.

Regardless of the effect sought through colour selection, there is no getting away from the need for green. It is the backbone of any colour scheme and should always be in evidence. There is a whole range to choose from: fresh apple greens will complement white and yellow, and warm bronzy greens will set off orange and scarlets. In a single-colour garden the presence of greens is particularly important and should be used to maximum effect.

Everything in a garden has colour, not just flowers, but foliage, walls, buildings, paths and seats. Together they offer the opportunity for endless experimentation and variety. If the hard landscaping has been inherited with the garden, the colour of brick walls, gravel and so on must be taken into account before embarking on a colour scheme to which they might be unsympathetic. A new site offers a rare opportunity: a chance to create the design, with the colours, of the gardener's dreams.

Left: Colour on its own cannot make a garden, but it is one of the most powerful instruments in the gardener's hand. It can shock, soothe or seduce; the gardener is in control.

Top left: Geranium × *oxonianum* 'Claridge Druce' under roses and border phlox contributes to a running variation on a theme of pink and mauve. A precise and limited colour scheme allows for subtle shifts of tone.

Bottom left: Foliage can be just as much a source of colour as flowers. Here, variegated hostas, meadowsweet, bamboo and golden catalpa form the basis of the colour scheme, while highlights of the same colour are provided by day lilies and helianthus.

Top right: Single-colour gardens are deservedly popular. Variety must come from shapes and textures rather than colour. Here, white 'Blizzard' tulips, grape hyacinths, forget-me-nots and pansies nestle beneath *Viburnum × carlcephalum.* It is the geometic rank of tulips which keeps the composition alive and anchors the display.

Bottom right: Some colours have to be used sparingly because they are so strong. In this detail the bright red of *Lychnis chalcedonica* is isolated in front of a delicate curtain of the cool grey weeping pear. Both plants benefit from the juxtaposition.

Harmonizing Colours

Each of us sees colour differently, and one person's idea of bright harmonies may be another person's chamber of horrors. Nevertheless, there are certain basic guidelines which will help to produce harmonizing colours. Thereafter it is up to the individual to satisfy his or her tastes and to find the combinations that do most justice to the size, style and situation of a garden, a garden "room" or a flowerbed.

With colour, almost more than any other element in garden design, economy is the key. A few colours used carefully will be far more effective than a fussy mixture. Too many colours, used indiscriminately, will tend to cancel each other out and look either muddled, frantic or simply unattractive.

Colour harmonies can be made by several means. The simplest way is to use several varieties and tones of one colour, plus greens of course. This can be fun, but it is rather limited. Alternatively, one main colour can be combined with closely related colours – think of late summer borders of scarlet, oranges and browns or those intriguing mixtures of steely blue and grey foliage spiked with flowers of white and midnight blue. Another way, which is perhaps the hardest, is to

Above: On the colour wheel, blue and grey are neighbours and offset each other well. Grey is accommodating and will act as a foil for many other colours.

Above right: Blue and gold are contrasting colours, but can be made harmonious by using one in a pale form and one in a dark form. Here the rich blue of *Geranium himalayense* is combined with the paler blue

of *Veronica gentianoides* and the soft yellow leaves and heads of Bowles' golden grass (*Milium effusum aureum*).

Below left: Different tones of one colour make a harmonious combination. Here, yellow is the dominant theme leading through the border, from *Achillea* 'Moonshine' on the left, through golden-leaved shrubs and trees, to *Rosa* 'Golden Wings' on the right.

choose two colours some way apart on the wheel and to link them with an intermediate colour. This effect is often seen in rose gardens, where pale pink roses are tied to the soft blues of catmint and lavender by grey foliage, always a useful linking colour.

Colour harmonies can also be used to allow a large part of the spectrum to appear in one garden, by progressing from cool creams and yellows through warmer reds and oranges to purples and blues. Along the way it is possible to make a whole range of small contrasts and variations depending on taste and space, but the general progression will remain the same.

Colour relationships work not only through their relative positions in the spectrum but also through the strength and amount of colour used. A good guide is to have one or at most two colours that are dominant in strength but not in area, with other colours supporting in decreasing ranks.

Never forget the importance of green. It is often spoken of as if it were one colour, overlooking the fact that there is a whole range of different shades which can be just as useful in creating harmonies as any other colour which has a range of tones.

Below: Blue and red make a bold contrast, but here they are drawn together by intermediate colours such as pink, lavender and mauve. Using intermediate colours allows the creation of schemes that pass through several strong colours; if the design is well paced the effect can be wonderful. Gertrude Jekyll used intermediate colours in this way in her grand Edwardian flower borders.

Below right: Strong colours need to be used sparingly, as the culmination or highlight of a colour scheme. Here, deep red azaleas form a dense and dark base, leading upwards into lighter-textured pale pink, and finally into the airy, white structure of a magnolia tree. Strong colours used in tiny flashes have a very different, less startling effect than dense blocks of colour which hide every leaf.

One-colour Gardens

These have become popular in recent years in the wake of such famous examples as the white garden at Sissinghurst. They represent an extremely disciplined form of gardening in that the gardener has to work with a very limited palette. This can have its advantages: the emphasis is thrown back on to the elements of shape and texture, which is never a bad thing, and it suits small gardens because the simple and economic use of colour saves them from the clutter trap of having too many colours squeezed into a limited space. Larger gardens may use the single colour theme in just one small area, and in a garden where colour is used in an extravagant and complicated way this can come as a moment of relief from the hurly-burly. This is certainly true with a white garden which seems so clean and neutral to an eye that has been romping through the whole spectrum. Above all others, a white garden allows the viewer to appreciate the forms of the plants and the flowers: by removing the element of strong colour, the white palette gives a unique clarity to a planting scheme.

Single-colour gardening can be based on any colour – red, yellow, grey, blue, brown have all been used, as have black and white. Parallel herbaceous borders have been divided up into single colour sections facing each other across a path. Whichever colour is chosen, three things will remain paramount: the need for many shades of the chosen colour, the occasional contrasting colour, and the liberal use of greens throughout the garden or bed.

Above: In the famous "White Garden" at Sissinghurst grey and green are used as foils. The very formal design gives substance to the garden in winter, and there is much underplanting of bulbs to extend the season.

Left: Rosa rugosa 'Blanche Double de Coubert' has a relatively brief flowering period but it makes a delightfully cool combination with snow-in-summer (*Cerastium tomentosum*).

Right: Roses, pinks and peonies make a scrum of compatible pinks. The hard landscaping of steps and verandah, rather than contrasting foliage, provides the structure.

Even within a single colour there are many variations and degrees of density with which to make contrasts. A blue garden will almost certainly be improved if it contains the gamut of blues, from the midnight purple of *Salvia × superba* through the royal blue of agapanthus to the lavender and palest amethyst of violas and crocuses. It may contain more grey and silver foliage than green, but the overall effect will be a fanfare of blueness. There is no reason why a blue garden should not contain the occasional splash of another colour. Nature may do it for you, just as the dense blue-grey of rue will always throw up its crop of yellow flowers. The occasional splash of white will never seem out of place in a blue garden, while a steely autumn picture of juniper, rue, *Euphorbia characias wulfenii* and santolina can be enhanced by a streak of screaming pink schizostylis (kaffir lily). Select harmonious or contrasting colours to suit the mood.

Top right: Experimentation is needed when finding different shades of a colour to put together. Scarlet and pink are not automatically comfortable bedfellows, but with the chaperones of rich greens and plentiful greys to keep them apart, the effect is one of warm harmony and unity.

Right: There is no need to take too strict an approach to single-colour gardens. A little latitude will positively improve the look of a scheme, provided the principal colour (and therefore mood) remain dominant. Here, an array of blue, white and mauve delphiniums combine perfectly to produce an effect that is more than just an exercise in monochrome.

All-green Gardens

From time to time most gardeners long for an all-green garden. It is a longing for clarity and simplicity, for a rest from the business of gardening. The inspiration may be found in a formal garden: picture a white-painted weatherboard house with a long verandah overlooking still trees and emerald lawns striped with the shadows of beautifully clipped hedges. Or a more intensively planted garden may appeal, perhaps a dappled grove carpeted with choice woodland plants. Whatever the inspiration, an all-green garden is almost certain to be restful and easy on the eye. There is an easy-going naturalness about green gardens, even when made in a formal style.

Green gardens happily lean toward formality because in the absence of other colours they are free to fall back on the elements of texture and design. Some of the most striking green gardens are exclusively topiary gardens, which can be breathtaking displays of trained and tailored evergreens.

In a less formal context there is a huge range of all-green plants to choose from; plants, that is, which have green flowers as well as green foliage. Look at all the different greens in a flowering plant of *Euphorbia amygdaloides robbiae* or *Alchemilla mollis;* there is everything from dark green to pale grey-green and lime. A good green garden can incorporate every shade; emerald, olive and khaki all have their uses.

A green garden is a way of making the most of the simplest palette on offer, but it will also benefit from other discreet colours such as brown. There are brown, black and green barks to be had, and there is the russet and silver indumentum underneath the

Left: A green garden can throw the emphasis back onto the line, colour and texture of nearby buildings and paths. Here it highlights the configurations of the brickwork, the gateway and the floating forms of the "lollipop" bay trees. A shady courtyard is made into a delightful haven by this cool, formal approach.

leaves of some species of rhododendron. Grey foliage is not always sucessful in a green garden, as most grey-leaved plants are sun lovers and come from more naturally colourful plant communities.

Do not banish colour from a green garden. As with any single-colour garden, a little of the colour's close relatives (yellow and blue) can be incorporated with good effect. White also blends in very comfortably with green. *Tiarella*, *Aruncus*, Solomon's seal and primroses all offer a gentle touch of colour without moving away from that green-upon-green woodland feel. For the palest pinks, add Tellimas or dicentras.

Variegated foliage has a place in a green garden, but can by contrast look very artificial when surrounded by simple greens. It should be used sparingly. Most variegated foliage shows its best colours in full light and tends not to be successful in shady gardens. Slight shade is less of a problem to these plants and a dull corner will benefit from bright variegations.

Far left: Any one-colour garden is always improved by a touch of another colour. White or pale blue are the most discreet and perhaps best additions to green, as they enhance the feeling of purity and simplicity. Green itself has a whole range of tones, from the yellows of box and spiraea, as here, to sea greens, greys and blues. A mostly green garden is relaxing compared to an over-fussy floral display.

Left: Clipped shapes within the hedges echo the forms beyond: box spirals and tall conifers, box balls and stone balls, spiky phormium leaves and complementary patterns in the pathway.

Above: Variegated foliage has a most useful role to play in green gardens. It can add variety and provides a means of highlighting certain shapes and areas. Ivy and euonymus can be particularly useful.

Contrasting Colours

The colour wheel shows how the principal contrasts in colour are made – red with green, blue with orange and yellow with purple – but countless bold combinations can be used. These are strong effects, highlights to be used in garden design in a similar way to harmonies, but more sparingly. If a garden is overloaded with severe contrasts they cease to be effective. For instance, a golden-leaved conifer can make a brilliant highlight in the all-green days of winter, but plant a dozen of them and the effect is devalued.

A variety of smaller contrasts, in colour as in texture, are the stuff of interesting gardening. They keep the eye entertained and moving along. Sharp contrasts, like purple hazel next to yellow elder or a blue spruce with a yellow cypress, can draw attention and focus a garden, but they also hold up the progress of the eye, whereas smaller, gentler contrasts allow the eye to flow along. Indeed, the most harmonious of planting schemes will need a little contrast to keep it

Below left: Red has the ability to make green, its opposite on the colour wheel, all the more intense. Here, one form of the excellent, vibrant climber parthenocissus changes colour after another form, the autumn contrast being used to emphasize the line of the wall.

Above: Strong colours can have strong effects. This deep scarlet rose contrasts just as much with blue as it does with shell pink, when all colours are delivered in the same volume. The tiered effect – blue rising to red, rising to pink – is satisfying and clear.

alive and add that certain spark of the unexpected. A garden without enough contrast becomes a dull affair.

Colours which at full strength would war with one another can make good companions when one of them is used in a paler tint. The strong, creamy yellow of *Anthemis* 'Wargrave' would look crude beside royal blue delphiniums, yet if the misty lavender of *Thalictrum delavayi* were to be substituted for the delphinium there would be an interesting contrast, and the speck of yellow in the heart of the thalictrum flower would tie the two colours together. For a more gradual contrast, the thalictrum could be placed between the anthemis and the delphinium.

Contrast of foliage colour can be just as telling as that of flower colour, and this should be borne in mind when planning a garden. Schemes which are

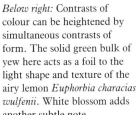

intended to carry a great deal of bright flower colour will not require so much contrast or variety in the foliage: a reliable matrix of good stable greens will provide the best platform for floral pyrotechnics. By contrast, a garden which relies more on permanent shrubby plantings and evergreens will benefit from a greater range of contrasts in foliage colour.

Colour contrast can be made part of the whole garden design with certain areas set aside for strong hot colours, in direct contrast to other pale, cooler areas. These colour pools need not be kept separate in enclosed areas of the garden; instead, contrast can be used to enhance and distinguish the different sides of a more open prospect.

Remember that the effects made by colour depend upon the light in which they are seen. A really startling contrast may be devalued by siting it in shade, but, conversely, this effect can be used to temper an unwanted, unavoidable clash of colours.

Above: In a largely yellow colour scheme, a contained touch of deep maroon presents a strong highlight and focus that emphasizes the different lighter shades. The maroon is made more intense by the contrast, and the yellow is saved from being uneventful.

Below right: Contrasts of colour can be heightened by simultaneous contrasts of form. The solid green bulk of yew here acts as a foil to the light shape and texture of the airy lemon *Euphorbia characias wulfenii*. White blossom adds another subtle note.

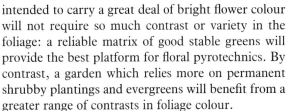

Left: A gentle colour scheme of mauve and lemon can be given a sparkle by the addition of some rich blue and bright yellow, forming a greater contrast on the fringe. Grey helps to tie together the lemon and mauve. This late summer border gives a good impression of the flower and foliage effects that can be achieved with a planting of perennials and annuals. The main emphasis falls on the yellow *Achillea taygetea* and *Helichrysum* 'Sulphur Light', with their respectively flat and clustered flower heads and

texturally interesting foliage. A companula, to the right, gives height, while the delightful floriferous annual, *Xeranthemum annuum*, fills the foreground. Although it is drawing to the end of the growing season, the plants remain attractive. Fading flowers and mature foliage can have their own charm – subtlety compared to the vividness of high summer extravagance. The whole makes an enchanting scene. Notice the discreet supports around the rose bushes at either side.

TEXTURES

Texture works with shape and colour in a garden to create movement and harmony for the eye. In contrast with themselves and each other, these three elements produce a constantly changing variety of interest, bringing the detail of the garden to life. The greater the range of textures, the greater will be the interest throughout the space.

It is easy to forget that everything in a garden has its own texture; not only are there the textures of foliage, grass, flowers and bark, but also those of water, paths, walls, gravel and all the other areas of hard landscaping. Texture is a more discreet element than colour or shape, and a wide range of textures will not clutter a garden so much as highlight its other elements. So it is worth trying to incorporate plenty of different textures in all aspects of the garden.

We are made aware of texture in different ways; partly through direct sight and touch – we can see and feel if a leaf is rough and hairy – and partly through the way light falls on surfaces – we expect shiny rhododendron leaves to be smooth and firm or a glistening, wet stone-flagged path to be harder than gravel. This indirect visual appreciation of texture needs to be part of the planning of texture in a garden as much as the tactile element.

Hard landscape features can be softened by the use of textures. Consider the use of "green" steps, where the risers are planted with ivy or some tiny cotoneaster; think of deep cobbles or precise herringbone bricks with emerald green moss in every joint. The features themselves also offer a wide range of textures, from hard concrete to fine footstep-deadening grit. In a precise, formal garden, where much of the design is dictated by architectural features, large quantities of polished marble can look perfect on walls or underfoot, most usually in the form of a well-proportioned staircase. By contrast, in a minimalist style, where incidental details are more appropriate

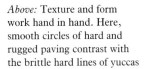

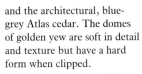

Above: Texture and form work hand in hand. Here, smooth circles of hard and rugged paving contrast with the brittle hard lines of yuccas and the architectural, blue-grey Atlas cedar. The domes of golden yew are soft in detail and texture but have a hard form when clipped.

Above: Textural contrasts need not be extreme to be effective. The roughness of this gravel is suitably offset by a gentle mixture of soft shapes and textures, seen in both the foliage and the adjacent surfaces. The delicate, mounding Japanese maple rightfully takes centre stage.

Left: The tall Chusan palm has its own internal contrast of textures. Hard, flapping leaves stand above a rugged hairy stem. A woodland floor, rippling with bluebells, complements the softness of the trunks to produce a calm, gentle aspect. Although the tree is distinctly exotic in appearance it is frost hardy. It does, however, need full sun, fertile, well-drained soil and shelter from strong winds.

Above: Texture can be a matter of scale. Here the spiky flowers of the dwarf laurel *Prunus laurocerasus* 'Otto Luyken' combine *en masse* to form a soft carpet of green and white. As a contrast, the light glossy texture of box is clipped into a hard wheel shape to be doubly effective. Colour and form underline the textural contrast. The whole effect shows the highly original nature of garden design.

than clearly delineated patterns, a great river-washed boulder will combine a gentle shape with a hard texture without imposing uncompromising order.

The range of textures to be found in foliage is immense, but they can reasonably be grouped into the following categories: feathery, soft, felty or hairy, rugged, spiky, hard, smooth or shiny.

Feathery leaves make you instantly want to touch them. Some, like fennel and ladslove, release a perfume when touched. There are the green or purple domes of the dwarf maple, *Acer palmatum dissectum*, the tougher birch 'Trost's Dwarf' or the fern-leaved elder. There is the billowy foliage of 'Boulevard' cypresses, the brittle delicacy of dicentras or the flowers themselves of the smoke bush, *Cotinus coggygria*, which is smothered in panicles of wonderful, fluffy blossoms during summer.

Softness comes in many guises, from the swaying fountains of bamboos and ornamental grasses to the simple eloquence of moss. Ferns offer some deliciously soft textures over a long season. Meadow grass rippling in the wind must surely be one of the garden's most seductive softnesses, while in a border plants like *Alchemilla mollis* will act as a gentle foil for more vigorous shapes.

Feltiness or hairiness is often to be found on large leaves, like those of *Hydrangea sargentiana* and *Bergenia ciliata*, or on the undersides of some species rhododendron leaves which can have a rich indumentum of grey or russet. Lambs' ears (*Stachys byzantina*) is a favourite with children, and many people like to stroke the cerise velvet flowers of *Salvia buchananii*.

Ruggedness shows up well in the striking corrugated leaves of veratrums, rogersias, *Viburnum davidii* and

V. rhytidophyllum, and the vast umbrella leaves of *Gunnera manicata*. There are barks too, flaky, deeply corrugated, striped, or even peeling in shreds and tatters.

Spikiness appears most often in the sword-like foliage of irises, crocosmias, phormium and yucca, and in the prickles of holly and eryngiums. Acanthus, morina and eryngiums also have spiny flowers.

Hard textures are found in shiny broad-leaved and needle-bearing evergreens, in the rigidity of yuccas and in the tight surfaces of topiary and cushion plants like *Bolax* or *Hebe* 'Boughton Dome' (which is as crusty-looking as a new cottage loaf).

Glossy leaves grace evergreen shrubs like laurel, aucuba and griselinia, but there is just as much shine on the foliage of herbaceous plants like galax or asarum. Remember that some barks can be shiny too, especially some species of cherry and birch.

Opposite: Amid a generalized soft planting of ferns and primulas, the striking textures come from the shiny surface of the water and the rugged bark of the silver birch. These elements together produce a balanced effect.

Top left: In a planting of soft shapes and textures, the hard lines of stepping stones can be used to give clarity to the structure of the garden.

Top right: The combinations of texture and form can vary greatly. The shape of this pampas grass is undeniably stiff, yet the flower plumes are

soft and yielding. The dome of 'Jackman's Blue' rue has a broad, draping form that matches its soft texture.

Bottom left: Texture is often deceptive. The purple euphorbia is far softer than the surrounding cotoneaster branches, yet their geometric structure would lead you to expect them both to be hard. Greater contrast of form would benefit these textures.

Bottom right: The leaves of this purple cordyline and the surrounding griselinia are equally hard, yet the contrast of form is extreme.

STYLES

The style of a garden is largely responsible for its atmosphere, whether it is neat and geometric, relaxed and informal, busy and colourful, or still and discreet. The choice of style is often influenced by other gardens that have been seen and admired. Try to be open-minded about the styles you look at, and consider not just their personal appeal, but also how they would suit your house and family use, and how much maintenance they would create and when. Styles which rely on a very detailed planting to look correct will require a great deal of summer attention which you may not be able to give. On the other hand, a style which is architecturally complex may be more expensive to construct but far easier to maintain during the growing season. Some of the great historic garden styles have been extremely simple in terms of plant material, relying more on the form of the land, on water and buildings, and such staples as grass and trees. This restrained approach can produce stunning results, whatever the scale of the site. Let period styles be a source of inspiration, a starting point rather than something to copy slavishly. It is too easy to let period style become a cliché: draw the best from it and make it your own. After all, every style was modern once. By giving serious consideration at the outset to style, ideas are often enriched and crystallized and the temptation to simply fill the garden with a mass of favourite plants avoided.

Left top and bottom: Classical formality or cottage garden? You must decide what suits your house, your household (children and pets as well as adults) and your pocket. It is also important to consider how much time you are prepared to put into gardening and the length of time you are likely to stay before moving. Choosing the right style will maximize the pleasure you receive.

Above left: Select a design appropriate to your interests. The clear lines of a modern designer garden can be obscured by rich planting so may not suit the plant lover.

Above right: With care, you can make your own style by mixing unlikely elements. The combination of classical urn, cottagey pots and modern paving works as a satisfying composition of shapes and colour. The attention given to the paved design allows other details to be simpler.

Below: If time and money are plentiful, the Victorian style may be for you. But would you always want a garden so rich in detail in all its parts, so formal, so ostentatiously gardened? Might you prefer a simpler, classical approach to formality, that gives order to a space without such abundance?

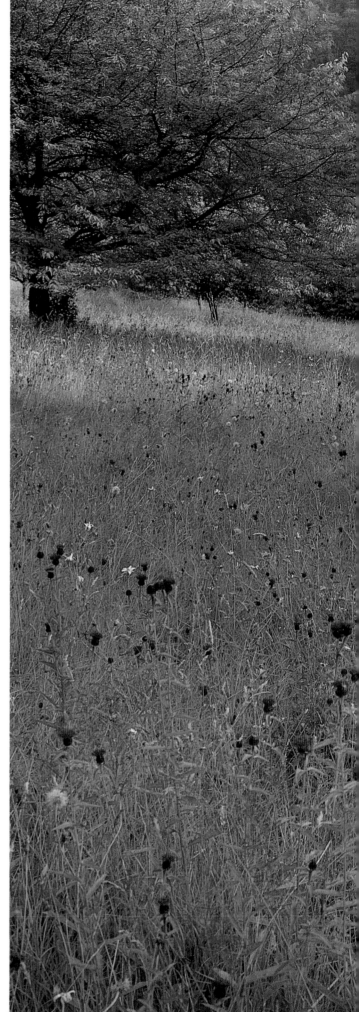

Wild

Most gardeners understand what is meant by a wild garden even though it is really a contradiction in terms. How can a garden, a man-made creation, be truly wild? The main characteristic is that nature is apparently allowed to have the upper hand over the gardener, but in a successful wild garden this is never actually so. The gardener produces this illusion by keeping maintenance to a discreet minimum and by choosing plants which will not take advantage of this kind of freedom. It is a quiet lyrical style of gardening, a balance between the truly natural and the contrived which is surprisingly difficult to achieve.

The fashion for a more relaxed approach to gardening first appeared in the late seventeenth century, when large gardens often included a "wilderness": an intersecting network of paths and vistas running between areas of trees and shrubs, and sometimes hedges. This was wild only in that it contrasted with the more rigidly formal gardens nearer the house. Wild gardening as we know it today was pioneered in the late nineteenth century by the writer William Robinson as a reaction to the ostentatious formality of the high Victorian period. In *The Wild Garden* (1870) he advocated naturalizing "perfectly hardy exotic plants under conditions where they will thrive without further care". It was he who first persuaded the hybrid daffodil out of the bed and into the long grass; yet even he was content to have areas of more closely managed formality around the house.

Today, the notion of wild gardening has become associated with the idea of nature conservation, and one hears more of putting back native plants than

Far left: Naturalized bulbs, like these anemones and small early daffodils, are perfect for creating decorative drifts of colour in a wild garden. The grass here would not be cut until mid-summer, allowing the foliage of the naturalized plants time to feed the bulbs and die down first. Wild daffodils self-seed readily in these conditions.

introducing foreign ones. We have become aware of gardens as living communities, not just of plants but also of birds, animals like hedgehogs and squirrels, insects, fungi, and even lichens.

Certain rules of thumb are worth remembering when creating a wild garden. First, the garden needs to be big enough to have its own identity to avoid looking like a small shabby part of an otherwise well maintained garden. It may be advantageous to separate the wild area visually from the rest of the garden. Second, it is usually more appropriate to keep wild gardening at some distance from the house. Close contrast with a neat house will make a wild garden look muddled rather than relaxed and comfortable.

The wild garden should be planned for minimum maintenance. Lawns may even become flower meadows, cut as hay in late summer, with paths mown through them for access. Safe old trees should be left to decline gracefully and woodland plants should be cultivated beneath them. Use plenty of bulbs and shrubs which can compete with grass and require next to no pruning or spraying. It may be a good idea to introduce a pond if the time is available to maintain it. Above all, do not overplant: nature is an economical gardener and gains her best effects very simply, with just a few plants.

Left: A wild-flower meadow makes a superb transitional zone between garden and country. Wild gardening, when it is successful, can be sheer magic.

Below: In damp woodland, primulas, ferns, bluebells and forget-me-nots multiply. Such a display needs weeding in spring but later in the year requires minimal attention.

Left: This early summer scene has a wonderfully fresh and relaxed quality. Vigorous roses look well in turf, and can be allowed to sprawl freely. Try to choose mildew-resistant varieties, and then leave them.

Below left: Much of wild gardening is a matter of keeping the peace. Having established wild flowers where you want them, the general maintenance regime should allow them to increase freely, apart from the most vigorous.

Below right: An informal pond cannot be beaten for imparting that wild look, even when, as here, exotic plants are combined with native ones. Ponds also provide a habitat for wildlife, including fish, amphibians, insects and certain birds.

Right: A simple hazel-nut walk can be transformed into a garden with a minimum of planting. Self-seeding bluebells are given that little extra spark by the addition of a few scarlet tulips.

Below left: Wild gardening should be simple, but can still be subtle. Here, native foxgloves and the wild *Rhododendron ponticum* make a perfect early-summer combination alongside a soft path. Purples can be all the more opulent in shade.

Below right: Wild flowers may often be small, but *en masse* they are just as effective as larger garden flowers, if a little less precise. These buttercups contribute just as much to this scene as the pink pokers of the cultivated bistort.

Topiary

Despite the vituperations of those who regarded topiary as "pastry cooks' gardening", it has always had a loving following somewhere. Whatever topiary might do for the style of a garden, there is always pleasure to be taken in the sheer craftsmanship of creating and maintaining it. In manageable quantities, making topiary is fun.

The clipping of yew, holly and box played an important part in seventeenth-century gardens and came to the fore again in the grand formal gardens of the high Victorian era. Large gardens of the twentieth century have often made bold use of topiary, and it has long been a part of the cottage garden tradition.

The continuing appeal of topiary stems from the fact that it is an effective (and also inexpensive) means of creating the structure of a garden. A fine hedge with knife-edged finials marching on top is every bit as much a part of the garden's structure and ornament as a stone wall would be. A well-placed and freestanding topiary specimen, in whatever style, will command just as much dramatic attention as a fine statue.

Topiary is essentially a formal style of gardening. It is the imposition of the gardener's will upon the plant, a living sculpture. This degree of artificiality immediately commands the onlooker's attention and makes competition from mere flowers seem rather petty. Consequently, topiary is best used where it has the space to be seen on its own terms. The faintly comical mixture of topiary and a gentle jumble of flowers in cottage gardens is perhaps why topiary there has tended to be humorous in inspiration.

Whole gardens of topiary are best kept simple. The point of concentration should be in the contrast of curves and straight lines, of light and shadow, of earthbound or floating forms. A lawn or clean gravel is all that is needed to set off these living sculptures, but you can extend the interest by adding a little coloured foliage such as golden yew, or some simple washes of colour provided by bedding plants.

Topiary is not in itself a labour-intensive craft. Only the amount of topiary you have will make it a chore, especially if ladders are needed. Patience and skill are the keys. Once the shapes are fully formed, an annual clipping is sufficient for yew and box, carried out at the gardener's convenience during autumn or early winter. Topiary can be made out of holly and bay too, but there is no doubt that yew is much the best. Good topiary is slow to take shape, which is why so many topiary gardens conveniently begin life with a more diverse planting until the topiary develops its own singular authority.

Left: This great topiary cartwheel is almost a garden in itself. It is made entirely of box, both the green and yellow forms, giving structural contrast throughout the year. Interplanting is restrained.

Below: Strong, towering forms produce a maze-like effect, which offers new vistas at every turn. A bold structure like this can cope with a loose, informal underplanting.

Above: Single-colour bedding emphasizes the geometric design in this scheme of great clarity and simplicity. There is contrast in the hard paths and the play of sunlight on the imaginative shapes.

Top left: These three-sided pyramids of yew make a wonderful abstract sculpture. They would be difficult to maintain without the use of a small scaffold: very tall topiary specimens always present difficulties of this kind.

Top right: Box bushes will respond well to hard pruning. This old specimen has been cut back to its framework of branches and the new growth has been cloud-pruned to form a clever vegetable poodle of considerable charm.

Below: Spiral box sentinels of this size require many years of skilful training on a wire frame. Specimens that have already been trained are expensive: weigh your means against your patience.

Left: A living chessboard of topiary makes a magnificent conversation piece. Note the contrast of straight and curved lines. Irish yew (on the perimeter) is too weak to make good upright cylinders and always leans. Purple and grey always complement topiary.

Below: Yew can be shaped more tightly than any other tree or shrub that is suitable for topiary. These flattened balls look as hard as the winter frost upon them.

Top left and right: The precise hedging of a parterre or knot garden is just as hard to maintain well as more fanciful pieces of topiary. In topiary it is always the straight lines that take time to perfect. The job is made easier if a stretched line is used as a cutting guide.

Cottage

The best words to sum up the cottage garden style might be unpretentious or unsophisticated. It is a style in which a random variety of plants is grown, not particularly for the subtleties of careful plant association but simply as favourites, because they are loved for their own sake or are useful in some way. The garden in which they grow will have a small-scale, purely functional framework, without any grand vistas or extravagant hard landscaping. This is because a cottage garden is essentially an elaboration of a working

garden, a fruit and vegetable garden made pretty by flowers with the minimum of expense.

The cottage garden was developed by people who could not afford designer gardens, in the days when cottage meant a humble dwelling in a rural setting rather than a desirable small house in the country. So, for instance, paths were of simple local materials, no wider than absolutely necessary, and lay where necessity required – for instance, from the front door to the garden gate, from the front door round to the back door or from the back door to a garden shed. Gates were simply made, perhaps of painted wood rather than metal. A rustic fence or boundary hedge kept passing farm animals out and would have been of native plants such as holly and hawthorn, forming a transition from garden to country.

Pursuing the theme of a productive garden, in a modern cottage garden the trees should be fruit trees wherever possible, or at least blossom trees of some kind. Apples, pears, plums and cherries will all help

Left: In the soft light of evening this cottage garden seems to merge with the countryside beyond, with the fields seen through a screen of old espalier apple trees and roses trained over a rustic arbour and fence. Free-seeding has helped to produce the relaxed plant groupings in the foreground; it also quickly gives a look of maturity.

to create the right atmosphere, as will nut trees such as hazel or almond. If there is space for a large tree, a walnut might do. Try to avoid large upright conifers. Evergreens such as holly or yew will look more appropriate and they can be clipped into shapes which add a touch of fun and formality to the garden if required. Lawns should not play an important part in a cottage garden. Open spaces suitable for lawns would in a real cottage garden be used for vegetables, so if you need grass for children grow it under fruit trees.

Colourful plants, or perhaps herbs, in simple pots by the door will look right. Make the most of vegetables and fruit bushes, letting them be part of the garden design. Do not be afraid of using rows of vegetables, herbs, bedding plants or flowers for cutting, especially alongside a path. There is no need to grow only old fashioned flowers because it is how the flowers are used and grouped that creates the cottage style not what type they are. Choose as many scented plants as can be fitted into the space available, especially climbing roses and honeysuckle.

The overall effect should be of fussy well-tended order, a comfortable mix in which all the plants are allowed to run together. There will be plenty of weeding, but also an opportunity to grow all your favourite plants in rich profusion.

Far left: Foxgloves, clematis and lovage grow freely in an informal border, backed by low, simple architecture that seems at one with nature.

Below: This arbour is engulfed by a luxuriant growth of mixed climbers; plants drape over the path, giving the scene an intimate mood.

Left, top right and centre right: In cottage gardening, the planting is visually more important than the structure. Paths can be overwhelmed with plants – just so long as you can get by – and the built structure of the garden should be made of simple materials. Smart, sophisticated materials look out of place. Local stone or brick are ideal materials for walls and paving. Rough-cut timber or rustic logs are most suitable for arches.

Bottom far left: Built features in a cottage garden should be well made but simple, like this wicket under a nut arch.

Bottom left: Topiary, often whimsically shaped, is a traditional feature of many cottage gardens.

Below: This excellent example of dry-stone walling shows high quality construction and the use of sympathetic materials. The pink hue in the stone complements the foxgloves. Simple furniture is entirely appropriate.

Bottom right: Showy wild flowers, like foxgloves and herbs, strike a suitably unpretentious note in a cottage garden. Lavender makes an attractive lining to paths, tempting passersby to pick it. Flowers for drying, like helichrysums, honesty and Chinese lanterns, fit in well.

Modern

It is ironic to think that every historical garden style was once the latest thing, fresh and exciting. But what makes a garden modern today? Certainly not the plants themselves, for the world contains no more un-explored continents to offer us startling new introductions as it did during the last 400 years; and while we can reconstruct or draw inspiration from period styles to make something new, the result would not immediately be called a modern garden.

The most clearly modern tendency in gardening is to follow the leads of modern architecture and painting towards a minimalist style, using plenty of clean, modern hard landscaping materials and a much reduced palette of plants. The plants, such as grasses and bamboos, are often chosen more for their foliage and architectural qualities than for their flowers, because the modern style springs precisely from the contrast of shapes and textures between plant and plant, and between plant and hard landscaping.

Due to this predominance of hard landscaping, the modern style is especially suitable for town gardens and courtyards. Here sculpture can bring life to this kind of precise, discreet garden, and it looks more at home than in some traditional styles. Water can be used in mirror pools, trickling over pebbles or in fountains to bring light and movement to the design.

Below: Modern gardens tend to use few plants and there is an emphasis on line and hard landscaping. These pebble arabesques are unashamedly modern, yet are inspired by the parterres of earlier periods and the decorative style of Spanish and Moorish architecture. Could this open space happily stand further complication of its lines?

Left: High-quality materials, such as marble and slate, deserve the attention drawn to them in this angular garden. The fountain and the stylish, sweeping pergola add movement to the design.

Above: An "outdoor room", complete with tiled floor, cleverly uses the contrast between the rough texture of grass and the smooth texture of stone. The linear pattern lengthens the garden.

There are so many different modern paving materials that the possibilities for interesting effects are endless. Concrete paving slabs come in all sizes and colours, from simple rectangles to hexagons. Bricks offer a wonderful range of colours and opportunities for patterned textures. Wooden decking is increasingly used in warm dry climates as a means of surfacing outdoor areas, and it can easily accommodate sudden changes in level.

Another development of modern architecture has been the large plate glass window, which has helped to bring the garden into the house. Equally, everyone likes to have a living area outside in the garden, where the family can eat, read or amuse themselves when the weather permits. These two factors have combined to blur the distinction between indoors and outdoors. Swimming pools have further emphasized this ambiguity and have also introduced another form of hard landscaping into the garden, a feature that requires careful placing and design. Materials usually found indoors have come to be used outside, and it is not unusual to see ceramic tiles on the floor and walls of a patio, as well as in swimming pools. Where shade is needed for outdoor living, modern gardens have made use of specimen trees with ornamental bark set off by a gravel surround, so that the beauty of the trunk becomes a feature in itself.

It is in the modern garden that the curve, the organic shape, has found its proper home. Curved lawns, curved pools and curved paving marry in well with this flowing, informal style.

Above left: Unashamedly artificial curves are perfectly at home in the hard landscaping of a modern garden. The angular pattern of the paving only serves to accentuate the curves of the low retaining wall. Modern grey slabs and a sweep of old dark bricks are effectively juxtaposed.

Above: The modern style suits small courtyards and town gardens. In this example, the relationship to the house is enhanced by the use of quarry tiles on the steps; they give warmth to the scene and are probably seen from a vantage point inside the house as often as from the garden.

Left: The large simple shapes, made possible in modern architecture by the use of concrete, find a complement in natural forms: the spiny disks of cacti contrast splendidly with the smooth rectangles of paving. Gravel is a discreet foil to both.

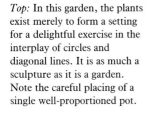

Top: In this garden, the plants exist merely to form a setting for a delightful exercise in the interplay of circles and diagonal lines. It is as much a sculpture as it is a garden. Note the careful placing of a single well-proportioned pot.

Bottom left: Sculptural foliage, water, and hard landscaping blend well together. The clever tunnel-stepping-stone contributes liveliness and a sense of direction to this carefully poised composition of mixed materials.

Bottom right: Here a rather ordinary back yard has been transformed into an attractive outdoor room. The emphasis is on gravel, paving and the wooden supports for the "roof", which gives a feeling of privacy and seclusion

without making the space dark. The pale gravel also helps to keep it light, as does the delicate statue on tip-toes. Modern gardens make a good setting for modern sculpture; a sympathetic environment can be made around it.

Victorian

The interiors of Victorian houses were known for their fussiness and crowding detail; so it was with the gardens of the high Victorian period. Labour was cheap and numerous gardeners could be employed, removing worries about whether a garden style might be labour intensive or not. The period was also marked by a passionate interest in scientific discovery and the cultivation of those plants which were being introduced from far-off countries. These two factors led Victorian gardening away from eighteenth-century debates on the aesthetics of design towards an interest in plants for their own sake, for their collectability as specimens. The result was a style of gardening as formal and ostentatious as gardening has ever been. Everything was kept very dressy indeed.

Above: The Victorians loved to use formal vases, and to plant them up with striking specimens for the summer. Yuccas have been used here, to top off two already enormous vases that have been raised on pedestals to frame the hedges and the path. The Victorians were not in the least afraid to be a little pompous, or to gild the lily.

What the gardens of the great houses did one day, the villa gardens of the new suburbs did the next but on a smaller scale. Whereas in the eighteenth century country landowners had vied with each other for supremacy in good taste, the new one-upmanship was in the material contents and the sheer quantity of plants used in a garden.

Typical features of the period include close-shaven lawns, frequently changed bedding schemes, parterres, extravagantly winding paths, iron pergolas and arches, cast iron seats, urns and balustrades, and

Below: Victorian gardens made the most of ironwork, and of roses. The elegant top of this gazebo and the swags of roses between its pillars make a fine wedding-cake feature.

the very generous use of specimen trees at the expense of open space. Conservatories, glasshouses and vegetable and fruit gardens were beautifully and precisely maintained. Formality was the keynote in all things, whether the garden was full of curves or straight lines. Nothing was discreet: all the work was for show.

Even specimen trees were clipped and evergreens such as holly and yew were used a great deal for the purpose. Weeping trees were especially favoured as specimens, not least of which was the weeping holly. Monkey puzzles sprouted on every lawn with a pretence to fashion. Evergreen shrubberies were common and made much use of three laurels: spotted laurel, Portugal laurel and cherry laurel, largely because they withstood the sooty Victorian town

Left: Grandeur in miniature was the keynote of Victorian villa gardens. Here there are terraces with imposing central steps, but all in rather light materials. The planting is used to emphasize the central axis, with pairs of clipped box and griselinia flanking the steps. The use of coloured gravel and rope-tile edging adds to the sense of order.

atmosphere so well. Roses were the great favourite and could be trained hard. Small, perfectly-edged island beds would be cut into lawns to house specimens such as a potted cabbage palm or a mass of red-hot pokers, surrounded by rings of brightly coloured annuals. Gravel paths were popular, kept perfectly clean and well raked with a rope-tile edging. Even tarmac came to be used for its precise looks. Urns were common and were planted rather than used as ornaments in themselves. In short, the Victorian style can offer some unforgettable eye-opening effects.

Above: Victorian gardens were places of entertainment and education, as much as havens of peace. Aviaries like this were common and were used to house collections of newly discovered, extraordinary birds. Conservatories housed exotic plants in a similar way.

Left: The Victorians loved formal fountains, especially when they were set in a large pool. With electric pumps and countless reproduction fountains, similar effects can readily be achieved today.

Below: Fashionable Victorian gardens never shied away from complicated features. Economy of design, or of labour, was not respected: in the great country houses of England, entire bedding schemes could be changed overnight, while weekend guests dined and slept.

Above: Roses, bedding, a planted urn and lots of white paint make a typically Victorian combination. The late nineteenth century saw a considerable fashion for the idea of charming cottage gardening and roses around the door. Here, a modern interpretation of picket fencing is successfully coupled with a chinoiserie bench (a style popular from the 1760s) and Victorian-style planting.

Top right: A box-edged parterre in Victorian style complements a good cast-iron seat and elaborate jardinière. Centrepieces like this were common in formal gardens. The contents could be changed regularly as plants came into flower under glass.

Bottom right: No lawn could be too well maintained for Victorian taste, so, if you have the patience, a fine lawn should be your aim. Specimen trees were used a great deal, including forest conifers and, of course, the monkey puzzle. Bedding was often used under the canopy of young specimen trees or on its own, in small, well planted island beds.

Parterre

A good parterre is about as stylized a piece of gardening as you will ever find. It turns the surface of the garden into a picture, a pattern complete in itself. In principle it is one of the simplest of garden styles, however complex the geometry of the pattern itself may actually be.

Knot gardens were a feature of seventeenth-century gardens and consisted of a square plot upon which lines of dwarf shrubs were interwoven to form a symmetrical pattern. The style developed, under French influence, into the parterres of the early eighteenth century. Here a larger area was divided with small hedges into all kinds of shapes, such as animals, crests, arabesques and leaves. The areas between the hedges were filled variously with grass, flowers, shrubs, or coloured substances such as gravel, fluorspar, sand, coal, crushed brick and glass. Clipped evergreens were also used, in pots or in the ground, to add a further dimension to the patterns. Much later, in the mid-nineteenth century, the grand parterre was revived in England by designers such as Nesfield and Barry, and fountains were regularly used as the centrepieces.

The parterre may not be a style which will appeal to a keen plantsman, as the opportunities for growing a large range of plants are few. Its appeal lies instead in the precision of its lines, its contrasts of colour and its relation to the adjoining architecture of the house.

Below: Strictly speaking, parterres are filled with blocks of a single colour. However, an alternative approach is to use them as island beds filled with a mixture of shrubs and perennials. These will give varied colour and interest in summer, and still leave you with an ornamental pattern of hedges in winter. The garden will have two distinct identities, the one abundant, the other linear.

Left: Part of the attraction of a parterre is the wide variety of surfaces that can be combined with the structural planting and the different effects that can thereby be achieved. Paths can be gravel – discreet or highly coloured – or paved, as here, or even of grass. The object is to make a pleasing pattern with whichever materials you select.

Above: Plain blocks of colour help to emphasize the shapes and structure of a parterre and to draw attention to the overall pattern by the way colours are repeated. The choice of colours is endless, from subtle pastel shades or single-colour schemes to outrageously bright contrasts. All can be made to work in different, appropriate situations.

A parterre will complement even the most modern of houses because it is a pure geometric design. The modern style of heather-and-conifer garden of the last twenty years is simply a form of arabesque parterre.

A parterre needs to be kept separate from the hurly-burly of a mixed flower garden so that its lines can be appreciated without distraction. An encircling hedge is often all that is required to do this. The Victorians loved to use a grand balustrade to mark the perimeter. With a hedge all round it, a small parterre garden could be made a part of a much larger garden at some distance from the house, but the symmetrical facade of a house is undoubtedly the best backdrop for this sophisticated style of gardening.

Dwarf box is the traditional hedging material for parterres, but yew, cotton lavender, berberis, germander and lavender can all be used. There is no reason at all to be limited to a traditional range of plants, either for hedging or for in-filling. The spaces between hedges could even be filled with water or pebbles instead of the usual bedding plants or bulbs. The same opportunities are offered in the use of modern hard-landscaping materials, producing a wealth of detail in the surface of the paths in a small-scale parterre. Modern sculpture or a modern fountain can be used instead of topiary specimens. Parterres are an unashamed contrivance, to be enjoyed for their bold structure and artistry.

Left: In this modern knot garden the gravel background has been kept deliberately simple to emphasize the pattern of the box hedging.

Below left: Part of the pleasure of a parterre is to be able to walk among the beds, making your own patterns as you cross. A parterre that has no central axis has the appeal of an open-ended maze.

Right: This parterre, in the Victorian manner, has typical vibrantly coloured spring bedding that will be changed again before summer. There is a lot of work in maintaining grass paths but, in a garden of this size, gravel might seem very stark. The huge vase centrepiece could be replaced by topiary, a traditional ornament of parterre gardens.

Below: Vegetables and herbs do not have to be grown in straight rows. They can be surprisingly ornamental in a parterre, and access for picking could not be easier.

Japanese

Japanese gardens have throughout history set out to provide a tranquil environment around the house. They possess an aura of calm which is rarely matched in western garden styles, and almost every element in their composition is symbolic of some aspect of nature or human life. Today the symbolism is not so strong and many gardens in Japan tend to use these symbolic elements for traditional and aesthetic reasons rather than for their meaning. For a westerner, perhaps the best approach to Japanese gardens is to draw from

them the means of arriving at that special stillness and to use it like any other garden tool, instead of trying to produce faithful copies in a foreign land.

Much of that tranquillity derives from an economical, almost minimal use of materials. Each element, whether built or planted, seems heavy upon the ground and settled there. Even water is still or flows gently downwards; you do not find fountains in Japanese gardens. The garden is designed to give the impression of the natural landscape at its most serene. The man-made geometry of some western garden styles is abhorrent to the Japanese.

It is precisely because Japanese gardens discreetly suggest nature, instead of copying it, that they can be created in a space of any size, however small. (At its most extreme, this becomes the miniature landscapes of bonsai.) Western gardeners can learn much from this clever use of small spaces.

The key elements involved are stone, water and a wealth of greenery, arranged in asymmetrical but well-balanced configurations. Flowers, such as irises,

Left: A true Japanese garden is calm and discreet, full of light and shade and contrasts of hard and soft. The paths are gentle and indirect and there is minimal planting.

Far left: Restful Far Eastern gardening can be a wonderful source of inspiration, even when there is no intention to fully reproduce the style in a Western garden.

peonies, lilies and chrysanthemums, play a relatively unimportant part. Groups of stones or boulders can be used to represent mountains and evergreens are clipped to depict boulders, while flat stones may form a gently weaving path. Straight lines are avoided. Water will be present, either as a waterfall, a pool with islands or simply suggested by flowing white sand. Commonly used plants include trees such as plums, cherries and maples and bamboo. Coniferous trees such as pines and juniper are often clipped to form floating cloud shapes, or they can be encouraged to take on a weatherworn appearance. Most significantly, all these plants are used sparingly and are rarely allowed to rub shoulders with one another.

Fences and screens, of materials such as bamboo or grasses, are more common than walls for dividing the garden. Often a loggia is provided from which to view the garden and a lantern of stone or metal is carefully placed to light the path at night or to offer reflections in the water of a pool.

Essentially, a garden in the Japanese style is intended to offer peace and quiet contemplation to its owner and his or her guests, a designer's garden rather than a plantsman's garden. Restraint is everything, with order, harmony and decorum as the guiding principles behind a scheme.

Above: Waterfalls and watercourses are a major element in Japanese gardens and are intended to suggest high mountain streams. Bridges and stone lanterns are also important, symbols of a safe pathway. The cut-leaved, domed Japanese maple (*Acer palmatum dissectum*) is a popular plant for Western versions of Japanese gardens.

Above and bottom far right:
Japanese gardens contain many
traditional elements which can
be used to suggest an Oriental
style. Water is vital. Favourite
plants, such as maples, plums,
pines and bamboos, will
produce the right flavour,
especially when set in a carpet
of moss. Low mounding
evergreens can be used as a
substitute for mosses. It is a
style that can be adapted to
any size garden, as can be seen
here, where a small courtyard
and an expansive landscape
have been equally well served.

Bottom right and above right:
When there is no real water,
an impression of a stream or
waves can be created by raked
sand or gravel or a bed of
small stones. Where there is
real or imaginary water there
are stepping stones; here,
wood, stone and foliage
combine to present a crisp,
clean effect.

Above far right: Bamboo is
commonly used to make
screens and bridges and well
constructed features like this
example would be an asset to
any Japanese-style garden.
Stone lanterns of traditional
design are an emphatic
Japanese statement.

Classical

In all art forms the classical style is one in which a logical, well-considered form is used as the structure upon which to hang the individual expression of the artist – and so it is with gardens. A classical garden is one which has a structure designed to be pleasing in itself, rather than the largely functional layout of the traditional cottage garden. Within that structure, the planting may be as unrestrained and romantic as you wish, but it will always be seen in relation to the structure of the garden as a whole.

It is no surprise to find that most of the formal period styles of gardening have come under the heading of classical gardens, and there is no denying that symmetry and formality lend a garden the strongest of structures. However, the planting can be vibrantly colourful and extravagant or contained, minimal and quiet. This is the great advantage of a classical garden: its good bones will support all manner of fleshing out.

Throughout history it has been the classical gardens which have survived, from the green simplicity of an eighteenth-century landscape park with its lakes and temples to the geometric razzmatazz of Baroque gardens. But the twentieth century has seen the development of classical gardens on a much smaller scale, where the blend of domestic architecture and plantsman's gardening have complemented each other perfectly. English gardens like Sissinghurst

Below: Classical gardens have strong bones – a clear and attractive structure which can then be enriched by planting. Light and shade and the qualities given to a design by the inclusion of water are almost more important than the overlay of planting, which need not be colourful.

Left: Symmetry plays an important role in classical gardens, repetition of parts being the easiest way of producing balanced arrangements that are strong and visually satisfying.

Above: The formal structure of a classical garden, frequently composed of walls, hedges, paving and sculpture, should be coupled with a sympathetic, complementary selection of plants.

(designed by Vita Sackville-West and Sir Harold Nicolson) and Great Dixter (by Sir Edwin Lutyens) and Dumbarton Oaks (by Beatrix Farrand) in the United States have proved that gardens rich in architectural and structural detail will happily support the most exuberant of planting and win the affections of all serious gardeners. In gardens like these, form and content reach a most satisfactory balance, which surely is the essence of a classical garden.

A well-designed garden deserves to be well planted, and when making a classical garden it is worth planting carefully with an eye for shape, colour and texture. The plants may form part of the structure itself, in hedges or recurring patterns of specimen plants. Water, either standing, running or as a fountain may form part of the design. Even within a small garden it is possible to make use of vistas and focal points, while ensuring that the open spaces intended to be part of the design do not fall prey to a clutter of specimen plants. It is too easy to let the planting obscure rather than enhance the design.

Well-built walls, doorways, arches, steps, paths and pergolas will all enhance the quality of the garden structure, and occasionally a good-sized urn or vase will add distinction. So will an attractive garden bench carefully placed. Good quality hard landscaping can be expensive, but it is undoubtedly the key to success when making a classical garden. Few great gardens, however, were made in a season, but were built up gradually over the years. This is the best way to approach your own plans for a classical garden.

Left: Classical gardens, in relying on a strong structure and plan, tend to use a good deal of hard landscaping, often of antique appearance.

Right: Period features such as parterres can be introduced into classical gardens. The twentieth-century idea of separate "garden rooms" fits in well with the classical tradition, allowing different planting styles to be used within the various sections of the overall design.

Bottom right: Simplicity of structure is one of the keynotes of classical gardens. The emphasis here is linear.

Below: High quality materials skilfully combined with simple planting, as here, will always produce a classical garden.

Subtropical

The so-called subtropical garden is really a trick. We are used to seeing in our gardens plants from all over the world, from the most extravagant rhododendron to the most delicate alpine primula; but usually these plants come from a climate broadly similar to our own. In the subtropical garden, the aim is to present a picture of a totally different climate in which the usual range of temperate plants will not grow. To do this is inevitably a deception, but a satisfying one.

The subtropical style of gardening involves using a range of plants which might seem more at home in a much hotter climate, although they must of course be able to grow in our own gardens. It is achieved by selecting those plants with the most appropriate foliage; but perhaps more importantly, it is achieved by avoiding those plants which are commonplace in temperate gardens. The absence of certain plants is just as telling as the choice of plants used.

By the same token, subtropical gardens are often best sited in an enclosed area where the presence of the temperate world outside cannot dilute the effect you are trying to achieve. The same goes for garden architecture, furniture and hard landscaping. It is better to avoid the hallmarks of other garden styles such as classical urns and familiar, traditional garden seats and paving techniques. Instead, try to keep hard surfaces as informal as possible. Gravel is the most discreet option but clay tiles are another possibility. Stay with unsophisticated materials wherever possible. Cane or bamboo seats will look right.

Water can be important in creating a subtropical garden. If you want to give the impression of a hot dry climate, then a pool or a fountain is ideal. If the aim is

Left: The great paddle-shaped leaves of cannas always look suitably exotic, especially those forms with bronzed foliage. Although in temperate parts of the world cannas are grown mainly for their impressive leaves, their large flowers can produce a brilliant tropical effect, coming in bold shades of red, orange and deep pink, taking complex forms.

to reproduce a jungle effect, running, trickling or dripping water may be more appropriate, with moss and ferns growing alongside to enhance the effect.

Subtropical climates tend to produce large, lush foliage and this should be imitated in your choice of plants. The paddle-shaped banana leaf is to be found in cannas and lysichitums; spiky rosettes are found in yuccas, cordylines and potted agaves; araucarias can be useful too. For sheer size of leaf, there is no beating the Chusan palm, *Trachycarpus fortunei*, and paulownia and ailanthus trees can be stooled to produce huge leaves. Gunnera and *Rheum palmatum* both produce huge herbaceous leaves in damp soil and in similar conditions bamboos and phormium can be used to give an exotic touch. In dryer conditions, *Melianthus major* offers lush blue-grey foliage. Climbers such as passion flowers, gourds and menispermum can add a tangled, jungle flavour, and daturas in pots will provide wonderfully exotic trumpet flowers rather like a hibiscus. In general, however, foliage is a better tool than flowers in creating the effect of an alien climate: it can offer the promise of subtropical flowers without ever giving the game away.

In some climates it is necessary to create the subtropical effect under glass or at least partial cover, where the higher temperatures and reduced winds will better suit many large-leaved plants.

Far left: As long as plants look exotic and foreign, they can be used, no matter how many continents the result actually represents. The jungle effect is enhanced by running water.

Below: The combination of potted aspidistra, Chusan palms and a reflecting pool helps to create an "oasis" look. The palms produce fragrant yellow flowers.

Right: Palm fronds and handsome large leaves are the hallmarks of the colonial-style subtropical garden. Tall, mature palms create the ideal, lush impression.

Below left: Even where the climate is temperate, and especially in coastal gardens, there is scope for using plants that impart an exotic flavour, such as the yuccas flanking these steps. Simple touches like this, combined with the use of suitable hard landscaping materials, can make all the difference to a design. Such strategic use of plants and features is a device that will serve any garden style; one ideal element can crown the effect.

Below right: Given overhead cover, you can grow a wide range of large-leaved plants, both hardy and not-so-hardy, which in the open would not look as lush and exotic because of the wind and the drier atmosphere. *Rodgersia podophylla* (as underplanting in the centre) is perfectly hardy in an open space, but looks and is at home in the cool, moist shade beneath taller foliage plants.

Right: In a hot, dry climate the sound of trickling water from a fountain is always welcome. It is a reminder of fresh peacefulness in the oppressive heat of the day. The sound of a stream smacks much more of greyer, cooler climates with plentiful rain, so it is less appropriate to a subtropical garden.

Above right: The dry heat of central America and Africa can be simulated by the use of succulents and cacti. Where soil would be expected to look dry, gravel or pebbles can be successfully used as ground cover. Select light shades of stones and other surfaces to suggest arid conditions.

Container

Never let it be said that container gardens are second best to gardens in the soil. They may be labour-intensive, but, as a reward, they can be as rich and extravagant as your pocket and patience will allow.

Containers solve many problems for would-be gardeners. They are the answer for a paved town courtyard and a roof terrace ten storeys high, and an excellent solution for people who cannot bend easily to dig. They are an ideal finishing touch: an array of window boxes can complete a house front. Whatever the reason, the choice of containers is enormous.

However, certain ground rules need to be borne in mind. You need to consider the work involved in occasional changes of soil and the ease of access; most important of all, you need to consider watering. Do

Above: Pelargoniums provide a bright summer display in this formal garden. Pots of flowers are set into permanent containers allowing for change during the season. The empty pots provide winter ornament.

Right: Potted citrus trees are a feature of Italian gardens. The orangeries of English historic gardens were built to overwinter such trees which were then displayed outdoors during the summer.

the containers have adequate drainage? Is there a water supply nearby? Will you be able to use liquid feeds? What will happen if you are away for a weekend or on holiday? Watering is by far the greatest chore of container gardening and it needs to be done generously and regularly. Rain is never adequate on its own and can fool you into thinking the containers are wetter then they really are. Automatic irrigation is well worth considering for a large container garden.

Below: Alpines are the perfect plants for stone or imitation stone troughs. Although most of these plants need perfect drainage they will still need watering in dry weather.

It is important to decide whether to plant for a 12-month display or to let the containers remain empty during the winter. Remember that many plants which would be hardy enough in the ground may succumb to the cold when their roots are raised up in a container open to frosts. Frozen, waterlogged soil can also burst containers as it expands. Conversely, containers in sun can get very hot in summer and your choice of plants needs to be governed by this fact: it is all too easy to bake the roots of plants.

With these practical points in mind, you are free to choose from the gamut of container gardening styles. Formal courtyards can be graced with potted bays, sentinel cypresses, camellias or bamboos. In addition, some especially beautiful pots may look best not

planted but used as an architectural contrast. Large concrete planters can be filled with trees and shrubs, almost as if they were in the ground. Stone troughs can be planted as miniature gardens of alpines or screes, but they can equally be filled with a single carpeting plant as a piece of living sculpture.

In a more cottagey style, tubs, pots and even baskets of all shapes and sizes can be clustered to form splashes of colour, by doorways or lining steps. Window boxes and hanging baskets blend in well with this style and provide an opportunity for bold or restful incidental planting in prime locations.

With the aid of a circulating pump, even water can be a feature of container gardens, either as a small fountain or trickling over pebbles from one container to another. Certainly such details add great charm.

Right and below: Container gardening need not be formal. A glorious clutter of interesting, well-filled pots can look splendid and can give a Mediterranean air to your garden. Only remember that every pot you use is another one to water. Hanging baskets are the hardest of all to keep moist. All sorts of containers make interesting planters so there is no need to stick to commercially available ones, as long as you remember to provide drainage holes. Copper wash-tubs or polythene-lined baskets make attractive tubs, and bought pots can be painted and decorated to suit the style of your garden.

Bottom: An arrangement of containers that is loosely symmetrical is a very appealing way of arranging a busy mixture of pots and harmonious plants.

Opposite, top and bottom left: A rigidly formal arrangement of containers is a useful way of accentuating strong, adjoining architectural features.

Opposite, bottom right: Pots and troughs, when well placed, are a form of sculpture in themselves. The effect is enhanced here by simple, single-species planting. The row of tulip-filled containers is sited to echo the curve of the parterre behind.

THE
STRUCTURAL
FRAMEWORK

SURFACES

In the garden, surfaces have both a practical and a visual function. They are used for walking, sitting or playing on, and they also provide an area of rest for the eye, a space between the profusion of the planted areas. The visual element is particularly important as surfaces define the space and layout of the garden, and their design should be given a great deal of thought. The materials should be chosen with care; they should be sympathetic to their surroundings, taking into account the mood of the garden and the materials of the house and any other buildings or walls. Never employ too many different materials, especially in a small garden, as this will create a restless effect in an area usually dedicated to relaxation.

There are two types of surface: soft and hard. Soft surfaces, mainly lawns, are better for occasional use and dry weather, and for covering large expanses, as they tend to be easier on the eye than hard surfaces. Hard surfaces are best for constant use and wet weather, and for smaller areas of the garden. Generally speaking, hard surfaces are expensive to install but cheap to maintain, while soft surfaces are relatively cheap to create but expensive to keep in good condition during bad weather and heavy use.

For a garden to look its best, all surfaces, whether they are soft or hard, should be properly laid and well maintained. Being such prominent features, any carelessness will affect the whole garden.

Grass

Lawns provide a calm contrast to the hard surfaces or planting groups that may surround them. Their shape and design should be determined at an early stage of planning the garden as they will greatly influence its whole appearance. The shape of the lawn should complement other features, such as flowerbeds and pools. Square or rectangular lawns have a formal look which is well suited to larger gardens but can be a little dull in small town gardens, and they have the advantage of being easy to lay out and mow. Informal, irregular shapes are more satisfying and lively and are particularly suitable for small gardens, but any curves should be sinuous rather than acute otherwise the lawn will be rather difficult to mow.

If games such as croquet or tennis are envisaged, the lawn should not slope and efforts should be made to level it, using steps between different levels if necessary. However, a gentle slope can add to the charm of a lawn and give it character, particularly in large gardens, and a lawn sloping away from a house can give the illusion of increased size.

Lawns can be made by either sowing seed or laying turf, both on well-prepared ground. If lawns are to be practical and used regularly then they should contain tough grasses such as rye, while finer turf with more fescues and bents in it should be kept for decorative lawns. If the gardener is making a new garden from an existing field, it is possible to tame the grass over a period of time. However, stubborn perennial weeds are likely to disfigure the sward and get into the borders until they are completely eradicated, which may take a few years.

If part of the lawn is constantly used as a path, stepping stones will prevent wear and tear (see page 130). Sink them into the lawn to just beneath its surface so they are easy to mow over. Regular paving stones set in a straight line will suit formal gardens.

Some areas of grass and flowers can be left semi-wild and only cut a few times a year, after the flowers have died back. This can be done in meadow-like areas that contain daffodils and crocuses or a mixture of herbaceous spring flowers.

Mowing Lawns can be formal (*above*) or informal (*right*), according to their context. The way the grass is mowed can make all the difference to the appearance of the garden. A clear edge (*opposite*) or the lack of one (*right*) can also dramatically alter the character of a lawn. Formal edging, such as stones, should be below the level of the lawn for easy mowing as raised edging makes it very difficult to trim the lawn effectively. Plants can also be used as edging around lawns.

PREPARING LAWNS

Lay turf or sow grass seed in April or September, when the weather is damp and the soil is warm and moist, ideal for growing grass. Avoid preparing lawns in hot weather.

If any part of the lawn suffers from moisture problems, install a drainage system. Either use drainage pipes laid diagonally or, in particularly extreme circumstances, in a herringbone pattern, the system being connected to a main drain or ditch. Alternatively, dig trenches and fill them with small stones and rubble.

Prepare the soil some months before sowing seed or laying turf to allow enough time for a second weeding. Remove perennial weeds using weedkiller or by hand; weedkiller is more thorough, especially on heavier soils such as clay, where roots can snap off and lie undetected in large lumps of compacted soil.

Once weed-free, break the soil into a fine tilth and lightly but firmly compact it. Make sure the surface is flat, with no bumps or hollows.

Keep the freshly prepared surface moist but do not over-water.

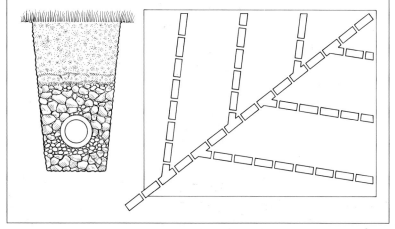

Above: If regular passage is made across a lawn, stepping stones can be incorporated to prevent wear. These can be of wood, as here, or stone; wood should be treated with a preservative. Each one should be slightly below the level of the lawn.

Above: A lawn can provide a restful area for the eye as well as a pleasant surface to walk on. In shrubberies and leafy parts of the garden, grass presents a tranquil counterbalance to varied foliage.

Right: In gardens which are visually very busy, a lawn holds together the various elements – hedges, paths, seats, ornaments, borders, trees, shrubs and gates – with the peaceful sweep of its subtle surface.

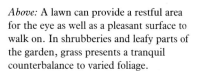

SOWING

Grass seed should only be sown on well-prepared ground, free from all weeds, otherwise the lawn will look coarse and untidy. The area to be sown should be marked out in square yards (metres), either with strings attached to canes stuck into the ground, or by lightly drawing lines straight onto the soil itself.

Scatter the seed at the rate recommended on the packet, usually about 1.5oz per sq yard (50g per sq metre). The seed can be left or it can be covered with a light sprinkling of sieved soil. If birds are a problem and the area is not too large, it may be necessary to protect the freshly-sown lawn with netting to prevent the birds eating the seed and dusting themselves in the soil. Keep the soil moist; germination should occur within three weeks.

Left and above: Lawn can be laid in almost any shape that the gardener chooses. However, the need to cut the grass has to be borne in mind: be wary of making the lawn too complicated, otherwise a lot of time can be wasted mowing. When laying a curved surface, for example on banks (*above*), be certain that cutting will be possible with a lawn mower. Lawn can be laid round borders of almost any shape (*left*) and can be allowed to fade out under trees and shrubs. Plants overhanging grass are very attractive but they can become a nuisance, partly because they hinder mowing but also because they can cause the grass to die beneath the shadow of their dense foliage.

LAYING TURF

It is better to pay extra for turf that has been specially grown from grass seed rather than buy meadow turf, which is likely to contain many weeds. Turf comes in rolls, and these need to be laid as soon as possible, or at least unrolled to prevent the grass from yellowing.

The turf should be laid in staggered rows, with the joints offset from each other, in the manner of bricklaying. Make certain that the turves butt up close to each other. Do not end a row with a short piece of turf; rather, move the nearest full length out to the edge and fill the gap with the short piece. Firm the turves down to form a flat, even surface and fill in the gaps between each turf with sieved earth, packing it down well to form a good bond.

Do not allow the turves to dry out; they should have rooted within two weeks, when they can be walked on.

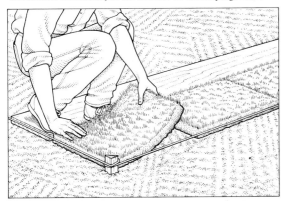

Gravel and Bark

Gravel can be used to create practical and attractive garden surfaces. It has a smooth look about it and is easy to lay; it also has the advantage of being relatively cheap. Many people enjoy the satisfying crunching sound that it produces under foot, indeed, some use it as an early warning for anybody approaching the house. Gravel does, however, need a bit more care and attention than some other surfaces to keep it neat and in place as it is easily spread to adjacent lawns and flowerbeds, spoiling the effect.

Being a soft material, gravel flows around corners and is ideal for filling irregular shapes. In small gardens or courtyards, the whole ground can be covered with it, with plants growing through in one or two places for a natural look. Gravel can also be used to complement other materials such as brick, stone or grass, providing interesting textural contrasts.

The warmth of orange and brown gravels has a lot to recommend it in the garden, but there are also many grey and yellow chippings to choose from. In addition, plenty of gravels are made from local stone, and these are useful for tying up paved areas or walls made from the same material.

Gravel areas can benefit from a solid, fixed edge, such as a kerb of stone or lengths of wood, to keep it in place, although for a less formal effect it can be left to merge in with surrounding areas, or the edges can be softened with overhanging plants.

Chipped or shredded bark is another popular material for creating visually and physically soft surfaces. Its somewhat unruly appearance and tendencies make it unsuitable for formal areas and, because of its natural affinity with wood, it is generally used in wilder parts of the garden. Bark is particularly suitable for woodland areas, where its colour and texture blend in well with the trees.

Bark is one of the best materials to use in areas where children play as it is relatively soft. Heavier pieces of bark are better than composted bark, which is more like peat in consistency, and tends to be more difficult to control.

Bark and wood chips will not necessarily stay in place, even with kerbing of some kind, as regular use by pedestrians and birds searching for worms will scatter it far and wide. Logs can be used to edge the area to provide some restraint, and these will be in keeping with the natural look of the surface.

The Japanese make the most of the amorphous nature of gravel in their tranquil gardens which are especially designed for contemplation. Here, a deep layer of gravel is laid and then raked into patterns, often swirling to resemble water flowing around stones. With sensitive treatment, these ideals can easily be transferred to any garden, provided that the surrounding areas conform with the stark, minimal approach of the Japanese original.

Left: In informal settings, gravel makes an ideal surface, flowing around flowerbeds.

Below: In a woodland setting, dark stones or bark make a soft, sympathetic path.

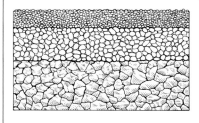

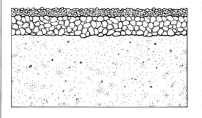

Gravel in formal gardens
Gravel is particularly effective when used in formal patterns where it can be mixed with other materials, such as brick (*left*). It fills the spaces naturally and lacks the harshness of concrete or other hard surfaces, and it has a visual affinity with grass. Different colours (*below*) can be used to enhance the pattern, but care must be taken to avoid the different gravels getting mixed up. Gravel should be raked regularly to maintain an even pattern and to remove debris; any weeds should be uprooted.

Bottom right: Practical stepping stones can be incorporated into paths that are composed of gravel.

Above: Gravel is a versatile material, suitable for formal and informal settings. This elegant parterre is perfectly highlighted by the neat gravel path. The main disadvantage of the material is that stones tend to spread onto adjoining surfaces like lawns.

LAYING GRAVEL
Gravel can be laid in three ways; the last technique is the most durable. The first method consists of a 3in (7.5cm) base of well rammed hardcore covered with a 2in (5cm) layer of compacted coarse gravel, with a final 1-2in (2.5-5cm) top covering of finer gravel, rolled flat for a good finish. The second involves a 3-4in (7.5-10cm) layer of hoggin over which is spread and rolled about 1in (2.5cm) of compacted gravel, and this is scattered with a covering of loose gravel. The third method, for a hard-wearing finish, involves a base of concrete covered with tar and gravel.

Gravel Although the individual stones in gravel vary in colour and size, they present a very uniform surface which usually looks fresh and uncluttered. This clear-cut quality can be seen in the surround to this pool (*left*). The band of gravel helps to emphasize the clean lines and serenity of this formal feature; few other materials would be as effective. The gravel surround of the circular flowerbeds (*below right*) also produces a clean finish, the surface providing an ideal background for the hard lines of brick and the softer inner circle of hedge. As well as being decorative, the circular brick edging is a functional barrier that prevents the gravel from spreading.

Bark Bark is not an elegant surface material but it has a soft appearance that can be reassuring to the eye. Its physical properties correspond to the visual impression it makes. It can be particularly useful where children run and play. Bark is also a good material for creating contrasts with hard surfaces. Where beds are top-dressed with gravel, as in rock gardens (*above*), bark makes a good choice of pathing material. It can also be used to create a bridging area between two different surfaces, such as decking and grass (*right*).

Decking

Part way between a hard surface and a soft one, timber is very much in harmony with the garden, and timber decking (areas of wooden planking) is used a great deal for constructing areas of relaxation. Decking can provide terrace space either at ground level or, in some cases, higher up.

Timber is a versatile material and it can easily be cut and shaped to create a wide variety of designs. Most decks are built just above ground level, but they really come into their own when built on hillsides so that they project out as high platforms, giving elevated views of the garden and the surrounding countryside. With such platforms, it is possible to leave holes in the decking through which the branches and tips of the trees below can emerge, giving the impression that you are sitting high up in the tree tops. With houses that are built on steep slopes, this is the only realistic way of creating a flat area immediately outside the house without major earthworks being involved to level the site.

As decking is relatively light, it can be used at an even higher level on the roof to make an ideal sitting-out area or roof garden, and the added advantage here is that it protects the roof below from wear and tear. Decks at all levels can also have pergolas constructed above them to give the feeling of a veranda. If climbing plants are grown over at least part of the structure, they will provide a cool and shady area to enjoy during hot, sunny days.

A much more exotic kind of deck can be built in trees, usually in the form of tree-houses. These have a special appeal for children, but people of all ages find them fascinating. Of prime importance is safety, both in the strength of the structure and the construction of safety rails around the edges. It goes without saying that the tree must be sufficiently large, sturdy, healthy and mature to take the weight of the deck and a number of occupants.

Structures at ground level are well within the capabilities of most people. The decks should be supported on joists which in turn need to be supported by brick or concrete piers or walls; a damp-proof membrane should be placed between the joists and the piers or walls. All the wood must be treated with preservative, which is available in a variety of colours. Higher structures, especially those on sloping hillsides, are likely to need the aid of an architect or structural engineer in their design. If in doubt, seek professional advice when constructing any deck, so as to avoid accidents.

Wooden decking The versatility of decking means that it can be used as a single surface (*left*) or stepped over several levels on sloping ground (*below*). It can merge into the rest of the garden or it can be enclosed and used as a courtyard. If a large expanse of decking is used in combination with groups of tables and chairs, it can serve as an open-air room, with a floor but no containing walls.

Left and below: Decking makes an excellent surface for roof gardens and can form the basis of an attractive retreat. It is pleasant to look at and, because it spreads the load, can prevent the underlying roof from being damaged. There is no reason why decking, like other surfaces, should not be decorated with containers (*left*). Plants can be grown in pots and tubs, and these can be moved around and replanted with the changing seasons. Climbing plants can be grown up posts and trellis. Decking can also be used as an extension of the living area (*below*); there is plenty of room for outdoor furniture.

Variations on decking Wood is a very versatile material and can be used in situations where it would be difficult to use other materials. Deck construction is relatively easy and, compared with building materials such as concrete, timber is light. This means that structures and level surfaces, often as platforms, can easily be erected on problem slopes in the garden that might otherwise be difficult to maintain. On a steep site it may be desirable to create a series of terraced decks to cover most of the slope (*left*). Various additions can be made to the platform of a deck. More interest can be created with guard rails that are not only functional but decorative (*below left*). Built-in furniture – seating and possibly a table – can also be added. Either the whole or part of the deck can be covered with slats, in the style of a pergola (*below right*); this is particularly appealing in hot climates where cross-pieces can support a variety of climbing plants.

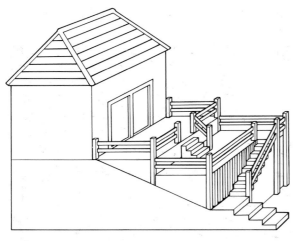

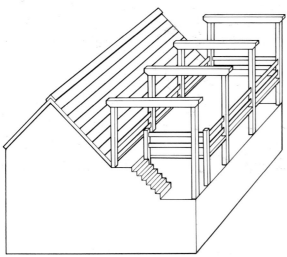

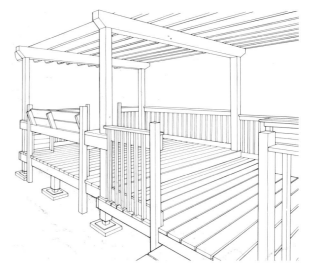

SAFETY AND CONSTRUCTION

Great care must be exercised in the design and construction of decks since they can be very dangerous, especially in wet weather. They must be well-built, made with the best and strongest materials, and securely attached to firm foundations. Those decks built above ground level should have a handrail, and any steps and planting holes should be well-illuminated or edged with a painted white line.

Most decks are likely to be built of softwood which will need to be planed to avoid splinters. This will inevitably make the deck slippery in shady areas and wet weather, but preservatives will help to keep moss and algae at bay. Alternatively, brush the surface regularly with a stiff garden broom or apply an algicide, or nail small-mesh galvanized chicken wire over the deck. Treat steps in a similar manner. The whole structure should be regularly treated with wood preservative and none of it should rest on damp ground. Any broken or rotten boards must be replaced immediately.

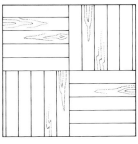

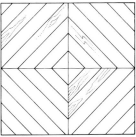
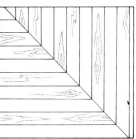

Patterns (*left*) The planks of decking do not have to be laid in simple parallel lines. There are numerous patterns to choose from and these can be highly decorative. With complex patterns it is essential to work out the framework below the deck so that all the planks are supported.

Top left: Decking can be used to create a clean, neutral finish that is easy to live with. Here, an uncluttered deck, sporting some modern furniture, provides a sitting-out area beside a pool. The simple parallel lines of the planking are offset by the planting of pampas grass beyond.

Left and above: It is much better to define the edge of an area of decking rather than allowing it to tail off. These two treatments are very different. The straight line (*above*) mixes well with the foliage, while the log-palisade finish (*left*) blends perfectly with the stones and water.

Paving Stones

Areas that are constantly used, like paths and patios, are best made with a hard surface. Paving stones are a convenient and relatively cheap method of covering both large and small areas.

The choice of paving will depend on many factors, including the character of the garden and other materials used, as well as cost. The best slabs are undoubtedly of real stone and York stone is particularly attractive. Unfortunately this, and stone in general, is very expensive, although occasionally it is possible to buy second-hand slabs at a more reasonable price. Reconstituted stone and concrete slabs are readily available and much cheaper, but imitation riven stone and coloured stone should be used sparingly as they can look rather garish. Brightly coloured slabs are visually uncomfortable to live with in grey climates, where their brilliance is likely to jar with the rest of the garden; accordingly, they tend to look better in hot, sunny climates. When they are used, colours should not be mixed as this will create a restless pattern in what should be a restful area. Plain concrete slabs will make a more subdued surface, especially when they have begun to weather and take on the patina of age, which, as a rule, is a very useful quality.

Paved areas should be almost level, with enough slope to allow water to soak away, either to a drain or into the garden. The larger the slabs, the easier they will be to lay, although weight may prove a hindrance. Avoid using small slabs if covering a large area, to reduce the amount of work and time involved. Slabs can be laid in regular patterns, either like a chessboard or offset from each other, like brickwork. Varying sizes can be employed to create irregular but more interesting designs, and broken slabs can be used to create crazy paving, but this must be done well in order to be a success.

The difficulty with using paving stones is that they are not easy to lay in irregularly-shaped areas. One way around this is to fill as much of the space as possible with whole slabs, and leave the edges free for an alternative material, such as cobblestones embedded in concrete. In larger areas of paving, it is possible to break the monotony by leaving out the occasional stone and planting the space instead. Alternatively, large tubs or urns can be placed in appropriate positions, but if the containers are heavy and the paving is not laid on a base of hardcore, the slabs may sink, creating an irregular, dangerous surface.

Left and above: Paved areas in the form of patios and terraces are indispensable close to the house (*left*). These surfaces should be level and even, and suitable materials for such surfaces include paving slabs and bricks. Different coloured slabs can be used if the tones are muted. Concrete is practical and easy to lay, but a large expanse of it can be hard on the eye. Solid foundations are needed for most main pedestrian areas and wherever heavy plant pots and furniture are likely to be positioned. Leave uneven surfaces (*above*), however attractive they might be, for areas that receive little traffic; they are excellent for an informal finish.

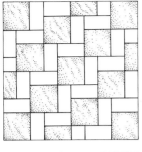

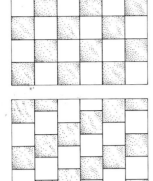

Paving slabs (*above*) Concrete slabs are available in a wide variety of sizes and colours. The simplest designs (*top right and bottom right*) have the advantage of being easy to lay. They blend in with their setting more readily than complicated and difficult patterns (*top left and bottom left*), a point that is relevant in areas designed for relaxation. In the right place, however,

detailed patterns can be interesting to look at and their creation can give a lot of enjoyment. It is best to work out the pattern on squared paper before buying slabs so that the exact requirements can be calculated. Lay out all the slabs before securing them, then the whole pattern can be seen. Only cement them into place when you are happy with the effect.

Left and above: Paving slabs are suitable for surfaces in both formal (*above*) and informal (*left*) garden designs. When paving has been newly laid it can stand out rather starkly; it tends to look better if covered with lichen, which gives it the patina of age. An informal effect is created when plants are allowed to flop over the edges and grow between the cracks in the paving.

LAYING PAVING

If the surface of the ground is well compacted and the paving slabs large, it is possible to lay them directly onto soil using sand to level them. However, if there is any risk of the slabs sinking then it is best to lay a hardcore base first.

Take off the turf and lay any drains that might be necessary. Next, level the site, allowing a gentle slope as little as ½in per 3½ft (1cm per 1m) in one direction, preferably away from any buildings, towards a drain or flower bed. To level the site, place a datum peg in one corner of the area so that the top is at the desired level of the surface of the sand that will support the paving slabs. Mark the proposed levels of the soil and hardcore on the peg. Place similar pegs at 6ft (1.8m) intervals across the site, progressively moving away from the datum peg, and then level them by spanning adjacent pegs with a length of wood bearing a spirit level. The tops of the pegs

should reflect the line of the gentle drainage slope.

Once the ground is level, compact the soil and ram down a 4in (10cm) layer of hardcore to form the foundations of the paved area. Next, lay a 2in (5cm) layer of sand, raking and rolling it until it is level with the tops of the pegs. The slabs can then be laid directly onto the sand. Check that each slab is level using a spirit level, making allowance for the drainage slope, before going on to the next one.

Do not set the slabs too close together as this will draw attention to any irregularities in their shape. Short strips of wood can be used as spacers between them so that an even gap is left around each slab, but check the slabs by eye to make certain that they are aligned in all directions. The joints can be pointed to help prevent grass and other weeds growing up between the slabs: brush dry cement or sand over the surface until all the gaps are filled.

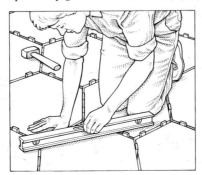

LAYING CRAZY PAVING

Choose the pieces of paving carefully so that they fit together reasonably well, like a jigsaw puzzle. This will create a more attractive surface as it will reduce the amount of cement needed to fill the joints in between each piece. Try and use the same type of material throughout; any variations in colour and texture have to be handled well to look good.

Bed down each piece in cement rather than sand and, using a spirit level, make sure each paving stone is level before laying the next one. Try not to use small pieces around the edge of the area as they can easily become detached. Alternatively, lay some form of kerbing or edging. Point the joints with mortar.

The shape of paved areas When laying out paving there is no need to restrict yourself to rectangular shapes. Broken and irregularly shaped slabs can be used to make crazy paving (*top and bottom middle*), which can be fitted into almost any shape. Rectangular slabs can themselves be shaped or interstices can be filled with other materials. There is great variety in the paved areas illustrated above, although rectangular slabs have been used in most of the designs.

Bricks and Tiles

Brick is ideal for surfaces and paths within the garden. It is a sympathetic and versatile material and its colour and texture mellow well, blending in with most designs. Bricks can be laid in a variety of patterns, both simple and complex, either used on their own or in conjunction with other materials.

Bricks are available in a wide range of colours; if possible, select a tone which fits in well with the colour of the house and any other nearby structures. Avoid white bricks as these are likely to stain and become rather unsightly with time, while frost-proof housebricks are a good choice as they are readily available and should last well. Clay brick pavers offer more scope in shape and design than housebricks; they come in a variety of colours and textures and are best used for decorative surfaces. Granite setts can also be used, either on their own or mixed with other materials; these are extremely hard-wearing cubes of grey stone which are similar to bricks but slightly irregular in shape. They can be laid in many herringbone, weave and circular patterns in the same way as brick, but the resulting surface will be a little uneven, which can make chairs and tables unstable.

From a safety point of view, bricks can be very slippery, especially if they fall in the shadow of a north wall, which encourages the growth of moss and algae. These can be removed by vigorous and regular sweeping or with an algicide. Tiles too can be very slippery, and for large outside areas it is best to use non-slip ones to avoid any accidents.

Tiles are made of hard-fired clay and, depending on the composition of the clay and the temperature of the firing, they can be very durable. Quarry tiles are popular for paving; these are unglazed, geometric in shape (usually square or octagonal) and regular so they can be used to make formal, smooth surfaces. However, they are very difficult to cut and should be reserved for areas with long, straight edges rather than complicated, curved perimeters.

For a more decorative effect, use glazed paving tiles which come in different shapes and colours, often with painted motifs or designs. The more decorative tiles look best in the strong sunlight of hot climates. As glazed tiles are both fragile and relatively expensive, they should only be used in small quantities. Fragments of tiles can be used to make floor mosaics.

Brick and tile patterns It is easy to create a wide range of patterns and designs with bricks and tiles because the units are relatively small. Specially shaped and coloured tiles (*above*) can be used to make unusual three-dimensional patterns. More conventional bricks (*right*) can be used to produce quite complex designs, although it may be necessary to trim them. The use of more than one colour extends the range of design possibilities.

LAYING BRICK

Bricks are laid in many geometric patterns, including the traditional herringbone arrangement. They can be set on their sides or ends to expose different faces, enabling more complex designs to be created.

Bricks can be laid in the same way as paving stones, on a 2in (5cm) layer of sand over 4in (10cm) of rammed hardcore. The use of a hired plate vibrator will help to settle them firmly and evenly in the sand.

For extra stability, especially if heavy loads are likely to pass over the area, a layer of dry-mix concrete can be used instead of the sand. Concrete is also useful under the edges of the paved area to keep the edging bricks in place. Ideally, edges should be reinforced with a kerb or low wall. The gaps between the bricks should be even and can be filled with sand or dry cement brushed into them. This will help prevent weeds disfiguring the paved area. Tiles need a more solid base and should be laid on concrete and grouted with cement.

Pavers and bricks Modern pavers (*above and right*) are ideal for paths and larger areas of paving. Their regularity and uniformity of colour make them especially useful for modern designs, where clear, crisp lines are required. Pavers are available in a range of colours and sizes, making them excellent for complicated patterns. Older bricks are less regular and vary a great deal in colour, making them more sympathetic for paths and larger paved areas in mainly traditional gardens. Pavers have the big advantage of being frost-proof, whereas many bricks are not. It is essential to check whether the latter are frost resistant before buying them, or the surface may fracture in cold weather.

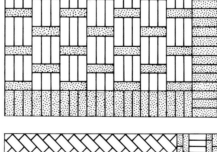

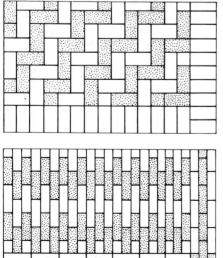

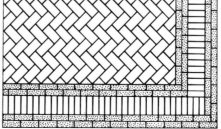

Designs for bricks and pavers Being small, both bricks and pavers can be used in a very wide range of designs (*left*), many of them extremely complicated; the herringbone pattern is particularly popular. The most satisfying designs, both for paths and for larger areas such as terraces and patios, need an edge pattern of some sort. This contains the main pattern and prevents it drifting off unsatisfactorily as it reaches the margins of the paving. Different coloured bricks or pavers can be worked into the pattern for variety when a large area is being covered, but colours should be selected carefully.

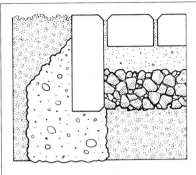

BRICK EDGING

Unless the edge of a brick surface falls against a wall or a similar structure, it must be contained within a permanent restraint to stop it moving.

Timber treated with preservative can be used in the form of edging boards. Nail some stakes onto the timber and drive the stakes in until the timber lies flush with the ground.

Alternatively, use bricks set on their edges embedded in a 4in (10cm) bed of concrete. This will create a more decorative and formal edge.

New and old paving Brick surfaces fit in well with a garden. Even when laid in complicated patterns they do not detract from the rest of the garden. Each of the patterns illustrated here fits comfortably in its setting. In a patio (*above*) the new bricks used have been cemented into place. A path (*right*) has been made from old bricks, using sand as an infill. Some of the bricks have suffered frost damage. Quite different effects are created with pavers and tiles. A courtyard at the back of a house (*below left*) has a surface of modern pavers. The Victorian tiles providing an attractive paved area at the front of another house (*below right*) are in keeping with the age of the building.

Concrete

Concrete is a hard, unyielding material that is used in the garden as a foundation for structures as well as a surface in its own right. Like tarmac and asphalt, it is mainly used for drives and other hard-wearing areas, particularly those around sheds or greenhouses to make large, flat surfaces for storing or mixing materials. In spite of its rather cold and unattractive appearance, it does have the advantage of being cheaper than most other paving materials; it is also very strong – particularly if it is reinforced – and relatively easy to lay compared to other surfaces.

Concrete does not look attractive enough to be used on its own in areas intended for relaxation, especially if it is introduced in large, unrelieved expanses. It will eventually acquire the patina of age, but this will take several years and will never fully disguise the harsh appearance of the material. However, concrete can be made to look much more acceptable and less harsh if its surface is brushed while still damp to reveal a pebble or gravel aggregate. This mellow, soft appearance is better suited to a garden setting.

There are other ways of texturing concrete to make it look more interesting. On some even surfaces it is

possible to press objects, such as strong-veined leaves, into the freshly laid concrete so that a decorative impression is left when they are removed. Alternatively, designs, abstract or otherwise, can be drawn in the semi-wet concrete, but these must be done well to be successful. Do not forget that it is virtually impossible to remove any marks once the concrete has set. Avoid making the impressions too deep as they will only create an uneven surface, unstable for furniture, and the grooves will collect dirt and water. Make sure there are no rough edges.

Concrete can be used in association with other materials; small areas can be decorated with large pebbles or cobblestones which are embedded in the wet concrete to create a pattern (see page 123). This may be uncomfortable to walk on, but it does make an attractive surface for a little-used spot. Concrete can also be tarred and covered with gravel while the tar is still wet, giving it a permanent gravelled surface. Alternatively, it can also be coloured by the addition of special pigments, but this is rarely satisfactory as the end result can look too garish and artificial for the natural garden environment.

Improving concrete Concrete is a harsh material for the garden but it will look softer and more sympathetic if treated before drying to expose its aggregate, thereby creating a patterned, textured surface (*left*). Another way to make concrete blend in more effectively is to split it up into small units (*above*). Here, the use of long slabs, softened with plants and interspersed with stones, is a very effective way of breaking up the surface.

EXPOSED AGGREGATE

Scatter dampened pebbles or gravel over the freshly laid concrete and tamp them down. After the concrete has hardened, but not quite set, use a stiff scrubbing brush and a gentle spray of water and brush away the concrete to expose the aggregate.

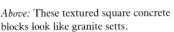

Above: These textured square concrete blocks look like granite setts.

Below: Circular concrete stepping stones make attractive small units.

Right: A large area of concrete can be brushed while wet, to expose the aggregate, and impressed with lines, thus suggesting crazy paving.

LAYING CONCRETE

The area to be concreted should be dug out to a depth of 6in (15cm) and the final extent should be marked out on all sides using wooden shuttering. This is made from planks of wood nailed to upright posts and encloses the ground that is to be covered. The top of the shuttering marks the finished level of the concrete, therefore it must be accurate, allowing for a slight slope for rain water to run off.

Hardcore is laid and rammed down to a depth of 3in (7.5cm), on top of which is laid the same depth of concrete. The concrete must be levelled-off; this is done by tamping it down with a length of wood that extends right across the width of the site, with the shuttering as a depth guide. Cobbles can be embedded or patterns made in the semi-wet concrete for a more decorative finish.

In wet or frosty weather, the concrete must be covered until it has set. The wooden shutters can be removed after about a week, and the concrete can be walked on once it is fully set, a few days after the shuttering has been removed.

If the area is extensive, it may be necessary to lay the concrete in several sections, each one being laid in turn with a separate set of shuttering. After the shuttering has been removed, the gaps left behind must be filled with a proprietary expansion compound.

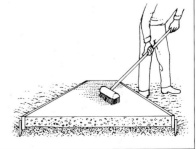

Mixed Materials

An exciting way of using materials is to mix them. Different materials are particularly useful for emphasizing various aspects of a design; they can break up large expanses into smaller plots and accentuate different levels, as well as defining a change of purpose in an area. Contrasting materials set in geometric patterns can act as guidelines; parallel lines of bricks set lengthways in paving will lead the eye towards some focal point, a statue or a view for example, but laid in intricate patterns, they will act as a focal point in their own right. Either will enhance the design.

Whatever is done, the imaginative use of materials will give the garden a unique and personal character, but mixed materials should be handled sensitively and not overdone for the greatest effect.

There are many combinations of materials that can look very pleasing, creating areas of excellent textural contrast. Brick and stone slabs, for instance, complement each other, as do brick and gravel, and stone and gravel. Blocks of tiles can be laid on their edges in a paved area; cobbles and flints set in concrete can be used on their own to cover small areas or they can be mixed together for a patterned surface. They can also be combined with other materials such as brick, granite setts and stone in durable, attractive designs.

Scraps of left over materials from other projects can be combined and used in much the same way as crazy paving. Be careful not to make a main path too irregular and avoid combining materials that deteriorate at different rates as this may make an uneven, dangerous surface; wood is likely to rot before any surrounding brick or stone has crumbled.

Sometimes artefacts can be incorporated with dramatic effect. For example, a millstone can be embedded in the centre of an area of gravel or cobblestones and surrounded by radiating circles of bricks, granite setts or tiles set on their edges.

Mixed materials look better once the surface has aged and mellowed. Often the brashness of new materials can clash, the brightness of newly-cut sandstone with raw brick, for instance, but once they have weathered, they will become aesthetically more compatible. Lichen and moss will help to blend materials together; these can be encouraged by coating the appropriate surface with a thin solution of cow dung and water or liquid seaweed fertilizer.

Left and above: A paved area can look interesting if more than one material is used in its construction. A certain amount of skill is required to visualize the finished surface, but working it out on paper beforehand helps a lot. These circles of brick and crazy paving (*left*) are very effective but need careful laying. Pebbles of different colours can be laid in a great variety of designs, including flowers and triangles (*above*).

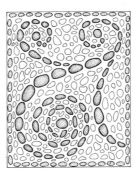

Above left: Paths that are not main thoroughfares can be more incidental in appearance. Stepping stones set in gravel are ideal for an informal path. Try to ensure that the stones are set at a distance of a stride apart for comfortable and relaxed walking.

Above right: An informal path of small paving slabs has been set directly on the earth. This casual method of laying means that the path can easily be moved, but it does create an uneven and therefore potentially hazardous surface, unsuitable for hard use.

MOSAICS

Both abstract and figurative mosaics can be created using a variety of pebbles and cobblestones. Work out the design on graph paper, and recreate the pattern using different coloured pebbles and stones in a mixture of sizes. These should be set in cement and firmed down.

Above: A delightful informal area has been created around a formal layout of circles and straight lines. This has been achieved by laying pebbles and intersecting them with paths of bricks radiating from a central water feature. The containers of plants have been placed on the brick lines for aesthetic reasons and they can be moved to make different patterns. The green of the foliage enlivens the surface.

123

MIXED MEDIA SURFACES

Some areas of the garden, such as large expanses of patio or terrace, or courtyards, can benefit from decoration to break up the monotony of an otherwise uniform surface. A combination of materials can be used to make attractively patterned and textured surfaces. Given the number of different materials available, the choice of colours and patterns is myriad. Surfaces can be laid to take pedestrian traffic or to form hard areas that are largely ornamental. Variations in shape and thickness have to be taken into account when laying and bonding materials. Large, heavy objects, such as millstones (*bottom*), can be laid directly on compacted earth or sand. In areas where there is light pedestrian traffic, bricks and whole paving slabs can be laid directly onto a sand base. In general, however, a firm foundation should be provided with a base of rammed hardcore. Bricks, pieces of stone slab, tiles, blocks or pebbles should be bedded in concrete laid over such a base. Smaller stones, such as gravel, can be left loose, but these, too, should be spread over a base of compacted hardcore. In pedestrian areas, the surface should be as near level as possible so that there is no risk of people tripping up. Unless they are flat, large pebbles bedded in concrete are very uncomfortable to walk on and are best confined to surfaces where there is little or no traffic.

Uncomfortable and hazardous surfaces Mixed materials can look very attractive but can be uncomfortable to walk on in anything other than stout shoes. Avoid using irregular stones (*left*) or large pebbles (*below left*) in areas where there is a good deal of traffic.

Wood (*below*) can be mixed with other materials – bark is appropriate – but wooden surfaces can become very slippery and are best used on paths away from trees and shrubs. A covering of small-meshed galvanized wire netting is rather ugly but it gives a good grip.

Granite setts Granite setts are a very versatile and decorative form of paving. They can be used as solid paving on their own or mixed with other materials of a different colour or texture. They can look particularly good with gravel or stone chippings. The smallness of each individual unit allows granite setts to be laid in various patterns, including complicated geometric designs (*left*) as well as much simpler linear schemes. The concentric circles of setts (*below right*) echo the curve of the lawn and are complemented by the shaped bush; the circular bench around the tree adds the finishing touch. The principal disadvantage of granite setts, however, is that they are not very pleasant to walk on in thin shoes, so avoid using them on main pathways.

Above left: An advantage of materials that come in small units, such as bricks, granite setts or pebbles, is that they can be used in a wide variety of patterns. With complicated geometric designs it is often sensible to draft the proposed configuration on paper first. An alternative course is to work the pattern out on the ground. Once the pattern is complete, a mixture of sand and cement can be worked into the gaps between each piece to bond the units together for an even surface.

Left: Interesting patterns can be made using large pieces of irregularly shaped stone. Usually the pattern can only be worked out on the ground with the available pieces of stone. Begin by selecting one or two key pieces and then fit other pieces around them, finishing off with some form of edging. This can be heavy work, even when lifting is minimized by the use of levers. The imaginative gardener can, however, produce a feature unique to his or her garden.

125

PATHS

Paths are important elements as they direct the eye as well as the foot. They are used in the garden for both practical and visual reasons. As well as providing a way for people to circulate, paths also form a framework, delineating lawns and individual flower beds or defining various parts of the garden.

As a practical feature, a path can be used regularly as a means of getting from one place to another; for example, from the gate to the front door. This type of path will receive a lot of heavy use, irrespective of the weather, and should be built of hard weather-proof materials so that it will stand up to the constant wear.

On the other hand, a garden path is often more decorative than practical, to be used for slowly strolling along while admiring plants or chatting to a companion. This tends to be a fine weather activity and presents no real hardship to the surface; soft materials, such as bark, grass and gravel can be used.

From a visual point of view, the choice of materials will depend on what is sympathetic to the house and other structures in the area, and what is appropriate to the style of the garden. Paths must be constructed on solid foundations, with a slight camber (upward curve) to drain rain away from the surface.

Formal Paths

Most formal paths are intended to be used frequently and their construction should reflect this. One great fault with many paths is that they are too narrow. As a rule of thumb, such thoroughfares should be wide enough for two people to walk comfortably side by side. This is particularly true of paths that are made for ambling along, as nothing is worse than having to talk over your shoulder as you progress around a garden. Functional paths should be even more generous in width to allow easy access, and if you want to have plants spilling over the edges of the path, do not forget to make allowance for these decorative effects; pushing past wet or thorny bushes on the way to a gate or doorway is not pleasant and can be dangerous.

The shape or direction of a formal path will mainly depend on the overall design of the garden, but paths with a definite function should, on the whole, be straight and direct, otherwise people will start taking short cuts, especially between well-used areas such as the back door and the dustbins, or the house and the garage. Paths meant for wandering along can be more serpentine; it is always rather exciting not to know what lies around the next corner. A meandering path can also give the impression that the garden is longer and wider than it really is.

Formal paths can be constructed from a wide range of materials. Close-clipped grass can look very smart, but for a more hard-wearing finish, one of the most traditional and best-loved materials is brick. The relatively small size of each unit allows for a wide range of patterns to be used. If they are laid in lines along the length of the path they tend to accelerate the walker's pace and at the same time make the garden appear longer than it really is; bricks laid widthways across the path have the opposite effect: they slow the walker down and make the garden seem smaller.

Stone slabs are another traditional material, one well-suited to older houses. The only drawback is that they are rather expensive. Concrete slabs can be used instead, but these tend to be harsh and unsympathetic to the eye. Concrete itself makes a very practical, if not particularly attractive, path; it is certainly more acceptable used in small rather than larger areas, but it should be left for the more functional paths. Its appearance can be improved by brushing the surface before it has completely set to reveal the aggregate (see page 121). Gravel, in spite of being loose, can be used for both formal and informal paths, but if it is to form the main pathway it must be well contained by edging of some sort.

All formal paths should be regularly checked for any weeds growing in or through them. The weeds can be removed by careful hand weeding, or an appropriate herbicide can be applied instead.

Straight paths Paths play an important role in the garden's design, as these three examples show (*left, above and right*). The treatment of paths can vary considerably and their impact will vary accordingly. All three of these paths are straight and yet they have quite a different effect on their surroundings. The materials, the edging and the positioning are all important factors in shaping a garden and creating its atmosphere. The gravel path (*left*) is the least formal of all the paths, the herringbone motif (*right*) is the most decorative, while the entrance path (*above*) is primarily functional, leading through the front garden to the gate.

Above: Granite setts make a simple but effective diamond pattern in a gravel path.

Paths of mixed materials (*below*) The combination of two or more materials can totally transform a path into a very handsome feature. The attraction may lie in the pattern formed, the varying textures of the materials, their different colours or a mixture of all three. Care needs to be taken in getting a level surface; the path should preferably be laid on a solid concrete base. An edging that gives the path solidity can enhance the pattern.

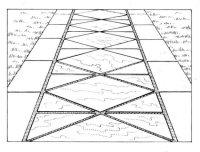

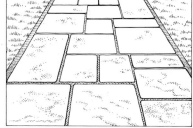

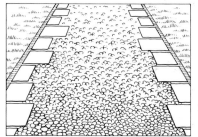

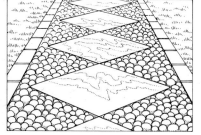

Above: When grass paths are well maintained, they are wonderfully soft to look at and blend sympathetically with plants. They are also relatively cheap to create. However, they do need constant mowing if they are to be kept in good condition. Such paths are not at their best in wet weather, being unpleasant to walk on and easily damaged. Plants cascading over them create brown patches and make mowing difficult, while paths that lie under trees can become bald. In spite of these drawbacks, in many situations grass is the only obvious material for paths; it is one of the best choices of pathing to use among shrubberies and borders for an informal, natural look. Paths that curve away, like the one above, are especially attractive, drawing the viewer on to see what is growing around the corner in the neighbouring part of the garden.

Informal Paths

Some paths are markedly informal, both in use and in appearance, and they will give a relaxed and casual feel to the garden.

One of the most informal pathing materials is chipped or shredded bark. This has a loose, shaggy appearance and looks very much at home in wilder or more neglected parts of the garden, especially woodland. Paths through woodland areas always look best if they are as informal and as natural as possible. This also applies to pathways through large areas planted informally with bushy shrubs.

Gravel or other stone chippings can look informal and decorative, especially if the path has no defined edges or if it is swamped with flowering plants. Indeed, planting has a lot to do with the style of a path, and the more the edges and line of the path are blurred, the more informal it will look. Gravel paths in particular look very good with a few plants spilling over them from neighbouring borders. For safety reasons, regularly trim or cut back any vegetation that has become too abundant.

Delightfully informal paths can be created in an orchard, a meadow or a patch of wild garden by simply mowing a swath through the long grass. No preparation is needed for this natural pathway and the beauty of it is that you can change the direction of the path to create different routes and vistas every year without any trouble.

On a more practical level, many large flower borders need some form of access so that they may be tended. Such paths only have to be wide enough to allow the gardener to slip between the plants without causing damage to roots or growth. A similar path can be constructed along the back of a border in front of a hedge; wading through a lush growth of plants makes cutting a hedge very difficult and clearing up the resulting clippings all but impossible. The surface should not be made of any permanent material as there may be a need to change the route from time to time; a beaten earth track with a gravel topping is both simple and appropriate and ash, a traditional country material, can also be used.

Left and above: Informal paths may make a more humble contribution to the garden than formal, main highways, but they help to create a relaxed and restful atmosphere. There is no urgency in their given course and they allow the garden to be enjoyed at leisure. They can be constructed of simple, plain materials, crazy paving being especially appropriate, as is rough-cut grass, ideal for wild, meadow-like areas.

129

Above, right and below: Informal paths appear to wander at will, leading into the heart of the garden's growth. Their natural flow helps to create a romantic atmosphere, which can be heightened by planting that softens their edges, merging vegetation and paths into an organic whole. Yielding surfaces, such as gravel, soft bark and grass, are more suitable than paving of stone, brick or concrete, materials which convey an impression of purposefulness that is more appropriate to main paths which are used a great deal.

STEPPING STONES

Position whole or broken pieces of paving slabs and test the stride-length. Mark out the shape of each stone using a trowel and remove the turf. Lay the paving ¾in (1.5cm) below the surface of the lawn on a 1in (2.5cm) bed of sand.

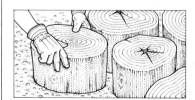

WOOD AND GRAVEL PATHS

An informal and attractive path can be made from logs and gravel; the wood should be treated with preservative. Make sure all the logs are the same height to ensure that the surface is even. Lay them close together, almost touching, on a sand and gravel base, and firm them down. The gaps between the logs should be filled with a mixture of sand and gravel, and the surface brushed with a stiff outdoor broom.

STEPS

Having more than one level, whether natural or man-made, can add considerable interest to a garden, but either ramps or steps are necessary to move from one point to another. Where the slope is gradual, a ramp or sloping path may be sufficient, but for steeper slopes steps are necessary, a curved flight being best for unusually steep ascents.

Steps make an exciting and dramatic feature in the garden. Standing at the top of a flight the lower area spreads before you, but approaching from below, the upper area may be wrapped in mystery until the steps have been ascended. Steps that curve up and away through bushes, with the top out of sight, give a touch of enticing secrecy to the garden, and few can resist the impulse to climb them to find out where they lead and what lies beyond.

It is important that steps should fit in with the look of the garden, and informal steps should be much more fluid and less severe than formal ones. Formal flights of steps are a structural feature, part of the basic framework of the garden, while informal flights are more of a decorative accessory. Formal staircases can be straight and angular or almost sculptural in concept, with double flights curving around to meet the lower level, or diverging to finish some distance apart. Informal steps can produce a gentle curve or a sharp zigzag, and they are usually less exposed than formal steps, perhaps hidden away in a corner of the garden, winding up a gradual slope.

As well as being functional, steps can also act as important focal points, drawing the eye towards them in expectation. It is essential, therefore, that as well as being structurally sound, such steps should be attractive and well designed.

A wide range of materials can be used to construct steps. Apart from cost, the main consideration should be to use materials that blend in well with the paths and other structures within the garden. Another vital factor to consider is safety; in certain places, most notably moist and shady sites, non-slip surfaces should be used whenever possible. As long as safety is not impaired, it is perfectly acceptable to plant up the sides of steps, even occasionally on some of the treads, although make sure enough of the tread is showing to enable the climber to ascend easily and securely, with a sure, uncluttered foothold.

Above: Informal steps have a "take-it-or-leave-it" air, but they are likely to lead somewhere interesting, like a hidden walled garden or a wooded area. They are most tantalizing when their full extent cannot be seen.

Left: Formal steps link different levels of a garden on a clearly defined axis in a definite and self-conscious way, even when the edges are softened by planting.

Formal Steps

Steps can either be built into a bank or slope or they can be constructed as freestanding structures that project out from a rise. The latter is a particularly formal device associated with a regular design, and is usually used in conjunction with highly finished retaining walls and terraces.

Formal projecting steps should be built on a grand scale as a small flight will look insubstantial and give the impression of being merely an afterthought. Since projecting steps form an integral part of the surrounding structures, they must be planned in advance. They are more difficult to construct than built-in steps because, being freestanding, they have to be self-supporting, whereas those built into a bank have their weight catered for.

Projecting steps are usually constructed from stone or brick and must be tied well into the adjoining structure. They are often constructed as part of a retaining wall and built at the same time. It is important that they are well built on good, firm foundations so they are safe and sturdy.

Stone and brick are the most appropriate materials for formal steps. Stone steps are undoubtedly the most visually satisfying but stone is an expensive material. Brick is very popular because, among other reasons, the small units make it very versatile to use. They must be frost-proof and match the materials of any nearby structures.

On a truly grand scale, grass can be used. It is best if grass steps are reinforced on the leading edge with bricks or some other solid material. They are very difficult to maintain because of the problem of mowing them, and they are also prone to wear and tear; depressions can be dangerous, making it easy to trip over the top of the solid riser. Wood is another option; leading up from decking, a flight of wooden steps is an excellent finishing touch. They should be made using a timber framework so that the treads are not in contact with the soil. Concrete, in the form of slabs or pre-formed step units, is suitable for formal designs, and it is possible to buy non-slip slabs which are useful for shady areas of the garden.

Above: There is no mystery in a short flight of steps but the materials used and the positioning of features can give it an individual character.

Left: A long series of steps is visually exciting, drawing the eye and enticing the garden visitor to ascend and explore. The mystery deepens when, as here, bushes obscure the full sweep of the steps. It is a good idea for long stairways to have flat "resting" areas at regular intervals. These can be more interesting if they correspond with cross-paths.

Ramps (*below*) In gardens where it is only possible to move from area to area by ascending or descending steps, it is often useful to incorporate a ramp. This may be to give access to wheelchairs (when a wide ramp would be needed), but it is more likely to facilitate gardening needs like moving wheelbarrows about.

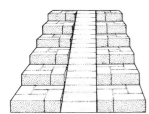

Above: Grass steps generally need to be on a grand scale; here, they look splendid with formally clipped hedging.

Left: Wooden steps have a light, ordered appearance that contrasts with foliage.

Below: Stone steps nearly always have a solid, safe appearance because the treads tend to be deep and the risers shallow. Here, the curved shape creates the impression that they are flowing through the gate, into the courtyard.

TYPES OF STEPS

There are two basic types of steps: freestanding and cut-in.

Freestanding steps are built between one flat area and another, and they are keyed-in to the retaining wall so that the two structures do not pull apart. They must be well constructed and sturdy, built on a firm foundation. The steps should be laid on a base of approximately 4in (10cm) of hardcore and covered with a 4in (10cm) layer of concrete.

For cut-in steps, each step should have a foundation of well-rammed hardcore. If you are using small paving material, such as brick or granite setts, these should be set in concrete or cement and the joints securely bonded with cement. Concrete or stone paving slabs need to be bedded down on pads of cement on top of the hardcore base.

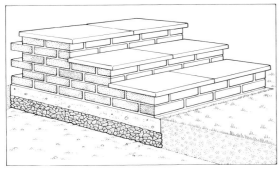

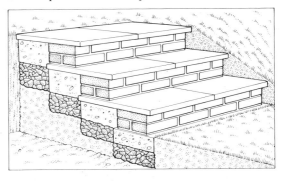

Informal Steps

Informal steps are often much narrower than their formal counterparts, but it is still a good idea for them to be at least as wide as the path leading up to them otherwise they will look out of scale.

Use sympathetic materials for informal steps, or soften hard materials by mixing them. Timber is a good choice, particularly well suited to woodland settings. Wood can be used in a number of ways; cut in half lengthways, the flat surface forming the tread, logs can be embedded into an earth hillside. Alternatively, large slices of tree trunk can be arranged in a flight ascending a slope; they can also be driven into the earth to resemble a palisade. Again, logs or lengths of preserved wood can be used for risers with well rammed earth or gravel in the treads. Old railway sleepers are effective, cut to length and embedded in a bank. Use either softwood or stone for cantilevered steps if space is limited; these are a novel way of enlivening a flat surface and, tucked away in a corner cut into a wall, they make an interesting feature. They

must, however, be very firmly supported from underneath and well constructed for utmost safety.

Concrete can be made to look informal by roughening its surface while semi-wet to create a textured finish. This is good for shady areas as it gives some surface grip against moss; otherwise non-slip paving stones should be used. For curved steps, use brick or stone as both are versatile materials. Old brick gives a sense of maturity, and stone built into a slope will lend a rural flavour. Crazy paving is a good mixed medium to use for a particularly informal look.

Another feature of informal steps is that they often have vegetation growing beside them. This helps to integrate the structure into the garden, giving the steps a softer, more natural look than is the case with formal designs. Plant up the sides of the steps, but only plant sparingly on the steps themselves unless they are very wide. As with informal paths, regularly cut back vegetation growing on or near the steps so safety is not impaired by trailing or exuberant growth.

Above: Planting to blur the edge of a short flight of steps helps create an appealing effect.

Left: Mixing dimensions and materials makes an informal flight of steps blend into the garden in a picturesque manner. When using materials of irregular shape, it is particularly important to ensure that they are firmly anchored so that there is no chance of them tipping or being dislodged.

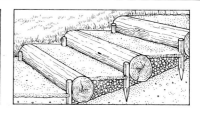

MAKING LOG STEPS

Use wood treated with preservative and make sure all the logs are the same diameter. Excavate a regular slope in the bank and compact the surface using a rammer. Drive a couple of strong stakes in at the base where the first step is to go and snugly fit a log behind the stakes, bedding it down in the soil. Firmly pack a layer of hardcore behind the log to form the base of the second step, and cover this with gravel.

SAFETY

To avoid slippery surfaces, regularly and vigorously brush each tread with a stiff garden broom, using an algicide if necessary. Wooden steps can be covered with fine-mesh galvanized netting and concrete steps should be built with non-slip treads.

It is important to make sure that the steps are firm and sturdy; all blocks, bricks and slabs should be well secured so that they do not move under foot. Handrails of wood or rope will help to increase safety, especially for the elderly, and all wood must be treated with a preservative to stop it rotting.

Only plant on the margins of the steps and not in awkward places on the treads, otherwise the plants will obscure the view of the step.

STEP DESIGN

All steps should be carefully designed. Do not build garden steps that rise very steeply in a restricted space. Rather, they should rise gently and gracefully, with as much emphasis on their appearance as on their function. Aim for a safe, easy climb.

Steps need to provide a generous foothold and both the height and depth of each step should be regular.

The width of the staircase must satisfy the demands placed on it, be it constant access or occasional use.

The relationship between the height and depth of steps is critical, both for comfort and safety. Steep or very low risers should be avoided as they are often difficult to judge; shallow and deep treads are equally difficult to negotiate as they do not fall within the natural walking pace of most adults.

Above: Railway sleepers are heavy and make stable risers for steps.

Making simple steps Simple steps are generally best made from materials that are ready to hand (*below, left to right*). Irregularly shaped stone can be used for crazy paving. Wooden steps need to be treated with a preservative, cross-sections of logs should be of long-lasting timber and risers of split logs should not be too wide. Wooden treads can have a covering of fine-mesh wire to prevent slipping.

EDGING

Not all surfaces need to be edged but it often adds the finishing touch. In some cases, edging is used for purely ornamental reasons, but in others, edging is required to help keep the surface material in place, or even to hold back soil in flowerbeds. With brick surfaces, edging has a dual function. On the practical side, it helps to prevent the edges breaking away or sinking, and from a visual point of view, decorative edging can add considerably to the effect of a path or a more expansive paved area.

A brick surface can be edged in a variety of ways (see page 119), according to the look of the garden. A level course of bricks can be set in cement or concrete, but a more decorative effect can be created by sinking bricks into the soil at a 45° angle, to give a toothed effect. Many special edging tiles can be purchased for brick paths, especially Victorian styles which include those with scrolled tops, known as barley sugar tops, and those with a castellated finish. These look particularly good in small town gardens and in association with weathered brick or gravel.

Concrete is more difficult to edge. The most commonly seen edging is round-topped lengths of concrete, but these are rather municipal and not very attractive. A better finish is to use a row of granite setts or even bricks positioned around the edge of the concrete area. Paving slabs need some form of edging, and a line of bricks or granite setts can often add to the interest of the material. These should be laid flush with the surface rather than raised.

Gravel requires a raised edge to prevent the stones mixing with bordering soil. Any of the materials already mentioned can be used, although brick and granite setts look the most handsome. In a more informal setting, use thin logs of wood.

Plants themselves can be used as edging. Low clipped hedges of box (*Buxus*) make very effective edging, especially to brick or stone. Other plants can be used for a more informal edge; lavender (*Lavendula*), for example, is ideal as it can be clipped into neat shapes; it is also deliciously fragrant and will perfume the air along the border or path.

Left and above: The linear or sinuous quality of a path is emphasized if it has a uniform edge. The line is broken if plants are allowed to flop over it at irregular intervals, although a row of a single species of plant, such as these hostas (*above*), will soften the line but highlight the whole sweep. Here, the rounded shape of the abundant leaves complements the geometric brickwork. Clipped hedges, for example of box (*left*), produce a harder line, ideal for a parterre or the borders of a knot garden.

Solid edges A solid edge of logs (*above*) gives a neat but soft finish. It can also act as a support for adjacent beds, to prevent them encroaching on the path. These colourful ceramic bricks (*right*) separate the soil from the gravel and complement the flowers. Individual stones (*below left*) also help to define a path precisely, while sunken edging (*below right*) allows for a well finished lawn.

Decorative edging Various forms of decorative edging (*right*) can be used for paths. Second-hand, frost-free bricks (*top row*) are among the cheapest materials; they can be laid in a flat row or angled for a serrated effect. The gaps between the vertical bricks can be filled with cement to make a small wall. The diagonal bricks can be left resting on one another with or without bonding. Bricks and tiles (*middle row*) define the edge of the path and also give it some support, especially if they are concreted or cemented into place. Edging tiles can be plain or ornate, with pretty decorative tops. They are ideal for a Victorian garden. Wire edging (*bottom row*) is versatile and can simply be pushed into the soil.

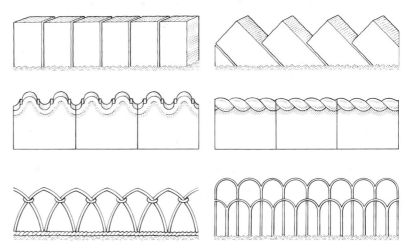

Left: Loose stones provide an effective surface for a sunken edge to a grass path; this recess allows a lawn mower to be run right along the edge.

Above: The barley sugar twist on Victorian tiles makes a lively boundary to a path, helping it race away out of sight.

Below: Edging to irregular paving can be soft, with plants disguising the irregularities, or pronounced, as shown by this strikingly shaped lawn.

Below left: Plants help to soften hard architectural lines. A mixture of plants makes an irregular edging while using a row of the same kind creates a more formal effect. Here, the bushy lavender almost forms a hedge containing the steps.

Below right: Edging is used to finish paths and paved areas and also to confine beds and borders. Here, uncemented bricks are used to form a circular surround to a small bed, with concentric circles of foliage and flowers.

BOUNDARIES

Unless you are lucky enough to have a ha-ha – that is, a sunken fence or deep, steep-sided ditch – around your garden, you will need to construct some form of boundary. The beauty of a ha-ha is that, unlike a barrier, it allows uninterrupted views, visually merging the garden and the countryside beyond into one continuous, harmonious vista.

Most gardens must have some form of physical barrier around them, partly to keep the world out and partly to keep the garden in. A boundary also defines the limits of a garden, and at the same time provides a backdrop for displaying plants and other features such as statues and decorative garden furniture. With the exception of hedges, most forms of boundary can be used to support climbing plants of one sort or another for a decorative effect. This allows the gardener to pick his own colours and textures to soften the harsh outlines of walls and fences.

The choice of boundary material will greatly affect the overall appearance of the garden. Although many fences, walls and hedges are used as screens, they should not always turn the eye inwards; any vistas beyond the garden should be framed with well sited gaps in the boundary.

Hedges

Hedges make both good and bad barriers. On the positive side, they form a marvellous background to plantings, the colours and textures being fully complementary. They also allow the wind to filter through rather than creating a solid barrier which can cause wind turbulence. Hedge plants are relatively cheap to buy and no real skills are required in planting them. On the negative side, hedges may take several years to reach maturity and, having done so, they need regular maintenance in the form of trimming and feeding. It is also difficult to grow climbers over a hedge as this will interfere with clipping.

There is a wide range of hedging materials from which to choose. Some, such as yew (*Taxus*) and holly (*Ilex*), are evergreen and will form a permanent screen. Others, for example, hazel (*Corylus*) and hawthorn (*Crataegus*), are deciduous and so lose their leaves in winter, although some deciduous trees, notably beech (*Fagus*) and hornbeam (*Carpinus*), retain their brown and withered leaves throughout the winter. These make a dry rustling sound when the wind blows them, which appeals to some people but is thought to be rather menacing by others.

The colour of hedges can vary considerably. There is a range of both coniferous and deciduous hedging plants that will give different shades of green, from dark to light and on through to yellow and even purple. Yellow and purple should be used with care; large blocks of light yellow can be too bright as a general background, while purple can be too solid and leaden. Yew and holly provide a sombre green that is very good in a formal setting but can be a little oppressive in a small garden.

Tapestry hedges are an interesting option, but these are best used as a feature of the garden rather than just a background, since they are visually very lively and can be a little distracting. Here, a mixture of hedging plants are used, planted in alternating colours. Common green and copper beech are a popular choice for such hedges, but there are other equally pleasing colour combinations.

Not all hedges need to be neatly trimmed and manicured. In gardens with plenty of space, informal hedges of rose (*Rosa*) or barberry (*Berberis*), for example, can be grown and left to take on their natural, wild-looking shapes.

Holly and thorny hedges like hawthorn and barberry deter unwanted visitors, but the thorns are a menace to the gardener if the hedges are planted near a border that needs weeding.

Previous page, left and above: As well as forming physical barriers, hedges help to define spaces, preventing the eye from being distracted by what lies beyond, thereby forming private secluded areas. They can also create a sense of mystery by hiding other parts of the garden; openings through them provide tantalizing and enticing glimpses. The autumnal colouring of certain hedging plants is another asset.

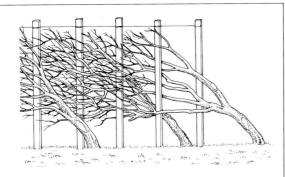

LAYING A HEDGE

An overgrown deciduous hedge can either be pruned back into shape or relaid as a new hedge. To relay the hedge, cut out any dead wood and thin the hedge (which will promote new, dense growth). Then cut halfway through the main stems, bend the tops over and weave them through a row of stakes. This will train in the old growth.

Top right and above: Although hedges are composed of living plants, they can be architecturally massive and dense, particularly evergreens, making wall-like enclosures that can create a feeling of isolation and security.

Above: An attractive, almost floating hedge can be created by planting trees behind a conventional hedge and then training them to form an upper tier. This creates an unusual and interesting hedging feature, one that emphasizes the horizontal element of the garden and allows only a partial view of what lies behind it. The horizontal layers will initially need to be trained along wires and branches from adjacent trees will need tying together. Limes (*Tilia*) make ideal trees for this kind of training, which is known as pleaching. A heavier stilt hedge can be made from hornbeam (*Carpinus*). When aiming for this layered effect, the lower hedge is best planted on the sunny side; if a hedge does not get sufficent light it will be drawn and thin. This type of hedge casts an area of dense shadow so underplant appropriately.

TRIMMING

A hedge should be shaped as it matures. This is normally done by sloping the sides inwards slightly so that the top is narrower than the bottom. This shape is known as a batter.

The reason for having a batter is to allow maximum light to reach the lower leaves so that they remain healthy. It also prevents large quantities of snow weighing on the top and splitting the hedge open in winter.

With formal hedges, the slope should be even along its whole length. To do this, frames known as formers are constructed with the desired batter, and strings are stretched between them along the hedge. These act as a guideline to create a level surface.

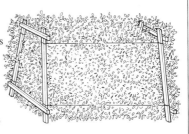

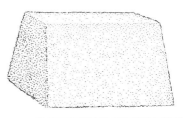

Above: A stilt hedge makes an impressive canopied entrance to a garden.

Left: Dense, dark hedges make good backgrounds against which to see light foliage and flowers, but they also take moisture and nutrients from the soil.

PLANTING AND MAINTAINING HEDGES

Hedges should be well cared-for if they are to look their best. The soil along a new hedge-line should be well dug, even double-dug if possible, with all perennial weeds removed and plenty of organic compost or farmyard manure incorporated. Choose plants that are about 2ft (60cm) tall and plant them in autumn or spring. A single row planted 1-2ft (30-60cm) apart, depending on type, is usually sufficient for most gardens, but for a thick hedge, a double row with the plants staggered is necessary.

Water the plants in and lay a mulch of grass cuttings or some other organic material. With the exception of conifers and slow-growing evergreens, the plants should be cut back as soon as they have been planted to promote bushy growth.

Water regularly, especially in dry weather, until the hedge is established and the plants have developed good root systems.

Once a hedge has reached its full size, it should be trimmed regularly, the number of annual clippings depending on the speed of growth of the plant. Hedges of large-leaved plants, such as Portugal laurel (*Prunus lusitanica*) or holly, look better if they are pruned with secateurs rather than a hedge trimmer, as the latter tends to cut leaves in half, giving an untidy finish.

Not all hedges need cutting. Informal hedges of rose or barberry can be left to their own devices apart from some general pruning to keep the plants healthy and vigorous.

To help maintain the hedge in good condition, regularly clear out the bottom and feed it in spring with a general fertilizer or organic material.

Above: Archways and gaps through hedges are always inviting and their positioning should be well thought out. Often only a glimpse of what lies beyond is needed.

Right: Hedges of uniform colour are best as backdrops. Avoid mixed or tapestry hedges and variegated leaves as these tend to make the background look too busy.

Walls

Walls are a popular choice of boundary, ideal for the utmost privacy. They give a solid, secure feeling and, at the same time, provide a uniform but handsome background for plants. Their colours and textures often make them attractive in their own right, and their warmth and strength make them suitable for climbing plants. They need not be confined to external boundaries, and can equally well be used as internal screens or as supports for hillsides, raised beds or terraces. Internal walled gardens offer the opportunity to create a miniature garden and peaceful haven within a larger whole.

Walls have their drawbacks, high costs being one of them. In small gardens they can also be rather claustrophobic, especially if they are tall and cut out a lot of light. When built in certain positions, walls can also create turbulence as they cause strong winds to eddy, which plays havoc with border plants.

Brick is still the favourite construction material for walls, and it should be chosen to match the walls of the house or any other existing buildings. Stone is another sympathetic walling material, although it tends to be rather expensive. If possible, local stone should be used to conform with the character of the area; this will also be much cheaper as lower transport costs are involved. Stone is a versatile material that can be bonded with cement or constructed as a dry-stone wall. Tufa, an unusual, porous rock, is appealing as it can be planted up. Only use it to build retaining walls which support little pressure.

Concrete blocks are relatively cheap and easy to use but they can look severe and unyielding in a garden setting. For a less solid wall, use geometric pierced blocks. These are light and airy but they tend to have a coldness about them, although their appearance can be softened with climbing plants.

Above: This low retaining wall divides two levels of a garden. Although it is essentially functional, holding back the earth of the upper level, the choice of materials and the planting make it a decorative feature. Aubrieta and heather grow in abundance here.

Left: A solid boundary wall makes a splendid support for climbing plants. Wires need to be fixed to such walls so that plants can be trained up them. When such a wall is well exposed to sun, a microclimate is created at its base in which relatively tender plants that might not survive in more open positions are likely to thrive. This allows for a much greater variety of plants.

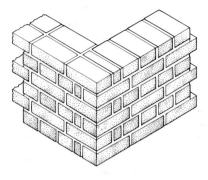
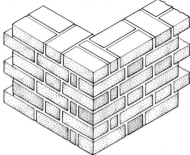
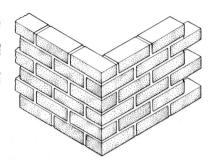

The construction of brick walls Brick walls can be constructed in several different ways (*above*). The different bonds that can be used are chosen partly for their decorative quality and partly for the strength they give a wall; for example, a retaining wall supporting a hillside must be a double thickness, whereas one supporting a shallow flower bed can be a single thickness. A wall consisting of more than one thickness of brick must have ties through the wall to prevent the two layers from pulling apart. The tie bricks, which show their ends, are known as headers. Those that are laid lengthways are known as stretchers. The various bonds illustrated (*above, left to right*) are English bond, Flemish bond and running bond, all different combinations of headers and stretchers. The running bond is used for single skinned walls.

Decorative treatment of walls Brick and concrete blocks are most widely used in the construction of walls but many other materials are also suitable. Furthermore, there is great scope for adding decorative finishes through a range of varying textures and colours. Some of the most attractive finishes are achieved using local materials. Flint (*below left*), alone or combined with other materials, lends itself to various treatments and sandstone (*below*), which varies in colour from region to region, is much used where it is available. Decorative tiles (*left*) are attractive but may pose problems. They may look altogether too busy for the garden environment, and their glazed surfaces are not hard-wearing. Their permanent coloration and patterns mean that any plants will have to be carefully selected.

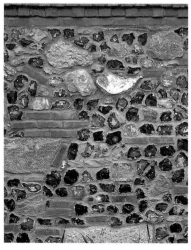

Above left: A fence topping a low wall forms an effective barrier but is much less heavy to look at than a solid wall to the same height. A railing fence, as here, allows light to reach plants in the border at the base of the wall.

Above right: Painting walls a light colour helps to cover up any blemishes in brickwork and creates a surface that reflects light into the garden. This is particularly useful in small or basement gardens in part or full shade.

Below left: Tall brick walls form a very good background to a garden, especially if the bricks are of a sympathetic colouring. As well as providing a backdrop for border plants, they can also provide support for climbers.

Below right: Planting in beds and borders backed by walls should take into account the colour and texture of the materials the walls are made of. The orange and yellow primulas bring out the red in the stone wall.

PLANTING AGAINST WALLS

Using nails and ties to secure plants against a wall is not a recommended practise, as the nails will need to be replaced regularly and this will damage the wall. Instead, attach horizontal wires between vine eyes. These are wedge-shaped pieces of metal with holes in the top, through which the wire passes. The wire can then be tightened with tensioning screws so it does not sag.

Wooden trellising is an attractive alternative. Fix the trelliswork to the face of the wall with screws and plugs, using 1-2in (2.5-5cm) thick wooden blocks as spacers so the trellis is held clear of the wall.

For a more informal look, use wire mesh. Wire livestock fencing can be used on large walls behind borders; if you are growing very heavy, dense climbers, use plastic or plastic-coated metal mesh for good support.

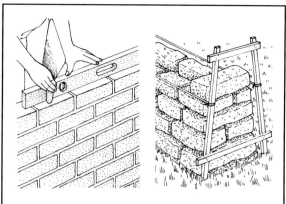

BRICKLAYING TECHNIQUES

When bricklaying, lay a ½in (1.25cm) layer of mortar along each course and butter the head of each brick with the same amount of mortar. Firm down each brick and check that it is level. Level the whole course before building upwards by spanning it with a spirit level and, with the end of the trowel, tapping down any bricks that are not level. Also check vertically with a spirit level that each course is exactly above the previous one.

For dry stone walling, use a former as a guide when placing the stones so that the sides slope slightly inwards. Construct the ends with several courses of uniform edging stones alternated with through stones, and fill in the cavity formed between the front and back facing blocks with small stones, tightly packed in the space.

Below left and below right: Walls in formal gardens are often used as supports for climbing plants. In more informal or rural situations, strands of ivy make an appropriately casual cover. However, care must be taken that this vigorous climber does not become too rampant and take over. Although both these walls are fairly low, they provide some protection for plants as well as giving them encouragement in the form of radiated heat.

Rustic stone walls Such walls have a charm that is difficult to beat and they rarely look inappropriate, especially in a cottage garden. Ornaments, such as urns, will make the walls look more formal. A capping of some sort, whether it be flat slabs (*top*), blocks set on end (*above*), or simply a rough dome of cement (*left*), helps to finish off the feature. Without it, a wall tends to look incomplete. Capping also serves the practical function of shedding rainwater, thus protecting the internal fabric of a wall. Steps associated with walls should be constructed of a sympathetic material and built in an appropriate style for an integrated effect.

Fences

Fences make slightly less solid boundaries than walls, but this is not necessarily a disadvantage, especially in attractive country areas where short fences will allow good views of the scenery. Fences tend to be easier and cheaper to construct and install than walls.

There are many attractive forms of fencing, handsome picket fences being a prime example. These are generally quite short and so are of little use for providing privacy, but they do have a delicacy that makes them particularly suitable for small cottage gardens in either town or country. They are often painted white, which adds to their charm.

There is a wide range of more solid wooden fences that can be purchased from garden centres, most of which are sold as pre-prepared panels that can be quickly erected between vertical posts that have been fixed into the ground. These include lap board, wavy-edge and woven panels.

A more formal and solid look can be achieved by constructing a close-boarded fence. Here, overlapping, vertical boards are nailed to two or three horizontal bars which are then attached to the secured vertical fence posts.

All wooden fencing should be treated with preservative, preferably not creosote as this may harm nearby plants. Alternatively, they can be sealed and painted. Erect the fencing so that the panels do not touch the ground; this will prevent the bottom being permanently damp and so prone to decay. Fill the gap between the bottom of the panel and the soil with a gravel board, a separate length of wood that can easily be replaced should it rot.

Old-fashioned iron fencing can look very elegant, while the more recent chain link, although not particularly appealing in its own right, can be quite acceptable if it is well covered with climbing plants. It does have the advantage of being relatively cheap, easy to put up and long-lasting.

Many fences can be extremely unattractive in spite of their obvious efficiency. This is particularly true in the country where they are designed to keep animals at bay rather than to create an attractive garden boundary. It is best to avoid fences that simply consist of livestock netting stretched between posts with one or two strands of barbed wire pulled taut along the top, although this can serve as a temporary measure while a hedge is growing.

Fences can be covered with plants, but this may introduce one or two problems. The extra weight of the plants and the wind resistance will increase the stress on the supports. Consequently, the fence should be as solid as possible in order to withstand such pressures. Furthermore, unless the climbing plants are species that can be cut to the ground annually, the fence cannot be re-painted, or re-treated with preservative to keep it in good condition.

Left and above: These two fences are markedly different in character. One (*left*) has been erected on a low wall. This is very much in character with the Victorian house beyond and is nicely in proportion with the wall. It gives some feeling of security, as well as allowing a view of the garden inside. The other example (*above*) is a simple post and rail fence. It is made from chestnut or oak that has been split lengthways, giving it a rustic air that is entirely in keeping with the country setting. If well secured, it will keep out large animals in rural areas.

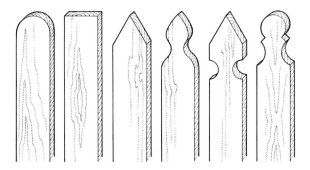

Decorative paling (*above*) For a more decorative finish, shape the ends of palings. The simplest designs are square, pointed or rounded, but more complex ones include intricately carved Gothic and ornate Queen Anne styles.

Fences Fences make less solid barriers than walls. They define a space but do not necessarily totally enclose it, allowing the planting within to relate to that beyond the demarcated boundaries. They can be informal (*above*) or formal (*below left and below right*). Often they are decorative features in their own right (*left*) and there is enormous scope for varying the construction and using different materials to make them highly ornamental. As a general rule it is advisable to keep formal fences free of climbers, especially those that need to be painted regularly. More informal ones, such as woven wooden hurdles, although decorative, can be clothed in plants and still remain functional.

Simple and sophisticated fence designs
Although the appeal of many fences is their simplicity, such as a plain fence made of wooden stakes (*left*), they can be handled in a very imaginative way (*below left*). Here, the curve of the fence echoes the details on the adjacent benches. Specially commissioned fences can be expensive, but when they are tailor-made they contribute to the unique character of a garden. Amateur carpenters can make their own (*below right*), suiting the style to the situation and using materials according to their means. The bottom rails of this fence almost touch the ground and will be liable to rot unless the ground underneath them is kept clear.

FIXING A FENCE POST
Drive a fence spike into the ground and check that it is vertical by holding a spirit level against each side. Install the post in the collar of the spike and tighten the integral bolts to secure the post.

Alternatively, set the post in concrete, with at least a quarter of the post below ground. Lay a hardcore base, position the post and brace it with battens. Before filling the hole with concrete, ram more hardcore around the base of the fence post.

Wooden fencing (*below*) This selection covers six types of wooden fencing. The three panels in the bottom row could be constructed at home but they are almost certainly cheaper to buy ready-made. The three in the top row are more individual designs but they are still within the scope of many amateur carpenters. The fence on the left is the easiest to construct, and is simply a matter of nailing horizontal planks to vertical posts. If rustic timbers are available, the fence on the right is probably the cheapest to make. Treat all wooden fencing with a preservative that is not toxic to plants.

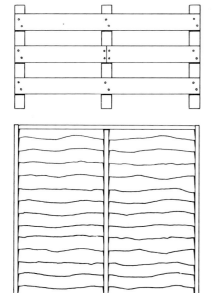

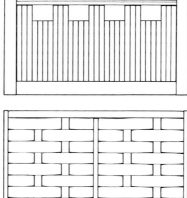

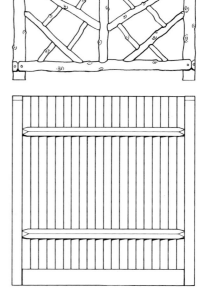

GATES AND GATEWAYS

The approach to a house or garden is often through a gate or gateway, and it is important that this first impression is given due consideration. The general principle in choosing a gateway is to select one that matches the hedge, fence or wall through which it gives access. If it is near the house or any other building then the gateway should be architecturally and stylistically in keeping.

The most popular materials for gates are wrought iron and wood. As a very general rule of thumb, the former looks better in town gardens and the latter in country gardens. Iron gates can look very smart when they are associated with brick or stonework; a tall, fine wrought-iron gate set in a high brick wall with tantalizing glimpses of a garden beyond will be a beautiful object in itself but, being strong, it is also practical and will provide good security. If privacy and security are needed then the gate should be a tall and solid wooden one, affording no views of the garden beyond to the passer-by.

Wooden gates can look very attractive set in hedges and fences, especially picket fences. They can be painted; black tends to be more popular in towns and white in the country, but it is really a matter of personal taste. Only choose a bright colour if it fits in with the setting. Alternatively, wooden gates can be treated with a preservative and left plain (creosote may be used if there are no plants near the gate), or stained with wood stain to bring out the grain.

Gates are heavy and need to be well supported, especially if there are children about who often delight in swinging on them. If the gate is set in a wall there should be no problems as long as well-secured, heavy duty hinges are used. Freestanding gates in hedges or fences should have strong wooden posts that are securely embedded in the ground, preferably in a 1ft (30cm)-deep bed of concrete, to stop them moving. For small gates the posts should be at least 4in (10cm) square and for larger gates, those leading to a drive or a field, for example, the posts should be approximately 8in (20cm) square.

The key to constructing a wooden gate is to make certain that the frame is rigid and will not sag, which will prevent the gate from shutting properly. This is normally done with the use of diagonal cross braces. Always use strong hinges and catches, and make sure all the gate furniture is in keeping with the style and status of the gate, be it simple or grand.

Left and below: The delicacy of iron gates allows the eye to pass through them to the enticing sight of the gardens beyond (*below*); the filigree metalwork is particularly attractive. Such views are invitations to step inside but the gates make effective barriers, especially if spearhead finials are used (*left*).

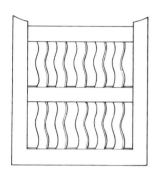

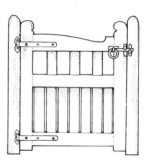

A selection of gates The range of gates commercially available is not as wide as it has been hitherto, but it is still possible to have them made to your own design by a skilled carpenter or blacksmith. There are many styles to choose from, including mostly functional (*top right and bottom right*), the more delicate (*top middle*) and rustic (*bottom middle*). Some are relatively easy to make at home (*top left and bottom left*). The choice of gate depends on its proposed function and position: heavier gates should be used in the walls, fences and hedges marking the outside property boundaries of a garden, while gates of lighter construction are suitable within the site, used just as much for decoration as for practicality.

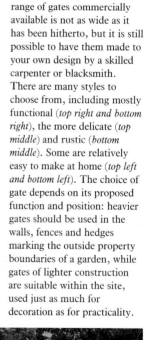

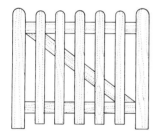

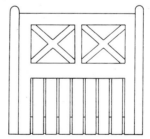

Fitting gates to their setting Gates in fences (*top left and top right*) should be designed, if possible, in the style of the fence. The gateposts should also be in keeping, as in both of these examples. For gates in hedges and walls there is much more choice of style and material. However, they should suit the weight of the boundary and be appropriate to what lies beyond. Delicate ironwork has the advantage of allowing a view of the garden and, although rather elegant, it complements wilder, meadow-like areas (*bottom left*) as well as more formal paths (*bottom right*). Gateposts should be substantial but not out of scale. Finials and palings can be highly decorative and add character and finish to the gate.

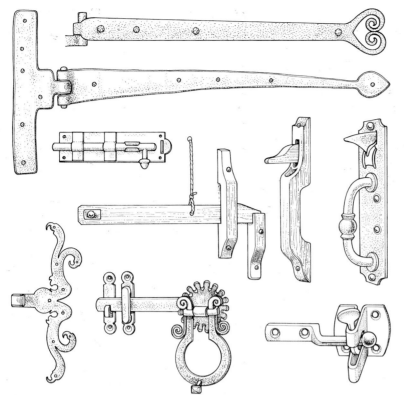

Above and below: It is important to choose a style of gate that is in keeping with its setting. These two wooden gates, in contrasting styles, would not be interchangeable.

Gate fittings (*above*) The choice of fittings can make or mar the appearance of a gate. Many hinges and bolts are designed to be decorative as well as functional but even a fitting that is essentially practical should be in keeping with the style of the gate on which it is to be used. When buying fittings, carefully choose those that are durable and in scale with the gate for which they are intended. A skimpy fitting will look wrong and will be short-lived. Fittings are either made of metal or wood. The latter are not commonly seen, but should be within the capabilities of many adept handymen. To last a long time they need to be made of a hardwood, such as oak. Most metal fittings are made of iron or steel, but occasionally they are of brass or bronze. Iron or steel fittings can be either galvanized or painted. Blacksmiths may accept custom-made orders.

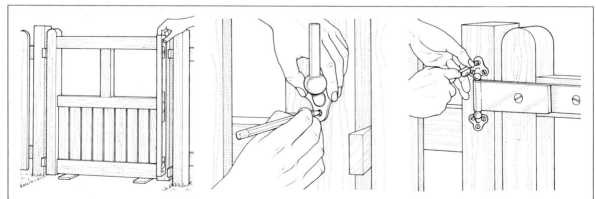

HANGING A WOODEN GATE

Prop the gate up 2in (5cm) above the ground, between the posts. Check that there is a clearance on either side of at least a ¼in (0.5cm) between the gate and the posts, so that it will swing open and shut without jamming; if necessary, plane off any surplus wood. Temporarily but accurately hold the gate in place with wooden wedges, and mark the position of the hinges on the gate and the appropriate post. Remove the gate and attach the hinges. Drill the pilot screw holes into the post, position the gate, ensuring that it is vertical and sits correctly in the space, and securely attach the butt end of the hinges to the post. Oil the hinges if they are stiff.

Decorative gates The design of ready-made gates is generally dull but, as all these examples show, gates can be very decorative objects in their own right. If a gate is needed, it is well worth going to the trouble of either making one or getting one made. Cast-iron gates (*above left*) are difficult to come by, but forged ones (*bottom left and bottom right*) can be made by blacksmiths, who often welcome the chance to fashion something different. Wooden gates (*right and below left*) may well be within the range of skilled individuals, or they can be commissioned from carpenters. Gates should always be made from the best materials and must be well maintained to ensure a long life. A neglected gate gives a garden a dejected, uncared-for appearance and mood.

GARDEN
FEATURES

Retaining Walls

Retaining walls are used in two ways in the garden; either they shore up a bank or slope to prevent it from slipping, or they form the containing walls of a raised flowerbed or lawn. Raised flowerbeds are particularly popular as features bordering patios and terraces; they will suit a wide range of plants, including alpines, which can be grown in the walls as well as in the beds. While both types of retaining wall are fundamentally functional, being in a garden they should also have some decorative merit; thus the choice of materials and style are of great importance.

In a formal situation, the best materials to use are brick, dressed stone or rendered concrete, either cast or in blocks. For a more informal garden, appropriate materials include wood, dry-stone walling and various decorative concrete blocks. If using brick, it should match or complement the colour of other structures and blend in well with the planting. Any of the various brick bonds can be used, but for walls that retain banks a double thickness of brick is required, with piers if necessary. A low wall built around a raised bed can be built using a single thickness, although a double layer will often look better. Foundations are required in both cases.

Dressed stone is attractive but expensive; dry-stone walling is a cheaper, less formal option that is best employed in areas where it is widely used. This is partly because it will look more in keeping with the surroundings, and partly because stone is likely to be cheaper and more abundant. Both reconstituted and imitation stone are popular choices, but these can look unnatural and garish, even though the colours do become more muted with age. Concrete is a harsh and unattractive material to use, but rendered with cement, incised with lines to give the effect of stone blocks, it can be more acceptable. Pierced concrete blocks are a relatively cheap way of building retaining walls, but such walls tend to look more functional than attractive.

It is also possible to decorate retaining walls by pressing objects, such as pebbles, shells, coloured glass or broken pottery, into cement on the surface. This must, of course, be done with sensitivity to the rest of the garden.

Wood can be used in less formal settings. Although a versatile material, it is less hard-wearing than stone and is prone to decay. All supporting timbers should be thick, in good condition and well soaked in preservative – avoid creosote if plants are to be grown up the wall or nearby. Old railway sleepers can be used to construct very solid retaining walls, and these will last for a long time because they contain tar. For a more natural look, use logs laid horizontally one on top of the other, the whole stack being well supported by vertical posts to stop the logs rolling forward. Alternatively, construct a retaining wall from logs driven into the ground vertically, like a palisade. In both cases, the logs should be as straight as possible so that they butt together snugly, preventing soil from spilling out between the cracks.

Left and above: In formal walls (*above*) as well as in dry-stone walls (*left*) holes and crevices can be left for inserting plants. This helps to soften these features, giving them a less functional, more decorative look, and it gives a vertical dimension to the planting.

Variations on retaining walls
There are retaining walls for
every situation. This rustic
stone wall (*right*) fits in well
with the rough hillside and the
woodland setting. The low
brick wall (*below right*) reflects
the brickwork of the terrace
and pergola above it, and
creates a flowerbed alongside
the path in which a variety of
plants soften the precise
brickwork. Without the raised
bed, the terrace wall would
look too tall and stark. Thick
and boisterous planting (*below
left*) is kept in check by low
retaining walls that surround
the beds. Railway sleepers are
easily used and are particularly
suitable for straight-sided
beds. They form stable,
informal walls and are still
relatively cheap to buy.

Above and right: As well as containing
beds, retaining walls are used to hold
back the soil from different levels of the
garden. Often there is little or no pressure
on the wall (*right*) and a largely decorative
structure can be built. Steps are often
necessary to gain access to the upper
levels. A retaining wall can also be built
into a sloping lawn (*above*).

Right: Some retaining walls are simply low surrounds to raised beds. Others, however, are constructed between two levels where the alternative would be a sloping bank. Sometimes a strong, massive construction is needed to hold back the earth of the upper level. In order to disguise its functional nature, a retaining wall, especially one that incorporates a number of features, can be a highly ornamental component of the garden. In this Italianate example, there is a grotto-like recess containing seating and a table, with a sweeping stone staircase linking the two levels. There are niches for statues as well as for plants, and cascading vegetation breaks up the sturdy, stone-built structure.

BUILDING A RETAINING WALL

If the wall is to support a great deal of weight, such as that exerted by a slipping hillside, it is essential to employ a civil engineer to plan and supervise the operation as it could be too difficult and dangerous for amateurs to tackle by themselves. The same safeguard applies to all retaining walls over 3½ft (1m) high.

Dry-stone walling can be used for retaining walls, but because there is no mortar to hold the wall together, only low walls should be attempted if the builder has no previous experience. If in doubt, employ a professional waller. Simple retaining walls, however, are relatively easy to build and well within most gardener's capabilities.

The earth must be removed from immediately behind the wall and, if necessary, held back by wooden shuttering. All retaining walls, apart from those built of wood, must have concrete foundations which are 6-8in (15-20cm) deep, with a width approximately three times the width of the wall. If the retaining wall has any weight behind it, the front section of the foundations must be deeper than the back, but low

retaining walls that are built around a raised bed will be sufficiently safe with shallower foundations.

With brick and stone retaining walls occasional gaps must be left in the mortar on the lowest level to allow water to drain from the bank or bed. Fill the area immediately behind these drainage holes with rubble to prevent them getting clogged-up with soil. Other gaps higher up in the wall can be left as planting niches and filled with colourful trailing plants such as aubrieta.

Allow the mortar to harden for about a week before back-filling the area behind the wall with soil. If the wall is to support a flowerbed, use a good potting compost for small areas, or for larger areas a home-made mixture of one part loam or good garden soil, one part grit and one part peat, coir or leaf mould, measured by volume. Put drainage material such as rubble in the bottom, and fill the bed with the compost, pressing it down firmly. The surface should be heaped up above the level of the wall, and this should be left to subside naturally before planting commences. If alpines are grown, add a top dressing of gravel or small stones.

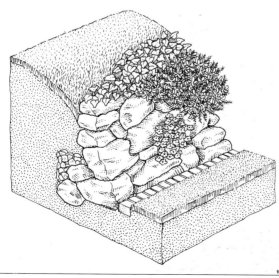

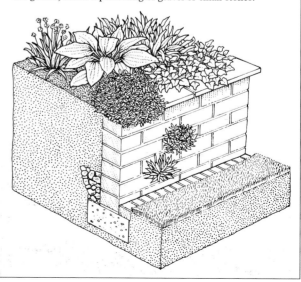

Materials for retaining walls
Irregular stones and dry-stone walling (*left*) make a very informal wall, much akin to a rock garden. Such walls are very suitable for planting in because of the gaps between the stones. This stone wall, surrounding a pool fed by a small cascade, suits the atmosphere and informality of this tropical-looking garden. A retaining wall of mortared brick (*below left*) is a complete contrast as it is much more structured and formal. Here, the regular brickwork echoes the wall of the terrace and pergola behind it, producing a unified appearance. The function of this retaining wall is to create a bed beneath a sunny wall that will hold its warmth and provide suitable conditions for tender plants.

Stone blocks can be used to make a regular, rather formal wall (*above*). This retaining wall, which has made a bed from a low rise in the garden, is attractively draped with plants; careful plant selection based on colour and form is needed to achieve this effect. Although regular in shape, rustic logs create a very informal wall (*left*), especially when the bark starts to peel off. This type of wall is particularly suitable for a woodland border; note the top covering of bark which ties in with the wooden wall. The logs will eventually rot and need replacing.

Rock Gardens

Rock gardens are usually planted with alpine plants. The rocks create a natural and decorative setting against which the alpines look at home; indeed, the rocky site provides the perfect, free-draining habitat with a cool root-run which alpines require if they are to thrive. Rockeries can be any size; they can vary from small arrangements built on patios where paving stones have been removed, to large features that take up most of the garden.

The site can be of any aspect but an open one with plenty of light and air is preferable. Although alpines will tolerate high winds they do not like draughts, so avoid constructing a rockery where wind is likely to be funnelled between buildings or trees. Rock gardens look best on sloping sites, but they can also be built on flat ground to make horizontal features.

The soil must be carefully considered. A free-draining loam is best if it can be obtained, otherwise a mixture of one part good garden soil, one part coir, peat or leaf mould and one part grit or gravel, as measured by volume, can be used; the grit or gravel is important as it will aid drainage. The soil used must be completely free of weeds, otherwise the rock garden may have to be dismantled so that the gardener can thoroughly weed the site.

Rockeries are attractive features in their own right and the choice of rock is important. If possible, use a local stone which will not only be cheaper but will also look more natural. Do not use lumps of concrete as these rarely look right, and in particular avoid using a soft stone that is more than likely to shatter and flake during the first frosts.

The rocks should be arranged so that they resemble the strata of a rocky outcrop rather than being dotted around on the surface of the soil. Each rock should be partially buried in the ground. This will create a more natural look and provide the plants with a cool root-run, as well as making the feature more stable so that people can walk across it to admire the plants.

For a more varied feature, certain areas of the rock garden can be given different soils so that a wider range of plants can be grown. Areas shaded from the sun during the hotter part of the day should have more organic material, such as peat or leaf mould, incorporated into the soil to make it more moisture-retentive; primulas love damp soil and these and other plants suited to moist conditions can be grown. Crevice plants can be worked into the vertical cracks between the rocks which will provide the sharp drainage that they require.

There is a vast range of plants that can be grown in rockeries but the majority flower in the spring. Try and include some summer- and autumn-flowering plants as well to give as much seasonal interest as possible. Rock garden plants need not be restricted to those from high alpine regions; many dwarf lowland plants are excellent choices. Small bulbs in particular can look very attractive in rocky settings.

Left and above: Rock gardens resemble miniature free-draining natural habitats. The rocks, stones and gravel of which they are made allow surplus water to drain away quickly and plants, especially alpines, seek out the moisture retained under the rocks.

Natural rock gardens Natural rock formations (*left*) make the best rock gardens; the small cushions of plants growing on this rock cliff appreciate its sharp drainage. However, few sites have a suitable outcrop, so natural-looking arrangements need to be constructed using imported rock (*above*). If possible, use local stone as this is more likely to harmonize with its setting than foreign material, which will look out of place.

Scree beds A natural scree consists of stones and pieces of rock that have fallen from a cliff and accumulated at its base. The free-draining conditions that are found in a scree suit a number of plants and can be created in an artificially constructed scree bed (*right*). The bed is best created on a slope but can be constructed on flat ground by building the bed up at one end. Dig out the soil and include a drainage channel to prevent any water collecting. Fill the hole with rubble or with pebbles. On top of this put a thick layer of gravel or small stones. Incorporating a few random outcrops of rock will help give the bed a natural appearance. Plant the scree bed with appropriate plants for a natural look.

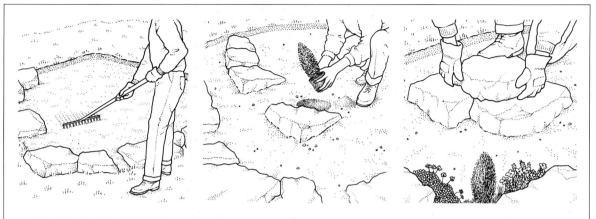

BUILDING A ROCK GARDEN

Clear the site and eradicate all weeds, especially pernicious ones, either by hand-weeding or using weedkiller.

Rocks are very heavy to move and the help of a second person is useful. If the pieces are quite large, hire a miniature mechanical digger. Roll or lever the rocks rather than lift them if possible; a soil or stone ramp built between different levels can be helpful. Always bend your knees when lifting.

Before building the rockery, assemble all the materials. Spread the rock around the site with the best side of each piece facing you. This will make the choice of pieces easier and lessen the number of times each stone will have to be moved as all the rocks are clearly displayed around you.

Arrange the first layer, burying each rock up to at least a third of its depth. If the pieces have any visible strata lines, they should all run in the same direction, preferably horizontally. Slope the rock backwards into the ground so that it gives the impression of an outcrop emerging from the garden; this will also ensure that rainwater runs back into the bed rather than cascading over the rocks, eroding the soil and

bed beneath. Each piece of stone should be firmed in very well so that it cannot move, even when stepped on.

Crevice plants can be planted while the rock garden is being built. Place them between two rocks as they are pushed together, making sure that the plant roots are in contact with the soil behind or beneath the rocks. Build up the outcrop, staggering each layer further back to form a series of terraces, allowing plenty of spaces for planting.

Once the structure is finished, arrange the rest of the plants, still in their pots, among the rocks. When satisfied with the arrangement, plant them, watering them in well.

All exposed soil will need a top dressing of grit or stone chippings. This will act as a mulch, keeping in moisture, as well as providing a free-draining surface around the bases of the plants. It also makes a tidier finish.

Contrary to popular opinion, alpines do need watering, especially in dry weather. Keep the rock garden free of weeds; if they do become established, it may be necessary to demolish that section of the rockery and thoroughly weed it before rebuilding the site. Preserve the plants.

Above: This rocky outcrop has been colonized by self-seeding plants; the planted stone container successfully complements the texture of the rock.

Left: Rock gardens need not be confined to rocky outcrops and slopes. Here, the combination of a rock garden and water feature allows for a wide range of plants.

Raised beds The conventional rock garden is constructed on either a natural or an artificial slope (*below left*) although alpines (the most usual rock garden plants) are increasingly being grown in raised beds (*left and below right*). These consist of walls enclosing a free-draining compost, covered with gravel and rocks. The strategically placed rocks create a more natural look and also provide plants with a cool root-run. If dry-stone walls are used, plants can also be established in the vertical sides. Even bonded walls can have planting gaps in them.

Below: It takes some skill to construct a natural-looking rocky outcrop using large blocks of stone; a covering of lichen and moss will give the rocks a weathered look. Allowance has to be made for planting pockets, not only in horizontal niches and ledges but also in vertical crevices.

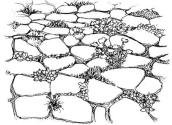

Growing alpines Alpine plants can be grown in a variety of attractive ways. Old walls (*top left*) make an ideal planting position, plants being established by sowing seed. In a well built rock garden (*top right*) plants can be grown in a much more natural way. Troughs and old sinks (*bottom left*) provide ideal conditions and look good on patios. Paving with gaps (*bottom right*) can reproduce the conditions of a rock garden, the plants' roots spreading beneath the stones. Such surfaces are especially good in association with aromatic plants such as thyme.

163

Screens and Trellis

Screens and trellis are similar to fences. They are principally used for concealing or dividing one area from another, and they can be decorated with climbing plants for a more attractive finish.

Solid screens are often used to hide an eyesore, such as an oil tank or a dustbin. They can also be used to mask off part of the garden, with only an archway cut into the screen that allows further exploration of the garden. These dense screens are usually made of wood and are available in a variety of different sizes and designs, to suit most styles of garden.

Other screens, made of wrought iron or wire netting, are open so that light can filter through, silhouetting the foliage or flowers that grow up the vertical surface. This type of screen will also provide a tempting glimpse of what lies beyond. Wrought-iron screens look particularly good used in association with brick or stone. For a more solid, permanent screen, pierced concrete blocks can be used, but the overall effect may look harsh and fussy, and the geometric patterns do not always complement the fluid lines of plants or the sweep of a lawn.

For a simple screen, stretch a length of wire netting between upright posts and cover it with climbers; evergreens will ensure that little of the netting is visible. Screens can also be constructed out of other materials such as bamboo canes; placed close together they will form a solid, ribbed barrier; set further apart, they will make a more open and decorative screen. For less solid screens, it is also possible to weave bamboo and other softwoods, while rough hurdles made from hazel (*Corylus*) or willow (*Salix*) are also available. These make attractive and appropriate rustic screens for less formal gardens.

Lengths of trellis tend to look more elegant than screens, and a great deal of thought should go into their design. The most elementary types consist of square or rectangular panels comprising horizontal and vertical laths that create a squared pattern. Common variations include laths that cross each other diagonally and laths that move on opposing diagonals from a central upright, to create a chevron effect. The panels are held between upright posts that should be concreted into the ground.

If the trellis is to support climbing plants, it must be made from relatively thick, strong laths, but as a decorative feature it is better to use a thinner wood so that the overall appearance is graceful and stylish. The more ornamental trelliswork is often associated with archways or pergolas laid in sweeping lines with finials on each post. Rustic trellising can be constructed from rough poles.

All screens and trellis must be well secured to posts concreted into the ground as the wind can exert considerable pressure on them, particularly if they are covered with plants. If they are not painted then they should be treated with a preservative other than creosote, which is harmful to plants.

Screens and trellis Screens and trelliswork can be used to create visual barriers, partially or completely blocking a view. They can also provide supports for plants. When an example is highly decorative (*left*), it is often better left plain, uncluttered by plants, but in most instances it is the planting that makes the structure ornamental (*above*). Tantalizing glimpses through a screen or trellis are often more appealing than a full view, encouraging the viewer to explore futher.

Above left, above right and right: Screens and trellis can be highly decorative or quite plain. There is great scope for the imaginative gardener to produce something unusual.

Ready-made panels (*below*) These are commercially available in a variety of designs. Many are made of wood but some can be created from concrete blocks (*top centre*). Rustic hurdles (*top left*) are rather rough and informal in appearance and look best in rural situations. These and other rustic and woven panels (*top right*) cannot be cut to length as easily as other forms of wooden trellis, which come in many patterns (*bottom row*).

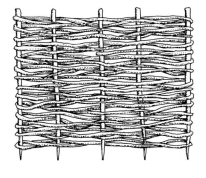

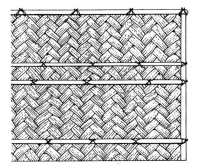

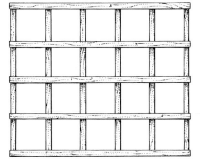

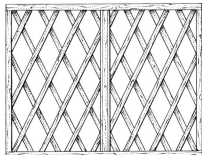

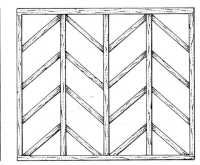

Arches

Arches make attractive decorative features, ideal for enlivening a garden. They are most frequently seen creating access points from one side of a barrier to the other in fences, walls or hedges, but they are also used freestanding as pure ornament, clothed with climbing plants such as clematis and honeysuckle (*Lonicera*). The more ornate arches, especially those made of wrought iron, are best left unadorned or only partially covered with rambling or climbing roses.

The positioning of arches should be carefully considered; they should be tied in with another structure or placed in an obvious position, such as at the beginning or end of a path, or at the dividing line between a lawn and vegetable plot. Arches can be used as very effective framing devices, to draw attention to a view, a statue or a water feature. An arch set in a wall or hedge will encourage people to walk under it and into the garden beyond; set over a gate, an arch will define the area as an entrance and give it presence, particularly if it is combined with a pathway.

As a purely decorative feature, position a plant-clad arch over a seat or path, or arrange several in a circle for an especially ornate effect.

There are several materials from which arches can be constructed. To a certain extent, the material is unimportant since it will be mostly covered with plants, but bear in mind that in winter the arch will be leafless. For freestanding structures wood or metal are best, as brick and stone can look rather heavy used in isolation. An arch which is sited in a fence, wall or hedge will look more integrated if it is worked in the same material as the boundary. For more of a feature, however, use contrasting materials: metal and wood look good in association with hedges; metal will also complement brick and stone.

Freestanding arches that are designed to carry plants are relatively exposed compared to other structures that support climbers. Therefore, they must be well anchored into the ground, preferably set in concrete, to resist the ill effects of the wind.

Arches and vistas The arch is a device that has been long used in garden design. The vista created by a series of arches adds mystery to a garden, the eye being drawn to discover what lies at the end of the sequence. They also draw the eye in a particular direction, framing an ornament of some kind. Arches can be solid architectural forms, as they often are when located at the points where paths intersect walls and hedges (*below*), but often they are no more than light supports for climbers such as roses (*left*).

Transitions A properly formed arch (*above left, above right and right*) marks the transition between one area of a garden and another in a way that an undefined gap in a wall, fence or hedge never does. An additional emphasis can be given by flanking an arch with urns, containers of plants or specimens of topiary. The shape of an arch and its method of construction should be in keeping with its surroundings. Planting can be used either to soften the edges of an arch or to disguise it, partly obscuring what might lie beyond. When constructing arches, make sure they are wide enough for the traffic they will have to take; if necessary, allow extra height for any plants that might hang down, such as wisteria.

MAKING A RUSTIC ARCH

Use rough wooden poles for this arch, either with or without bark. The wood must be treated with a preservative other than creosote. Arrange the bracing poles in a decorative, secure pattern and construct the arch using V-shaped or cross-halved joints, fixed with nails and screws.

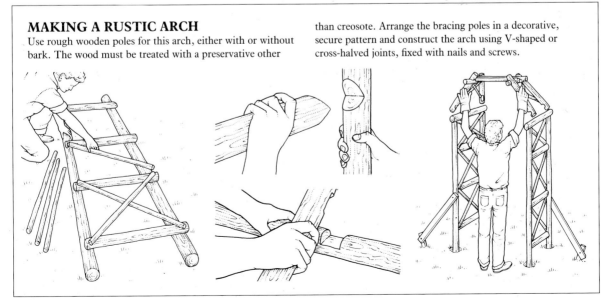

Pergolas

Ornamental walkways are often covered with wooden or wrought-iron frameworks holding climbing plants; these structures are known as pergolas. Although they are mainly used as decoration, in hot countries they have an additional, more functional role of providing shade. From the point of view of design, they add a vertical element to the garden and a texture that is light and airy and full of interest.

Pergolas can either consist of a series of disconnected arches or they can be one continuous tunnel. In hot climates they are more likely to stretch along a network of paths to give protection from the sun, but they can equally well be used in shorter lengths, covering a single path or even a small part of one. They must be well integrated into the surroundings so as not to look out of place; a pergola placed in the middle of a garden with no obvious purpose or sense of direction will look totally wrong. If it covers a main path, or marks the beginning or end of such a path, it will take on more significance. The effect of a long pergola can be enhanced by a point of focus at the end, such as a piece of sculpture, a view, a bold planting scheme or a simple seat.

In order to create areas of shade, pergolas must be well covered with climbing plants. A single species often produces the greatest impact: a dramatic golden tunnel of laburnum or frothing masses of headily-scented climbing roses can be breathtaking and spellbinding, enticing the viewer to walk through the pergola. Many climbing plants are suitable, but make certain that any thorny ones, such as roses, are properly trained and well tied in. Pergolas do not necessarily have to display ornamental plants; they can equally well be used in the vegetable garden to support runner beans or marrows.

Depending on style, pergolas can be constructed out of brick, wood or metal. Ready-made, highly decorative wrought-iron pergolas must be bought but brick and wood structures can be home-made. When building a pergola, be generous with the width as this will narrow once the structure is covered in plants.

In formal settings, brick piers look elegant and imposing. They must have concrete foundations and it is a good idea to place an iron scaffold pole up the centre of each column to reinforce it. The wooden cross-members must be of a substantial thickness, otherwise they will look out of character with the piers. This is a solid structure that will bear a considerable weight of plant cover.

Wooden pergolas are easy to construct. Use thick timber so the framework will not only be able to support the weight of the climbers, but it will look as if it is able to do so; psychologically, no-one will enjoy walking under a structure that looks flimsy even if it is not. Make certain that the uprights are well embedded in the ground, concreting them in if necessary, so that the wind does not push the structure over or move it out of line. A more informal pergola can also be made out of rustic poles, but this will look lighter so should carry delicate climbers.

Formal and rustic pergolas Pergolas add a delightful geometric element to a garden; they also provide additional planting possibilities to sites that do not have wall space for vigorous climbers. Structures can be rustic and made from whole or split logs (*right*), or they can be more formal, made from smooth timber (*above*). Both examples support roses.

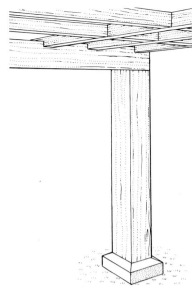

Supports for pergolas There are many different pergola designs, each with different construction methods. All supports must be very strong in order to carry the weight of vigorous climbers and withstand strong winds. Wooden supports (*left*) need to be made of sound wood. Hardwoods, such as oak, are the best, but softwoods can be used as long as they are treated with an effective preservative. Creosote is poisonous to plants and not suitable. The base of each column should be sunk at least 24in (60cm) into the ground and embedded in concrete. Brick or stone columns (*right*) need to have foundations. To give extra strength, it is advisable to insert a steel rod in the centre of the column when the foundations are laid; a galvanized scaffold pole is ideal. Cap any stone or brickwork to prevent water getting inside the cavity.

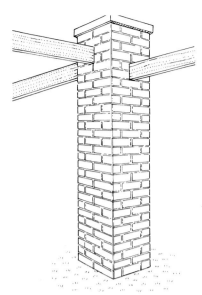

Pergolas with a purpose A pergola that is simply stranded in the middle of a garden, leading nowhere, usually looks forlorn. It is only when a pergola forms part of a real or visually important axis in the garden that its full potential can be realized. These three examples show how important the focal point of a pergola can be. Seen in winter, one pergola leads purposefully to a gate that gives access to an orchard (*left*). Another wooden pergola, wonderfully decked in roses (*below right*), ends at the edge of a garden. Brick-piered pergolas tend to be the most solid and robust-looking. The vista through this example (*below left*) terminates at a fountain, which cuts across the line of vision. Grass is only suitable underneath if there is enough light; where a pergola supports a dense canopy, lay a paved or gravel path.

Scale and weight Pergolas tend to look best when they have been designed on a generous scale. The grace of the shallow arch and the gentle curve along the length of this pergola (*above left*) creates a wonderful atmosphere, even when the covering climbers are out of leaf. Sturdiness also adds to the character of a pergola (*above right*). Even with delicate trelliswork there is an underlying feeling of strength here, mainly because of the substantial beams used for the roof. However, many pergolas are little more than a framework to stroll under, and these rely on the plants that climb up and over them for their attraction (*right*).

Pergola design (*left and right*) Pergolas are designed to be seen as an architectural whole from outside as well as from within, framing a vista. There are many variations of shape, scale and degree of ornamentation; the two examples shown here are particularly ornate. In both cases, the detailing might be too small to be seen if plants are allowed to climb all over the pergolas. Iron frames (*left*) have the disadvantage of needing to be painted at regular intervals, which can present problems when the structure is carrying a mass of climbing plants. The plants will need to be removed before painting can take place. The chinoiserie pergola (*right*) has an ornate roof which should only be lightly covered with plants.

Left: A trellis pergola has several points in its favour. Despite looking light, a structure made in this way is surprisingly strong as the members are mutually supportive. Furthermore, it has the great advantage of providing plenty of fixing points for tying in scrambling climbers. Roses are the ideal plants to train over this sort of structure. Although they are vigorous, their foliage is not so dense as to obscure the pergola.

Below: Pergolas constructed of stone piers create quite a different impression from those made of box sections of trellis. These look sturdy and walking beneath them inspires confidence in their strength. They require less maintenance than pergolas of trelliswork, but a disadvantage is that they lack convenient tying points. Climbers must be tied either to eyes fixed in the stonework or to wires attached to the columns. These should be checked regularly to be sure they offer plants the necessary support.

Pergolas from the inside The interior of a pergola is as important as the view of it from outside; indeed, the very sight of one draws you towards and into the defined space. The appeal of many pergolas is that they provide shady walks and, if large enough (*above left*), places to sit in dappled shade. In some, the cross members are too far apart to provide much shade (*left*), but the repetition of the columns and horizontal bars along their length creates the impression of a tunnel. If a pergola is too enclosed by foliage, it is difficult to grow plants under it. On the other hand, if too many plants are grown along the inside of a pergola, or if they are too vigorous, the path can become difficult to negotiate (*right*).

Arbours

An arbour is the name given to a structure, natural or otherwise, over which plants grow, creating an enclosed area of dappled shade, often containing a seat. It is a romantic, decorative feature suitable for gardens of any size.

Both wood and wrought-iron arbours can be bought ready-made, but some models are insubstantial and flimsy, so manufactured units should be carefully inspected before being purchased. Arbours are also relatively easy to make. To a certain extent it does not matter what they look like because the framework can be covered up with climbing plants.

The simplest arbours do not involve any framework at all but are carved out of solid bushes or thick hedgerows. These take time to grow to a sufficient size, and they should be trained from the start to ensure an even coverage of foliage. If an existing bush is opened up it might take a while for the areas that have been cut to grow more leaves. Yew (*Taxus*) is an ideal material for a natural arbour but many other faster-growing evergreens can be used. It should be remembered, however, that the faster the growth, the more clipping will be required to keep the arbour neat. A suitable climber can be trained over an arbour to highlight and embellish the feature.

Wood is the most practical, versatile material to use for arbours as it is relatively cheap and the arbour can be constructed on site. Ready-cut, prepared wood is ideal for making smart, elegant structures, especially if thin wood is incorporated into the framework. This type of wood can also be used to build a much more functional, less decorative feature and, being a strong material, it will take the weight of a mass of climbing plants. The alternative is rustic wood in the form of poles; these will provide a strong but less regular framework, one that is more in keeping with rural or wild settings. It is also possible to use panels of trellis as the basis of the arbour, but these will need strong supporting posts.

All the joints must be well made and fastened with galvanized bolts and nails. Strength is important as the framework will not only have to bear the considerable weight of climbing plants but also the force of the wind. The main uprights should be well embedded in the ground, preferably in concrete.

Arbours can be used to support a wide range of plants, but particularly decorative arbours, such as those made from wrought iron, should only be partially covered. The more delicate and thin-leaved the plants, the more sunlight they will admit. Plants with open habits, such as roses, will provide the right density of cover, so the ornamental metalwork can be enjoyed as well as the flowers. Less formal wooden arbours can have a thick covering of foliage and flowering plants; this will create more shade and give greater protection from the elements.

Above: Typically elegant gazebos and belvederes are purely architectural features that need to be well sited.

Left: Foliage creates shade and a sense of intimacy, as seen in this unusual, informal arbour built in an area of stonework and evergreens, where the roof is constructed out of living plant material.

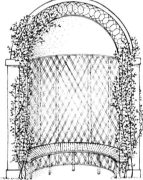

Above: Arbours are suitable features for quiet, secluded parts of the garden, a cover of foliage and flowers adding to their appeal as places of retirement. Although the clothing of vegetation may be quite dense, it rarely makes these structures rainproof.

Trellis arbours (*above*) Pretty arbours and summer houses can be constructed out of trelliswork, a versatile material that can be adapted to a variety of shapes, whether open or relatively enclosed. The use of trellis simplifies the tying in of climbing plants.

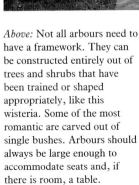

Above: Not all arbours need to have a framework. They can be constructed entirely out of trees and shrubs that have been trained or shaped appropriately, like this wisteria. Some of the most romantic are carved out of single bushes. Arbours should always be large enough to accommodate seats and, if there is room, a table.

Right: The most commonly seen arbours are built frameworks with climbers scrambling over them, the amount of shade offered depending on the density of the foliage. Roses create a dappled shade, heavier when used in conjuction with climbers like honeysuckle. Such scented flowers are particularly appealing.

WATER FEATURES

Water was one of the earliest features to be introduced to the garden. It is considered particularly precious in countries with hot, sunny climates, but it is just as appropriate in more temperate conditions under much greyer skies.

Water adds sound and texture to a garden and, as ornamental details, water features will attract attention, drawing the eye towards them. Water can be spread in a vast sheet or it can be kept to a smaller area, such as a pool or rill, partially hidden by vegetation. Running water, either splashing in a stream or playing in a fountain, introduces a pleasing sound and creates a lively atmosphere. It brings movement and

moving images that sparkle with every ripple and splash. Conversely, the mirror-like surface of still water has a superb reflective quality which adds further scope to a design. Another benefit of water in the garden is that wildlife will be more plentiful.

It takes a certain amount of planning and effort to introduce a water feature in a garden, and such a project should not be undertaken lightly or without a firm commitment to success; a wrinkled black or greying plastic liner, half-filled with dirty water, does little towards producing an attractive garden. If in any doubt about your construction abilities, employ a water garden specialist to do the job for you.

Below: The addition of a water feature can transform a garden. Most people find it relaxing to be near water, enjoying the calming influence of the reflections in a still or broken surface. A water garden, especially one with moist margins, offers an opportunity to grow a wide range of beautiful and colourful

plants. Furthermore, features associated with water, such as bridges and stepping stones, make attractive additions to the garden. Water can be introduced on any scale, from a large area of the garden devoted to a series of streams or waterfalls to a small pond or even an ornamental container.

Pools

Pools are one of the most popular garden features. They can be any size, from a small, formal raised structure built on a patio, to a full-sized lake. They must be sited where they will receive plenty of light; the water plants themselves will provide ample shade and protection for wildlife.

Formal gardens are best served with ponds that are regular and geometric in shape: circles, squares, ovals and rectangles are all suitable. For an elaborate feature, use a more complex shape such as a cross, a hexagon or a dumbbell shape. Triangular pools can be constructed, but these tend to look better in modern gardens where they are more likely to fit in with asymmetrical designs. The pool should be edged in a formal way, with paving stones or bricks. Any planting should be within the pool itself and is best restricted to one or two choice water lilies or a few marginal plants with impressive foliage.

Informal ponds can be of any shape but they are usually sinuous in outline. They should be well integrated into the surroundings and blurred at the edges with waterside planting that starts on the banks and moves down into the water. Informal ponds are often constructed in association with bog gardens, and once fully planted, these wet, spongy features will help merge the pool into the landscape.

There is a wide choice of construction methods and materials to choose from, the major ones being concrete, butyl rubber liners and pre-formed shells. As a general rule, more irregular shapes are easier to construct using liners or pre-formed shells rather than concrete; concrete is best reserved for formal and raised structures. The disadvantage of pre-formed shells, however, is that you are restricted to the shapes on offer and it is difficult to blur their edges with planting; once installed, they should be edged with stones and plants. It is much easier to disguise the edges of pools made with butyl rubber liners, and these flexible liners can accommodate virtually any shape of pool, sinuous or angular.

Plant the shallows of the pool with marginal plants, keeping the marshy area around the pool for bog plants. Place water lilies on the pool floor, along with other deep water aquatics; these should be planted in planting baskets and carefully lowered into the water. Introduce several clumps of submerged plants and floating aquatics to help keep algae at bay and to encourage all manner of wildlife.

Above: Splashing fountains, waterfalls or more lively cascades add the pleasure of sound to the light-catching qualities of moving water.

Left: Marginal aquatics usually look out of place in a formal pool, where water lilies are the most appropriate plants. With less formal pools, however, marginals make a distinctive contribution.

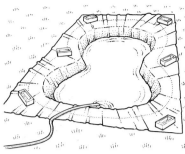
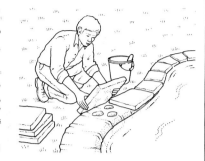

USING A BUTYL LINER

Create the outline of the pool on the ground using a hosepipe. Excavate the site, keeping the topsoil for use elsewhere, but discard any heavy subsoil. Build up or reduce the sides so that they are all level; if the garden is on a slope, it may be necessary to construct a strong bank using some of the spare soil. Make some areas of the pond deeper than others to allow for plants that require different depths.

Once satisfied with the excavation, line the pond with a 2in (5cm) layer of soft sand to prevent any stones from puncturing the lining once it has been filled with water. If any vertical faces are too steep for the sand to adhere, use damp newspaper, (you can use this alone for small ponds).

The dimensions of the butyl liner should be as follows: the length of the pool multiplied by twice its depth will give the length of the liner; the width of the pool multiplied by twice its depth will give the width of the liner, plus about 18in (45cm) in every direction to allow for overlap into the ground around the pool margins. The liner must be well secured.

Stretch the butyl liner across the pond, holding it in position with slabs of stone placed around the edges. Slowly fill the centre of the liner with water from a hosepipe; as it fills, the liner will sink into the hole, taking shape as it does so. Once the pool is full of water, trim the liner, leaving an 18in (45cm) margin all the way around. Smooth this down and dig a trench in which to bury the edge of the liner. Cover the margins of the pool with stone or concrete paving slabs so that the edges of the liner are well masked; alternatively, add a layer of soil to accommodate plants. It is also possible to use turf but this is likely to go brown where it comes into contact with the liner unless it goes right down into the water; grass edges are also difficult to mow. Be careful never to puncture the lining; although repair kits are available, the patch will always be a source of weakness.

Pool shapes and surrounds In the design of pools, like that of many other garden features, there are great possibilities for varying the shape. In addition, there is considerable scope for treating the surrounds of pools in different ways, as these examples show. A hard surround with flagstones makes an interesting stepped edge (*above*). A more natural finish is created by grass, plants and stone running right up to the pool edge (*above right*). The rim of the raised pool (*right*) is cleverly disguised by a closely clipped hedge, an attractive option. The delicate irises are perfect for this design. Care must be taken in planting small pools such as these; an incautious approach can soon lead to overcrowding.

Marginal planting There is great scope for the imaginative planting of the margins and bog areas of pools and ponds (*right and below left*). A great number of plants thrive in moist conditions; bog plants require a wet environment but will not tolerate periods of inundation, while marginal plants prosper in standing water. Both types of plants are useful for masking and softening the area where land and water meet, integrating the feature into the adjacent landscape. Many of these plants look particularly attractive when planted in large drifts. Foliage is often more important than flowers. Around a big pond, large-scale planting always looks better than the restless effect produced by dotting plants about at random.

Reflections Much of the appeal of water lies in the way its surface reflects sky, clouds, surrounding vegetation and waterside features such as statues. Water also reflects light back onto surrounding plants and features, the flattering illumination enhancing their appearance (*right*). If there is no room for a pool, a simple tub of water can be used to create a small-scale watery mirror (*below left*). Although best if the surface is kept clear, it is possible to grow a few plants in a small container.

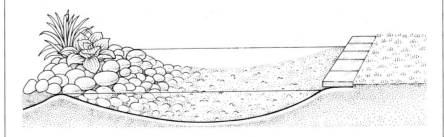

MARGINS

It is important to get the margins of a pool right, making a suitable interface between two different surfaces – water and grass for example – and disguising the edge of the liners that are commonly used. Many potentially attractive pools are spoilt because the wrinkled edge of the liner is visible. This can be hidden by plants, paving slabs (*right*) or by a beach of pebbles and gravel (*left*); the last will encourage wildlife.

Right: A pool and bog garden together form a natural-looking association. The hard edge of a pool betrays its artificiality, but this is blurred when the moisture-loving plants of the bog garden hang over the water's edge. Water lilies and similar plants enhance the natural effect. The red and yellow flowers add a splash of colour in what is predominantly a foliage-led area; much interest is generated by the contrasting shapes of the different types of water plants and shrubs.

Left: A wide range of plants can be grown in the permanently moist conditions of a bog garden, many with superb leaves that are interesting for their forms and colours. Flowers are often an attractive bonus. Good foliage plants generally have a long period of interest and are likely to make a contribution for the whole of the growing season. Irises are among the many plants enjoying the moist conditions around this pool. Their long, narrow leaves contrast well with the rounder shapes of water lily pads, hostas and the umbrella-like marsh marigolds.

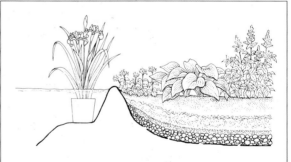

MAKING A BOG GARDEN

The bog garden should be constructed at the same time as the pool, using one large piece of liner for both features.

Excavate a 12in (30cm) basin next to the pool. Its edges must be the same height or a little higher than the bank of the pond, but the interconnecting lip must be a little lower than the pool. Spread a layer of coarse grit or gravel over the soil to aid drainage.

When the pond is lined, continue the liner over the lowered bank and across the bog area, and then tuck in the edges in the same way as for the pond. Puncture the liner in a few places and cover the floor with a layer of gravel to prevent the holes becoming clogged-up. Add a layer of well-rotted farmyard manure before filling the basin with a mixture of loam and leaf mould.

Above: Bog gardens are sometimes extensive but they need not cover a large area. Because they are recreations of natural habitats, it is important that bog gardens have an organic shape; straight rows of plants rarely look good. A sinuous line of moisture-loving plants can create the illusion of running water even where there is none.

Canals and Streams

A garden with naturally-running water is a rare blessing; most people have to be content with constructing artificial streams using pumps to recycle the water. However, impressive and realistic results can still be achieved by artificial means.

The design of a canal or stream very much depends on the garden and whether there are any natural slopes down which water can flow. Running water does not require a steep gradient, and if no slopes exist it is quite easy to construct one with a sufficient incline to keep the water moving. Informal streams can be incorporated into rock gardens or natural, wooded banks; install a pool or create a spring at the top of the slope and construct another pool at the bottom of the stream, from where the water is recirculated by means of a submersible pump.

Streams that are irregular in width, depth and direction can be made with a strip of butyl liner, much in the same way as the construction of pools or, if the watercourse is very irregular and includes waterfalls, it may be easier to use several pieces of liner instead of one large strip. The joints should have a good overlap of liner, a minimum of 6in (15cm) depending on the steepness of the slope, the uppermost piece pointing in the same direction as the flow of the stream.

It is also possible to construct streams using concrete and waterproof cement. The ground beneath the feature should be well compacted, with a layer of hardcore for extra support to ensure that the finished, set concrete does not crack.

When using either a liner or concrete, be certain that the bed of the stream is flat so that the flow of water will cover and disguise it completely. If using concrete, you can implant rocks in the semi-wet concrete along the margins to give a more natural appearance. With a liner, any rocks must be placed on the bank overhanging the channel so that they do not come into contact with the liner and risk puncturing the material in any way.

For a more formal feature, a straight-edged canal built of concrete and cement can be built between regularly shaped pools.

Left and above: A natural stream flowing through a garden makes a superb feature. Simple planting on the margins, for example of ferns (*left*), is often the best way to integrate a stream into the landscape. There are, however, a large number of plants that relish moist waterside conditions, and more detailed planting can produce charming effects with foliage and flowers (*above*). Hostas and irises in particular lend themselves to streamside planting, especially when clustered together in groups.

Below: A canalized stream can look particularly attractive if there are small fountains placed at regular intervals along its length. Such a watercourse needs a formal setting, although the straight lines of the canal can equally well be softened by adjacent planting.

Above left and above right: Moving water always adds a touch of sparkling excitement to a garden, especially if it is bouncing off rocks and plunging down waterfalls. The visual effect is important but so, too, is the sound generated by running water. This can pervade the whole garden, giving it a unique atmosphere. If there are no natural waterfalls in a flowing stream, it is well worth creating small artificial falls by constructing dams or forming miniature rapids by the careful placing of stones and large rocks.

Left: A slow stream quietly meandering through a garden can be just as attractive as a fast moving torrent, although its appeal is very different. Because the flow is gentle, plants can be allowed to spread out into the water with no fear of them being washed away. The floating margin creates a natural look. Plants and the sky are reflected in the calm surface. Note the very effective stone edge.

Left: Rustic logs make an attractive bridge that is suitable in an informal setting. The logs must be checked periodically to ensure that they have not decayed.

Below: Some form of non-slip surface is a wise precaution on wood, especially if the bridge has no safety rails. Wire mesh is best; nail it securely in place over the boards.

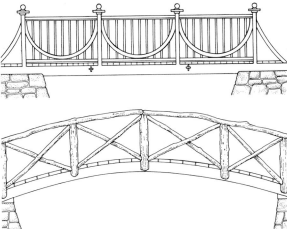

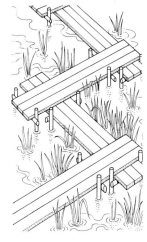

Duckboards Duckboards (*left*) are a simple but effective means of bridging broad stretches of water and, more particularly, of creating paths through extensive bog gardens. The supporting posts should be driven well into the ground, so this is not a technique to use if the pond or bog has a butyl rubber liner. Both the posts and the planks need to be treated with a preservative. They should also be checked regularly to ensure that they are sound. The boards can be laid in patterns.

Bridge design There are many ways to vary the design of a simple wooden bridge (*above*). The crossing can be flat or curved, a curved design adding to the bridge's strength by thrusting the weight towards the banks. Handrails are generally necessary for the safety of pedestrians, and there are a variety of different ways in which the posts and rails can be treated in a decorative manner.

Right: A crossing such as this colourful bridge will enhance the unique character of a garden. A purpose-built bridge, on a scale appropriate to the path it is carrying and the water it is crossing, is more likely to add a distinctive touch than a ready-made one.

Fountains

The sound of falling water is soothing and gives the impression of coolness. A fountain also keeps water moving and this will help prevent the growth of algae in a pond, as well as oxygenating the water for fish and other aquatic animals.

Fountains are most usually associated with pools. The simplest kind consists of a pump submerged under the water with the fountain nozzle just above the surface; various spray patterns are available. Stand the pump on a pile of bricks or a wooden framework, if necessary, to bring the nozzle up to the correct height. The fountain head will not be obtrusive as interest is focused on the water, but it is possible to disguise it by burying it in a pile of stones with the water emerging from the top. For more of a feature, install a sculptural fountain, which can be placed in the centre or at the edge of the pool. It is essential that such fountains are attached to a secure base and care must be taken not to puncture the pool liner.

The height to which the water is thrown should be carefully calculated in relation to the size of the pool; even the slightest breeze can blow the spray sideways and possibly right out of the basin. For this reason, do not be too ambitious with small areas of water.

Not all fountains are freestanding. Water spouts can be attached to a wall or any other vertical surface, perhaps built into a sculpture, mask or gargoyle, from where they will shoot water into a pool or basin below. When installing such a device, provision must be made for draining it during the winter or when hard frosts threaten, with their punishing effects.

A bubble fountain is another option. This produces a simple, low bubble of water and, placed within a rocky outcrop edged with flowers, it can successfully imitate a spring. A bubbler can also be placed in the middle of a millstone set in a bed of pebbles; the water will emerge from the centre of the stone and wash over the edge, through the stones.

Figurative fountains Fountains come in numerous guises. A classical figure pouring water from an amphora (*left*) is an attractive if well-used motif; the single trickle of water and the green vegetation produce a lovely cool effect. In another figurative fountain (*above*), the liveliness of the water seems to express the exuberance of the figure. The cherub is best placed in the middle of a pool, and the classical figure to one side, as here.

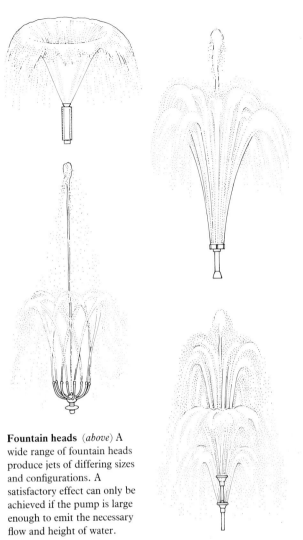

Fountain heads (*above*) A wide range of fountain heads produce jets of differing sizes and configurations. A satisfactory effect can only be achieved if the pump is large enough to emit the necessary flow and height of water.

Below left: The water of a fountain is not necessarily collected in a pool. Here, water splashes onto stones and pebbles before draining into a reservoir located below them. The variety of different stones used adds much interest.

Above: Stainless steel is a material much used in modern fountains. In this example, water flows out of the tallest cylinders filling those below till they brim over, spilling into a pool below: a pyramid of moving water.

PUMPS

A pump is the power behind all artificially moving water, giving the impression of an uninterrupted flow.

There are two types of pump: submersible and surface. Advice should be sought from the supplier as to which pump will supply the required rate of flow. Submersible pumps are suitable for small water features: they will operate a fountain or lift sufficient water for a modest stream. They are quiet and easy to install; simply place the pump on the floor of the pool, on a pile of bricks if necessary to bring it up to the right level. Surface pumps are much more powerful and should be used to shift large quantities of water over considerable distances or heights. A surface pump can operate a large fountain or a waterfall and, with the addition of a T-piece, it can operate more than one feature at the same time.

The power supply must be provided by an armoured cable that is buried in a trench at least 2ft (60cm) deep. As an extra safety precaution, the cable should be fitted with a residual current device which will cut off the supply should there be a short circuit. Any outdoor sockets must be weatherproof. As a word of warning, water and electricity can be a fatal mixture, and if there is any doubt on the part of the gardener as to his or her ability to install an electric pump, then a qualified electrician must be called in.

Right: A solitary fish, stranded eternally on the shore, spurts a single jet of water into a pool. Delivery nozzles can usually be changed to vary the jet. The Buddha and spouting stone fountain add to the Eastern flavour.

Below right: There are many appealing figurative fountains available that are suitable for small pools. These include wildlife associated with water, such as seals, birds and fish, as well as miniature, angelic-looking statues.

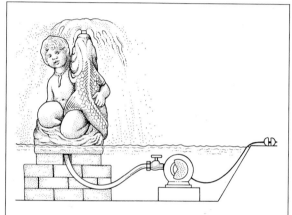

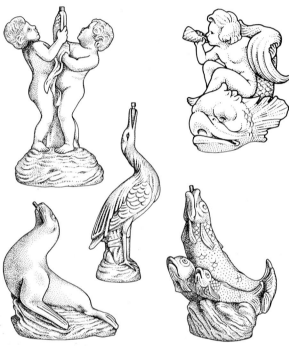

INSTALLATION

The fountain should be fixed onto a stable base positioned just below the water level. The pump must also have a firm base and should be located for ease of access so that the filter can be cleaned regularly. The waterproof cable can be led to a power point through the side of the pool with suitable fittings, but it is easier to take it over the edge, hiding and protecting it with rocks and plants.

Variations on fountains A large ornate fountain (*above left*) demands a dominant position in formal surroundings. However, the spot should be free from strong winds otherwise the water will be constantly blown beyond the pool. Masks are often used to deliver water to pools; the slightest trickle of water (*above middle*) falls from a mask hidden by foliage into a shallow, stony pool. Masks are frequently used as keystones in arches (*above right*) or as ornaments on walls.

Cascades and Waterfalls

Moving water is always a joy in the garden, but while gentle streams satisfy the needs of many gardeners, the thrill of faster-moving and tumbling water excites even more. Both waterfalls and cascades really come into their own in large gardens where they can be exploited on a grand scale, but they can also form excellent focal points in small gardens.

Waterfalls can be built into streams, a series of which form cascades, or they can consist of water falling from one pool to another. If built into a stream, a waterfall should look as natural as possible and be constructed so that water actually tumbles over rocks and does not just drip down behind them along the butyl lining. Select smooth, regular rocks with flat faces that will fit snugly against the vertical face of the lining and fill in any gaps with waterproof resin. Arrange the waterfalls so that they match the lie of the land or, conversely, re-landscape the surrounding garden in order to make the waterfalls appear as natural as possible. If your garden does not have a natural slope, you will have to construct an artifical mound out of heavy soil.

Use a pump that is strong enough to produce a good flow of water, as water gushing down a waterfall is much more impressive than a lacklustre trickle. Narrowing the part of the stream that contains the waterfall will make the flow seem stronger, but do not use this trick too often otherwise it will become obvious. A series of waterfalls with white, frothing, tumbling water will make an exciting cascade and create an excellent centrepiece.

In a small garden, it is very easy to construct two pools at different heights, either with a liner or pre-formed units, so that one drops water into the other. They can be connected by a short channel, curved to contain the water, or they can be left as separate units with a rockwork wall between them, allowing water to pour over the slightly lowered rim of the top pool into the pool immediately below.

Pools are not necessarily needed for waterfalls. A delivery hose can be placed at the top of a wall or rocky outcrop so that the water cascades down the face. Alternatively, a rock, real or otherwise, can be carefully positioned and firmly fixed to a vertical face so as to form an overhang, with a delivery hose bedded above it. In both cases, a collection tank with a pump in it is placed at the bottom of the feature, hidden among rocks and foliage.

Left and above: There is a magical quality to water tumbling over mossy rocks. The movement is arresting to the eye, encouraging long periods of peaceful meditation, and the sound is soothing, sometimes making itself heard throughout the garden. A sloping site, natural or otherwise, is necessary for the construction of natural-looking waterfalls; artificial mounds are quite easy to build.

185

Below: An interesting waterfall can be created by allowing water to fall down a vertical face. It is best seen as a wide sheet, perhaps overflowing from a pond. The visual and sound qualities are quite different from that of a conventional waterfall.

CONSTRUCTION

Two or more pre-formed plastic shells can be used to make a cascade. The rigid pools are set in an ascending sequence of holes, each one lined with sand. The liners should be slightly tipped back, with an overlap from one to the next. It may be necessary to line the overlapping sections with butyl rubber. Careful placing of stones and plants around each liner will create the impression of a stream passing through a series of rocky pools. The pump should be located in the bottom pool, with the exit pipe disguised by rocks. The water, fed back to the top of the slope, can re-enter the topmost pool either as a spring, emerging from the rocks, or by welling up to the surface.

Rocks and waterfalls Well placed rocks are the making of a good waterfall. They break the flow and cause the turbulence and lively sound that make waterfalls such attractive additions to a stream (*above*). The water does not have to be moving fast. Even a broken trickle can make an attractive sound and keep the rocks glistening (*above left*). Substantial rocks and increasingly large pools have a particular grandeur (*left*). If the watercourse is not a natural one it will need to be lined with a liner or concrete.

Moving water and plants

Flowing water contributes a great deal to the character of a garden, but in addition it provides conditions that suit a number of plants. Many plants, for example primulas and meconopsis (the blue poppy) (*above right*), are happiest when surrounded by the very moist, buoyant atmosphere created by moving water and generally do poorly if not given these conditions.

Ferns also relish moisture and are among the most suitable plants for the banks of shady streams. Many other plants such as lysichiton (*right*) cannot be grown without an abundant supply of water. The charm of streamside planting relies heavily on creating the effect of natural plant groupings, but no effort is needed to achieve this green and mossy, romantic watery corner (*above*), only patience.

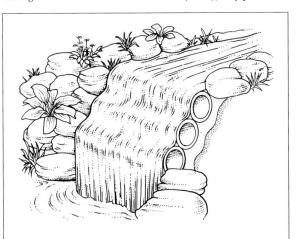

STAIRCASE

A cascade or water staircase can easily be constructed using sections of plastic or ceramic pipe set one above the other, creating an uneven surface for water to flow over. The pipes are embedded in cement or concrete. Smooth plastic is unlikely to provide a very good key for the cement: drill large holes in the underside of the tubes; some cement will enter and hold the pipes fast.

ORNAMENT

Ornamentation has long been a feature of garden design and it is a unique way in which the gardener can stamp his own imprint on the garden for a truly personal touch. Although some ornament is religious or commemorative, such as a small shrine dedicated to a god or goddess, or a stone erected in remembrance of a beloved pet, the majority have little or no symbolic function. Generally speaking, decoration is mostly a matter of pure self-indulgence, something that looks good, is appropriate to the setting and will give a great deal of pleasure in the garden.

Ornament exists in many forms, including sculpture, statuary, sundials, columns, finials, urns and grottoes. Not all ornament is inanimate; there are moving abstract sculptures and enlivening topiary figures. The particular style employed is entirely a matter of personal taste: statuary can be classical or contemporary; *trompe l'oeils* and *objets trouvés* can be serious or surrealistic.

Whatever your choice, ornament can stand out and act as a point of interest or it can merge in with surrounding features for a more subtle effect. As well as being attractive in its own right, it should also work well within the garden as a whole and complement the planting. The overall effect must be one of harmony and integration.

Sculpture

Sculpture is a general term that covers most three-dimensional objects that have no function other than a decorative one; a piece of sculpture is an object to be appreciated and enjoyed. Its success relies on an underlying sense of proportion and relationship of space as well as the manual skill of a good sculptor.

To be aesthetically pleasing, a sculpture does not have to be representational, that is to say, it does not have to resemble a realistic figure or an animal, or an object like a basket of fruit. Instead, it can be a simple block of stone or wood that has a pleasing shape or an interesting texture. A cube of stone, for instance, if it is carefully erected in a sympathetic setting, can work very well, often better than something elaborate.

Sometimes sculpture is symbolic; it may contain a message or have an association with a particular phenomenon or experience. A figure of Neptune rising from the waves, for example, would be most appropriate placed in or near a water feature, and in order to be successful, a Japanese sculpture — a lantern, a tower or a buddha — should be placed in an oriental-looking context. Most sculpture benefits from a backdrop such as a hedge or wall, a plant-clad trellis or an "architectural" plant. Classical sculpture tends to look best in more formal settings; it can look especially pleasing in association with another stone structure such as a terrace or a paved walkway. Some modern sculpture is best in informal settings; a figure standing partly hidden by shrubs can be very effective, or one peeping from behind a group of trees. Modern pieces also look good near plants that echo the shape of the sculpture.

All sculpture should be carefully chosen. Only select pieces that you personally like and which you feel will enhance the garden. Do not overburden the garden with too many different items, otherwise you will detract from each individual piece and the effect will lose its impact: one thoughtfully chosen, well positioned sculpture will be more impressive than indifferent pieces scattered around at random.

Commissioning original sculpture can be very expensive and the alternative is to buy a reproduction, but be selective and pick the most authentic-looking piece. Stone, real, reconstituted or artificial, is one of the best materials for garden sculpture; bronze is also excellent, although it is rather dear.

Displaying sculpture In an Italian Renaissance-style garden (*left*) individual figures are scattered distantly along the top of a wall, looming over a path. The pairing of two contrasting figures on a low balustrade (*right*) makes an imposing formal group and creates a focal point, whereas Cupid hunting among the flowers (*above*) is altogether more relaxed.

Below: A pale figure stands out in the distance, offset by the greenery all around. The eye is immediately drawn to such a figure, which acts as a focal point. The statue is all the more eye-catching because it seems to float above the planting in front of it.

PLACING SCULPTURE

Choosing the location for a sculpture is extremely important if the work is to look effective. The best approach is to decide where you want an object and then set about finding a piece that will suit the location. However, more often something irresistible is acquired which must be accommodated in an appropriate setting. Some pieces will dictate a likely location: a Bacchus will look most effective reeling out of the bushes, while a formal statue is ideally placed in a niche or in a more commanding position such as on a pedestal or balustrade.

The most dramatic results can be obtained by positioning a sculpture at the end of a vista. Alternatively, it can be placed at the sharp bend of a path, or at the junction of two paths, so that the piece can be seen from both directions. Sited centrally at the back of an area, it can act as a focal point, but set asymmetrically to offset the curve of a flowerbed, the object will create a more relaxed and informal effect. For greater formality, doorways and stairs can be flanked by sculpture. Sculpture can also be used as a counterpoint to a particularly bold plant, or it can be used to distract the eye from a less sightly feature such as a compost heap.

For the most dramatic impact, place a sculpture in front of a clear-cut background so that it stands out: a smooth hedge or a wall is ideal, as long as it is higher than the statue itself. For the opposite effect, sculpture can be hidden away and used as a means of surprise.

Above: Without its pedestal, this statue of a classical figure would be insignificant.

Right: Gothic figures and fallen columns make a magnificent although apparently random sculptural grouping.

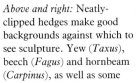

Above and right: Neatly-clipped hedges make good backgrounds against which to see sculpture. Yew (*Taxus*), beech (*Fagus*) and hornbeam (*Carpinus*), as well as some conifers, are among the best as they present a solid, uniform, green backdrop. Avoid variegated or tapestry hedges, where the backdrop can be too fussy to see the figures clearly.

Some pieces of sculpture, such as this dancing figure standing in front of a formal garden (*above*), fit well in many settings. Other pieces, such as the modern frog (*above right*) and cranes (*right*), need more careful placing. The frog works best partially hidden, as though it were a living thing, and likewise with the bronze cranes, which look like real birds as they stand in tall grasses beside the water.

Left: Woodland is an ideal setting for this piece of sculpture, the twisting, slender forms of the entwined figures reflecting the shape of nearby tree trunks.

Below: Although sculpture is often serious, it can also be light-hearted. Here, a bucolic youth celebrates in a time-honoured way, adding a touch of levity to the garden.

Small-scale sculpture Small figures rarely look right in isolation as they tend to be dwarfed by their surroundings and so lose their impact. They frequently need to be placed on a pedestal to lift them up to eye level (*above*), which will make more of a feature of them. Another way to give small figures emphasis is to place them on a low base, surrounding them with plants grown in flower beds and in urns (*left*). This figure seems to dance, floating above brightly-coloured flowers.

Above: A substantial plinth takes the weight of this massive kneeling figure; the base also provides a visual anchor for the sculpture.

Pedestals Pedestals (*right*) can be of a wide range of shapes and sizes; they can be plain or decorated, matching the sculpture they support.

Above: This sculpture depicting two figures is itself quite small, but the pedestal doubles its height, transforming it into an imposing and handsome formal garden ornament.

Sculpture and foliage The worked surfaces of pieces of sculpture contrast well with the texture and shapes of foliage and bark. This is never more apparent than when a figure (*above*) or a more abstract piece (*left*) seems to be wandering out of the greenery; then the effect is particularly subtle. The contrast can also be strong, even when the plants are a little more distant (*above left*).

Decorative Details

Apart from sculpture, there are other ornamental features which can be used to liven up and decorate the garden in all manner of ways.

Columns can be employed for purely aesthetic purposes, or they can be functional, acting as supports and pedestals. They may be simple, with a smooth surface, or fluted to accentuate their length, with either plain or highly ornate capitals (the moulded crowns). Used as decoration, columns can be positioned in such a way as to frame another feature, such as a gateway or view; a tall Grecian column flanking a doorway will look elegant and imposing. Columns can also be used to form colonnades and as supports for pergolas.

In many small gardens, a complete classical column will look out of place, but a section of a column that includes the capital, hidden in a corner and half covered with ivy, can blend in well and look very effective. In a large, leafy garden which has a timeless quality, columns can be used to create an interesting feature. They need not stand upright; they can be placed on their sides, either whole or in a number of pieces, to simulate a classical ruin.

Obelisks are four-sided columns, usually made from stone, that taper to a pyramidal form. They often have inscriptions on one or more of their faces, an arcadian ode or, in the case of a commemorative monument, an elegy. They make interesting and elegant decorations when used in pairs to mark doorways, or at the top or bottom of a flight of steps. Larger examples make good focal points, especially set at the end or intersection of a series of paths or avenues, or in the centre of a circular lawn.

For the finishing touch, add a finial to a wall or column. These ornamental pieces, often in the shape of a fleur-de-lis or a pineapple, or a more simple spherical or pointed design, can stand on gateposts and other features. Urns can be used instead of finials, either as containers or simply as ornamentation. Unless they are very large, they usually look best on some sort of pedestal. There is an extremely wide range of different styles of urn available. Antique examples come in a number of materials including stone, terracotta, bronze, copper and lead, although reconstituted stone reproductions are a popular alternative.

Above: Urns need not be filled with plants to have visual impact. Here, the rounded empty pot contrasts well with the slender, linear planting around it. The raised position of the urn allows its decorative surface to be appreciated.

Left: The contrast of the solid but spiky growth of the plant with the shape and decoration of the urn in which it grows is perfect as they fully complement each other. The background planting makes the picture even more satisfying; a frothy collection of bedding plants would not be at all effective.

Urn selection There is an almost inexhaustible range of urns on offer from which to choose. In this selection (*below*) all have strong character. The central three, the largest representing autumn, are decorative in themselves and could not be planted up; they would look best standing on pedestals. The smaller two would make ideal adornments placed on walls, and the top and bottom urns can be used either by themselves or containing plants. If large enough, they could stand directly on the ground, but both would be displayed better if they were raised on low pedestals.

Urns for planting Urns for planting always look best if they are on the generous side so they can be filled with a mass of plants (*top and right*). However, large pots are heavy and should be placed in position before they are filled with compost. Smaller urns (*above*) make ideal objects with which to ornament the tops of walls, although they may need to be secured on high walls so that they are not swept off by the wind.

195

Below: The gateposts flanking a gate give
an impression of the style of the garden
beyond. In this example, the stone balls
topping the gateposts help to make an
impressive entrance.

Obelisks Their smooth, geometric shape
makes obelisks stand out from their
surroundings in the garden. These
architectural forms make strong focal
points; this can be seen in the example of
an obelisk positioned in a border among
colourful, spiky agapanthus (*left*), and in
the very different example (*below left*) of
an obelisk set in isolation in a formal pool,
repeating the shape of the tall, slender
trees close by.

Right: The clean lines of these
columns inevitably lead the
eye to the sculpture in the
garden beyond. The columns
are themselves ornamental
because of the effective, well-
proportioned ball finials that
add a finishing touch.

Classical columns Although both these columns (*below*) have the same physical function, one looks solid and heavy while the vertical flutes make the other look much lighter.

Left: The tall, elegant finials surrounding this garden create a strong, rhythmic vertical emphasis, which is repeated in the columnar yews and in the building beyond.

Above: The mysterious character of this narrow, almost claustrophobic garden compartment is intensified by a curious spiral column topped by an oversized ball.

Finials (*above*) There is a very wide range of finials available, many of which, like the three illustrated, take traditional, refined forms. New examples are usually made from reconstituted stone or cement. Because of their weight, they need to be fixed to the tops of walls or columns securely, so that there is no risk of them being dislodged by strong winds. Increasingly they can be found made from lightweight fibreglass, but this does not weather like stone.

Above: Finials can often be used to create links between different areas of a garden. Here, the ball on the gable is picked up on the column in the foreground. The repeated use of softening creepers makes the echo more obvious.

Niches

A niche is a decorative alcove and, when built into a wall, it can also provide a place for displaying a piece of sculpture or an urn.

To incorporate a niche into a wall, the wall must be thick enough to take the depth of the niche, that is to say, more than one brick deep. It is also advisable to build the niche into the wall at the time of construction, rather than have to partly demolish the wall at a later date to accommodate the niche.

There are many designs suitable for niches. The most popular is semi-circular with a domed top, but the sides can equally well be straight and the niche box-like; a number of ornamental examples have fluted surfaces with shell-head tops. Niches are frequently set flush with the brick or stonework but can be delineated with a decorative raised edging around them. This can be extended to create a sill at the base of the niche and a canopy over the top. While the conventional niche is smooth-sided and formal, it is possible to create a rougher finish, perhaps a little irregular in shape, more similar to a small grotto. This should not be decorated but left to weather; in a cool, damp, shady position, it will soon develop a thin coating of moss and lichen and take on a natural, informal appearance.

A niche does not have to be restricted to a stone or brick wall; with careful design and skilful management, an alcove can be cut into a hedge to liven up an otherwise flat surface. For the best results, use a compact, small-leaved hedging plant like yew (*Taxus*) and create a simple arched shape. This needs to be well maintained for the most dramatic effect.

To a certain extent, the position of a niche will be determined by its intended contents. A figure, religious or otherwise, can be set high up looking down on the viewer, but while a full-length statue can be placed at ground level, other sculptures require an eye-level location; an urn full of plants, for example, should be positioned at a height where it can be fully appreciated as well as easily watered.

Larger niches can be created at ground level to house a bench or even seats and a table, although these tend to be more appropriate in large, formal gardens. Ground-level niches of any size can also contain a flowerbed planted with shade-tolerant species. Niches can also be incorporated into water features; they make handsome wall fountains with the spout emerging from the back of the alcove and falling into a pool or basin below. For a more decorative feature, install a figurative fountain.

Above and right: If a wall is deep enough, niches are a valuable way of adding decoration to the garden. A small one set in a wall at eye level or above might accommodate a bust (*above*) or a similar small sculpture but, on a grander scale, niches can become major features in their own right (*right*), lavishly planted and ornamented with large scale sculpture.

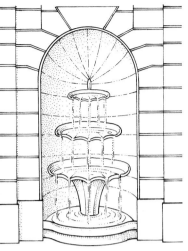

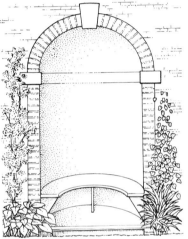

Above left: Many niches have curved crowns and these can be decorated in various ways. The shell shape, dating back to the seventeenth century, has been much used.

Above: Large niches are almost apsidal in scale and can be used to house water features, such as the tiered fountain (*top*), and even seating (*bottom*).

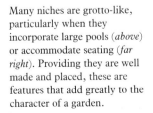

Many niches are grotto-like, particularly when they incorporate large pools (*above*) or accommodate seating (*far right*). Providing they are well made and placed, these are features that add greatly to the character of a garden.

Right: Architectural detail in brick or stonework can be used to make a niche look more conspicuous.

199

Grottoes

Grottoes are mostly small caves, either natural or artificial, some of which are highly decorative, often housing an ornament of some kind. Buildings that are obviously not caves but are adorned with plentiful stones or shells are also known as grottoes. It is believed that they were originally sacred shrines that housed gods, goddesses or water nymphs. In the past these features have mostly been constructed in large, formal gardens as picturesque features and cool retreats from the sun, but today they are no longer associated with such grandeur and can be accommodated very successfully in smaller sites.

Among garden features, grottoes call for the greatest imagination and flair in their design. True grottoes should either be sculpted out of a rock face or cliff, or dug into the ground, perhaps in association with a mound or a suitable grassy bank. As few gardens have the benefit of a rocky outcrop, it is most likely that the gardener will have to construct a small hill out of which the grotto can be carved.

At their simplest, grottoes are shallow caves, not much more than hollows, while complex ones can involve a warren of tunnels and underground chambers. Those built either totally or partly below ground should have walls and domed roofs of stone or brick. These grottoes should be provided with a drainage system to take away any water that may accumulate on the floor. Above ground, structures can be built of preserved wood or brick.

It is a good idea to leave a vent in the roof, not only for ventilation but to admit a shaft of sunlight. If all or part of the walls are then covered with glass bottle-bases, a most effective atmosphere can be created as they will reflect the light and produce an eerie glow. The structure should also be surrounded by trees and bushes to give an authentic, dark, cool effect. Finally, an ornament, a statue of a god or goddess, or some kind of water feature, such as a wall fountain, can be introduced to enliven the interior.

Potentially, grottoes can be one of the most dangerous garden features, especially if built below ground, and so great care must be taken in their construction to ensure that they are safe and sturdy. Caves in particular should be given much attention, to ensure that they do not collapse. The most complicated grottoes are major projects which should not be undertaken lightly, and professional help should be sought to ensure that roofs and walls are totally secure. The internal decoration, however, is enjoyable and well within the grasp of most gardeners.

Left and above: Although both these grottoes are likely to have similar dark and damp interiors, their exteriors are very different. One, appearing as a black hole in the hillside, is like the original grottoes, which were either natural or man-made caves. The other has an ornate and classical architectural entrance with an iron gate, which gives little idea of the interior.

Right and below: Many grottoes have facades in keeping with their interiors and sunken entrances. It is typical of many that they have a Gothic flavour (*right*) which seems to pay homage to their primitive origins, but these are often rather run down or decayed (*below*). This is mainly because they are old and have not been maintained, but as long as they are safe, this suits the character of the feature; indeed, many of the grottoes that have been built or refurbished in recent times have emulated this state of decay. Grottoes are best set out of the way in an isolated part of the garden.

Above: These four faces are typical of keystones set in the entrance arches of grottoes. They epitomize the character of these garden features, which have their origins in pagan places of worship. The figures represented guard the grotto and also act as a forewarning of the earthy, primitive world within. Carvings of this kind are also found inside. A certain degree of skill is required to make these grotesque masks, but cement reproductions are readily available. They can be adapted into wall fountains, with water spouting out from their mouths into a pool or decorative sink below.

DESIGN AND DECORATION

Authentic grottoes are mysterious and secretive. For the greatest effect, they should be hidden away in a corner of the garden, off the main track so that they are suddenly chanced upon. Vegetation and rough stonework will help hide the entrance, which might be approached by a winding path that inevitably draws the inquisitive towards the unseen grotto. If possible, a damp situation should be chosen, as this will allow ferns, mosses and other lush, green growth to surround the approach and doorway, adding to the sense of adventure. If a grotto has a waterfall or stream flowing by the entrance, with careful engineering, this could be diverted inside to provide a delightful water feature.

The entrance itself can be protected by a gargoyle or the head of a mythical beast. Once inside, decoration can be anything from the bizarre to the primitive, or it might reflect the religious origins of the form. Grottoes provide a unique opportunity for the imagination to run riot without the gardener having to re-design the rest of the site to match or accommodate them.

The walls can be decorated with murals or they can be covered with mosaics of odds and ends, shells being especially popular. The use of glittering materials that pick up any rays of light is very effective; broken pieces of glass or mirrors, faceted if possible, and pieces of broken porcelain will supply a charmed atmosphere. Not only can the walls be decorated but the ceiling as well, creating a room without boundaries, again, part of the grotto's mystical quality. The floor can be left as trampled earth or it can be covered with cobblestones laid in a pattern.

Odd shafts of light can be allowed into the interior through small roof lights or long pipes leading out through the walls into the open air. When visitors are expected, candlelight will add to the romance. Water can be introduced, and masks and small figurines enhance the Gothic feel of a grotto, which should still retain much of the mysticism and idiosyncrasy of a holy shrine. Strange, artificial stalactites can be made out of cement, as can a mass of other three-dimensional effects. Not everybody likes to create a bizarre illusion however, and many prefer to keep the grotto simple, with just one or two mysterious touches such as a hidden niche or dimly-lit statue of a god or goddess.

Such places are often damp and cold, even on a hot day, and few people remain inside for long. However, a grotto could contain a bench, possibly built into the wall, for those who wish to linger in the special setting.

Left, top right and bottom right: Grottoes are usually decorated with sculpture, shells and other small objects, including pieces of glass and mirrors, that catch and reflect any light that penetrates the gloom. Water is also often a feature, an allusion to sacred springs.

Wall Ornament

As structural components of gardens, walls have more to offer than just protection and privacy. They can be used to display a variety of ornamentation, although attractive old walls are best left unadorned. Some forms of ornament can be built into the wall while it is being constructed; these are likely to become permanent features as they will be difficult to remove without damaging part of the wall.

A modest form of built-in decoration is a simple coping placed on the top of the wall, often used to complement fine stone or brick. More of a feature can be made if tiles or slate are used to complement the fabric of the wall. Piers or columns are a means of creating a functional but decorative structure: they may be there primarily to support the wall, but they are also ornamental and can be used to break the monotony of a flat surface. Another way of decorating a wall is to create a small round or square window, which can be left as an open space or covered with a metal grill. This will allow a glimpse of the area beyond, encouraging the observer to explore further, while from a distance the feature will look like a picture hanging on the wall.

Fixed patterns and designs using different coloured bricks can be incorporated into the wall at the time of building, and certain bricks can be left slightly proud of the wall surface to form a raised pattern. A less subtle form of decoration is to use pierced concrete blocks in a geometric pattern. These can be used on their own or built on top of an existing low wall, their angular appearance used as an asset in a suitable, linear design, or softened by climbing plants.

Applied decoration does not need pre-planning and can be used to add variety to existing walls. Urns, balls, obelisks and finials all look effective placed on the tops of walls, and framing columns or piers next to gates or doorways can be highly decorative. A more creative approach is to attach items to the wall. These can be in the form of ready-made pieces of sculpture, such as decorative masks, or perhaps a few unique pieces found in an antique shop. Another possibility is to make a mosaic out of fragments of coloured tiles and porcelain embedded in cement.

None of these effects should be overdone or allowed to become too dominant; they need to be subtle in order to blend in well with the garden.

Left and above: When decorating walls, many gardeners are happy to use only plants. However, a variety of different kinds of sculptural decoration can be applied, both on the face of a wall and on its top, and these help make blank architectural features more interesting. Sometimes a decoration is most effective when combined with plants. The mask (*left*) seems to be commenting on what is taking place above its head. The decorative circular niche (*above*) may originally have housed a sculpture.

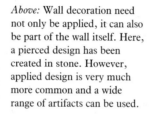

Above: Wall decoration need not only be applied, it can also be part of the wall itself. Here, a pierced design has been created in stone. However, applied design is very much more common and a wide range of artifacts can be used.

Ceramic dishes These shallow dishes (*left*) can easily be fixed with cement as applied wall decorations.

Right: Medieval-style masks and gargoyles add levity.

Below: Individual letters like these are beautiful and can occasionally be obtained from dismantled shop fronts.

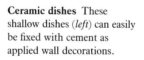

Above left: Most applied decoration is expensive, but interesting designs can be created from inexpensive or even free items. Shells and pebbles are always decorative and weather well.

Cast shell shapes (*above right*) Although shells themselves are frequently used as decoration, embedded in wet cement (only a small area should be worked on at a time), shell shapes can also be cast in plaster.

Appliqué Decorative applied work is called appliqué. (*above left and above right*). It is best to lay out the pieces before attempting to fit them in position. The simplest method is to create them as panels, which can then be attached to the wall. Medallions can be used, personalized with silhouettes. Other possibilities include panels made from items collected during a holiday, or from discarded domestic oddments, including broken china, coloured glass and pieces of tile.

Below: Hollow ceramic planters are another way to decorate walls. They are ideal for growing trailing plants. Such containers must be well fixed as they can be heavy when filled with compost.

Above: Extended walls with this degree of finish are now prohibitively expensive to build. However, the details, including the coping, banding and niches, can be copied successfully on a small scale.

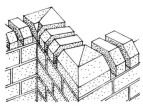

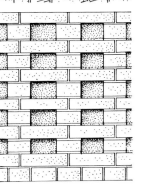

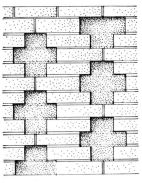

Decorative walls Walls can be ornamented without applied decoration. The surface of a simple brick wall can be varied in many ways; one way of making a pattern is by recessing bricks or leaving them proud of the wall when they are laid (*bottom left and right*). The coping of a wall (*top left and right*) lends itself to decorative treatment.

Sundials

Sundials make popular and attractive garden ornaments. These days they are primarily used as decoration rather than as time-pieces, but as such they add a tranquil air of historic timelessness to the garden. Although old sundials are expensive to buy, there are many good reproductions available, and sculptors and blacksmiths will often be delighted to take commissions to produce original works.

There are two types of garden sundial: one that is placed in a horizontal position on a pedestal, and one that is fixed vertically to a wall. Essentially, each one consists of a dial and a gnomon — the sloping piece that casts the shadow. The gnomon is usually made of metal, either brass or bronze, although stone ones are sometimes seen, and the dial can be made of metal, engraved stone or slate; the smooth texture of the latter makes it particularly popular. More contemporary designs made of metal and perspex can also be found. If freestanding, the sundial should be placed on a pedestal made of stone or cast cement; this must be low enough to enable the observer to look down onto the face of the sundial. If the sundial is fixed to a wall the dial should be clearly visible.

The basic structure of a sundial is very straightforward, but there is plenty of room for imaginative decoration. The gnomon can be made of plain metal or decorative wrought iron; numbers denoting time can be simple or ornate, following any preferred design. Quotations can be engraved on to the dial; anything about the passing of time is appropriate. On a wall, the dial can be painted.

Sundials need careful positioning at a particular time of day, with the shadow of the gnomon showing the correct hour. From a functional point of view they must obviously be sited in a location which receives full sun throughout the day; even if a sundial is to be used for purely ornamental reasons, it should still be placed in a sunny spot as it will look out of place in the shade. A prominent location will take full advantage of their aesthetically pleasing qualities.

Sundials make ideal central features in open, circular, paved or gravel areas, and they can look particularly handsome when placed in the middle of a series of radiating paths or borders. Set in the heart of a herb or rose garden they add true character. They also make an interesting focal point in an otherwise uninterrupted expanse of lawn. Used as an accessory rather than a centrepiece, a sundial can be placed on a terrace or in a sunny courtyard.

An attractive alternative to sundials are armillary spheres, globes of concentric metal hoops showing the progress of the planets across the sky.

Left and above: Some of the best sundials are the simplest. All they need is a stable plinth and somewhere to stand in the sun; this last point is particularly important but is often overlooked. A patina gives them the romance of age but, if they are to be used to tell the time, make certain that the face does not become so moss-covered that it obscures the numbers and the time cannot be read.

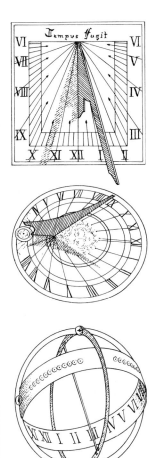

Mounting a sundial A sundial must be mounted correctly if it is to read accurately. The angle of the gnomon or style (*right*) to the horizon should be the same as the latitude of the place where it is set up. The gnomon should point along the meridian or earth's axis so that its shadow falls directly below it at noon.

Fixed sundials Some sundials are portable but most are mounted in fixed positions. In garden settings they are conventionally placed on a horizontal plane (*above*), but they can also be vertical (*right*), as is more frequently seen on the side of buildings. The armillary sphere (*below right*) is an attractive alternative to the sundial.

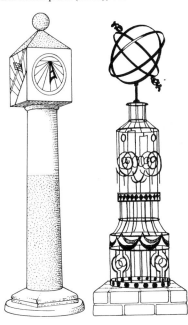

Columns for sundials Stone or a stone substitute are the usual materials for sundial columns (*above left*), although fancy wrought iron (*above right*) can be used for a more decorative effect.

Variations on sundials Sundials need not just be conventional flat dials with gnomons (*below*). They can also be multifaceted (*above*); such sundials must be made specifically for the area where they are to be installed. Alternatively, three-dimensional designs (*left*) can be constructed, and these give great scope for unusual and imaginative treatment.

Above: The armillary sphere is more sophisticated than the sundial, doing more than telling the time. It also demonstrates the movement of the heavenly bodies and, among other things, gives information on the equinoxes. Armillary spheres are set with the gnomon, (here, the straight line passing through the centre of the sphere), along the meridian; that is, it points due north at midday. A sphere needs to be mounted at eye level.

Right: Do not be deceived: some pieces that superficially resemble armillary spheres are simply sculptures.

Topiary

Topiary can be considered a living sculpture, not only in the sense that it is made up of living material which grows each time it is clipped, but also because it sways and changes shape when blown by the wind. As long as you have the patience to wait until it is mature, topiary is the cheapest form of sculpture and can be had for the price of the original plant. However, buying ready-formed topiary can be expensive because of the amount of time it has taken to bring the plant to maturity and to train it.

Topiary as a form of garden sculpture is expressive of the gardener's tastes, and the range of shapes and designs are infinite, as wide as the gardener's imagination. They can be purely geometric — cones, pyramids, spheres or spirals – or they can be representational, depicting a bird or an animal. Simple shapes can be carved directly from mature shrubs, but more complex shapes need a former which will act initially as a training frame and then as a guide for subsequent trimming; pieces that stick out, such as animals' tails, particularly need some kind of support until the plant is mature.

There is a wide range of trees and shrubs that can be used for topiary. Slow-growing species are best because, although a bit more patience is needed to await their maturity, the plants will need less clipping and retain their shape better. While fast-growing plants can be used, they quickly become loose and ragged and need a lot of attention in order to keep any consistent and recognizable pattern. Fast-growing plants, such as privet (*Ligustrum*), should only be used for simple shapes, while the slow growers, for example yew (*Taxus*) or box (*Buxus*), have a much tighter habit, good for more complicated figures.

Topiary need not be confined to plants growing in fixed positions, it can equally well be practised on container-grown shrubs placed singly or in small groups. This means that even in a small garden where the majority of space is devoted to paved areas, it is possible to have miniature pieces positioned at strategic points, and these can easily be moved around to create different arrangements. Bay (*Laurus*) can be successfully accommodated in containers, with the growth shaped into spheres or cones.

Left and above: Topiary is one of the most delightful forms of garden ornament, often lovingly created by gardeners themselves. There is great scope for the imagination as well as skill with the shears. Some specimens are representational, like these birds sitting enthroned in regal majesty (*left*). Others are more geometric in shape, such as this spiral (*above*).

MAZES

In the long history of maze making, hedges, stones and turf have been used to form intricate patterns. Two of the many possible patterns are illustrated above. The most familiar planted mazes consist of a complex of paths walled by hedges, trimmed to head height or above. These may take years to reach full maturity.

Below: This row of topiary could almost represent chessmen lined up for a game. Yew, one of the most suitable trees for topiary, only needs trimming once a year. However, if time is available, two cuts will keep it neater. Scaffolding will be needed to trim the taller pieces.

Above and right: Topiary need not be restricted to pieces on a grand scale (*above*). It can equally well be created on the much smaller and more intimate scale of these animals shaped from box (*right*). These have been grown in Versailles tubs and make an interesting contrast alternating with the box "tubs". Simple shapes are easier to maintain than more intricate designs, and this is particularly relevant when it comes to clipping large specimens. Pot-grown topiary can generally be moved easily to different settings.

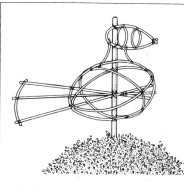
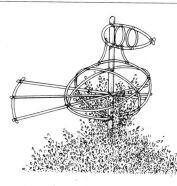

CREATING TOPIARY

The first step to creating successful topiary is to choose a suitable site. This should be done carefully as topiary can take up to ten years to mature, a time-consuming mistake if it is in the wrong position.

Next, the shape must be decided upon. Sometimes an existing bush, or the configuration of the young growth on a new bush, will suggest a form. In such cases, shaping will be easier as it will follow the natural lines of the plant. Solid and simple forms can be clipped from existing trees or started from scratch. Cutting into bushes will expose bare areas of wood, but these will soon leaf over and within a year or so the piece will be quite presentable. Geometric shapes are deceptively difficult to clip, especially those with flat surfaces. Use plumb lines to get vertical faces; wooden templates and jigs are also very helpful in getting the correct line. Spontaneous, asymmetrical shapes are easier to create and can be done by eye.

Figurative works are in some ways easier because any accidental variation, short of cutting off a tail or head, is much less likely to show. These can be shaped from a solid bush if they are not too complicated, but the most detailed figures are best created from young bushes trained from the beginning over sturdy wire formers.

Train a few thick stems along the main elements of the former. Loosely tie in the shoots with tarred string to allow them to grow. Do not try to force older shoots in a direction in which they do not want to go as they are likely to break; young pliant growth is better for complicated shapes. Growth is rarely uniform, especially when shoots have been bent downwards, and the side facing the sun is likely to grow fastest. Try to accommodate such quirks of nature into an asymmetrical, irregular design.

Topiary does not have to be a single colour; plants of different shades can be planted and trained together.

Clipping is best done with garden shears. Use the tips rather than the full length of the blades, as the latter are likely to create flat areas. For intricate details use secateurs, which are more adept at fine pruning. It is best to start at the top of a figure, cutting out and downwards.

Left: Pleaching is another way of training plants, as seen in this row of trees forming a screen on stilts.

Above left and above: Topiary often introduces elements of fun and humour, even in grand, formal gardens.

Trompe l'oeil

A *trompe l'oeil* is a painting or decoration that creates an illusion, tricking the viewer into seeing something that is not really there. With a bit of imagination and ingenuity, it is possible for the gardener to create any number of original, deceptive devices using plants, paintings and sculpture.

As practical features, they are mainly employed in small gardens to give the impression of space, so that the garden seems bigger than it really is. However, they can be used in any garden in a jocular way to create an amusing and witty trick of the eye.

Classic *trompe l'oeils* are created by painting pictures that look three-dimensional. It is possible to use this technique in a small garden by painting windows on a wall that reveal an apparently pastoral vista; this will be especially effective in a town garden where the painted scene will contrast with the true urban surroundings. Similarly, doors or gateways can be painted; a half-open gate with a glimpse of what lies beyond will deceive the observer into thinking the garden has another part to it.

Another example of *trompe l'oeil* is the careful positioning of a large mirror on the wall of a small basement garden or other enclosed area to give the impression that the garden is twice its actual size. Again, another trick is to attach trellis to a wall so that it gives the illusion of perspective: the typically horizontal battens should be arranged so as to point towards some imaginary vanishing point, taking the eye with them into the supposed distance. This is most effective when the impression given is that of a tunnel or corridor. A further method is to use a single panel on a side wall that narrows towards the far end, again in the direction of an imaginary vanishing point, making the space look longer. Plants can be used in a similar fashion: tall trees in the foreground with progressively shorter, thinner ones behind will give the illusion of distance. Pale flowers, misty blues for example, planted at the end of a border will make the border seem longer; conversely, brilliant colours planted at a distance will draw the end of the garden towards the viewer.

More illusions can be created by painting murals, of woods for example, that form a backdrop against which the garden is viewed, but the problem with this is that a painting does not change with the seasons. It is possible to create whole borders on a flat surface, with one or two real plants in front to add to the three-dimensional effect. Three-dimensional *trompe l'oeils* can be created by using artificial flowering plants and trees made from plastic or silk. This kind of illusion should be used with care and is only suitable for certain types of quirky garden where such materials can be assimilated into the overall style. Real statues and other ornaments such as urns can also be placed in front of a decorative mural.

Left and above: The illusions created by *trompe l'oeil* can introduce an element of fun into the garden. Flat walls can be transformed by painting (*left*) or by trelliswork (*above*) so that they present an impression of three-dimensional architecture.

Above left and above right: The use of trellis to distort perspective has a long history. It has often been combined with elaborate architectural features (*above right*), although the wooden laths are simply attached to flat walls. Planting can enhance the impression created by *trompe l'oeil*, but the perspective should not be obscured (*above left*).

Illusions of perspective At its simplest, *trompe l'oeil* creates an illusion of depth by using painted lines or trelliswork (*below*) that suggest a receding perspective within necessarily uncomplicated architectural forms. These architectural fantasies can be elaborated so that even a tiny garden can seem like a courtyard in a palatial complex.

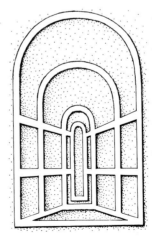

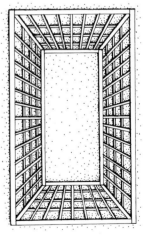

Left: Painted *trompe l'oeil* allows more scope for inventive decoration than trellis does. Dull blank walls can be enlivened with views that you might expect to see there, such as a window or door, or the image of a landscape can create the illusion in an urban setting that countryside lies just beyond the garden. The technique is particularly useful for increasing the apparent size of a small garden. The use of large mirrors, although not strictly *trompe l'oeil*, can also make a garden seem larger.

OBJETS TROUVES

Many less conventional garden ornaments start life as quite ordinary, often functional, objects. The range is limitless, but they should be chosen with care; incongruity can have its place and often makes a welcome impact, but it can be overdone and detract from the garden.

A surprising number of man-made objects, such as old wooden wheels, millstones, disused beehives or dog kennels, can fit well into the landscape, and chimney pots, either used on their own or as containers filled with plants, are often seen. The more esoteric railway signal posts and road signs feature in some gardens, and old tools also have their devotees. Not all *objets trouvés* are man-made, some are natural items: a carefully placed stack of logs, stones or old weather-worn tree stumps can all be used effectively. Tree stumps can be left on the surface of the ground with their interesting, tangled roots exposed, or part of the stump can be buried to give the impression that it has been there for a long time. Shells and antlers are other favourite decorative ornaments that are often seen.

The placement of *objets trouvés* must be considered with great care. Some pieces are best in formal settings, used perhaps as focal points; others work well in informal designs, apparently carelessly abandoned. The more surrealistic objects should be positioned in such a way as to create witty or amusing scenes that possibly tell a story.

Recycled objects Recycled objects have long been used as ornaments for the garden. Many old jars from a pre-plastic era (*right*) make attractive plant containers. This example has a spigot hole that allows for drainage. If there are no drainage holes, old jars can be used to hold planted plastic pots. The millstone (*far right*) has been converted into a table that looks at home in a garden setting. Terracotta pots and jars, including those once used in the house, are ornamental, even without plants (*below*). This medley includes old rhubarb forcing pots, which are no strangers to the garden.

Above: Home-made sculpture can be made from all kinds of recycled objects and *objets trouvés*. The springs here may well be a witty reference to "spring in the garden". The scope for this type of sculpture is infinite, but avoid overwhelming the garden with too much junk as it will lose its impact.

Containers

The use of containers for growing plants has a long history and their popularity has never diminished. Containers are decorative objects in their own right, but they are also practical. They allow the gardener to introduce plants to soilless areas like steps, patios and terraces, and facilitate a variety of fresh, seasonal changes in the garden.

The range of containers available is almost inexhaustible. There are ornamental and plain, informal and formal ones, and it should not be difficult to find a suitable container for any position that is required. The material of the container is relatively unimportant except as an aesthetic consideration, although some types of terracotta are susceptible to damage from frost and this should be borne in mind in cold areas. If the containers are to be on a balcony or roof garden then those of fibreglass or plastic will be much lighter than stone, terracotta or metal, and will reduce the load on the structure.

Containers can be placed on their own or used in groups; larger ones look better in isolation while smaller ones look best collected together, especially if they are all different shapes and sizes. The appearance of a lone container is important, while in a group, it is possible to hide one or two that are not so attractive.

Classical urns tend to look more appropriate in formal settings, while wooden containers are more informal in design, although an arrangement of carefully-planted, painted Versailles tubs can look very smart.

Wherever it is positioned, a container should always have a firm base as a pot full of moist compost is very heavy. In most cases, particularly with very large tubs, it is best to put the container in the final position first and then fill it with compost and plants to save having to move it when it is full.

Virtually any plants, including vegetables, can be grown in containers, but all will need more care than those grown in the open garden. The key to success is not to let the containers dry out, but at the same time never to allow them to become too wet. They will need constant watering, which will leach nutrients out of the compost, so the plants will also need regular feeding during the growing season.

To facilitate drainage, all containers should have holes in the bottom, preferably covered with a layer of stones, shards or coarse gravel to prevent them from clogging-up and to provide an easy passage for excess water. The compost should be free-draining but capable of retaining sufficient moisture for the plants' needs from one watering to the next.

Left and above: Container-grown plants add much to a garden, and a wide range of vessels can be used, either singly or in groups. Some containers, including recycled coppers (*above*), are so impressive that they deserve to be displayed in isolation. Often, however, the appeal of plants is enhanced by the way containers are brought together. An old stone sink makes a lovely arrangement with clay pots containing different species and varieties of sempervivum (*left*).

Left and below: The ornamental quality of a container is often as important as that of the plants growing in it (*left*). Some containers can simply be used to house less attractive containers, including plastic pots, in which plants are growing. Pot-grown plants can just be dropped into decorative containers during their peak display and then replaced when their season is over. An attractive box for this purpose (*below*) is not difficult to make.

Troughs and sinks Old troughs and sinks (*below and right*) are particularly suitable for growing alpines. Glazed sinks can be made to look like weathered stone by coating them with a mixture of peat and cement. Sinks and troughs look best mounted above ground level.

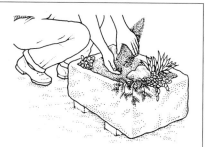

RECYCLING A SINK

A sink can be turned into a trough by covering it with hypertufa, a mixture of cement and fine peat. Clean the sink and apply a layer of adhesive. Apply the hypertufa to the sides, including the inside down to just below the intended soil level. When completely dry, paint the sink with mud, liquid seaweed fertilizer or a stiff mixture of cow manure and milk to encourage the rapid development of moss and algae. Place the sink in position before filling it with a free-draining potting compost and planting it up.

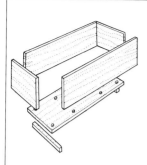

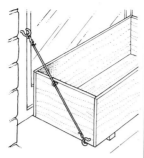

WINDOW BOXES

Window boxes are all but constantly wet and therefore need to be made of marine ply or hardwood, or a softwood that has been treated with a preservative (not creosote). Corrosion-free screws and fixings should be used. Holes in the base and some form of feet must be provided to facilitate drainage. Firmly fix boxes in place.

Above: Troughs and rough-hewn stone containers are normally planted with alpines, but they are also suitable for dwarf conifers and bulbs, provided they are deep enough to hold sufficient compost.

Below: Terracotta flower pots can be painted in striking patterns, as seen in these examples. Here, the contrasts between the shapes and textures of the foliage are an integral part of the effect.

Above and right: Groups of container-grown plants look good when assembled on patios, especially in corners or to one side of a door. However, they should not be allowed to encroach on paths to the extent that they pose a hazard to pedestrians. Variety in the containers, and in the planting, will greatly increase the interest of a collection. Regular watering is essential, especially during hot weather, and feeding during the growing season will ensure good plant growth.

Terracotta Terracotta is a traditional material for containers and remains popular because the colour and texture of the material is sympathetic to plants. Almost any plant looks good in a terracotta pot, whether grown in the garden, the greenhouse or indoors. There is a very wide range of shapes and sizes available, both plain and decorated (*left and below*). Firing at high temperatures is needed to make pots frost resistant, so not all pots can be safely left outdoors in areas that experience cold winters. The principal disadvantage of terracotta pots is that they dry out fairly quickly in hot summer weather. If planted up, the containers must have drainage holes; otherwise, fill them with plants still in their original flower pots.

Herb pots and planters
(*above*) Herb pots and strawberry pots have apertures in their walls to take plants at different levels. They can be used for a wide variety of ornamentals as well as for the plants they are designed to take. The pots should be rotated on a regular basis to ensure that all plants get sufficient light. These pots look attractive with tall planters, which can be glazed or partially glazed.

Below: Many terracotta pots have moulded decoration, such as this basket pattern, and a suitable planting is needed to complement it.

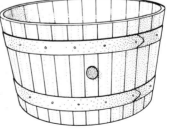

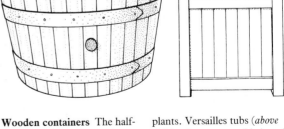

Wooden containers The half-barrel (*above left*), a simple wooden container for plants, has a certain rustic charm and will give many years service if the wood is treated with a preservative. Do not use creosote, which is harmful to plants. Versailles tubs (*above right*) suit a more sophisticated setting. These should be made of a hardwood and, as with half barrels, there should be drainage holes in their bases. Ready-made tubs are also available in fibreglass.

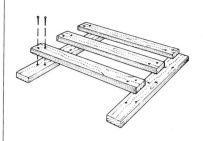

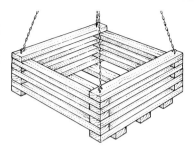

MAKING A BASKET

An attractive wooden hanging basket can be easily constructed from a few slats of wood. The slats should all be of the same length; about 30cm (12in) will do. The wood must be treated with preservative (not creosote) to prevent it rotting, and the base strips attached with corrosion-free screws. The slats for the sides should have a hole drilled in each end, just large enough to take a stout galvanized wire, which, when passed through, holds them together. Turn the wire over on the underside of the container and secure it with staples. Thread on alternate side pieces, as shown, and bend the remaining wire into a loop.

Below: Terracotta pots often look attractive combined with recycled containers. Here, a container is combined with ornamental chimney pots.

Right: Careful positioning is often needed to make the most of a container. The pendulous habit of a fuchsia is shown off in a pedestal-mounted pot.

Left: Attractive arrangements of spring bulbs such as tulips can make a splendid display in terracotta pots. Summer and autumnal planting can follow.

Above: Long-flowering plants for containers include pansies and the Mexican daisy (*Erigeron karvinskianus*), an effective combination of flowers.

LIGHTING

If the garden is to become an important part of the home and used in the same way as other rooms, it is necessary to provide outside lighting so that the space can be used in the evenings, especially when the weather is warm in the summer. Outdoor lighting is also important from a safety point of view so that people can see where they are going in the dark; it should also help deter intruders.

There are many types of lighting, including blanket cover from a lamp high up on the house. This will provide general illumination and act as security lighting as well. By contrast, a series of lamps set along a path or drive will light that area but the rest of the garden will be dark. Alternatively, different features can be spotlit: trees, ponds or statues can all be lit in isolation to give the garden interest and form at night. Highlighting features in this way creates a dramatic backdrop that is not only seen from the garden itself but also from within the house through key windows. These lights are generally installed low down so that they shine up at the chosen feature. Water can be lit from below the surface as well as from above; illuminated fountains and waterfalls make exciting and spectacular night-time features.

Treat outside lighting as you would lights inside and avoid overall coverage, restricting it to particular areas. Allow for different circuits so, for example, you can have a private meal on a terrace with soft lighting, without the surrounding area being lit up around you. Smaller, softer lights, such as fairy lights, are no more difficult to install than other lights, and candles and torches can be very effective.

There is a large selection of external light fittings on sale that will supply just the right amount of light in the right place, and many of these are unobtrusive during daylight hours, especially if they are hidden in the vegetation. All light fittings must be specially designed for outdoor use; never try to adapt lamps originally intended for use indoors.

While the gardener should be encouraged to choose the location of lights and to work out the general design of the scheme, if there is any doubt at all as to his or her ability to carry out the actual wiring then it should be passed over to a professional, as electricity is particularly dangerous in the damp environment of the garden. Any mains feeds should be of armoured cable and this must be buried at a minimum depth of 2ft (60cm) below the ground.

The garden at night Gardens are rarely used at night, except in summer, but an imaginative use of lighting can open up a whole new world (*left and above*). Lighting can be functional or it can be atmospheric; functional lighting allows people to find their way around and see what they are doing, whereas atmospheric lighting illuminates various parts of the garden, possibly individual plants, to create a relaxing ambience in which people can enjoy themselves. Electricity is now widely used for garden lighting but gas and oil can be used as well. Candles and flares can also be employed if adequate precautions are taken.

Light fittings A wide range of light fittings (*below*) is available for use in the garden. A standard, hard-wearing, general-purpose light (*top*) can be used to floodlight drives or paths, good for security reasons. The two below are movable fittings that can be pushed into the earth. These are generally battery operated, although there are some that work on gas. Below these is a lantern; these old fashioned-looking lights are decorative and functional fixed outside a door or marking a gateway. The bottom set of spotlights are for immersion in ponds, under fountains or on side walls, to illuminate the water.

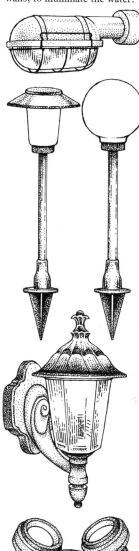

Above: Floodlighting certain features in the garden can create dramatic night-time vistas from the house and from within the garden.

Right: Lighting bollards are a good method of obtaining localized light along a path.

Below left: Spotlights or floodlights shining through plants can magically transform their daylight appearance.

Below right: Soft light filtering through from other areas that are illuminated can create an intimate atmosphere.

GARDEN FURNITURE

As the garden is an extension of the home, a place to sit and enjoy the surroundings rather than somewhere to just grow flowers or vegetables, it is important to have good, comfortable garden furniture which looks as attractive as possible.

There is a vast range of chairs, benches and tables to choose from; some are sufficiently robust and weatherproof to remain outside throughout the year, while others need to be taken inside for the winter and during inclement weather.

Permanent furniture is usually made of wood or wrought or cast iron; both are quite unyielding and may need cushions if they are to be used for any length of time. Inside summer houses, which get a certain amount of protection from the weather, cane furniture can look very effective, especially once it has begun to age.

Movable furniture comes in a range of materials, including plastic. Many of the modern designs are quite comfortable but their visual appearance leaves much to be desired. For example, folding aluminium chairs and tables are practical but generally look temporary and add little to the overall appearance of the garden, although they are useful as a back-up in case of a sudden influx of people. Traditional deck-chairs, on the other hand, give the impression of leisure and blend in well with their surroundings. Unfortunately, they can be dangerous if children are around as it is easy to trap fumbling and inquisitive fingers when putting them up or dismantling them.

It is also possible to have built-in furniture in the garden, for example, around a barbecue. Seats or benches can be constructed out of stone or brick as part of a wall, or they can be made using thick wooden slats suspended between parts of a low wall; tables can be constructed in a similar way. This type of seating will be very hard and often cold and will certainly need cushions. Much thought should go into their design and placement, however, because once they are in position they cannot be moved easily.

As well as placing seats in obvious sites, on a terrace for example, some should also be set in key positions where certain aspects of the garden can be enjoyed, such as beside a pond or a fragrant climber. Position a seat to catch the early morning or evening sun. Seats in the shade are always welcome, especially in the summer, as are those tucked away in an arbour that provides protection from light showers. Garden tables should be sited in shady spots as they are mostly used in summer for dining alfresco.

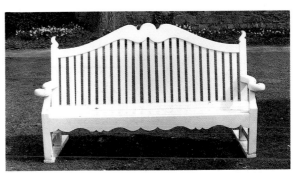

Opposite: Furnishing an area near the house with a table and chairs simplifies outdoor eating and entertaining. A paved patio with an even surface makes an ideal location, although the climate will dictate the extent to which the area is used throughout the year. Furniture not used during winter should be stored under cover.

Strategic seating Seats and benches need careful placing (*above left, above right and right*). The top of a flight of steps or the end of a path are natural resting places. A warm wall makes a good backing, as do beds of scented plants. Whether seating is in sun or shade, commanding a view or hidden away will depend on personal taste.

Benches Three common kinds of benches are illustrated above: rustic seating for a cottage garden (*top*), an elegant Lutyens-style bench (*middle*), and a simple, attractive teak bench (*bottom*).

Above: Seating that can easily be moved about has many advantages. Its position can be altered to suit the changing seasons and to take advantage of shelter and sun. The wicker canopy of this movable seat is functional as well as decorative, giving additional protection from the weather; it is an unusual, pleasing piece that would make a focal point in a garden. Some benches and chairs are fitted with wheels.

Simple seats Seats need not be of very complicated construction. It is perfectly possible to make them out of a single slab of stone (*left*) or a balk of timber (*below*) (note the topiary "back" and "arms"). Whatever material is used, the supports must be sturdy and firmly bedded. Carved or plain supports would suit a stone slab. A simple wooden seat is effective and easy to make.

LESS CONVENTIONAL SEATING

Not all seating need be purchased at the local garden centre; there are many types of seats that the gardener can construct by hand, often with the minimum of effort.

The easiest seat is simply a log or large piece of stone placed in a suitable position to provide a resting place. Another simple seat is a thick plank of wood supported on two pieces of tree trunk or balks of timber inserted into the ground; the uprights should be solid and treated with preservative. Grass or herb seats make delightful features: construct a hollow seat from wood, stone or brick which has draining holes in the bottom, covered with a thin layer of drainage material, such as rubble. Fill the seat with compost, water well, top up with more compost and firm the surface; it is now ready for planting. Grass seed can be sown or turfs laid; these will give the quickest result. Aromatic herbs can also be used; thyme is a fragrant and wonderfully resilient plant, while mint and chamomile are popular alternatives. Grass needs regular trimming, herbs demand less frequent attention; all need watering during dry spells.

Another type of resting place is the hammock. It is possible to buy modern swing seats on frames, but a hammock slung between two trees can hardly be bettered on a warm summer's day. Such hammocks can be bought or easily made from canvas or knotted from string or rope. Do not forget that the most important part of the hammock is the supports; these must be very strong and the hammock firmly secured. Healthy, mature, solid trees are ideal.

Combining seats and plants Seating that is built in conjunction with plants can make an interesting feature in the garden. Delightful, plain tree-seats (*above*) can be constructed to encircle a tree trunk, which acts as a back rest. A hole should be left in the centre of the seat large enough to allow the tree to grow. Other seats can be built using shrubs as part of the framework (*left*). These need regular clipping to keep them neat. Shrubs can also be used as a backdrop (*opposite*), here emphasizing the colour of the stone and creating a very interesting focal point.

Left: This beautiful tree-seat has been built over pebbles and tiles. Grass gets badly worn around permanent seating and can be difficult to mow.

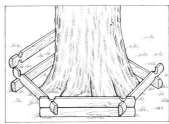

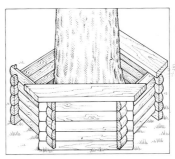

MAKING A TREE SEAT

Create a shady seating area under a favourite tree by building an attractive and practical tree seat. This simple design can be made from split lengths of logs and three lengths of planking. The logs should be treated with a preservative, but not creosote, which could kill the tree. Cut the logs to length, allowing room for overlap, so that they will form a hexagon around the tree. Make notches in one edge only of the first three logs and last three logs. Other logs should have notches cut on both edges, shaped so that they fit snugly into one another. Plane the top edges flat if necessary so that the planks will not rock and then drill holes to accommodate dowel pegs. Drill matching holes in the planks, position them and insert the dowels for a tight, secure band.

Above and left: An ornate, leafy chair, wittily painted green, and an elegant seat are fine examples of old, highly decorative wrought iron furniture. These deserve good care and should be washed and repainted regularly.

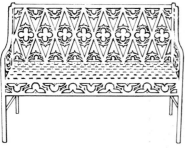

Right: There is a comfort and price advantage to seats made with cast-iron end-pieces and simple wooden slats.

Cast-iron furniture In the Victorian period, cast-iron garden furniture was manufactured in a wide range of designs, such as these gothic and romantic examples (*left*). Old pieces are expensive and difficult to come by, but reproductions are available.

Right: A variation on the traditional wooden deckchair, this elegant set of chairs with a matching table is made from wrought iron, the chairs having canvas upholstery. Because of their light construction, these pieces can be moved about as needed. They are, however, best on a good, level surface. To prolong their life, they should be put away when not in use so the canvas does not rot.

Below: Although much furniture of cast cement and artificial stone is very plain, these materials can be treated in a highly imaginative way, as this set of chairs and table demonstrate. Both these materials are long lived and they are fairly maintenance free, although with very fanciful designs there is the risk that comfort will be sacrificed to visual appeal. Cushions on the seats would help to make these chairs more welcoming.

Above: When painting garden furniture, decide whether you want pieces to stand out from or blend with plants and other features. This ornate wooden bench has been painted white and blue to show off its detail.

Left: A seat running round the edge of a Japanese gazebo provides a seating area that is shaded from the midday sun, but it cannot be moved.

Below: Well used furniture, like the collection of wicker chairs in this paved bay, adds a touch of homely comfort to a garden scene.

Below: This wrought-iron chair once had a refined elegance, but it now takes on the guise of a modern piece of sculpture. Even when furniture is old and possibly too unstable to use, it can still look attractive in the garden when employed in a decorative rather than practical way.

GARDEN STRUCTURES

Most gardens have at least one structure in them apart from the house itself. Some, such as sheds and greenhouses, are practical, while others, summer houses for instance, are more for pleasure. These structures should be chosen to blend in with the style of the garden and any buildings in the vicinity.

Sheds often have little aesthetic appeal but can be effectively disguised with a trellis or screen supporting climbing plants. Wood is more sympathetic than most other materials, but if you are building on a grand scale, brick or stone sheds can be constructed. Such structures can be covered with climbing plants, as can those of wood, but the latter will have to be stripped of creepers to carry out maintenance.

Greenhouses can be difficult to site. Although they need an open, sunny aspect, for visual reasons they should be tucked out of the way rather than placed in a prominent position. Wooden-framed greenhouses are better insulated, but those with aluminium frames are easier to maintain.

Summer houses, either totally enclosed or with one open side, can look very handsome when they are found, nestling in a secluded corner of the garden. Make sure they are big enough for two or more people to sit comfortably, preferably at a table. Pavilions are an original and exciting alternative; they are usually constructed to cover a bench or seat and are often set at the end of a path or avenue.

There are plenty of smaller structures that can be used around the garden, partly as decorative features and partly as practical objects. Dovecotes are popular; the design is up to the individual and, although good examples can be bought, the gardener can always make his or her own. Beehives are also attractive, especially the old-fashioned white ones which add a cottage atmosphere to the garden. These can be functional – a home to bees – or purely decorative.

Follies can be built but, generally speaking, the garden must be quite large in order to accommodate them. They come in many forms including buildings, monuments and ruins. Ruins are easy to construct; rather than completely dismantling an old disused brick or stone shed, do so only partly and allow it to become overgrown with ivy and moss.

Left and below left: Summer houses, gazebos, belvederes and pavilions are all evocative names for a romantic type of building that forms an ornamental feature in the garden. Large summer houses are often functional pieces of architecture used for sitting in, to admire a view or a fine piece of planting. They are sited where they allow a more intimate appreciation of the garden than is possible from the house. Although many summer houses are open-sided and airy, they do need a roof to provide some protection from both sunshine and sudden rainy outbursts.

Opposite: A summer house can be an important architectural feature of the garden, its significance underlined by the way it is sited. Here, a highly ornate summer house forms part of an elaborate scheme, terminating a pergola that covers a pathway running beside a large pool.

Above right and right: Many small summer houses are used as purely ornamental features. Such structures, clothed in climbers like ivy, often form a focal point along an axis of a garden. They can also serve as a quiet retreat in a shady, wooded area, where the planting is wilder.

Garden sheds Every garden needs its shed (*above left, above right and below*). There are many items that need to be stored, including hand tools, lawn mowers, potting composts and pots, chemicals and fertilizers, as well as overwintering plants. Much garden furniture also needs to be stored during winter or when not in use. Since a shed is so indispensable, it is worth making an effort to integrate or decorate it. One solution is to disguise a plain shed by training creepers over it (*below*), but unless they are kept on trellis slightly away from the building they can be difficult to keep in check and can make the building damp. The addition of architectural details such as decorative bargeboards can transform an ordinary shed, as can bright or delicate paintwork (*above left and right*). Louvres are attractive and useful; they help to maintain a free flow of air through a shed without allowing rain to penetrate.

Above: A summer house can be incorporated into a garden of almost any size but care must be taken in getting the scale right. In a really small plot, a scaled down summer house can still take up too much room, even appearing oppressively dominant if it is solid-sided. In this situation, and even in the larger garden, it is often better to build an open-work structure. This can provide a shady area in which to sit, although it will not give protection from wind and rain in the way a more solid structure can. The open-work summer house can be left unplanted but provides an ideal support for climbers. Being light and airy, it blends in with the garden and is an important architectural feature, adding much to the character of a design.

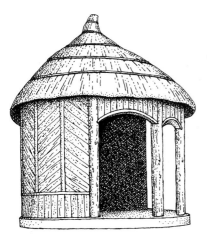

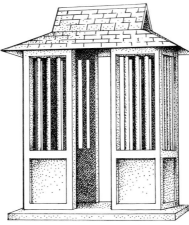

A wide range of materials is used for roofing. Thatching is often used in rustic designs (*above left*), while more conventional summer houses may have tile or slate roofs (*above middle*).

Above right: A Japanese-style open-sided summer house is roofed with sheet metal.

Conservatories A conservatory can make an elegant extension to a house, combining the warmth and comfort of a room with uninterrupted views of the outside world. It need not be restricted to the conventional garden, as this one on a roof garden demonstrates (*left*); the siting of the conservatory affords breathtaking views of the city. With the use of modern materials it is not necessary to stick to straight, small-paned pieces of glass. This allows the use of sinuous curves to create attractive roof shapes (*below*). These materials are light as well as flexible.

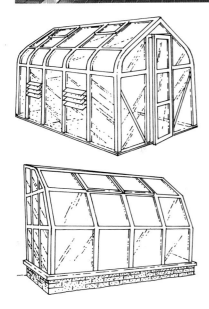

Greenhouses (*above*) The use of aluminium frames has allowed more flexibility in the design of greenhouses, both as freestanding buildings and as lean-tos; aluminium is a strong alloy.

Above: Dovecotes have long been a feature of gardens. Now they are usually decorative structures to house ornamental birds, but previously they were built for pigeons that were bred for food. Some dovecotes are elaborate freestanding buildings, but those most commonly seen are made of wood, erected on poles, as here, or attached to walls.

Follies and ruins Follies and ruins (*above*) help to create a romantic landscape. A ruin can be constructed from recycled materials, or an existing building – such as an old brick or stone outbuilding or a pigsty – can be distressed. Although conveying an impression of decay, a ruin must be securely built; make sure there are no loose bricks or unstable piers.

Left: Shrines and temples, sometimes plain but often ornamental, provide an opportunity for highly personal expressions of taste and homage.

Above: The original function of some highly ornamental buildings is obscure. This was probably the public side of a gardener's bothy (living quarters).

Above: The competent amateur carpenter could easily make dovecotes of simple, traditional design.

Right: Buildings beside water should fit in with the tranquillity of the setting. This circular boathouse sits squat and protected among the trees, with its doors facing towards the water.

Below: An imposing shrine is set at the top of a flight of stone steps. The shape of its pediment echoes the steps below.

THE PLANT
SELECTOR

TREES AND SHRUBS

The design of every garden, whatever its size, should include trees and shrubs. Even in the smallest plot there will be a suitable location for a tree, which will introduce the valuable element of height, and there are good compact selections of many shrubby species which will give substance to the overall composition. In addition, trees and shrubs create shade and a superstructure which allows a whole new collection of plants to be grown.

The choice of plant depends on the function it is expected to fulfil within the design. It is important, particularly in small gardens or where a single specimen is required to create a focal point, to be certain that the plant will justify the space it occupies. Size and shape are factors that should be considered for year-round effect: there are small compact strains of many plants as well as larger, vigorous ones; forms range from tall and columnar to pendulous. The foliage, flowers and fruit, bark and colour of young twigs all influence the visual scene while fragrance is always an added bonus.

Larger species should be positioned with care as they will create shade and block out light as they grow. Some of the most vigorous ones may interfere with the foundations of buildings and nearby drains if sited too close to them. For example, *Populus* species can be particularly problematic.

Left: Evergreen conifers – including cultivars of abies, chamaecyparis, cupressus and picea – create a stunning picture in golden- and blue-greens all year round. Changing light and atmospheric conditions will show the wide range of shapes, sizes, colours and textures to good effect. The flowering heaths used here add a bright seasonal note. A pleasing pattern, enhanced by the healthiness of the plants.

If blocking out an undesirable view outside the garden or breaking the linearity of a wall is a priority, then use quick-growing species. These plants often make large trees when mature, so a strict pruning regime will need to be carried out regularly. Quick-growing species are also very useful in creating an air of maturity early in the life of a garden. Often, as in forestry, a quick-growing tree is planted alongside a slower-growing species as a nurse and is removed as the latter gains size. I have seen balsam poplars (*Populus balsamifera*) coupled with a beech tree. The poplars grew quickly and, as the beech gained height, the lower branches of the poplars were removed. Once the beech had made 15ft (4.5m), the poplars were felled. Another slow-growing species which benefits from a nurse is English oak (*Quercus robur*).

Left: Three birches make strong vertical accents as they snake up through an understorey of ceanothus. Even in winter the trunks will remain arresting features of a simple composition.

Right: The appeal of this planting relies on contrasts of habit as well as of flower and foliage colour. The pink flowers of the hibiscus and foreground heather harmonize with the maroon foliage of *Cotinus coggygria* 'Royal Purple'. In habit and leaf shape the cotinus contrasts with the *Eucalyptus gunnii* behind it. Spiky heather and rosemary contrast with the broad, variegated leaves of the impressive dogwood.

Above: The foliage of the fine, spreading *Acer pseudoplatanus* 'Brilliantissimum' opens pink and later turns bronze and then greenish yellow. Here the lobed leaves make a sharp contrast against the tight, controlled shapes of clipped *Chamaecyparis lawsoniana* 'Fletcheri' behind.

Left: The bright red autumn foliage of *Acer palmatum* makes a strong focal point in a relaxed planting of shrubs, ferns and perennials. A well planned seasonal effect.

Large trees already present in the garden can create considerable shade. Try to work with rather than remove the tree; it is possible, through careful pruning, to significantly reduce and raise its canopy, letting in light without markedly altering the tree's impact.

There are many shrubs and small trees that are adapted in the wild to growing in the shade of taller trees and require these conditions to thrive in the garden. These include both evergreen and deciduous species: *Aucuba japonica*, *Juniperus × media* 'Pfitzeriana' and *Prunus lusitanica* provide good, all-year-round dense foliage. To this quality mahonias, some viburnums and many rhododendrons add blossoms in winter and spring. *Acer palmatum*, *Philadelphus coronarius* 'Aureus' and *Pieris* species are also grown for their foliage which colours spectacularly for extended periods, adding an additional season of interest to that provided by the flowers.

When designing a garden it may be that a plant is needed that is of interest throughout the year. Alternatively the garden, or a specific section of it, may need to be designed to be at its best during one season of the year. Many trees and shrubs have interesting features in at least two seasons and there are some outstanding ones that are attractive in three seasons. Among the best are many viburnums, particularly *V. opulus* 'Aureum' with its beautiful golden foliage, large panicles of white flowers in late spring and bunches of translucent red berries from late summer into the autumn. Other outstanding plants are sorbus, crataegus and prunus species that combine good foliage with flowers, fruit and bark; dogwoods with flowers, autumn or variegated foliage, and fruit; and witchhazels with winter flowers and autumn colour.

In winter the main feature is the bark. This may have a shiny, polished appearance as in some cherries;

a peeling or flaking texture that reveals layers of differing hues as in birches, *Acer griseum* and *Pinus bungeana*; or brightly coloured twigs from the previous season's growth as found on many willows (*Salix* species) and shrubby dogwoods. To get the best effect from willows and dogwoods it is necessary to prune them hard in early spring at least every other year.

There are many trees and shrubs that flower in early or late winter when frosts are at their worst. These always perform most successfully if planted in a sheltered spot away from the morning sun which can damage frozen flowers by thawing them too quickly. Remember that the blooms will be shown to their best advantage against a solid backcloth, so grow winter-flowering species near conifers or broadleaved evergreens or in front of a wall of a contrasting colour.

Spring is the time for flowers. They range in colour from the pale yellow racemes of *Stachyurus praecox* to the bright pinks of the flowering cherries. Choose the most garishly coloured ones with care so as not to clash with other spring-flowering plants. Young foliage can also have an impact, with delicate cream, pink and coppery leaves unfurling in the sun.

In summer the vegetation is at its height. Flowers are at their most abundant with lilacs, mock oranges and buddlejas covered in a mass of blooms. The dense cover of leaves makes a rich background to all the other plants in the garden. Colours range from the dark maroon of *Cotinus coggygria* 'Notcutt's Purple' or 'Royal Purple' to the blue-green of *Cercis siliquastrum*, the grey-green of *Pyrus salicifolia* 'Pendula' and the yellow-green of *Robinia pseudoacacia* 'Frisia'. The shape of the leaves – varying from the perfectly rounded to very narrow and feathery – and their size – they may be large or very small – are characteristics that affect the visual impact of the garden and can be used in very effective juxtapositions.

Autumn is the time when the canopy thins out and the garden begins to wind down, but still there are late flowerers such as *Abelia* × *grandiflora* and *Hydrangea paniculata*; *Clerodendron trichotomum* and *Callicarpa bodinieri giraldii* make a show with many berries that complement their startling foliage colour. Pyracanthas, cotoneasters and berberis are also good in berry, while maples, amelanchiers and euonymuses have beautiful foliage.

Right: Quercus coccinea 'Splendens', the only named form of the scarlet oak, colours gloriously in autumn. Arboreta and the many other plant collections throughout the world are often the best places to evaluate the ornamental qualities, speed of growth and ultimate size of trees when assessing their suitability for the garden. This oak will eventually make a tall tree in excess of 90ft (27m).

Quick-growing

Acer negundo   z 3
Ash-leaved maple or box elder
This rapid-growing deciduous tree can reach 30ft (9m) and has pinnate ash-like leaves, 8in (20cm) long, and a bushy habit. The bright green young shoots carry hanging clusters of pale pinkish-brown flowers before the leaves in spring. Cultivars include 'Variegatum', with irregularly white-bordered leaflets, the golden-yellow leaved 'Auratum' and the less-vigorous 'Flamingo', which has pink young leaves that mature to green with white and pink markings. Will tolerate some shade.

Ailanthus altissima (above)   z 5
Tree of heaven
This deciduous tree rapidly reaches 45ft (14m) with a spreading habit. The ash-like leaves are 1-2ft (30-60cm) long and turn yellow in autumn. Female trees bear small panicles of yellow-green flowers in late summer and early autumn, followed by bunches of bright red, winged fruits. It grows from seed in most soils and in some areas is rather a weed. For a tropical-looking bush cut back hard each spring; the strong shoots carry leaves over 3ft (90cm) long. Resistant to atmospheric pollution.

Alnus glutinosa 'Aurea'   z 4
All alders grow easily in virtually any soil and are especially suited to moist conditions. This cultivar has pale yellow leaves, which are most conspicuous in spring and early summer, fading to pale green as the summer progresses. With similar features is A. incana 'Aurea', the grey alder, the young yellow shoots contrasting well with the bright, red-tinted catkins during spring. It makes an attractive shelter-belt subject for an exposed garden. Alders bear woody cones which stand out in winter.

Aralia elata   z 3
Japanese angelica tree
A tall, suckering deciduous shrub or a small, thinly-branched tree, the doubly-pinnate leaves are the main attraction of this plant. These are up to 3ft (90cm) long and form ruffs at the ends of the branches. 'Aureovariegata' has yellow margins and splashes on the leaves, and 'Variegata' has creamy-white margins and blotches. The variegations turn silver-white in autumn. Plant in deep fertile soil, in a sheltered spot to protect the leaves from strong winds. The cultivars stand out best when grown against a dark backcloth.

× Cupressocyparis leylandii   z 6
Leyland cypress
This forms a noble tree of a dense, columnar habit. It is one of the fastest growing of all evergreen conifers, capable of reaching 100ft (30m) when mature. It makes a fine specimen in a large garden providing it is correctly sited and tended. The foliage is borne in irregular, slightly drooping sprays and is aromatic if crushed. Useful as a screen or windbreak, it grows well even in poor soil and tolerates alkaline soils and coastal conditions. 'Castlewellan' has yellow foliage.

Liriodendron tulipifera (above)   z 5
Tulip tree
Fast-growing and deciduous, this tree can reach 40ft (12m) in 20 years. The peculiar leaves are four-lobed, glossy green in summer, turning to clear butter yellow in autumn. The tulip-like flowers are greenish-yellow with orange centres and are sometimes followed by woody fruits. Young trees flower less readily. The leaves of 'Aureomarginatum' have greenish-yellow margins. Succeeds in all fertile soils, including chalky.

Pinus sylvestris   z 3
Scots pine
Characterized by its red-brown young bark, this fast-growing conifer will reach 100ft (30m) after many years. For the smaller garden choose 'Aurea', slow-growing with golden-yellow winter foliage, or 'Nana', a bushy, slow-growing dwarf form. Trees are densely conical when young, losing their lower branches as they age. The leaves are dark greyish-green, stiff, needle-like, and held in pairs. Small brown cones stand out against the foliage. Avoid damp, acid or shallow, chalky soils.

Populus × serotina 'Aurea'   z 3
Golden poplar
Also listed as P. × canadensis 'Serotina Aurea'. Like many poplars, this species is a rapid-grower and can reach 150ft (45m). It requires a fair amount of moisture to grow well; searching surface roots can damage drains and foundations so plant away from buildings. The pyramidal, juvenile shape develops into a densely branched, rounded canopy. Pointed leaves open golden-yellow in spring, turn greenish-yellow, and then golden-yellow again before falling in autumn. This cultivar is useful on wet sites.

Ribes odoratum (below)   z 2
Buffalo currant
This ornamental currant is a vigorous, deciduous shrub that grows to 5ft (1.5m) with a loose, erect habit. The shiny, dark green leaves are carried on upright stems, along with golden-yellow, clove-scented flowers during spring. Shiny black currants contrast with the rich orange-yellow autumn foliage. Prune out some of the oldest shoots in late winter. Suitable for most types of soil.

Shade tolerant

Acer palmatum (*above*)   z 5
Japanese maple
This plant will slowly make a small tree of 20ft (6m) with a low, rounded crown, but is best treated as a shrub. The species has palmate leaves, 2-4in (5-10cm) across, with five or seven lobes; these turn scarlet in autumn. Small, purplish summer flowers are followed by winged fruits. 'Senkaki' has coral red winter bark; 'Atropurpureum' is smaller, growing to 6ft (1.8m), with rich purple-red summer foliage. Grow in cool, moist loam, possibly in a tub or raised bed, sheltered from cold winds. Succeeds in dappled shade.

Aucuba japonica (*below*)   z 7
A shade-loving evergreen shrub that makes a dense, rounded bush, 6ft (1.8m) tall, with large, laurel-like, glossy leaves. Female plants bear red berries. 'Crotonifolia' has golden speckled leaves, 'Variegata' (spotted laurel) has gold blotches. For berries, grow the narrow-leaved, all-green female 'Salicifolia', with its sea green stems. Variegated forms retain their colour best on an open site, but all thrive in sunless positions in most soils.

Juniperus × media 'Pfitzeriana'   z 5
Pfitzer juniper
Ideal for growing as a lawn specimen or to break up the outline of a bed or border, this evergreen shrub is also useful as a tall ground cover. It reaches 10ft (3m) and spreads 10-15ft (3-4.5m); arm-like branches are set at an acute angle with drooping shoot tips. It has glaucous, scale-like juvenile leaves. 'Pfitzeriana Aurea' has golden-yellow young shoot tips and foliage; the latter turns yellowish-green in winter. Very versatile; good for alkaline soils.

Lonicera fragrantissima   z 5
The flowers of this semi-evergreen shrubby honeysuckle give off a strong scent during the coldest winter months. The small cream blossoms appear on part-naked branches from winter to spring, followed occasionally by red berries. Liven up the dull summer phase with a fast-growing clematis or other climber; this will scramble over the bush which can reach 6ft (1.8m). The deciduous *L. standishii* is similar and *L. × purpusii* is more vigorous. Prune out old wood in spring.

Mahonia aquifolium (*above*)   z 5
Oregon grape
This vigorous, spreading, suckering evergreen shrub reaches 2ft (60cm) in height and makes good ground cover. In spring, dense terminal clusters of fragrant yellow flowers appear, followed by black, bloomy berries that give the plant a bluish sheen. The spiny, glossy, leathery leaves can turn orange-red in winter and are up to 1ft (30cm) long. 'Atropurpurea' has rich reddish-purple winter and early spring foliage. 'Moseri' has bronze-red young leaves which turn apple green and then dark green in summer. Needs well-drained soil.

Philadelphus coronarius 'Aureus'   z 4
(*above*)
Golden mock orange
The leaves of this deciduous plant are bright yellow in spring, ageing to greenish-yellow. It makes a dense bush 6ft (1.8m) high, covered in scented, creamy-white flowers from early summer. Use in a mixed border, masking the lower stems with herbaceous plants such as *Euphorbia griffithii* 'Fireglow', which has orange-red flowers. Cut back the flowered stems immediately after the blooms have faded. Tolerates dry soils. Direct sun may bleach the leaves.

Pieris japonica (*below*)   z 6
This evergreen shrub can reach 4ft (1.2m) and has a compact, bushy habit. The young leaves are coppery-pink in spring, turning a darker, glossy green. Flower buds are decorative in winter, the long-lived waxy flowers opening in drooping panicles in spring. 'Daisen' has pink flowers, deeper when in bud; the leaves of 'Bert Chandler' turn from salmon pink to cream, white and then green. Needs moist acid soil; protect from cold winds and early frost.

Lawn specimens

Prunus lusitanica (*below*)   z 6
Portugal laurel
This can make an excellent specimen tree of 20ft (6m), doing particularly well on thin alkaline soil. The evergreen leaves are dark glossy green with red stalks. Small flowers appear in long, thin racemes in summer and have a sweet fragrance. Mature plants often fruit following a hot summer, the red fruits turning deep purple as they ripen. The less vigorous 'Variegata' has white-splashed leaves, flushed pink in winter; *P. l. azorica* has larger, brighter green leaves which are red as they unfold; *P. laurocerasus*, the cherry laurel, is less hardy and often used in hedging.

***Rhododendron* 'Blue Peter'**   z 5
This hybrid can grow to 6ft (1.8m), with a vigorous, upright habit and dark, glossy evergreen foliage. The large cobalt-violet and white flowers are funnel-shaped with frilled margins and are held in conical trusses. Each flower has an eye of deep purple spots. All rhododendrons need moisture-retentive, humus-rich, acid soil so suit a shady, woodland garden. Mulch in spring; no regular pruning is necessary.

Viburnum rhytidophyllum   z 5
A large rhododendron-like evergreen that grows in the dappled shade of trees. The drooping, long leaves are dark glossy green above with a thick grey tomentum underneath. Shoots are felty grey-brown. Upright clusters of white spring flowers are followed by small oval fruits which turn from red to black. Two or more specimens must be planted together to ensure fruiting. Plants can reach 6ft (1.8m) or more. 'Roseum' has rose-tinted flowers. Gives structure to a mixed border; ideal for alkaline soils.

Acer cappadocicum (*above*)   z 6
Notable for its brilliant autumn colour, this elegant maple makes a fine specimen, up to 70ft (21m) high, with a rounded crown. The broad leaves are bright green, five- to seven-lobed, and turn a rich butter yellow in autumn. 'Aureum' has leaves which turn from red to golden-yellow over several weeks. For attractive blood red young foliage grow 'Rubrum'; the leaves turn green in summer and reddish-gold in autumn. Needs fertile, well-drained soil.

Betula ermanii (*below*)   z 6
Grown largely for its stem colour, this Asian birch also has attractive yellow autumn leaves. A tree can reach 70ft (21m) when fully grown, but it is just as useful as a young garden specimen. The small glossy leaves have deep, parallel veins. The trunk has pinkish-white peeling bark while the branches are an orange-brown. On old trees the bark hangs from the branches. Plant with some thought as the beautiful bark colours are easily lost if not set against a dark backcloth such as evergreen shrubs. Grows well on most soils except shallow, calcareous types.

***Cedrus atlantica* 'Glauca'**   z 6
The blue-grey form of the atlas cedar is pyramid-shaped when young, with ascending tips to its branches, and reaches 110ft (33m) when fully mature. The silvery-blue, needle-like leaves are held in rosettes on plentiful short lateral shoots. The pale brown cones are up to 3in (7.5cm) long and sit topside of the branches. *C. deodara*, the deodar, has drooping tips, while the cedar of lebanon, *C. libani*, has level branches: both have grey-green foliage. All three trees develop a flatter habit when mature. Grows in most fertile soils.

***Cornus controversa* 'Variegata'**   z 5
This spectacular deciduous dogwood is ideal for a lawn where its horizontal, tiered branches can spread fully, giving it an architectural quality. The leaves have silver variegations, enhanced by clusters of creamy-white flowers in summer. In autumn the foliage turns purple-red and small black fruits may form. This species grows in most fertile soils, and benefits from shelter and sun. It can reach 15ft (4.5m) or more in height, and can spread to 10ft (3m), making this one of the most impressive of all foliage plants.

Davidia involucrata (*above*)   z 6
Pocket-handkerchief, dove or ghost tree
The extraordinary inflorescences of this tree are its chief glory. Each small flower is protected by two paper-thin white bracts which hang below the branches in summer. These bracts are between 4in (10cm) and 8in (20cm) long. The deciduous leaves are fresh green, heart-shaped and felted beneath. Green fruits litter the ground in autumn and winter. Plants can reach 30ft (9m), need rich, moisture-retentive soil and prefer a sunny, sheltered position.

Ginkgo biloba (below)   z 5
Maidenhair tree

This deciduous conifer is slow to establish but can reach 80ft (24m) with an open habit. The leaves are fan-shaped and two-lobed, pale green in summer, yellow in autumn. Plants are single-sex: male trees produce small catkins, females bear tiny flowers. The hard, yellow fruits smell of rancid butter when ripe. The nut-like seeds are edible. 'Pendula' has spreading, weeping branches. Resistant to atmospheric pollution.

Laburnum × watereri 'Vossii'   z 6

In late spring and early summer the golden chain tree is massed with hanging racemes of golden-yellow, pea-like flowers. This cultivar reaches 25ft (7.5m) and has extra-long racemes at 2ft (60cm). The deciduous leaves have three leaflets. It does not produce seed pods, which are poisonous in other laburnums, as are all the genus' parts. Train a late summer-flowering clematis, such as 'Ernest Markham', through its branches. Laburnums can be trained to form tunnels. Grows in most soils.

Magnolia stellata   z 5
Star magnolia

A fine shrubby magnolia that is covered with fragrant white blooms in spring which burst from silky, grey buds. Slow-growing to 10ft (3m), it has a rounded, compact habit. 'Rosea' and 'Rubra' have pink flowers. Plant in a sheltered position in rich, well-drained soil that receives plenty of moisture. Mulch regularly with organic matter. Avoid disturbing the roots and only prune if essential. Underplant with dwarf bulbs such as *Narcissus bulbocodium*. Tolerates alkaline soil and atmospheric pollution.

Metasequoia glyptostroboides   z 5
Dawn redwood

This deciduous conifer was known only as a fossil until it was rediscovered in 1941. It grows in a pyramid-shape, reaching 36ft (11m) in 25 years and ultimately 100ft (30m). The tapering trunk bears a light, airy canopy of feathery foliage, carried in opposite rows on short branches. The leaves are bright green in spring, turning golden-yellow in autumn. The shaggy, cinnamon-brown bark is attractive during winter. This tree grows well in moist soil and is resistant to pollution.

Salix caprea 'Weeping Sally'   z 4

Rarely growing to more than 6ft (1.8m), this small weeping willow is a female form of the larger goat willow, *S. caprea*, grafted on to a straight-species rootstock. It grows slowly into a graceful umbrella-shaped tree, the branches growing down to the ground, and bears soft silvery-white catkins in spring. The deciduous leaves are glossy green with woolly undersides and form a dense mass in summer, allowing little to grow under the tree other than spring-flowering bulbs.

Viburnum plicatum 'Mariesii'   z 4
(below)

This form of the Japanese snowball tree is best grown as a specimen shrub. Horizontally tiered branches make it a fine architectural plant reaching 6ft (1.8m) in height and spread. The flowers are made conspicuous by white, sterile, ray florets which form heads 2-3in (5-7.5cm) across. These are held above the branches in early summer and persist for many weeks. In autumn the leaves turn a rich burgundy-red. Grows in most soils including those over chalk; needs no regular pruning.

Fragrance

Cercidiphyllum japonicum (above)   z 5
Katsura tree

As the leaves of this tree take on their greyish-pink, vermilion and yellow autumn tints they release a delicious caramel-like fragrance. They begin coral-pink in late spring, turning sea-green above and bluish beneath. Small flowers appear before the leaves. In cultivation this large tree normally forms a small- to medium-sized specimen. *Helleborus orientalis* makes a good underplanting. Grow in a sunny, sheltered position, in any moist soil, preferably against dark evergreens.

Clethra alnifolia 'Paniculata' (above)   z 4

The sweet pepper bush grows to 6ft (1.8m) and is prized for its late-summer flowers which fill the air with a sweet fragrance. 'Paniculata' is a superior form with the near-white flowers held in terminal panicles. Its deciduous foliage is attractive year-round and turns a bright yellow-orange in autumn. 'Rosea' has flowers flushed pink. In warm areas black, peppercorn-like seeds follow the flowers. Succeeding in damp, acid soils, this plant is useful for woodland gardens. Good at the back of a border.

Daphne odora 'Aureomarginata' z 8
This is one of the most scented and hardiest of the early-spring flowering daphnes. Plants form a rounded bush, 4ft (1.2m) high with a 5ft (1.5m) spread. The tight clusters of purplish-red flowers, which fade with age, are complemented by the evergreen, gold-rimmed leathery leaves. 'Alba' has white flowers. Some protection is beneficial, especially from strong, cold winds, but the plants will stand some frost. Grow this species in moist, free-draining loam, in a situation where its fragrance can be savoured to the full.

Fothergilla monticola z 5
This deciduous shrub makes a rounded plant of 5 × 5ft (1.5 × 1.5m) in ten years. Small, bottlebrush flowers appear in spring, creamy-white and sweetly scented. The coarse, dark green leaves are up to 4in (10cm) long and turn orange and yellow in autumn, blending with the scarlet autumn hues of *Acer palmatum*. The leaves of *F. major* begin golden-orange then deepen to crimson-reds. Grow in moist, acid soil, in sun or partial shade, among heathers or evergreen azaleas. No regular pruning is necessary to maintain this plant.

Oemleria cerasiformis (*above*) z 6
Oso berry
A suckering deciduous shrub which bears male and female flowers on different plants. The small, bell-shaped, fragrant white flowers appear in very early spring, carried in pendulous racemes on erect stems some 8ft (2.4m) tall. The sea green leaves emerge on vigorous young shoots. Of little real interest during the summer, plant towards the back of a border. Fruits are plum-like, turning from brown to purple as they ripen.

Philadelphus 'Virginal' (*above*) z 5
In early summer the plentiful double flowers of this vigorous mock orange fill the air with their rich fragrance. It produces upright shoots 10ft (3m) tall and has deciduous leaves, 4in (10cm) long. The compact 'Belle Etoile' reaches 6ft (1.8m). It has 2in (5cm)-wide scented flowers with a reddish-purple blotch in the centre. This patch can be picked out in the mixed border with mauve-flowered herbaceous plants such as hardy geraniums. Easily grown, even on poor dry soils, it should be pruned straight after flowering.

Sarcococca hookeriana z 8
Christmas box
This spreading, shade-tolerant, evergreen shrub has erect stems that reach 3ft (1m). In late winter the small, pink-tinged white male flowers release a distinctive scent which is strongest on moist, mild days. Leaves are lance-shaped. The insignificant female flowers are followed by shiny black berries in early spring. *S. h. digyna* has narrower leaves and reddish-tinged stems. This species grows in any fertile soil, including that over chalk.

Styrax japonica z 5
This graceful plant makes a small tree which may reach up to 25ft (8m) and has slender drooping branches. It requires protection from cold spring winds and late frosts that damage the opening buds. The fragrant white flowers are pendulous and open in early summer. The roundish to oval deciduous leaves are dark shiny green. In cooler climates it is best grown in full sun, but some shade is necessary in sunny areas. Can be slow to establish but thrives in deep moisture-retentive soil with plenty of organic matter.

Syringa vulgaris (*below*) z 3
Hundreds of forms of the common lilac exist in cultivation as shrubs or small trees. They reach 5-10ft (1.5-3m) and have a tendency to sucker. The large, spring flowers, held in dense pyramidal panicles, have a delicious scent and can be white, pink, cream, purple or mauve, single or double. The heart-shaped deciduous leaves are fresh green in spring. Plant in any fertile soil in a sunny position, preferably towards the back of a border as it tends to become bare at the base. Deadhead, but avoid hard pruning which encourages growth.

Viburnum carlesii (*below*) z 4
The heavy daphne-like scent of this popular viburnum permeates the air in spring. Clusters of pink buds make pure white flowers, followed by jet black autumn fruits. The leaves are dull green above, grey below, and often take on orange-red autumn hues. A rounded shrub, 4ft (1.2m) high, it makes a fine specimen plant. 'Diana' and 'Aurora' have red flowers which turn pink; 'Charis' has red flowers which turn pink then white. Cut out suckers sent up by grafted plants. Easily grown in most soils, it requires little pruning.

Winter colour

BARK

Acer griseum (*above*)   z 6
Paperbark maple
This slow-growing, lime-tolerant tree grows to 40ft (12m) with an open, rounded crown. The polished, orange-brown peeling bark is fully developed on wood three or more years old. In spring the trifoliate leaves emerge buff yellow. They turn dark green, reaching 2-4in (5-10cm) across, and become deep scarlet-orange in autumn. Greenish-yellow flowers appear in early summer. Needs a moist soil. Grouped plants should be well-spaced.

Betula papyrifera (*above*)   z 4
Paper bark or canoe birch
During its first five years this deciduous tree develops a smooth, white bark which then peels away in sheets. This peeling continues throughout the tree's life, revealing new glistening bark beneath. It grows to 60ft (18m) but the canopy casts only partial shade, allowing other plants to grow at the base. The irregularly toothed leaves turn a rich yellow in autumn. *B. jaquemontii* is similar but has brown peeling bark. Grows in most soils.

Cornus alba 'Sibirica' (*below*)   z 2
The bright red, glossy, upright stems of this winter dogwood form a thicket some 6ft (1.8m) high; they are stronger in moisture-rich soils. The leaves are up to 5in (13cm) long and turn shades of plum-red in autumn before falling. For deep purple, almost black stems, grow 'Kesselringii', striking if combined with red- and yellow-stemmed forms. Plant in groups for the best effect, avoiding shaded positions. Cut the stems very hard back in early spring to encourage fresh growth; flowers and fruits will be sacrificed as a consequence.

Cornus stolonifera 'Flaviramea'   z 2
(*below*)
This dogwood is grown for its bright yellow and olive green stems which can grow to 6ft (1.8m) if cut hard back in early spring. The growth is vigorous and suckering, forming a dense thicket if left unpruned. The light green deciduous leaves are up to 5in (13cm) long and turn yellow in autumn. Choose a site where the stems can be illuminated by the winter sun. It will tolerate waterlogged conditions. Grow with the red-stemmed dogwoods for beautiful winter colour.

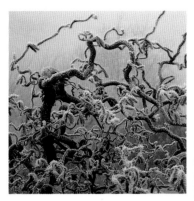

Corylus avellana 'Contorta' (*above*)   z 5
Corkscrew hazel or Harry Lauder's walking stick
The branches and the thread-like twigs of this deciduous bush are twisted and looped in a knotted mass. Reaching 10ft (3m), the plant is covered in spring with yellow male catkins and tiny, red, tufted female flowers. The leaves are up to 4in (10cm) long and more crinkly than the ordinary hazel; they turn yellow in autumn. Grows in most soils. Cut out vigorous suckers from the base. Plants look striking when seen against snow or covered in frost.

Leycesteria formosa   z 7
Himalayan honeysuckle or pheasant berry
This deciduous shrub has bright sea green stems which are hollow, upright and reach 6ft (1.8m) in a season. The young stems are covered with a glaucous bloom. Olive green pointed leaves are 2-7in (5-18cm) long; they turn yellow in autumn. In summer the white flowers emerge from purple-red bracts and hang in heavy racemes. These are followed by purple-brown fruits which smell of caramel. Grow in moist, fertile soil. Cut back to ground level in spring.

Parrotia persica   z 6
Persian ironwood
Grown mostly for its vivid red, orange and yellow autumn leaf colour, this plant also has beautiful flaking grey bark on its older stems. It grows as a spreading large shrub or small tree and can reach 25ft (7.5m) with a similar spread, the stiff, horizontal tiers of branches making an excellent winter silhouette. The flowers appear in late winter, conspicuous for their bright red stamens and lack of petals. Grows in most soils apart from highly alkaline.

Pinus bungeana z 5
Lace-bark pine

An unusual evergreen conifer, this slowly forms a low-branching specimen shrub or tree up to 40ft (12m) tall. The grey-green bark flakes away, leaving a beautiful jigsaw-like pattern of white, olive green, yellow, brown and purple. The colours change as more flaking occurs. The yellow-green, needle-like leaves are about 3in (8cm) long. *P. gerardiana*, Gerard's pine, has pinkish-grey bark that flakes to reveal brown, green and yellow wood. Grow both in full sun, avoiding shallow alkaline soils.

Prunus serrula (above) z 6
Tibetan cherry

The smooth bark of this tree resembles polished mahogany. It peels horizontally between large, pale brown lenticels which ring the trunk and stems. A tree is at its best after ten years when it is 15ft (4.5m) tall. Ideal for a lawn, underplanted with *Narcissus* 'February Gold' or similar. It grows in all soil types including alkaline. Plant in full winter sunlight, removing lower branches to gain trunk length. Polish the bark with a soft cloth to enhance the beautiful sheen.

Rhododendron barbatum z 8

Dense heads of crimson red flowers appear in spring on this evergreen rhododendron. It has deep purple, peeling bark, large leaves with sunken veins, and bristly young branches and petioles. It forms a very large shrub or a tree 30ft (9m) high. *R. thomsonii* has cinnamon-coloured bark and blood red flowers. Plant in semi-shade in moist, acid soil, mulching with leaf mould. This species is ideal for woodland. Water well until established. No regular pruning needed.

Rubus cockburnianus (above) z 5
Whitewashed bramble

A whitish bloom covers the arching, purple stems of this deciduous rubus. The lower surfaces of the pinnate, fern-like leaves are also bloomy. Small flowers are sometimes followed by black fruits. All shoots should be cut to within 1in (2.5cm) of the ground in spring to encourage new growth; this can reach 6ft (1.8m) on established plants. Will grow in shade or sun in most soils. Plant against a dark background in full winter sun, with *Eranthis hyemalis* beneath.

Salix alba 'Chermesina' z 2
Scarlet willow

Similar to the winter dogwoods in habit, the young shoots of this shrub are bright orange-red. Deciduous, pale green leaves open in summer. Prune hard back at least twice in spring to encourage fresh growth. Plants will reach 6ft (1.8m) in two seasons, considerably more if left unpruned. *S. alba* 'Vitellina', the golden willow, has bright yellow shoots. For contrast, plant with dogwoods such as the dark purple-stemmed *Cornus alba* 'Kesselringii'. Best in moist soil, especially near water.

Salix matsudana 'Tortuosa' z 4
Corkscrew willow

The twisted shoots and branches of this willow are dramatic against the winter sky. It makes a narrow, pyramidal tree and, once settled, grows to 20ft (6m) in ten years. The olive green twisted stems carry narrow, contorted, bright green decidous leaves in spring, as well as small yellow-green catkins. Train *Clematis* 'Bill Mackenzie' through it for yellow flowers and fluffy seed heads. Quickly regrows if cut hard back. Prefers moisture-rich soil, near water.

FLOWERS AND BERRIES

Camellia 'Salutation' z 7

This hybrid evergreen shrub grows to 6 × 6ft (1.8 × 1.8m) in ten years. The silvery-pink flowers are semi-double, 5in (13cm) across, and appear in late winter and spring. The leaves are matt green. Grow camellias in humus-rich, acid soil and mulch regularly with organic matter. Choose a sheltered spot, out of strong winds and protected from the early morning sun which can damage the flowers after frosts: a woodland garden is ideal. Water in the summer, especially until established.

Corylopsis pauciflora z 6
Winterhazel

The arching stems of this deciduous shrub can reach 6 × 6ft (1.8 × 1.8m). The leaves emerge pink and open a dull green, with good autumn colour. Drooping racemes of scented, bell-shaped yellow flowers are carried in early spring. *C. spicata* is larger, with yellow flowers and purple anthers; *C. willmottiae* 'Spring Purple' has purple-red winter shoots. Plant in deep, lime-free, humus-rich soil in some shade. Underplant with *Narcissus cyclamineus*.

Cotoneaster lacteus (above) z 7

This plant bears large clusters of small red fruits which last throughout the winter if they survive the attention of birds. Evergreen, leathery, oval leaves have deep-set veins and felted grey undersides. Creamy-white flowers appear in summer. It can be pruned to make a short, single-stemmed tree, but is more usually a free-growing shrub up to 12ft (3.6m) tall, with similar spread. The mauve flowers of *Clematis viticella* 'Abundance' will give interest in late summer. Grows in most soils.

Hamamelis mollis (*above*) z 5
Chinese witch hazel
One of the first winter-flowering shrubs, this has sweet-scented, golden yellow flowers with hardy strap-like petals, borne on bare, upward-growing branches. The light, open canopy reaches 10ft (3m). Hazel-like deciduous leaves are up to 5in (13cm) across, turning deep yellow in autumn. 'Pallida' has larger, sulphur-yellow flowers; *H.* × *intermedia* 'Diane' has rich copper-red flowers and good autumn colour. Slow-growing; do not prune. Plant in humus-rich acid soil in full sun.

Ilex verticillata z 3
Winterberry
This holly is quite unlike all others because of its deciduous nature. It forms a rounded shrub reaching 13ft (4m) in ten years. In winter the bare green-purple stems are clothed with long-lasting, bright red berries. An unusual shrub, also noted for its purple-tinged 1⅔in (4cm)-long leaves, which are particularly well-coloured in spring, turning yellow in autumn. The female form 'Christmas Cheer' has many persistent fruits. Needs acid soil.

Malus 'Red Sentinel' z 5
With fruits lasting into mid- and late winter, this crab apple is a valuable small- to medium-sized tree. The deep red fruits hang in large clusters from bare branches. They are preceded in summer by groups of white flowers. The deciduous leaves are 2in (5cm) long. It forms a round-headed tree 20 × 10ft (6 × 3m) after ten years. 'Golden Hornet' carries bright yellow fruits and is a useful pollinator for dessert apples. Thrives in most soils except those which are waterlogged; needs little pruning.

Pernettya mucronata z 7
Small, cup-shaped, white flowers appear in summer on this evergreen shrub, followed by dense clusters of shiny, marble-like fruits. 'Mulberry Wine' has large magenta berries, 'Pink Pearl' lilac-pink, and 'Alba' white. They grow to 2ft (75cm), making a rounded mass of wiry stems. The small evergreen leaves are held close to the red stems. Grow in acid soil, in sun or semi-shade; good in peat beds and for growing with heathers and callunas. Plant in groups, ensuring one plant is a male. Prune back straggly shoots. Makes useful ground cover.

Prunus × subhirtella 'Autumnalis' z 6
(*above*)
Autumn or winter flowering cherry
This tree grows to 16ft (5m) in ten years. Small, white, semi-double flowers appear throughout the autumn, winter and spring on bare branches; the blooms may be damaged by severe weather conditions. The 2in (5cm)-long leaves have yellow-bronze autumn colours. 'Autumnalis Rosea' has rose pink flowers. Plant in fertile, moist soil, avoiding frost pockets or very exposed positions. Can also be grown as a multi-stemmed shrub. Slow to establish.

Rhododendron 'Praecox' z 5
This rhododendron bears funnel-shaped flowers in late winter and early spring. Two or three crimson-purple buds form at the tips of each shoot and open rose-purple. The flowers are held well above the glossy dark green leaves which are aromatic when crushed. Plants are sometimes part-deciduous. Makes a compact rounded bush only 3ft (90cm) high. The purplish-pink, crimson-spotted flowers of 'Tessa' open slightly later than 'Praecox'. Grow plants in acid, humus-rich soil; mulch regularly.

Sorbus cashmiriana z 2
Kashmir mountain ash
From autumn onwards pearl white fruits are borne in dense clusters on the bare branches of this ash. They are ⅖in (1cm) across, have reddish stalks and last well into winter. The pinnate leaves are 9in (23cm) long with numerous grey-green leaflets that turn yellow in autumn. Soft pink flowers appear in spring. Makes a small rounded tree or large shrub, reaching 10ft (3m) in ten years. *S. hupehensis* (z 5) has smaller fruits tipped pink. Does not need pruning. Suitable for most soils.

Symplocos paniculata z 5
Sapphire berry
The ultramarine, jewel-like fruits of this plant are dazzling. Carried in dense clusters, they follow the fragrant, white spring flowers. Small leaves turn yellow in autumn. It forms a dense, twiggy shrub or small tree up to 10ft (3m) tall in ten years. Plants need cross-pollination and only fruit fully after several seasons. Grow in rich, deep, non-alkaline soil, in a sheltered spot in sun or shade. Fruiting is most prolific after a hot, dry summer.

Viburnum × bodnantense 'Dawn' z 6
(*above*)
This deciduous viburnum has a strong, upright habit and grows to 8ft (2.4m). Clusters of sweetly scented, tubular, pink flowers appear from early winter through to spring. In 'Deben' the flowers are pink in bud opening white. Leaves are bronze-tinted in spring, maturing to green and turning reddish in autumn. The purple-green stems darken as they age. Thin out some of the oldest flowering stems each spring when fully established. Suitable for any soil; reasonably frost-tolerant.

Spring colour

FLOWERS

Berberis darwinii (*above*)   z 7

Clusters of double, cup-shaped, orange flowers are borne by this evergreen barberry from early spring onwards. The dark green, spiny leaves have silvery undersides. In autumn dark purple, bloomy fruits appear and some older leaves turn fiery orange and fall. Grows to 6 × 6ft (1.8 × 1.8m) in ten years. Underplant with the bright blue-flowered *Brunnera macrophylla*. Grow in sun or shade; avoid dry soils. Use at the back of a border or as a hedge.

Cercis siliquastrum (*below*)   z 6
Judas tree

In spring the branches and trunk of this plant are covered with clusters of pea-like, pink flowers. These are followed by kidney-shaped glaucous leaves, which turn yellow in autumn. Purple-tinged seedpods appear in late summer. Makes a small tree but gives more flowers as a multi-stemmed shrub, reaching 8 × 7ft (2.4 × 2.1m) in ten years. Grow in full sun and well-drained soil. Plants need little pruning until they are five years old. *C. canadensis* is hardier (z 4).

Chaenomeles × superba   z 5
Japanese quince or japonica

Forms of this vigorous, small- to medium-sized thorny shrub include 'Knap Hill Scarlet', with orange-scarlet flowers, and 'Pink Lady', rose-pink. Loose-petalled flowers appear in mild winters, but the main flush is in spring. Dark green deciduous leaves follow. The fragrant, yellow fruits can be used to make jelly. Grow freestanding or as a wall shrub in sun or shade; avoid alkaline soils which cause chlorosis. Prune back the previous season's growth after flowering.

Cornus florida   z 5
Flowering dogwood

This deciduous plant makes a beautiful specimen shrub or small tree. It is covered in blooms in spring, each "flower" actually consisting of four, slightly twisted, petal-like bracts that surround the insignificant true flowers. The oval leaves take on rich autumn colours. It reaches 13ft (4m) in ten years and needs acid or neutral soil and shelter from cold winds and frost. No pruning required.

Cytisus × praecox (*above*)   z 5
Warminster broom

The spindly, green stems of this shrub form a mass that makes 4 × 4ft (1.2 × 1.2m) in eight years. In spring the stems are weighed down by pea-like, light yellow flowers. 'Allgold' has long-lasting yellow flowers, 'Albus' pure white and 'Buttercup' golden-yellow flowers. The small deciduous leaves drop early in the season. Grows in full sun in most soils. Plants tend to be short-lived; they have weak root systems and need staking in exposed sites. Prune if necessary after flowering, removing one-year-old wood: never remove mature wood.

Erica arborea 'Alpina'   z 7

During spring this form of the evergreen tree heath is awash with frothy white flowers which complement the feathery foliage. The blooms have a strong honey-like fragrance. Making 6ft (1.8m) in ten years, it is a fine specimen shrub and gives height to a heather garden. Works well with a basal planting of *Erica carnea* or *Calluna vulgaris* in their various forms. 'Riverslea' has purple flowers but is less hardy. Needs acid soil and full sun or very slight shade. Prone to damage by high winds or snow: only prune to remove damaged growth.

Exochorda × macrantha 'The Bride' z 5
(*above*)

The graceful stems of this deciduous shrub are covered with racemes of small, white saucer-shaped flowers in spring. Each flower has five petals. The light green, lanceolate leaves are 3in (8cm) long and turn yellow in autumn. Plants grow upright for the first few years and then develop arching shoots, making a rounded bush, some 6ft (1.8m) high and often wider. Grow in a sunny position, avoiding alkaline soils. Remove a third of the old wood after flowering to encourage new growth.

Forsythia × intermedia   z 5

Forsythia carries masses of early spring, yellow flowers before the leaves emerge. This vigorous hybrid will grow to 12ft (3.6m) in ten years, but can be kept smaller with regular pruning. Plants have an upright habit when young but form a rounded shrub when mature. 'Spectabilis' is the most floriferous form. Cut back one third of the oldest wood immediately after flowering to encourage new shoots. Easy to grow, it succeeds in sun in all soils.

Magnolia × soulangiana (*above*)   z 6
Tulip magnolia
Large, loose-petalled, sweetly scented flowers appear on bare branches in spring, the white petals shaded pink with purple bases. Oval leaves open later. A small tree or a multi-stemmed shrub, it reaches 16ft (5m) in 20 years. 'Brozzonii' has huge white flowers, 'Rustica Rubra' reddish-purple, goblet-shaped flowers and 'Lennei' has rose-purple flowers with white insides; it may have a second flush in early autumn. Needs shelter and a heavy soil, enriched with compost. A superb specimen plant.

Prunus 'Okame'   z 7
This cherry is renowned for its display of clear pink flowers, which are carried in profusion in early spring. The flower buds are equally attractive. Trees bloom over a period of 2–3 weeks, and in autumn the leaves turn attractive shades of reddish-orange. In winter there is the added attraction of brownish-red bark. Plants grow to 25ft (8m) and have an upright oval shape. Quick growing in most soils in a sunny position.

Rhododendron luteum   z 5
Also known as *Azalea pontica*, this deciduous shrub can grow to 5 × 5ft (1.5 × 1.5m) in ten years. It tolerates poorer and drier conditions than most deciduous azaleas but still requires acid soil. The winter buds and young shoots are characteristically sticky. Funnel-shaped, yellow flowers appear in round heads, in advance of the leaves; they have a very strong fragrance. The leaves are oblong, 4in (10cm) long, and turn rich shades of orange-crimson in autumn. Growth tends to slow with age. Pruning is usually unnecessary.

Stachyurus praecox (*below*)   z 6
From early spring onwards this deciduous shrub bears plentiful frost-hardy, pale yellow flowers in small rigid racemes. Long, oval leaves with dark veins open later and turn yellow in autumn. Stems are purple-green. It makes a domed bush 6 × 6ft (1.8 × 1.8m) in five years. Underplant with *Helleborus orientalis* and *H. niger* or use it at the rear of a border. *S. chinensis* has smaller, more numerous flowers. Plant in sun or semi-shade in fertile soil. Once established, prune out a third of the older wood every few years.

Viburnum × carlcephalum (*below*)   z 5
This deciduous viburnum carries large heads of scented, white, tubular flowers, pink in bud. The grey-green leaves often take on orange-red colours in autumn. A rounded bush of compact habit, reaching 5 × 5ft (1.5 × 1.5m) in ten years, it makes a good specimen, or can be grown in a border or large tub. Grows well in most soils, but avoid extremes of dryness or wetness, which damage the surface root system. Plants need sun or partial shade to thrive. Remove any suckering growths that appear at the base.

FOLIAGE

Acer pseudoplatanus   z 5
'Brilliantissimum' (*above*)
This sycamore is a slow-growing, small deciduous tree, reaching 12ft (3.6m) in ten years. The spring foliage emerges bright shrimp pink, turns pale yellow-green and then green during the summer. Autumn leaves are usually yellow. It has an architectural quality, forming a rounded, mop-headed shape after three or four seasons. Succeeds in most soils, in full sun. Remove wood affected by coral spot disease.

Aesculus neglecta 'Erythroblastos'   z 5
Sunrise horse chestnut
A beautiful, slow-growing, medium-sized tree with spectacular spring foliage. The leaves are composed of five leaflets, each up to 6in (15cm) long. They unfold bright pink in spring, then fade over a period of weeks to a pale yellowish-green and finally turn yellow-orange in autumn. Pale yellow flowers appear in summer. It can reach 25ft (7.5m). Grow in any good soil; choose an open position in spring sun, with some protection from larger trees.

Cryptomeria japonica 'Elegans'   z 7
This cultivar of the evergreen Japanese cedar has small, drooping, awl-shaped leaves that make a dense head. In spring the foliage turns blue-green, also the colour of new growth. It assumes brown-bronze tints in winter; the change is sometimes so dramatic the plant appears to be dead. A rounded coniferous bush or small tree, it grows to 8 × 8ft (2.4 × 2.4m). The reddish, peeling bark is only really noticeable on older plants. 'Elegans Aurea' turns green-gold in winter. Grows best in moist soils.

Larix decidua *(below)* z 3
European larch
This deciduous conifer is beautiful in spring as the leaves emerge; light green and needle-like, they are held in rosettes along the shoots and are set off by the yellowish-brown bark. In autumn they turn golden-yellow. Mature trees produce pink-purple female cones, along with smaller yellowish male cones. Quickly forms a large cone-shaped tree, reaching 60ft (18m); the branches droop with age. Avoid wet soils.

Photinia × fraseri 'Red Robin' z 7
(below)
This evergreen shrub makes its boldest statement in spring. Red leaves appear in autumn, the colour intensifying during winter, so that by spring the plant is covered with flaming foliage. Leaves continue to appear until mid-summer, when they turn bronze and then green with age. White flowers may open in spring. Plants can grow to 6ft (1.8m) in height in ten years, with a rounded habit. Mature specimens are a good support for a summer-flowering clematis. Plant in full sun, and add plenty of compost to the soil. Prune hard every few years.

Pieris formosa forrestii z 7
'Forest Flame'
An acid-loving evergreen shrub, ideal for a woodland garden. Fiery red foliage opens at the shoot tips in spring. The small lanceolate leaves change to shrimp pink, then white, and finally to dark green as summer progresses. Sprays of slightly fragrant, white, lily-of-the-valley-like flowers appear in late spring. Plants can reach up to 6ft (1.8m) in height when mature, and need little pruning. Avoid full sun and alkaline soils; add leaf mould at planting. Protect from cold winds.

Spiraea japonica 'Goldflame' z 5
An easily grown, deciduous shrub that reaches only 2ft (60cm) in height after ten years, this plant is a useful addition to the shrub or mixed border. In spring the brownish-red stems are adorned with new apricot-orange leaves; these turn orange-red and then golden-yellow as the season progresses. Reddish-pink flowers appear in summer. Grow as a specimen or in groups, avoiding strong sun (which can scorch the leaves) and dry and alkaline soils. Prune plants to ground level in spring to encourage healthy re-growth.

Viburnum opulus 'Aureum' *(above)* z 3
This yellow-leaved form of the guelder rose is useful in moist soil and for wilder parts of the garden. The deciduous leaves are 2-5in (5-13cm) long with five lobes. New spring growth is bright yellow, ageing to greenish-yellow during summer. It reaches 6ft (1.8m) in ten years and can be left unpruned; alternatively, a third of the oldest shoots can be cut to ground level every two or three years once the plant is established. Protect from strong, direct sun which scorches the leaves.

FLOWERS

Aesculus × carnea 'Briottii' z 4
This compact form of the red horse chestnut will reach 20ft (6m) in ten years, forming an oval-canopied tree. It has upright, 10in (25cm)-long panicles of deep reddish-pink flowers in early summer. The dark deciduous leaves are digitate and up to 1ft (30cm) across; they turn deep orange-yellow in autumn. The "conkers" (fruits) are smooth-coated. Plant in moist soil, avoiding high alkalinity, in full sun. Casts deep, unfruitful shade so best-suited to the larger garden.

Buddleja davidii *(above)* z 5
Butterfly bush
Fragrant, tubular flowers, held in large racemes, appear on this arching shrub from summer to early autumn. Deciduous lanceolate leaves are 4-12in (10-30cm) long and are light green with silvery-grey undersides. Forms include: 'Black Knight' (velvety-purple flowers) and 'Peace' (white with orange eyes). Grows to 10ft (3m) in five years in the poorest soils. Spreads by seed; can become a weed. Prune hard back in early spring to 4in (10cm) from the base.

Calycanthus floridus z 4
Carolina allspice
During summer this shrub bears red-brown, star-like, scented flowers on wood that is more than two seasons old. These are set off by the light green, deciduous leaves, which have downy undersides and are aromatic if crushed. In autumn the foliage turns yellow. It reaches 6 × 6ft (1.8 × 1.8m) in ten years, with a rounded habit. Grow in deep, rich, alkaline-free soil, in diffused shade, as found under a light tree canopy. Pruning is not necessary.

Crataegus laevigata 'Crimson Cloud' z 4
(*above*)
Also listed as *C. oxycantha*, this
hawthorn is a deciduous, spiny tree that
reaches 20ft (6m) with a rounded
crown. The small leaves are lobed, grey-
green, and often have attractive yellow
tints in autumn. However, the flowers
are the greatest asset. Held in dense
clusters, they are deep red with a white
patch at the base of each petal. 'Paul's
Scarlet' has double flowers. Bunches of
shiny red berries follow in autumn and
persist for at least six weeks. Prune only
to remove suckers. Avoid over-dry soils.

Deutzia × elegantissima 'Rosealind' z 5
(*below*)
The arching stems of this shrub are
covered with dense corymbs of pink,
five-petalled, fragrant flowers from late
spring to early summer. The oval,
deciduous leaves are slightly rough.
Plants reach 6ft (1.8m) and should have
a third of the oldest wood removed after
flowering. Train a large-flowered
clematis through the branches. Plants
need moist fertile soil and regular
watering during periods of drought.
Select a sheltered spot.

Enkianthus campanulatus z 4
A member of the heather family, this
deciduous shrub flowers in early
summer, producing clusters of waxy,
bell-like blooms, creamy-yellow with
red stripes. Growth is bushy and
upright, reaching about 13ft (4m) with a
spread of 8ft (2.4m); the base of mature
plants is open. The glossy green leaves
turn shades of orange, red and scarlet in
autumn. 'Red Bells' has more
prominent stripes. Cut back one or two
shoots each season. Plants need lime-
free soil and grow best in partial shade
in moist, deep, acid soil. They are
excellent for a woodland garden.

Halesia carolina z 5
Snowdrop tree or Carolina silverbell
This spreading deciduous shrub grows
12ft (3.6m) tall in ten years. Clusters of
nodding, pure white flowers cover the
branches in early summer. Four-winged
fruits follow as the flowers fade. The
deciduous oval leaves are pale green,
yellow in autumn. *H. monticola vestita*
has larger flowers that can be tinged
pink. Grows well in moist, acid soil,
high in organic matter in a protected
site. Takes two or three seasons to
establish; needs no pruning.

Kalmia latifolia (*above*) z 5
Calico bush or mountain laurel
This rhododendron-like evergreen
shrub is one of the most beautiful
summer-flowering plants for an acid
soil. In early summer the striking buds
open into clusters of pink flowers.
These last for several weeks, framed by
the narrow, glossy, mid-green leaves. It
makes a rounded bush, 10 × 10ft (3 ×
3m). Full sun is needed for maximum
flowering. Soil should be deep and
moist. Does not need pruning, except
for shaping when young.

Koelreuteria paniculata z 6
**Golden rain tree, Chinese rain tree or
Pride of India**
This excellent tree reaches upwards of
20ft (6m) in 20 years. Upright terminal
panicles, 1ft (30cm) long, hold small,
yellow flowers in mid- to late summer.
These are followed by three-lobed,
bladder-like fruits which are pale green
with a reddish tint, turning yellow-
brown in autumn. The light brownish-
green bark is also attractive. Needs full
sun and a well-drained soil; tolerant of
heat and drought, alkaline soil and
atmospheric pollution.

Kolkwitzia amabilis (*above*) z 4
Beauty bush
A hardy shrub with slender, drooping
branches, clothed in bell-shaped, pink,
yellow-throated flowers in summer. The
calyxes and flower stalks are hairy. It
forms a vase-shaped bush of 6ft (1.8m)
in ten years, and is suited to the rear of
a border. The small, deciduous leaves
are tooth-edged. Peeling, silvery-brown
bark gives winter interest. 'Pink Cloud'
has larger flowers. Grows in most soils,
needing full sun. Cut a third of the old
wood to ground level after flowering.

Paulownia tomentosa z 6
Princess or foxglove tree
Panicles of brown buds form in autumn
on plants that are at least five years old;
these open the following spring as blue-
mauve, foxglove-like flowers. Lobed,
deciduous leaves, up to 10in (25cm)
long, appear after the flowers. Reaches
16ft (5m) in 20 years. If only foliage is
required, cut stems hard back in spring
to produce vigorous shoots with
enormous leaves, 2ft (60cm) across.
Some damage to buds is likely in severe
weather, even in a sheltered site. Needs
deep, rich, soil and full sun.

Rubus × tridel 'Benenden' (*above*) z 5
This vigorous, shrubby rubus has arching, thornless, reddish canes and grows to 10ft (3m). The blackberry-like, deciduous leaves are lobed and turn yellow in autumn. In summer it carries 2in (5cm)-wide white flowers with clusters of yellow stamens. Good on most soils and happy in some shade. Prune a third of the oldest shoots out after flowering; new growth will reach 6ft (1.8m) in a year. This form has larger flowers than the type. Old shoots have peeling bark.

Syringa meyeri 'Palibin' z 3
Korean lilac
This smaller-growing relative of *S. vulgaris* is suitable for planting in a container as well as in the open garden. It grows slowly, forming a low, neat shrub 4ft (1.2m) high. During summer it is covered with small trusses of pale lilac-pink, fragrant flowers; this is particularly true of younger plants. The deciduous leaves are rounded, up to 3in (8cm) long, with a velvety texture; they turn yellow in autumn. Succeeds in any fertile soil and flowers best in partial shade. Pruning unnecessary.

Viburnum opulus 'Roseum' z 3
Snowball shrub
Also classified as *V. opulus* 'Sterile', this form of the guelder rose has creamy-white, snowball-like heads of sterile flowers which weigh down the spreading branches in summer. The light green deciduous leaves often turn attractive shades in autumn. Quickly reaching 12ft (3.6m), it can be left to form a mound; alternatively, a third of the oldest shoots can be pruned back in spring. Grows in all soils, even with extremes of dryness or wetness. Non-fruiting.

FOLIAGE

Berberis × ottawensis 'Purpurea' z 5
A vigorous, deciduous barberry which reaches 12ft (3.6m), it carries large, purple, ovate leaves along the upright, thorny shoots. Racemes of golden-yellow flowers form in spring, hanging clusters of red berries in autumn. Useful as an informal hedge or planted with white or gold variegated shrubs such as *Rhamnus alaternus* 'Argenteovariegata'. *B. thunbergii* 'Rose Glow' is smaller, with pinky-white leaves. Grow in full sun; avoid over-dry soils. Prune out a few old stems occasionally.

Cotinus coggygria 'Royal Purple' z 4
(*above*)
Smoke tree or bush
The leaves of this deciduous shrub open a deep wine red, changing through the growing season to a velvety maroon. They are rounded and turn shades of orange, scarlet and red in autumn. Plume-like panicles of pink blossom are at their best in late summer. The plant reaches 10ft (3m) if left unpruned, or it can be cut back each spring to produce vigorous 6ft (1.8m) shoots with large leaves but no flowers. Plant in rich, deep soil, in a sunny position.

Gleditsia triacanthos 'Sunburst' z 5
Golden honey locust
Vibrant, golden-yellow, late spring foliage characterizes this plant. The leaves are pinnate or bipinnate. It makes an elegantly branching tree, 13ft (4m) tall after five years; on older plants the bark is deeply fissured. It does not bear the vicious spines of the species. An ideal host for *Clematis macropetala*. Needs rich, well-drained soil, full sun and protection from winds as branches are brittle. Prune for shape when young.

Pyrus salicifolia 'Pendula' (*above*) z 5
Weeping silver pear
Few small trees are as graceful as this specimen plant. In spring the small, lanceolate leaves open with a silvery down and are followed by small clusters of creamy-white flowers. Reaching its full height of about 15ft (4.5m) in 15 years, its pendulous branches sweep to the ground. Mature plants have a mop-headed appearance. In summer the foliage is a cool greenish-grey. Spring-flowering blue or purple clematis make excellent companions. Grows in most soils and needs full sun.

Rhododendron yakushimanum z 6
This dome-shaped evergreen rhododendron has unusual young leaves that resemble silvery shuttlecocks. They appear from a collar of older, dark green, leathery leaves which are 2in (5cm) long and have brown, felted undersides. The silver hairs disappear as the leaves mature. Trusses of flowers open earlier, apple-blossom pink, fading to white. Very slow-growing, reaching 3-4ft (90-120cm) in ten years, it needs a well-drained, acid soil in some shade but no pruning.

Robinia pseudoacacia 'Frisia' z 4
Golden false acacia
Similar to, if more slender than *Gleditsia triacanthos* 'Sunburst', this tree has 6in (15cm)-long pinnate leaves that open bright yellow-green in late spring, turn green during summer and butter yellow in autumn. The petioles are orange. Mature trees bear clusters of pea-like white flowers in mid-summer. It grows rapidly, achieving 20ft (6m) in 20 years. Container-grown specimens establish themselves best. Needs moist, well-drained loam and shelter from winds.

Autumn colour

Sambucus racemosa 'Plumosa Aurea'
(*below*)   z 4
This form of the red-berried elder is one
of the finest deciduous shrubs for
golden-yellow foliage. The fern-like,
dissected, pinnate leaves are 3-6in (8-
15cm) long and wide. The largest leaves
are produced by plants that are pruned
hard back each spring: unpruned plants
bear large panicles of white flowers,
followed by translucent red berries. It
can reach 6ft (1.8m) but annual pruning
will reduce height and spread. Most
soils are suitable; some shade is good, to
protect the leaves from sun-scorch.

Sorbus aria   z 5
Whitebeam
In spring leaves emerge greyish-white
on this tree and turn bright green
above, with dense silvery-grey hairs
beneath. Autumn leaves are brownish-
yellow. In early summer 4in (10cm)-
wide panicles of white flowers appear,
followed by bunches of scarlet fruits. It
reaches 20ft (6m) in ten years with a
rounded crown. The leaves of
'Lutescens' have creamy-white hairs. A
fine specimen tree, it can also be trained
over a wall, archway or pillar. Most soils
are suitable; tolerates alkalinity.

Weigela florida 'Foliis Purpureis'   z 5
The leaves of this deciduous shrub are
flushed purple in spring and darken
during summer. Foxglove-like purple-
pink flowers appear in late spring along
the arching branches. 'Variegata' has
leaves with creamy-white margins and
pink flowers, while 'Looymansii Aurea'
has golden foliage and pale pink flowers.
Plants grow in all types of soil, reaching
2 × 2ft (60 × 60cm). To maintain good
leaf colour on established plants, prune
out a third of the old wood in early
summer after flowering.

FOLIAGE

Acer japonicum (*above*)   z 5
Japanese maple
The large, lobed, red-veined leaves of
this tree turn red in autumn. 'Aureum'
has golden-yellow summer foliage and
darker autumn colour; 'Vitifolium' has
fan-shaped leaves that turn plum-
purple; 'Aconitifolium' has dissected
leaves with orange-red autumn tints.
Groups of reddish-purple flowers form
from early spring. The spreading open
habit reaches 10ft (3m). Needs slightly
acid, moist soil; best in partial shade.

Amelanchier lamarckii (*below*)   z 4
Snowy mespilus or juneberry
Crimson, orange and red autumn foliage
adorns this plant. The small leaves open
coppery-pink. Plentiful sprays of star-
shaped, white spring flowers become
scarlet fruits in summer; these turn
black in autumn. 'Ballerina' has more
abundant pink-tinged flowers but less
striking autumn foliage. Makes a small
cone-shaped tree or multi-stemmed
shrub of 20ft (6m) in 20 years. Use
against a dark background or as a lawn
specimen. Plants need moist soil and
little pruning.

Euonymus sachalinensis (*below*)   z 5
This shrub has large leaves which turn
orange-red in autumn, enhanced by red
fruits with deep pink seeds. The leaves
open dark green and have a reddish
tinge in summer. Makes 13 × 13ft (4 ×
4m) in ten years. *E. europaeus*
'Atropurpureus' has purple summer
foliage and red autumn colour; *E. e.*
'Aucubifolius' has yellow and white
mottled leaves, tinted pink in autumn.
E. alatus 'Compacta' is the dwarf form
of 'Burning Bush' and has scarlet
autumn foliage and red fruits. Needs
sun; will grow on alkaline soil.

Fraxinus oxycarpa 'Raywood'   z 6
Raywood ash
This ash is beautiful in autumn when its
10in (25cm)-long pinnate leaves turn
reddish-purple. Clusters of creamy-
white, petalless, fragrant flowers appear
in late spring, developing into small,
orange-brown, key-like fruits. The
canopy broadens with age and makes it
a fine specimen tree, reaching 35ft
(10.5m) in 20 years. It casts only slight
shade, useful for underplanting. 'Flame'
has brilliant red autumn leaves. Grow in
any soil, in full sun.

Hydrangea quercifolia   z 5
Oak-leaf hydrangea
The large, deciduous, oak-shaped leaves
of this shrubby hydrangea turn bright
reddish-orange to purple in autumn.
From late summer the plant carries
conical panicles of white flowers which
fade to pink as they age and turn brown
in winter. Growth is slow, making a
rounded bush of 4 × 4ft (1.2 × 1.2m)
after ten years. Shoots tend to be brittle.
Thrives in sun or shade and grows in
most fertile, moist soils. Can be wall
trained. Pruning is unnecessary, but
plants will re-grow if cut back.

Liquidambar styraciflua (*below*)   z 5
Sweet gum
Similar to the maple, this tree differs in having alternate lobed leaves which release a distinctive aromatic fragrance when crushed; they turn red with hints of yellow, orange and purple in autumn. Slow to establish, it can reach 20ft (6m) in 20 years with a regular, conical canopy. Older trees have fissured bark. 'Worplesdon' and 'Lane Roberts' have more upright-growing branches and deep crimson-purple autumn foliage. Grow in full sun in rich, moist soil.

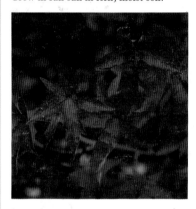

Malus tschonoskii (*below*)   z 6
Of all the crab apples, this species has the most spectacular autumn colours, the leaves turning yellow, then shades of red, crimson and orange. Clusters of rose-pink spring flowers are followed by yellow-brown fruits. This species has an upright habit, growing up to 25ft (7.5m) in height in 20 years, with a spread of 5-10ft (1.5-3m). Enliven the grey-green summer foliage with the climbers *Clematis macropetala* or *C.* 'Bill Mackenzie', which have bluish-mauve macropetals and yellow flowers respectively. Grow plants in sun in moist, rich soil.

Prunus sargentii (*above*)   z 5
Sargent's cherry
One of the first trees to colour-up in autumn, this has brilliant orange and crimson foliage. In spring the abundant pale pink flowers are followed by the leaves which open bronzy-red and turn dark green with strong veins. Chestnut-brown bark is a feature of older trees. It can reach 20 × 16ft (6 × 5m) in ten years. Grow singly or in a small group; underplant with spring bulbs such as *Narcissus triandrus* 'Thalia'. Best in full sun; needs moist, rich soil.

Quercus coccinea   z 4
Scarlet oak
During autumn the foliage of this tree turns scarlet, branch by branch, before falling; some leaves often persist until mid-winter. The leaves are up to 6in (15cm) long, deeply-lobed with bristly tips; they are light green in summer. Slow to establish, the tree reaches 23ft (7m) in ten years and ultimately 70ft (21m), with an open, broad crown. The red oak, *Q. rubra*, is over 100ft (30m) tall when mature, with 10in (25cm)-long matt leaves. Best in full sun, on acid soil. Tolerates pollution.

Spiraea prunifolia   z 4
Bridal wreath spiraea
The arching branches of this dense-growing shrub are ablaze with colour in autumn when the finely toothed leaves turn bright orangey-red. The branches can reach 6ft (1.8m) and are clothed in spring with button-like, double, white flowers. The leaves are mid-green in summer. Stands out against dark plants and works well with an underplanting of low-growing bamboos. Grows in moderate shade or full sun; avoid alkaline soils. Prune out a third of the older wood after flowering.

BERRIES AND FRUIT

Callicarpa bodinieri giraldii (*below*)   z 6
Clusters of lilac-purple fruits form on this deciduous shrub in autumn and can last for several months. The dull green, lanceolate leaves turn purplish at the same time. Small, mauve flowers appear in late summer. The upright stems reach 6ft (1.8m) after ten years. 'Profusion' is a particularly reliable form with larger fruits. Plant in acid soil with added leaf mould; may suffer in hot, dry summers on thin soil. Grow more than one plant to guarantee berries.

Clerodendrum trichotomum fargesii (*below*)   z 6
This shrub is a remarkable sight when mature. In late summer the delicate buds open into fragrant, star-like, white flowers, set in maroon calyxes. Electric blue fruits follow, held in the now deep red calyxes. The large, deciduous leaves have a fetid smell if crushed; they take on purple tints in autumn. It makes 8 × 8ft (2.4 × 2.4m) in ten years. Grow in some shade, in moist, non-alkaline soil. Prune out winter damage. The fruits glow in sunlight. Prone to whitefly, mealy bug and red spider mite.

Cotoneaster × watereri 'Cornubia' z 6
(*above*)
This semi-evergreen vigorous shrub is one of the finest tall cotoneasters. In autumn its branches are weighed down by bunches of bright red berries. These are preceded in early summer by clusters of white flowers. The small dark green leaves are lanceolate. Graceful with spreading branches, it makes 10 × 10ft (3 × 3m) in ten years. 'Rothschildianus' has clusters of yellow fruits and can make a small, single-stemmed tree. *C. × watereri* has large crops of orange-red berries. Grow in full sun or part shade in moist, fertile soil.

Malus 'John Downie' z 5
Probably the finest fruiting crab apple, this forms a medium-sized tree some 26ft (8m) tall when mature. The white, spring flowers are followed by small fruits which turn bright orange-scarlet in late summer and autumn. They are edible and used for jelly. 'Professor Sprenger' has amber fruits which persist into winter, 'Dartmouth' has large, reddish-purple fruits. Grow in full sun on moist, fertile soil. Prune to allow light in to ripen the fruit.

Pyracantha 'Mohave' z 6
This stiff-growing, evergreen shrub makes a 6ft (1.8m) vase-shaped specimen in ten years. Abundant small, white summer flowers are followed by orange-red berries that persist into winter, birds permitting. Leaves are dark green and shiny. It is good for windy areas and resistant to fireblight and scab. 'Orange Glow' has dark stems and large clusters of orange fruits. 'Shawnee' has orange-yellow berries that colour early. Full sun gives the best berries, on moist, rich soil.

Sorbus commixta (*below*) z 5
Scarlet rowan
This tree not only has clusters of large, bright red berries in autumn but also dramatic foliage colour. The large pinnate leaves emerge coppery in spring, turn glossy green in summer, then purple and finally flaming scarlet during autumn. It has a columnar habit when young, broadening with age, and reaches 16ft (5m) in ten years. *S. aucuparia* 'Beissneri' has shiny coppery-orange stems. Needs full sun and grows on most soils, including alkaline.

Viburnum opulus 'Fructuluteo' z 3
(*below*)
This form of the guelder rose carries bunches of translucent, lemon yellow, pink-tinged fruits in autumn. They are preceded by corymbs of white flowers. Large, lobed, light green leaves take on warm shades in autumn. For larger flowers and golden-yellow fruits which darken as they ripen, grow the cultivar 'Xanthocarpum'; 'Notcutt's Variety' has red fruits. The spreading habit reaches 8ft (2.4m) in ten years. Plants are tolerant of most soils, dry or wet. Prune out one-third of old wood annually, or leave to grow freely.

FLOWERS

Abelia × grandiflora (*above*) z 6
This semi-evergreen shrub carries pale pink, slightly scented flowers on its arching branches from late summer into autumn. It grows to 5 × 5ft (1.5 × 1.5m) in ten years, rarely any taller. Olive green ovate leaves are up to 2in (6cm) long. 'Francis Mason' has gold-variegated leaves. A good companion for autumn-flowering bulbs such as *Schizostylis coccinea*. Prune out a third of the old shoots in early spring; take care as the branches are brittle. Grow in moist soil, in full sun.

Ceanothus 'Autumnal Blue' z 8
One of the hardiest evergreen forms of the Californian lilac, this densely-growing, bushy shrub carries panicles of fluffy, dark blue flowers from late summer onwards. Green stems bear leaves that are shiny green above, grey below. Reaches 10ft (3m) in ten years. Use at the back of a border or as a host for a spring-flowering scrambling climber such as *Clematis* 'Marie Boisselot'. Can be wall-trained. Needs full sun and deep, rich soil. If damaged in winter cut hard back.

Hydrangea paniculata 'Grandiflora' z 4
Flowering from late summer into autumn, this makes a spectacular specimen plant. The huge panicles of white, sterile florets fade to pink before turning brown. Each panicle can be 18 × 12in (45 × 30cm). The broad leaves turn yellow in autumn. For the best flowers, cut back all shoots in spring to within two buds of the base: regrowth will be 10 × 10ft (3 × 3m) in ten years. Protect from strong winds if grown as a standard as the stems are brittle. Needs slight shade and deep, rich, moist soil.

CLIMBERS AND WALL SHRUBS

Garden walls present the best opportunities for growing climbers and shrubs that benefit from the support and protection offered, whether it be from the cold, the wind or the sun. Trellis, screens, pergolas, arcades, arbours and summer houses (see pages 164-173, 228-233) also provide good support for climbers and have an immediate impact on the garden while introducing a valuable vertical element.

Certain plants are better suited to specific structures according to their vigour and means of attachment. Reasonably vigorous twining climbers that provide adequate cover without swamping the structure are suited to pergolas and arbours. Either a single species, such as wisteria, can be used to create a spec-

tacular display at one time of the year or a collection of plants, including *Clematis armandii* and *Vitis vinifera* 'Purpurea', can be used to provide a succession of flowering and foliage interest.

Slow-growing scramblers, such as roses and *Jasminum nudiflorum*, that require careful tying in because they do not actually attach themselves to the structure, work well on small trellis screens; while self-clinging climbers such as ivies, *Schizophragma* and *Hydrangea petiolaris*, are best suited to walls which provide a suitable surface for their aerial roots or suckers to adhere to. The habit of a plant may also make it suitable for growing against a wall. *Kerria japonica*, *Pyracantha coccinea*, *Chaenomeles* species,

Right: Parthenocissus tricuspidata, the Boston ivy, is a vigorous climber that turns crimson-purple in the autumn. It attaches itself to walls by means of sticky tendrils and is tolerant of shady conditions.

Left: Pyracantha coccinea is a vigorous, evergreen shrub of stiff, erect habit suitable for training against a shady wall. In late spring or early summer it is covered with small, white flowers, which are followed by a plentiful crop of orange berries. These specimens, trained to great effect like espalier fruit trees, should be trimmed in early autumn.

Forsythia suspensa and *Robinia hispida* all have fairly stiff, upright stems that grow close to the wall and can be pruned and trained to fill the available space.

Climbers that hook their stems onto the support with the help of coiling tendrils need wires to wrap themselves around, or alternatively are well adapted to threading their way through other plants as they do in their wild state. When choosing a host plant the climber's vigour should be taken into account.

Many other factors will govern the choice of plants. The style of the garden dictates whether the plants should be slow-growing and neatly tied in to give a controlled form or whether they should be given a fairly free rein to grow at will. For example, the relaxed effect that is achieved by allowing honeysuckle to cascade over a structure with its scent mingling with that of other vigorous climbers, such as rambling roses and summer jasmine, is perfect for a cottage, romantic or wild garden. In contrast, a strictly pruned and flat-trained *Magnolia grandiflora* with its large, smooth, architectural leaves and single, stiff, waxy-white summer flowers, would be a fitting focal point in an enclosed courtyard.

It may be that a fast-growing climber is required to camouflage an ugly building or cover a trellis screen placed in front of an eyesore: *Persicaria aubertii* (the mile-a-minute or Russian vine), *Parthenocissus quinquefolia*, Virginia creeper and the related *P. tricuspi-data* (the Boston ivy), *Vitis coignetiae* (the crimson glory vine), *Celastrus orbiculatus* (the Oriental bittersweet), *Akebia quinata* and *Clematis montana* are all suitable for this purpose. However, these plants need a lot of space and require constant pruning or have to be replaced in order to prevent them from swamping all other nearby plants, lifting tiles or blocking gutters. Their speed of growth, which can be their greatest asset, has also earned them a bad reputation.

In fact most climbers are fast growers which need pruning and tying in to keep them under control. Some need near constant attention, others can be attended to once a year, either in the winter or in early spring or after flowering, depending on the requirements of the plant. It is always advisable to ensure that the structure is sound before the plant starts to cover it and that it is large enough to accommodate the plant when mature.

The aspect of the wall is an important consideration when choosing suitable plants to clothe it. A protected wall that receives the sun for most of the day is likely to be several degrees warmer than one that receives little direct sunlight. Marginally hardy plants can survive when grown against such south-facing, warm walls. For example, in areas where *Clematis montana* is perfectly hardy, *C. armandii* will require a southern aspect. Many Californian and Central American species such as the attractive *Ceanothus* and

Below: Climbers are particularly useful in the garden to create quick screens and an instant vertical element. Here, a large-leaved evergreen ivy, *Hedera colchica* 'Dentata Variegata', mingles with the autumnal foliage of *Parthenocissus quinquefolia*, the Virginia creeper, to create a "volcanic" effect. On the left is the herbaceous golden hop, *Humulus lupulus* 'Aureus'.

Right: Wisterias are fast-growing climbers with flowers that are generally violet-blue to mauve. There are also white- and pink-flowered forms of the commonly grown species which are attractive alternatives, as can be seen from this salmon pink variety.

Fremontodendron californicum will flourish in temperate climates when grown against a wall. *Magnolia grandiflora* makes a large freestanding tree in Mediterranean climates but will also survive and flower in areas where the summer rainfall is higher and season shorter when placed against a wall. The way in which a wall absorbs and then releases heat produces not only additional winter warmth and hotter summers but also extends the season, allowing the wood to ripen well and survive the winter cold.

In contrast, there are many plants that prefer shady situations – including *Jasminum nudiflorum*, *Kerria japonica*, *Garrya elliptica*, *Berberidopsis corallina* and *Lapageria rosea* – but this does not necessarily mean that they are frost-hardy; many shade-loving climbers are still tender. There are also a number of plants that tolerate the poorest conditions and are able to clothe seemingly inhospitable walls. These include ivies as well as the climbing *Euonymus radicans*, *Parthenocissus* species and *Hydrangea petiolaris*.

Camellias, winter sweet (*Chimonanthus praecox*) and *Jasminum nudiflorum* which blossom early in spring, when there is still a risk of frost, benefit from growing against a wall that does not receive direct morning sun, because this would defrost the blooms too quickly and damage them.

A notable way of extending the season of certain plants and adding a new dimension to a design is to grow climbers through other plants. The most vigorous climbers such as *Vitis coignetiae*, *Celastrus orbiculatus* and *Wisteria sinensis* are successful only in tall trees, but there are a number of other species that grow happily through shrubs without swamping them. Clematis are the most frequently used in this instance. Herbaceous climbers such as *Codonopsis convolvulacea*, *Tropaeolum speciosum* and *Lathyrus grandiflorus* are also well suited.

Left: Clematis 'Perle d'Azur' is an outstanding large-flowered cultivar, which is covered in blossom in late summer.

Below: Wisteria has traditionally adorned the warm, sunny face of many country houses. The scented, pea-like flowers are produced abundantly if specimens are pruned in summer, after flowering, and again, more severely, in winter, when plants are dormant.

Quick-growing

FLOWERS

Clematis × jackmanii (*above*)   z 5
A succession of large, velvety, purple
blooms cover this clematis from early to
mid-summer or even into autumn.
Cultivars include 'Gypsy Queen' (violet-
purple), 'Perle d'Azur (pale blue) and
'Comtesse de Bouchaud' (pink). Grow
through *Pyrus salicifolia* 'Pendula', with
its silver-grey foliage, and underplant
with *Allium christophii* and *Geranium
endressii*. Reaches 10 × 3ft (3m × 90cm)
in moisture-rich soil; prune hard in late
winter or early spring to within 3ft
(90cm) of the ground.

Clematis montana (*above*)   z 5
In late spring this plant is covered with
four-petalled, vanilla-scented, creamy-
white flowers. Use it to brighten a
north-facing wall or grow it through a
deciduous tree for early colour. Reaches
20ft (6m) in ten years. 'Elizabeth' has
soft pink flowers, 'Picton's Variety'
deep pink and 'Grandiflora' pure white.
C. montana rubens has pink flowers with
golden stamens and bronze foliage.
Plant with the roots in shade in moist,
rich soil. Prune immediately after
flowering to prevent rampancy.

Lonicera japonica 'Halliana'   z 4
The flowers of this honeysuckle open
white and change to orangey-yellow as
they age. They are produced throughout
the summer and have a strong
fragrance. Small, shiny, black berries
follow the flowers. The foliage is bright
green. It quickly covers a pergola or
garden structure, and can also be used
as ground cover. Grows in most soils, in
sun or shade. Prune hard back in early
spring to prevent growth developing
into a knotted mass.

Wisteria sinensis (*above*)   z 5
Chinese wisteria
Racemes of mauve or white scented
flowers appear in early summer, before
the long compound leaves. 'Black
Dragon' has dark purple blooms, 'Alba'
white. It achieves 30ft (9m) if grown in
full sun on a wall or pergola, and up to
100ft (30m) in a tree. Twines
anticlockwise; the hardier Japanese
wisteria, *W. floribunda*, spirals
clockwise. Cut back in late winter and
reduce shoots in late summer. In cold
areas protect from early frosts. Plant
containerized specimens year-round.

FOLIAGE

Aristolochia macrophylla   z 4
Dutchman's pipe
With heart-shaped, bright green leaves
some 12in (30cm) long, this climber has
a tropical look. It reaches 20ft (6m) in
ten years on a wall, fence, over a tree
stump or in a tree. Pairs of small
tubular flowers open in mid- to late
summer in the leaf axils; they are
greenish-yellow and purplish-brown.
A. tomentosa is less vigorous, growing to
10ft (3m), with smaller dark, evergreen
leaves. Needs a good fertile soil. Prune
lightly in late summer or early spring.

Hedera colchica 'Dentata Variegata' z 5
This Persian ivy has the largest leaves of
the genus and is an ideal evergreen
backcloth to autumn-fruiting climbers
and wall shrubs. The large, leathery
leaves are creamy-yellow with irregular,
rolled margins; when crushed they give
off a spicy smell. It climbs to over 12ft
(3.6m) over a wall or pergola. Virginia
creeper, *Parthenocissus quinquefolia*, is a
good partner, with its crimson autumn
foliage. Grows in sun or deep shade in
any good soil. Trim back frost-bitten
growth in spring.

Holboellia coriacea   z 9
A vigorous twiner, reaching 20ft (6m),
with glossy, evergreen leaves composed
of three leaflets. The spring flowers have
a sweet, strong scent. Cylindrical,
bloomy, purple pods follow in long hot
summers if the plant is in sun. Grow
through a tree with an open habit, or on
a sunny wall with other sun-loving
climbers such as the double, yellow-
flowered *Rosa banksiae* 'Lutea'. Plant in
fertile, well-drained soil and only prune
to keep the plant within bounds.

AUTUMN COLOUR

Akebia quinata (*above*)   z 4
After a mild spring and hot summer,
this vigorous twining shrub produces
dark purple, sausage-shaped fruits
which split to reveal black seeds bedded
in white flesh. The leaves comprise five
notched leaflets. Reddish-purple,
fragrant flowers appear from spring
onwards. It is evergreen in mild areas,
deciduous in cold. Reaching 33ft (10m),
it can be trained over a tree, hedge, wall
or pergola. Suits most soils; needs sun
to fruit. Prune after flowering, leaving
some branches if fruiting is likely.

Ampelopsis brevipedunculata (*below*) z 4

Grown for its attractive fruits, this climber can reach 8ft (2.4m). It has three- or five-lobed leaves, dark green above and paler and hairy underneath. The flowers appear in late summer, followed by masses of small fruits which turn from white to china blue to deep purple after a long hot summer. Grow in fertile soil, in sun. Plants need to be supported and trained, and are useful for covering walls and growing into trees. Fruiting and winter-hardiness is encouraged by restricting the roots.

Persicaria aubertii z 4
Russian vine

The tightly twining, hairy stems of this climber reach 25ft (7.5m) in ten years. It is one of the best plants for clothing old stumps, bare banks, garden structures, and unsightly fencing. The leaves are heart-shaped. Frothy, creamy-white panicles of flowers appear in summer, followed by rust-coloured seed heads. Cut some vines back to ground level in spring to prevent the plant becoming a tangled mass. Grows in almost any soil, in sun or partial shade.

Pyracantha coccinea z 6

This firethorn quickly makes a freestanding wall shrub 10ft (3m) tall. Evergreen, with sharp woody spines, the branches are covered with hawthorn-like masses of flowers in summer, followed by dense clusters of orange-red fruits. In a mild winter, fruits last until the following spring. The dark green leaves are oval and finely-toothed. Cut back long growths after flowering. Grow with other summer-flowering climbers. Grows happily on north- or east-facing walls, in any fertile soil; tolerates pollution.

Vitis 'Brant' (*above*) z 6

Also listed as *V.vinifera* 'Brant', this popular, hardy, fruiting vine is capable of growing to 30ft (10m) on suitable supports. It produces sweet, edible aromatic bunches of grapes, which are blackish-purple when ripe, covered in a beautiful waxy bloom. The leaves take on a range of deep reddish-purple tints in autumn before they eventually fall. Best grown against a wall, although it will also succeed on a pergola or arbour. Grows in most fertile soils and should only be pruned back if plants are getting out of control.

Vitis vinifera 'Purpurea' (*above*) z 6
Teinturier

The foliage of this remarkable cultivar opens grey-white in spring, turning red in the summer, darkening to deep purple in autumn. Like all grape vines, it climbs by means of tendrils and can reach 12ft (3.6m) in a single season. Prune during the dormant season, and in mid-summer to curb excessive growth – but never in spring and early summer as this causes profuse bleeding (an excessive flow of sap). Fruits are carried on one-year-old stems.

Shade tolerant

FLOWERS

Camellia japonica z 7

All cultivars of this shrub have glossy, evergreen leaves. 'Contessa Lavinia Maggi' has pale pink flowers with rose stripes; 'Adolphe Audusson' has blood red flowers; 'Alba Simplex' has white flowers with gold stamens. Plants reach 30 × 30ft (9 × 9m) and do best in moist, acid or neutral, peaty soil; mulch to prevent drying out which causes bud-drop. Good in a shaded, sheltered spot such as a north- or west-facing wall; complements ivies and spring-flowering bulbs. Deadhead and prune in spring.

Clematis 'Lasurstern' (*above*) z 5

This vigorous clematis can reach 10ft (3m). Blue flowers, up to 7in (18cm) across, cover the plant in early summer; a second flush of fewer, smaller blooms follows in early autumn. Eight broad, pointed sepals surround cream stamens. Grow in humus-rich soil with plenty of moisture, shading the roots with an underplanting of low-growing shrubs. In early spring cut out dead wood and shorten stems to a pair of healthy buds; in shade, reduce some shoots to 12in (30cm). Sun can bleach the flowers.

Clematis 'Nelly Moser' z 6

The flat flowers of this clematis are up to 7in (18cm) wide and are composed of eight pale mauve-pink sepals, each with a central purple bar which bleaches in sunlight. The plant either has two flushes of flowers in summer and autumn, or a slightly larger, early autumn crop, effected by hard pruning in early spring. Grow through another climber or wall shrub. Needs humus-rich, moist soil and shade for the roots. Prune as for *Clematis* 'Lasurstern'. Ideal for a shady spot.

Forsythia suspensa z 5

Bell-shaped yellow flowers cover this shrub in early spring. It can reach 25ft (7.5m) when trained on a wall, where the slender branches hang freely. Flowers are carried on the previous season's wood; prune immediately after flowering to promote new growth. The leaves emerge after the blooms and are a fresh green throughout summer. *F. s. atrocaulis* has purple-black young stems. Grow with clematis or other climbers for summer interest. Useful for a north- or east-facing wall and most fertile soils.

Hydrangea petiolaris (*above*) z 4

Also listed as *H. anomala petiolaris*, this climbing hydrangea clings with small aerial roots. Slow to establish, it reaches 10ft (3m) in ten years but eventually can make 50ft (15m). Flowers appear from early summer in large, flat clusters comprising off-white fertile heads surrounded by white sterile heads. In autumn the leaves often turn a rich yellow before falling. Peeling rusty-brown bark provides winter interest. Grows in most fertile soils and is very tolerant of pollution. Support and train until established; prune only to keep within bounds.

Kerria japonica 'Pleniflora' z 4

A deciduous suckering shrub with stiff upright growth that sits well against a wall. This is the vigorous double form reaching 10ft (3m) high, with deep golden-yellow flowers. 'Variegata' is more compact. The less common single form (*K. japonica*) has flowers that resemble large buttercups and a more graceful habit. The green stems set off winter-flowering plants such as *Viburnum* × *bodnantense*. Grow in moist, fertile soil. Suckers and older stems should be thinned after flowering.

Lapageria rosea (*above*) z 8

A sheltered, shaded or semi-shaded wall is essential to grow this tender evergreen climber. It will not stand strong sunlight and needs a cool, moist, acid soil, rich in organic matter, to grow well. Fleshy, bell-shaped pink flowers hang in clusters from the leaf axils in summer and autumn, set off by the leathery, heart-shaped foliage. The tough, wire-like, twining stems can reach 12ft (3.6m) with support. *L. r. albiflora* has glistening white flowers; 'Nash Court' has pink bells. Prune to keep in check or to remove dead wood.

Lathyrus latifolius (*above*) z 5
Everlasting pea

This perennial climbs to 6ft (1.8m) every year. The bluish-green leaves have tendrils which support the flattened winged stems. Purple flowers are held in dense racemes throughout the summer. Cultivars include the white 'Albus' and 'White Pearl', pink 'Splendens' and the dark purple and red 'Pink Beauty'. Useful for masking the bare lower parts of other climbers. Grows well in most soils. Takes several seasons to settle, dislikes being transplanted.

Lonicera periclymenum 'Belgica' z 4
(*below*)

The highly scented flowers of the "early Dutch" honeysuckle are cream, ageing to golden yellow with rose tints. They appear in spring and again in late summer. The "late Dutch", 'Serotina', has darker flowers which appear from mid-summer to autumn. Shiny red berries follow. Plants can reach 15ft (4.5m), the twining stems growing through other shrubs or trees. Plant in deep, shaded, moisture-retentive soil. Prune lightly after flowering.

Schizophragma integrifolium z 7

Related to the hydrangea, this plant climbs to 40ft (12m) by means of aerial roots. Lateral branches bear 1ft (30cm)-wide inflorescences of creamy-white flowers and marginal sepals that are white with dark veins. The heart-shaped, deciduous leaves are up to 7in (18cm) long. It is suitable for a wall, tree or tree stump. *S. hydrangeoides* is smaller and hardier (z 5) with reddish young stems. Grow in good soil and support the stems until aerial roots are established. Prune in winter if needed.

Tropaeolum speciosum z 7
Scottish flame flower

The deep-rooted, creeping rhizomes of this hardy herbaceous perennial produce long strand-like stems that reach 10ft (3m), climbing by means of leaf stalks. The deep crimson flowers appear from mid-summer until early autumn, followed by bright blue fruits set in persistent red calyces. The lobed leaves are pale green. Train on a wall through trellis or netting, or through a dark-leaved evergreen such as box or yew. Plant in cool, moist, humus-rich soil. Thrives in cool conditions: ideal for north- or east-facing positions.

FOLIAGE

Euonymus fortunei radicans   z 5

This leathery-leaved evergreen climber uses aerial roots to reach 12ft (3.6m) with a broad spread. It has a juvenile phase which ends when it stops climbing, at which point it produces larger leaves and flowers and fruit. 'Variegatus' has white-edged leaves, often tinged pink; 'Silver Gem' has white variegations; the foliage of 'Coloratus' turns reddish-purple in winter, especially on poor soil; 'Vegetus' bears deep orange fruits in autumn. Grows well in most soils, including alkaline. A good substitute for ivy, it needs no regular pruning.

Hedera helix 'Tricolor'   z 5

The evergreen common English ivy climbs to 30 × 15ft (9 × 4.5m) by means of aerial roots. The leaves of 'Tricolor' have broad, creamy-white margins, tinged rose red in winter. 'Goldheart' has yellow-centred leaves; the dark green leaves of 'Atropurpurea' turn deep purple in winter; 'Digitata' has deeply lobed leaves, 'Buttercup' rich yellow leaves that turn pale green with age. Grow up a tree or over a wall or fence. Tolerates shade and pollution. Cut out shoots reverting to green.

Humulus lupulus 'Aureus' (*above*)   z 3
Golden hop

This herbaceous perennial grows to 20ft (6m) in a single season, forming a mat of twining stems across a fence or over a pergola. The yellow palmate leaves are up to 6in (15cm) long, with three to five lobes. Small flowers appear in autumn, followed by cone-like spikes of aromatic (if rubbed) fruits. Needs moist, fertile soil. Cut back old growth in spring. Dry fruits can be used in arrangements.

Parthenocissus henryana (*above*)   z 7
The leaves of this deciduous, self-clinging vine have three to five dark green or bronze ovate leaflets with silvery-white veins. The foliage turns red in autumn, highlighting the dark blue fruits. The tendrils are tipped by sucker-pads which cling to walls or trees, reaching 30ft (9m). Needs some shelter in cold areas and moist fertile soil; leaf colour is strongest in half-shade. Growth can be rampant.

AUTUMN AND WINTER EFFECT

Azara microphylla   z 9

In late winter and very early spring the vanilla-like fragrance of this tender shrub fills the air. The yellow flowers have no petals but prominent stamens, and are held on the underside of the spray-like twigs in small clusters. Each dark green, evergreen leaf has a large leaf-like stipule at its base. Grows up to 22ft (7m), but even mature plants can be killed in a severe winter. Needs a moist loamy soil, and shelter from cold, drying winds. Prune in spring to remove dead or unwanted growth.

Berberidopsis corallina   z 8
Coral plant

The globular, berberis-like flowers of this evergreen climbing shrub are deep crimson and hang in clusters in late summer and early autumn. The leathery, oval or heart-shaped leaves are edged with spiny teeth. Plants can reach 15ft (4.5m) or more on a shaded wall. Does best in a lime-free, moist sandy loam, with protection from buffeting winds. Mulch after planting; prune to remove dead or unwanted growth.

Chaenomeles speciosa (*below*)   z 5

In mild weather flowers appear on the bare stems of this spiny shrub from mid-winter into spring. The species has scarlet or blood red flowers but there are many cultivars, including the pink, semi-double 'Phylis Moore', white 'Nivalis' and salmon pink 'Umbilicata'. Leaves are a glossy dark green. It reaches 8 × 15ft (2.4 × 4.5m) on a wall in fertile soil; best in partial shade. Prune all stems after flowering to within two or three buds of the base. This prevents breastwood developing.

Cotoneaster horizontalis   z 5

This deciduous shrub has stiff branches that grow closely against a wall or fence in a herringbone pattern. In spring they are smothered with small, scented, pink flowers (which attract masses of early bees), followed by red fruits that last well into winter. Tiny, glossy, dark green leaves turn orange-red in autumn. 'Variegatus' has cream-variegated leaves, suffused with red in autumn. It reaches 4 × 5ft (1.2 × 1.5m) and suits a dry, shady site, such as a north- or east-facing wall; succeeds in alkaline soil. Prune out old branches.

Garrya elliptica   z 7
Silk-tassel bush

Male plants have 6in (15cm)-long grey-green catkins which appear from mid-winter into spring. Female plants have shorter catkins but produce clusters of silky purple-brown fruits. Both have leathery evergreen leaves. Grows to 20ft (6m) in well-drained soil. 'James Roof' has larger leaves and longer catkins. An excellent host for the summer-flowering *Clematis viticella* which is pruned back in early winter. Tolerates pollution and salt; protect from cold, drying, east and north winds. Prune back long shoots.

Sun-loving

Jasminum nudiflorum z 5
Winter jasmine

Pale yellow, trumpet-shaped flowers appear on this plant's bare green stems from late autumn to spring, followed by glossy, dark green foliage. The strong, angular stems reach 15ft (4.5m) if trained on a wall; they can then be left to weep. Grow with other climbers such as the scrambling *Clematis × jackmanii*. Ideal for a north-facing wall, out of the morning sun (which scorches frosted blooms). Hardiest of the jasmines, it grows in most well-drained soils. Cut out old or dead shoots after flowering.

Parthenocissus tricuspidata (*above*) z 4
Boston ivy

This vigorous, self-clinging climber forms a dense covering on a wall and can reach 65ft (19.5m). The toothed, three-lobed leaves turn crimson in autumn before dropping. 'Veitchii' is a smaller form with purple young foliage and, after a hot summer, bloomy, dark blue fruits. Growing in most positions and soils, this rampant climber may require severe pruning of roots and, in summer, shoots to prevent it clogging gutters and covering windows.

Parthenocissus quinquefolia z 3
Virginia creeper

Growing to 50ft (15m) or more, this climber is ideal for high walls and trees. The leaves have five leaflets, dull green above, glaucous below which turn to bright scarlet, orange and crimson in autumn. Blue-black fruits are sometimes seen. Plant in any soil, avoiding deep shade, and support young shoots until the sucker-pads have taken hold. Grow with the evergreen, yellow-variegated *Hedera colchica* 'Sulphur Heart' for good effect. Cut plants back hard in summer or winter.

FLOWERS

Abelia floribunda z 8

This evergreen shrub grows to 10ft (3m) on a warm west- or south-facing wall. Young shoots are downy and red while the flowers are cherry red and appear in drooping clusters of two or three in mid-summer. The conspicuous calyces persist after the 2in (5cm)-long tube of petals has fallen. The leaves are rounded and glossy. Remove old and dead growth immediately after flowering, cutting shoots well back. Grow in moist, loamy soil and mulch heavily to prevent drying out in summer.

Bougainvillea glabra (*below*) z 9

Massed purple, papery floral bracts cover this rampant evergreen climber in summer. In 'Snow White' the bracts are white with green veins; in 'Magnifica' they are reddish-purple. 'Variegata' has creamy-white margins to its leaves. The coarse stems bear vicious backward-pointing barbs which hook over other plants; tie it in to any other support. It grows to 16ft (5m) in a sheltered, frost-free spot and rich, well-drained soil. Protect your eyes from the sharp barbs when pruning.

Campsis radicans z 4
Trumpet vine

Exotic trumpet-shaped orange and scarlet flowers appear in late summer on this deciduous self-clinging climber. They are borne at the tips of new shoots and are sometimes followed by spindle-shaped fruits. It can reach 35ft (10.5m) and will grow on a wall or tree stump or will clamber over a roof. 'Flava' has yellow flowers. Plant in any fertile soil, kept moist all summer, and support until the aerial roots are established. Prune back after frosts in early spring.

Ceanothus arboreus 'Trewithen Blue' (*below*) z 9

A large-growing Californian lilac with 5in (13cm)-long panicles of deep blue, scented flowers. It can reach 28ft (8.4m) and has flaking bark, downy younger shoots and broad, dark evergreen leaves. *C. sorediatus* 'A.T.Johnson' has bright blue flowers, while 'Autumnal Blue' is hardier with deep blue flowers. They will tolerate all but the thinnest alkaline soils and most are ideal for protected, coastal gardens. Prune only to restrict growth, after flowering (but prune deciduous forms in spring).

Cestrum parqui z 10

This tender wall shrub is deciduous except in very mild, sheltered areas. The narrow, lance-shaped leaves are 5in (13cm) long and have a pungent, spicy smell when crushed. Greenish-yellow flowers appear in mid- to late summer; they release a powerful fragrance at night. Shiny black berries follow. Plant near a door or window, or at the base of a bare-stemmed climber such as clematis. Grows to 7ft (2m) in most well-drained soils in a warm, sunny position. Prune in spring, removing some of the old growth.

Chimonanthus praecox z 7

Established plants begin to flower in the coldest winter months, filling the air with a sweet fragrance. The waxy, straw yellow blooms have purple centres and are borne on bare twigs. It reaches 7ft (2m) and can carry a climber such as *Clematis* 'Royalty' which will mask the large, coarse, deciduous foliage during summer. Grow in moist, well-drained soil in a sheltered, sunny spot. Useful on alkaline soils. Prune after flowering, taking out weak shoots. 'Grandiflorus' has deeper yellow flowers.

Clematis armandii (*above*)   z 7
An evergreen clematis which is strong-growing on a warm sheltered wall, where it can reach 15ft (4.5m). Each leaf is composed of three, long, dark green, leathery leaflets that make an excellent background to the creamy-white flowers. These are 3in (8cm) across, vanilla-scented and are carried in clusters from early spring onwards. 'Snowdrift' has pure white flowers, 'Apple Blossom' pink flushed sepals and bronze young leaves. Plant in shaded soil, enriched with organic matter. Prune hard and train after flowering.

Clematis **'Ernest Markham'** (*above*) z 5
Often considered the best of the red-flowered clematis, this reliable cultivar will produce velvety, petunia-red flowers for four months during summer and autumn, if pruned annually. Flowers are 5in (13cm) across, with six broad, rounded sepals. It reaches 8ft (2.4m). Grow through winter fruiting and flowering shrubs such as *Pyracantha* 'Mohave' or *Viburnum* × *bodnantense* 'Deben'. Also looks effective growing through silver-foliaged trees and shrubs. The roots need shaded, rich fertile soil.

Clianthus puniceus   z 9
Glory pea, parrot's bill or lobster claw
This evergreen or semi-evergreen wall shrub can reach 10ft (3m) with some training. It tends to be short-lived but is well worth the effort. Brilliant red, claw-like, 2in (5cm)-long flowers hang in clusters. 'Albus' has white blooms but is less free-flowering. The attractive pinnate leaves are 6in (15cm) long and have pale undersides. Needs a hot, sunny, west- or south-facing wall and very well drained soil. Pinch out growing tips to encourage bushiness. Prune in spring to remove dead wood.

Cobaea scandens (*above*)   z 10
Cup and saucer plant
This tender, tropical perennial will not stand frost and is raised annually from seed. The bell-shaped flowers are held on 10in (25cm) stalks. They are 2in (5cm) long, greenish-white when they open, turning mauve as they age. 'Alba' has white flowers. It rapidly grows to 10ft (3m), climbing by means of leaf tendrils. A fine gap-filler for pergolas or walls. Sow in spring after the last frosts in rich moist soil. Pinch out to get bushy plants with plenty of flowers.

Fremontodendron californicum   z 8
The large butter yellow flowers of this striking evergreen shrub appear from spring into early autumn. The three-lobed leaves are green above, with brown indumentum beneath. On a warm, sunny wall it quickly grows to 15ft (4.5m). 'Californian Glory' has larger, lemon yellow flowers, with a slight flush of red on the outside. Happy in poor sandy soil. Prune in spring to reduce growth; the leaf hairs can cause irritation to the throat and skin. Plants dislike being moved and are prone to dying suddenly.

Ipomea tricolor (*above*)   z 5
Morning glory
Large trumpet-shaped flowers open china blue in the morning and close by midday. They are up to 4in (10cm) long. 'Heavenly Blue' has clear metallic blue flowers. A short-lived, tender, twining perennial, it is usually grown annually from seed and is good on trellis, walls and pillars. Grow in soil enriched with manure or compost, in a warm, sunny position, and water well throughout summer. Dislikes root disturbance. Support with twigs to start climbing.

Jasminum officinale   z 7
Summer jasmine
This quick-growing climber will reach 25ft (7.5m) if trained. Night-scented white flowers are held in terminal clusters from summer to early autumn, set-off by glossy, pinnate leaves. Excellent for a wall or pergola near a house or sitting area, or it can be trained around a window or doorway. Combines well with other fragrant plants such as *Nicotiana alata*. In cold areas grow in a sheltered, sunny position, in any fertile, fairly moist soil. Avoid severe pruning; thin the green stems in spring.

Lathyrus odoratus   z 3
Sweet pea
The winged stems of this annual climber can reach 6ft (1.8m). Often grown up canes for cutting, it works equally well on walls or pergolas. Flowers come in a range of colours and are often highly fragrant. Picking the blooms encourages further flowering. Before sowing, chip the hard seed coats and soak for 24 hours. Grow in moist, loamy soil with plenty of compost. Remove seed pods immediately. Support young plants with hazel twigs.

Lonicera hildebrandiana *(below)* z 7
Giant Burmese honeysuckle

This strong-growing but tender climber can reach 70ft (21m). It has the largest leaves, flowers and fruits of all honeysuckles but is a shy flowerer when young. The flowers are up to 6in (⸱m) long, fragrant, creamy-white, chan⸱ng to rich yellow, and appear in termi⸱l leaf axils during summer. The roun⸱ed leaves are dark green. Spectacular on a pergola, trellis, wall or fence. Grow in moist, rich soil with the roots in shade, watering and mulching during summer. Prune lightly after flowering.

Passiflora caerulea z 8
Blue passion flower

The hardiest of the passifloras, this can grow to 15ft (4.5m) in a good season, climbing by means of twining tendrils, and is evergreen in mild areas. The flowers are likened to the instruments of Christ's Passion: the corona (crown of thorns) is striped purple, white and blue, against greenish-white tepals (the apostles); the stigmas (the three nails) are creamy-white. Flowers remain closed on dull days. Orange, egg-shaped fruits follow a hot summer. Grow in rich, well-drained soil and cover the roots with peat or grit in winter. Prune out winter-damaged shoots in spring.

Rhodochiton atrosanguineum z 9

The flowers of this perennial climber make an unusual addition to the garden, where it is grown as a tender annual. They are long and pendulous with large, bell-shaped calyces and 2in (5cm)-wide tubular corollas of a deep blackish-purple. Climbs by its twining leaf-stalks to reach 10ft (3m) in a season. It needs support and training. Plant after frosts, in a sunny spot in moist fertile soil. It may be short-lived.

Solanum crispum 'Glasnevin' z 9
(above)

A spectacular climber for a sheltered, frost-free wall in full sun. It grows to 15ft (4.5m) in well-drained, alkaline soil. Clusters of small violet-blue flowers open from mid-summer, continuing into autumn. Cream-coloured berries appear in autumn. It is semi-evergreen. Plant *Lavatera* 'Barnsley', with its pinky-white flowers, at the base, or grow it with the yellow climbing rose 'Golden Showers'. Prune in spring after frost, wearing gloves against the sap which is an irritant.

Sollya heterophylla z 9
Bluebell creeper

An extremely beautiful evergreen twiner, bearing clusters of nodding bluebell-like, sky-blue flowers in summer and autumn. Plants can reach 6ft (1.8m) and are effective if trained on a low wall or allowed to scramble through other shrubs. The leaves are insignificant. Grow in humus-rich, well-drained soil; where frost is likely, provide some winter protection.

Trachelospermum jasminoides z 9
Star jasmine

Hardy against a wall in frost-free areas, the stems of this self-clinging climber can reach 25ft (7.5m) on older plants. The sweetly fragrant flowers are 1in (2.5cm) across, white, turning cream with age. The evergreen leaves are glossy, thick and leathery. 'Variegata' has leaves splashed creamy-white; 'Wilsonii' has bronze leaves that turn deep red in autumn. Flowers appear on old wood, so prune immediately after flowering to remove dead wood or unwanted shoots. Grow in moist, rich soil for the best results.

Wisteria floribunda *(below)* z 4
Japanese wisteria

This wisteria grows to 30ft (9m), with 10in (25cm)-long racemes of strongly fragrant, bluish-purple flowers. After hot summers, velvety, bean-like pendulous seed pods may form. 'Alba' has white, lilac-tinged flowers in 2ft (60cm)-long racemes, while those of 'Macrobotrys' are up to 3ft (90cm) long. It is ideal for pergolas, arches or doorways. Plant in full sun, in fertile loamy soil. Train the shoots to prevent tangled growth. Prune in summer and winter to encourage flowering.

FOLIAGE

Actinidia kolomikta z 4

The leaves of this hardy deciduous plant are up to 6in (15cm) long and tricoloured, with green, white and pink variegations. It can reach 14ft (4.2m), with a twining habit that needs support. Young plants can be damaged because of their strange attractiveness to cats. Small, slightly fragrant white flowers appear in summer, sometimes followed by yellow fruits. Plant male and female forms for fruit-setting, in full sun for maximum leaf colour. Prune in winter to achieve a strong framework.

Magnolia grandiflora z 5

This magnificent evergreen wall shrub grows to 25ft (7.5m) in a warm position. The large, glossy leaves are dark green above, covered with fine, rusty-brown hairs beneath. Highly fragrant, creamy-white flowers appear in summer and early autumn. 'Goliath' has very large flowers. Underplant with *Choisya ternata* (z 7), which carries white flowers in the spring. Tie in stems to stop wind damage, pruning lightly in summer. Tolerates pollution.

Climbers for trees

Pittosporum tenuifolium z 9
This tender evergreen shrub thrives in coastal gardens, in mild areas. It has brownish-purple flowers which are honey-scented, and is noted for its pale, shiny, oval leaves, 2in (5cm) long, which have wavy margins. 'Purpureum' has mauve leaves, while those of 'Garnettii' have white margins. The mature foliage of 'Warnham Gold' is golden yellow. *P. tobira* has creamy-white, strongly fragrant flowers, similar to orange blossom. Grow in well-drained soil where plants can reach 30ft (9m). Prune only to keep within bounds.

***Robinia hispida* 'Rosea'** (*above*) z 5
This form of the rose acacia has pinnate leaves with many small, dainty leaflets, carried on bristly stems. It bears racemes of rose-pink pea-like flowers in late summer, and will grow to 10ft (3m). Train with *Wisteria sinensis*, which has pink and lavender flowers, or grow with *Ceanothus* 'Gloire de Versailles', which has china blue flowers. The best specimens are those grafted onto *R. pseudoacacia*. Useful in all soils, it is suitable for a dry spot and tolerates pollution. The stems need shelter.

***Vitis vinifera* 'Incana'** z 6
Dusty miller grape
This cultivar of the deciduous grape vine is excellent for decorative use in the garden. Plants can reach 12ft (3.6m) in a single season, climbing by means of tendrils. They are useful on walls, pergolas, bridges and fences. The grey-green leaves are covered in a cobweb-like down, which goes well with purple-foliaged shrubs, such as *Cotinus* 'Notcutt's Variety'. Grow in moist, rich soil. Prune back long shoots in summer and again in late winter to just above a pair of stout buds.

FLOWERS

Clematis macropetala (*above*) z 5
Growing to 10ft (3m), this early-flowering clematis has small, nodding, double violet-blue flowers from mid- to late spring. The silky, fluffy seedheads give a good show in autumn. The delicate leaves comprise three leaflets, each subdivided into three. 'Markham's Pink' has dark pink flowers, which are effective against the silver foliage of *Pyrus salicifolia* 'Pendula'. Grow with the roots in shade, in moist fertile soil. Cut back in autumn, leaving some shoots intact to enjoy the seedheads.

Clematis tangutica (*above*) z 5
The deep yellow, lantern-like flowers of this dense-growing climber look splendid bursting from the crown of a good-sized tree. Globes of silky feathery-tipped seedheads appear in autumn; flowers and seedheads are seen together for a while. Sea-green, finely dissected leaves provide the perfect foil. Grown on a wall or over a fence or hedge, it can reach 20ft (6m). Plant roots in shade and prune lightly in late winter if necessary, but not too hard. Raise named forms from cuttings.

Lonicera × americana z 5
This vigorous deciduous honeysuckle provides a spectacular display in summer. The fragrant, yellow-flushed, reddish-purple, tubular flowers are held in whorls at the tips of the shoots. It can grow to 30ft (10m) in a good-sized tree. The roots should be shaded and planted in moist, fertile soil. Prune lightly after flowering, removing weak and dead growth; cut a few stems to ground level to promote growth at the base which otherwise tends to become bare.

AUTUMN COLOUR

Celastrus orbiculatus z 4
Staff vine or climbing bittersweet
A strong-growing climber, its twining stems are armed with pairs of fierce spines at each bud. Choose a stout host tree such as a maple, birch, pine, larch, alder or lime, at least 20ft (6m) tall: it can reach 40ft (12m). The dense coat of rounded, deciduous leaves turn a rich golden-yellow in autumn. Brownish-yellow fruits split open in autumn to reveal bright red seeds set in a yellow lining, which persist all winter. Grows in most soils. Plant the self-pollinating hermaphrodite form to ensure fruiting.

Vitis coignetiae (*below*) z 5
Japanese crimson glory vine
Perhaps the most spectacular of all vines to grow in a large tree, it can reach up to 90ft (27m). The huge, broadly heart-shaped, deciduous leaves emerge dull-green in spring, with a rich felt of rusty hairs on the undersides. They turn brilliant scarlet, orange and crimson in autumn. Grow with *Clematis tangutica* for a stunning autumn effect. Needs a moist, rich soil to support the vigorous growth, and a sunny position. Prune in early spring to a plump healthy bud.

ROSES

Roses have always been an essential element in the garden, valued highly for the colour and scent of their flowers. Their hardiness varies widely depending on which part of the world they originated from. A few species are native to northern Europe; others came from an area stretching from southern France to the Middle East; while many roses introduced to cultivation in the late eighteenth and throughout the nineteenth century come from China.

In cold climates roses need to be chosen with care to ensure that they survive the winter; varieties bred from *Rosa rugosa* and *R. wichuraiana* are among those most tolerant of the extreme cold found in Canada, the northeastern United States and parts of continental Europe. Although roses require plenty of summer heat to ripen, their flowers tend to bleach and burn under intense sun.

Today, there are an enormous number of cultivars available to the gardener which often makes it difficult to know which to choose. However, broadly speaking there are three main groups – shrub, bush and climbing – each adapted to a different use.

Right: Many modern repeat-flowering roses make effective bedding plants. Here they are planted up in large blocks of a single cultivar but the same treatment can be used on a much more intimate scale. The impressive, mature trees at the back of the display provide a useful element of height.

Left: The sweet and powerful scent of many roses adds greatly to their garden value. The scented dimension of the garden can be enhanced by growing roses with excellent fragrant climbers such as honeysuckles and other richly perfumed summer flowers.

Below: 'Wedding Day', like other vigorous climbing and rambling roses, creates a wonderfully romantic effect when in full flower. Sturdy trelliswork, pergolas and old trees make suitable supports; think ahead and make sure the host structure or plant will be able to hold the mature rose.

Shrub roses include both the old-fashioned varieties bred mostly in the nineteenth century (such as 'Madame Hardy' and 'Cécile Brunner') and the modern shrub roses (for example, 'Marguerite Hilling', 'Frühlingsgold' and 'Fritz Nobis'), including the new English roses ('Graham Thomas', 'Gertrude Jekyll' and 'Mary Rose'), bred by David Austin and first marketed in the early 1980s. Shrub roses make large plants to 6ft (1.8m) high or a little more, which require little or no pruning and need space to look their best. Some give a single massive display early in the summer and nothing else for the rest of the season; others flower again later on, if less profusely; yet another group make a good display of hips in the autumn. All look good in a shrubbery or large mixed border, where the cultivars that flower only once can be part of a continuous display or a large-flowered hybrid clematis can be trained through them to extend the season of interest. In addition, some shrub roses are suitable for making hedges.

Most bush roses were created in the twentieth century. They are often planted en masse in rose gardens and require annual pruning in the late winter or early spring. They include the wonderful Hybrid

Left: Roses are available in such a wide range of colours that it is not difficult to select one that matches a particular scheme. Oranges and yellows suit old, mellow brick walls, while red stands out against the cream of many sandstones. Vibrant pinks are shown off by the subdued grey of this handsome lead tank.

Teas which are characterized by elegant but robust flowers and flower freely and continuously throughout the summer; (for example, 'Peace', 'Mister Lincoln' and 'Just Joey'); the Floribundas, which have multiflowered stems producing an abundance of colour for the whole summer (and are sometimes referred to as bedding roses); and the Grandifloras (such as 'Queen Elizabeth'), American hybrids with characteristics between Hybrid Teas and Floribundas. Grandifloras, as their name suggests, are taller (up to 10ft/3m) and have larger flowers than the Teas (3-5ft/1-1.5m) or Floribundas (2-4ft/60cm-1.2m).

Climbing roses combine the best qualities of other climbing plants with those of roses. In the wild they extend long vigorous stems towards the light through the branches of other plants, using their thorns to attach themselves. The most vigorous climbing roses are the ramblers (for example, 'Félicité et Perpétue', 'American Pillar' and 'Albéric Barbier') which send out long new shoots each summer. In the following year these shoots are covered with clusters of flowers along their entire length and should then be pruned away. Ramblers are best for clothing a large pergola, long wall or tall, sturdy tree. Less vigorous climbers (such as 'Climbing Etoile de Hollande', 'Maigold' and 'Handel') grow thick stems which flower over several years and sometimes reach a considerable height. They can be used for covering pergolas, trellis structures and smaller buildings. There are also some

shrub roses (including 'Madame Isaac Pereire' and 'Zéphirine Drouhin') that can be trained against walls, where they will grow twice as high as normal, or up a freestanding pillar or the uprights of a pergola.

There are a number of slightly tender cultivars ('La Follette', 'Desprez à Fleur Jaune' and 'Hume's Blush' among them) that in cool climates benefit from the protection of a sunny wall. In contrast, other cultivars flower abundantly against walls that receive little direct sunshine ('Albertine', 'Climbing Iceberg' and 'Madame Alfred Carrière' are excellent examples).

Roses are very versatile, rewarding plants. Their popularity never fails, reflected in the ever growing number of varieties available to the gardener. Choosing the correct plant for a particular site and design can be a daunting prospect. There is a lot to be said for opting for tried and tested varieties that have proved their worth in neighbours' gardens. However, at the risk of disappointment, you could gamble on a new plant that might be the making of your garden, adding a beautiful note or a delightful fragrance to a bed.

There are countless ways to use roses, not least being the formal rose garden which has enjoyed something of a revival in recent years, used as much in modern designs as traditional Victorian-style settings. Ranks of healthy, well maintained roses are a delight to behold, whatever the scale of the planting. Contrast with this the freedom of a cottage garden, and the versatility of the rose becomes clear.

For fragrance

CLIMBING

'Albertine' (*above*)   z 4
This vigorous, prickly, large flowered rambler will grow to a height of 20ft (6m) and is ideal for training along a hedge or low wall; it will also grow well into trees. The strongly scented flowers, which are a warm salmon or coppery pink, appear in one spectacular display in early summer. At the peak of flowering, well-grown plants have so many flowers that little foliage is visible. Prune back to younger stems after flowering to encourage new growth. The deep green leaves are prone to mildew.

'Climbing Etoile de Hollande'   z 4
A climbing sport of the hybrid tea 'Etoile de Hollande', this recurrent-flowering climber has clear crimson blooms with a very good scent. It flowers freely throughout summer, the blooms decreasing in number as the season draws on. Plants are fairly vigorous, growing to 25ft (7.5m) . One of the drawbacks of this rose in the hybrid tea form is that it has weak flower stalks, but this is an advantage in the climber where the drooping heads are brought more into view. It is also useful as a pillar rose.

'Madame Alfred Carrière'   z 6
Although of a mainly upright habit, this vigorous climber can be trained along a wall, reaching 20ft (6m) if pruned. The stems have few thorns and produce light green shoots; leaves are light green. The large, double flowers open white from pink buds, are hybrid tea-shaped and strongly fragrant. The display begins in early summer, peaks in mid-summer and continues to the end of the season. Good for a north-facing wall, a large pergola or to grow over a mature tree.

'Maigold'   z 4
This climber bears large, semi-double bronzy-yellow flowers with bosses of golden stamens in autumn. The flowers are reddish in bud, open quite early in the season and are highly scented. 'Maigold' is suitable for a wall, fence or pillar, or for growing as a loose open shrub in borders. It grows vigorously to 20ft (6m) and bears many thorny branches with glossy green foliage. Plants look effective against sand-coloured brick or stonework, or on wood. If deadheaded, they will produce a second flush of flowers.

'Zéphirine Drouhin' (*below*)   z 4
This bourbon rose can achieve 10ft (3m) in height, if trained as a climber, and is very popular because of its freedom of flowering and almost thornless habit. It produces sweetly scented, semi-double, carmine pink flowers continuously from summer to autumn. Flowering is improved by regular deadheading. Young growths are bronze-coloured. A vigorous grower, this cultivar can be used as a bush or a hedge as it is tolerant of heavy pruning. It is slightly prone to mildew and blackspot.

SHRUB

'Buff Beauty'   z 4
A very floriferous, vigorous hybrid musk which makes a shrub 6ft (1.8m) high with an equal spread. The flowers are carried in large clusters. They are varying shades of apricot and buff-yellow, semi-double or double, medium-sized and deliciously scented. The petals become paler at the edges as the blooms age. Plants begin flowering in summer and continue until autumn. The foliage is a rich brown-bronze when young, turning dark green as it matures.

'Frühlingsgold' (*below*)   z 4
Also listed as 'Spring Gold', this modern shrub rose will thrive in all soil conditions. Its branches quickly reach 7ft (2.1m) and then arch outwards. They are clothed with heavily fragrant, creamy-yellow flowers which reach up to 5in (13cm) across, each one bearing a cluster of golden yellow stamens. The flowers fade in hot sun. The main flush is in early summer with occasionally another show later in the year. The grey-green leaves complement the blooms. Plants are generally strong and disease-resistant.

'Madame Isaac Pereire' (*below*)   z 4
A very vigorous bourbon rose with large, double, strongly scented, deep pink flowers. These appear in clusters throughout the summer months, the best blooms often being produced late in the season. Earlier flowers frequently appear in the centre of the plant, later ones on the outside. The strong thorny shoots can reach 6ft (1.8m) in a single season, and mature plants grow to 10ft (3m) in height. This cultivar can also be trained as a pillar rose or pegged down: maintenance must be considered if the plant is pegged.

Borders

R. rugosa 'Blanche Double de Coubert'
(*above*)   z 2
This large, spreading shrub can reach
5ft (1.5m) high, with a similar spread,
and has a loose-growing habit. Large,
semi-double, fragrant white flowers first
appear in early summer and recur
throughout the season. The petals are
silky and slightly pleated. Hips, which
are large and reddish-orange, form less
readily than on the similar 'Alba'. Like
most derivatives of *R. rugosa*, stems are
prickly and the leaves have deep veins.

'William Lobb'   z 4
A damask moss rose which grows
quickly to 6ft (1.8m) or more, this is the
most vigorous member of this sweetly
scented group. Large clusters of flowers
are produced in mid-summer. These are
semi-double, crimson in bud, opening
purple and fading to grey-mauve with a
lighter-coloured base. The flower buds
and stalks are covered with green
"moss", typical of the group. The tall,
rather lank habit make it suitable for
growing up pillars and pergolas. Small
reddish thorns clothe the young shoots.

BUSH

'Betty Prior'   z 4
An outstanding floribunda which
combines health and vigour with a
wealth of long-lasting blooms. The deep
pink buds open as delicate, single pink
flowers, reminiscent of the wild dog rose
but held in large trusses. Blooms appear
from late spring into the autumn; they
become darker as the temperature falls
and the light intensity diminishes.
Flowers produce a spicy scent that
spreads generously. It forms a compact
sturdy mound 3-4ft (90-120cm) high,
making plants suitable for hedging.

'Fragrant Cloud'   z 4
Also listed as 'Duftwolke' and 'Nuage
Parfumé', this hyrid tea is a vigorous,
upright grower with large, exhibition-
quality geranium-red blooms. Flowers
are produced freely, mostly in summer
and again in autumn, with some
between the two flushes. They fade to
reddish-purple in hot weather and need
regular deadheading. Their scent is very
strong all season. The glossy dark green
leaves are resistant to disease, but may
need protection from blackspot in some
areas. Plants grow to 3ft (90cm) and can
be raised as standards.

'Mister Lincoln'   z 4
Cherry red flowers appear singly during
the summer following deep maroon
buds. They are large and very full and
have an exceptional fragrance. The
long-lasting blooms tend to flatten out
as they open, making a dramatic splash
of colour. They are carried at the top of
long stems, making them favourites for
showing and cutting. The glossy foliage
is medium to light green in colour and
makes an excellent foil for the flowers.
A tall plant reaching 6ft (1.8m) in
height, this hybrid tea is considered to
be one of the best red roses available.

'Peace'   z 4
If lightly pruned, this vigorous hybrid
tea will form a tall branching shrub,
upwards of 4ft (1.2m) in height with
large, full yellow flowers flushed with
pink, which become paler with age. The
colouring tends to vary from season to
season. The main flushes are in summer
and autumn, with a few blooms
bridging the gap. The flowers are
weather resistant and the strong-
growing, deep green, glossy leaves are
little troubled by disease. Excellent as a
cut flower, 'Peace' is much prized as an
exhibition rose.

'Saratoga'   z 4
The white flowers of this floribunda are
carried on the upright, vigorous bushy-
growing plant. The large flowers are
produced freely in irregular clusters and
are strongly scented. The foliage is dark
glossy green. The plant can achieve a
height of 3ft (90cm) or more. A more
compact white-flowered floribunda is
'Irene of Denmark', which grows 3ft
(90cm) at most, and produces flowers
freely which are tinted pink in bud and
open white, large and double.

SHRUB

'Cécile Brunner' (*below*)   z 4
Rarely growing more than 4ft (1.2m)
high, this shrubby rose is characterized
by its small neat leaves and delicate,
perfectly formed blooms. The small
flowers are blushed pink with deeper
centres, pointed when in bud and sweet-
scented. Plants flower recurrently
throughout the summer. Only
moderately vigorous, this cultivar
should not be hard-pruned: remove
weak growth and occasionally one or
two older branches. Valued for its neat
habit and useful for cutting.

'Ferdinand Pichard' (*below*)   z 4
Sometimes classed as a bourbon rose,
this hybrid perpetual shrub is recurrent
and free-flowering, producing semi-
double pink flowers with petals streaked
and splashed crimson, which tends to
deepen as the flowers age. The flowers
carry a good scent and appear in tight
clusters from mid-summer through to
autumn. They are particularly abundant
if the faded blooms are removed
regularly. Plants grow to a height of 8ft
(2.4m) and have a rather spreading,
bushy habit. The leaves are light green.

'Fritz Nobis' (*above*)　　z 4
This is one of the most beautiful of the modern shrub roses available. It grows to 6ft (1.8m) high and gives one spectacular display of flowers in early summer. The pale salmon-pink flowers are medium-sized, semi-double and open out flat like many of the old roses. In the centre of the flowers lie clusters of yellowish-brown stamens. 'Fritz Nobis' has a good scent and in the autumn bears dark red rounded hips which last into winter. Vigorous, it soon forms a finely shaped bush.

'Graham Thomas'　　z 4
Also listed as 'Ausmas', this English rose was raised in 1983 and named after the most influential of all the old rose enthusiasts, Graham Stuart Thomas. The flowers are tea-scented and appear throughout the season. They are double and of a glistening yellow, carried on slightly arching branches. Each flower is 4in (10cm) across and cup-shaped. Plants grow vigorously with a bushy lax habit. They achieve a height and spread of 4ft (1.2m). Other English roses raised in the 1980s with similar outstanding qualities include the pink 'Gertrude Jekyll' and crimson 'Mary Rose'.

'Madame Hardy'　　z 4
A vigorous damask rose growing to 6ft (1.8m) tall with clear green foliage, forming a strong bush. Cup-shaped when opening, the flowers expand to reveal a green eye surrounded by incurving petals which start off creamy pink-white before becoming pure white. They are of a medium size, double, carried in clusters and appear in a single flush in summer. The scent is delicious and fresh with a hint of lemon. A favourite among the old white roses.

'Marguerite Hilling' (*below*)　　z 4
A sport of 'Nevada' also sometimes listed as 'Pink Nevada', this modern shrub rose has great vigour and is a prolific flowerer for which it is very popular. It grows up to 8ft (2.4m) tall. The flowers appear in summer and are light pink with some deeper shading. They are slightly recurrent with odd flowers appearing throughout the rest of the season. Each flower is 3in (7cm) across and semi-double. Grow this cultivar towards the back of a border due to its large size. The leaves are small and dull and prone to blackspot.

'Nevada' (*below*)　　z 4
Spectacular when in full flower, this vigorous modern shrub is covered in blooms during summer, carried on long arching shoots. Most of the flowers appear in one main flush. They are scentless, semi-double, and open a creamy-white, becoming pink-tinged in hot weather, and fading white in duller conditions. The centre of the flower is a cluster of yellow stamens. As the blooms mature they become rather loose and untidy. Plants can grow to 11ft (3.3m) high with equal spread and are sometimes prone to blackspot.

***Rosa* × *alba* 'Maxima'** (*above*)　　z 2
White rose of York or Jacobite rose
Adopted as an emblem by the Yorkists, the origins of this historic *alba* rose are still undecided. It is characterized by its erect, thorny, dense growth and glaucous foliage. The flat ivory flowers are flushed with cream, scented and semi-double. 'Maxima' flowers in mid-summer and is tolerant of a wide range of conditions except shade. The flowers are not usually recurrent. In autumn there are oblong red fruits. Plants can grow to 8ft (2.4m).

Rosa glauca (*above*)　　z 2
Also listed as *R. rubrifolia*, this species rose is a tall-growing shrub which can reach 12ft (3.6m) with support, but is more normally seen growing freely to 7ft (2.1m) with arching branches. Distinguished by its beautiful blue-grey foliage, it has few thorns and deep pink flowers with white centres in summer. The flowers have long wispy sepals and are carried either singly or in small clusters. In autumn the leaves turn reddish and are accompanied by bright red, globular hips all along the arching, elegant branches.

***Rosa moyesii* 'Geranium'** z 4

One of the finest forms of this species rose, 'Geranium' is grown for its large, bright crimson-red fruits in late summer and autumn. The flowers appear in early summer and are bright red and single with overlapping petals. Plants form open-centred bushes, each with a few stout stems when mature. Some of the older shoots can be removed after flowering on established plants. The vigorous arching shoots are armed with sharp thorns and carry the light green foliage. Slightly more compact than the species and valuable for autumn colour.

***Rosa rugosa* 'Roseraie de l'Haÿ** z 2

Named after the rose garden of the same name to the south of Paris established by Jules Gravereaux, this richly-scented rugosa flowers throughout the season and is best planted in small groups. The vigorous growth can reach 8ft (2.4m), with an equal spread, carrying very large, semi-double loose flowers of deep crimson-purple with a velvety sheen and a strong scent. Each bloom is 4in (10cm) across carried among luxuriant, typical rugosa foliage. This form stands out among the rugosa group because of its distinctive wine-coloured flowers.

Rosa virginiana (*above*) z 4

Grown for its autumn leaf colours and brightly coloured hips, the young leaves of this species rose emerge bronzed, then turn glossy-green during summer and finally to fiery reddish-orange and yellow shades in autumn. They are accompanied at the end of the season by persistent, rounded, bright red hips. The stems are reddish-brown. The rather late flowers are pink with pale centres. Plants form dense rounded bushes with many shoots growing from the base to a height of 6ft (1.8m).

BUSH

'Allgold' z 4

Unsurpassed for the stability of its flower colour and for its numerous long-lasting flowers, 'Allgold' is a neat, compact, moderately vigorous grower which reaches to just over 2ft (60cm) high. The flowers of this floribunda open in early summer and last until late in the season. They are semi-double and of a deep golden yellow that never fades, even in hot sunny weather. The leaves are dark glossy green and resistant to disease. Plants resists rainy weather well, the flowers remaining unblemished by the water.

'Europeana' z 4

This vigorous growing floribunda may well need its flowers supporting if heavy rain threatens. This can be overcome by close planting so the plants give each other mutual support. Although this cultivar is susceptible to mildew in some areas, it is well worth growing for its striking, deep crimson flowers which are rosette shaped and carried in heavy trusses. Plants grow to 3ft (90cm) and have glossy, bronze-green foliage, which is coppery when young.

'Just Joey' (*below*) z 4

Unique for its coppery-orange flowers with lighter and deeper flushes, this hybrid tea is very free flowering and has an open spreading habit. The petals are often veined red, paling toward the edges which are wavy. The flowers appear singly or in clusters on plants growing up to 3ft (90cm) high and have some scent. Each one is fully double and can be up to 5in (13cm) across. The leaves are leathery and dark green. Flowers stand up well to rain and are excellent for cutting in the bud stage.

'Queen Elizabeth' z 4

One of the commonest pink floribundas with a tendency to produce a few blind shoots in the early part of the season, which eventually revert to flowering normally. It is a vigorous grower reaching 5ft (1.5m) or more in height with almost thornless stems and dark green glossy leaves. The flowers are very weather resistant and open a clear pink, fading as they age. They appear throughout the summer and autumn, carried either singly or in trusses, and are useful for cutting. Plants make an effective informal hedge.

'Starina' (*above*) z 4

A miniature rose achieving only 10in (25cm) in height, this plant is a vigorous grower with glossy green foliage and fully double, scarlet-orange flowers. This rose should be positioned carefully in a border so as not to allow it to become swamped by other plants. It is suitable for use as a pot plant, for bedding or as a miniature standard. As with all miniatures, 'Starina' resents root disturbance. The flowers are well-formed and last for a long time when used as cut flowers.

'Whisky Mac' z 4

The shapely blooms of this hybrid tea are gold with tints of bronze and orange; they are freely produced throughout summer. The flowers are quite fragrant, which is unusual among roses of this colour. Plants grow vigorously to 3ft (90cm) and carry holly-like, dark green glossy leaves which are tinted bronze as they unfold in spring. It is susceptible to mildew and damage by frost; this should be borne in mind when choosing a suitable position for planting, a protected, warm site producing the best results.

"Landscape" roses

GROUND COVER

'Nozomi' (*above*)   z 4

This miniature climbing rose will form excellent ground cover if left unsupported and planted 2ft (60cm) apart, as well as scrambling effectively along the top of a low wall. Its low arching habit means that it rarely achieves more than 18in (45cm) in height, but when supported it can reach 4ft (1.2m). Small, pale pink, single flowers appear in massed trusses. The leaves are glossy. Plants will also grow as weeping standards.

Rosa × paulii (*above*)   z 2

A hybrid between *R. arvensis* and *R. rugosa* that is excellent for smothering weeds because of its sprawling habit. A vigorous trailing rose, it will form a 3ft (90cm)-high shrub if hard-pruned. The long shoots are very thorny, carrying in mid-summer the single white or pink flowers with wedge-shaped petals, each one being 3in (8cm) across, with a central mass of golden stamens. The flowers are produced freely and have a slight scent of cloves. 'Rosea' has deep pink flowers with white centres.

'Max Graf' (*below*)   z 2

A hybrid between *R. rugosa* and *R. wichuraiana*, the long growths of this rugosa shrub lie prostrate along the ground unless trained. The dense foliage is effective at smothering weeds, but it can be difficult to weed among the prickly shoots before the leaves emerge. The scented flowers are single, pink, fading to white at the base of the petals, with yellow stamens. They are the size of large dog roses and appear once, but over a long season. Flowers sometimes appear in the autumn. The leaves are a glossy bright green.

'Snow Carpet' (*below*)   z 5

Also known as 'Maccarpe', this prostrate, creeping miniature bush rose was introduced to cultivation in 1980. It grows to a height of only 6in (15cm) with a spread of 20in (50cm), making it ideal for low ground cover. It carries fully double, pompom-like white flowers which are 1 ¼in (3cm) across. They appear in clusters, mainly during summer with some into autumn. The small glossy leaves are plentiful, adding to the usefulness of 'Snow Carpet' as ground cover as they smother weeds very successfully.

'The Fairy'   z 5

A weather-resistant and vigorous spreading plant which attains a height of 3ft (90cm). It is ideal as tall ground cover or as a low informal hedge and can also be grown as a standard. The small box-like leaves are deep green and shiny with a very healthy sheen. Large trusses of double soft-pink flowers appear later than most floribundas, and fade if the weather is hot. This is one of the few polyanthas available.

HEDGING

'Coupe d'Hébé' (*below*)   z 4

This vigorous shrub rose, which can grow to 7ft (2.1m), is usually described as a bourbon but is actually of mixed parentage; this gives it a rather loose growth pattern which makes it suitable for an informal hedge. Copious fresh glossy leaves form a dense barrier. The medium-sized double flowers are pink inside, almost white outside and fragrant, appearing quite late in the summer. The weak flower stalks cause the heads to hang downwards. Although this plant was introduced as long ago as 1840, its shapely outline is reminiscent of more modern cultivars.

Rosa eglanteria   z 2
Sweet briar or eglantine

Also listed as *R. rubiginosa*, this species rose has small leaflets which give the whole plant a spicy aromatic scent during damp weather. Plants grow with vigour to a height of 8ft (2.4m) and are excellent as dense informal hedges or as boundary plantings. The single pink flowers appear in clusters. Hips are bright red. 'Amy Robsart' has semi-double pink flowers and gold stamens; 'Lady Penzance' has fragrant leaves when wet and salmon-pink flowers.

Climbing roses

Rosa pimpinellifolia 'Hispida' z 2
Scotch rose or burnet rose
A moderately fast growing form which
suckers freely but grows little over 4ft
(1.2m) high. The stems are bristly, but
not very prickly. Freely-produced white
or creamy-white single flowers appear in
late spring or early summer in one flush.
The rather delicate foliage is bluish-
green and much toothed around the leaf
margins. The rounded hips are a deep
shining purple during autumn. A row of
plants will make a good informal hedge.
Cut out dead and damaged stems in
winter for the best effect.

Rosa rugosa 'Fru Dagmar Hastrup' z 2
(*above*)
Sometimes seen as 'Frau Dagmar
Hartopp', this rugosa shrub rose is more
compact than other rugosas, making it
suitable for hedging with the added
attraction of bright red hips throughout
summer and autumn, the size and
colour of small tomatoes. The leaves are
fresh apple green with impressed veins.
Plants respond well to winter clipping.
They flower over a long period,
beginning in mid-summer. Each bloom
is up to 3in (8cm) across, single, pink
with golden stamens, cup-shaped then
saucer-shaped when fully open. In
autumn the leaves take on attractive
golden-yellow shades.

'Tip Top' z 4
Growing to less than 2ft (60cm), this
vigorous, bushy spreading floribunda
has large, double, warm salmon-pink
flowers in large clusters, appearing
continuously over a long season. Plants
are rather prone to attack by blackspot.
Their low growth makes them well-
suited for use as edging plants or in
small beds. The leaves are dark glossy
green, complementing the flowers.

FOR GARDEN STRUCTURES

'Aloha' (*above*) z 4
This moderately vigorous climbing or
shrub rose reaches 5ft (1.5m) if grown as
a shrub or up to 10ft (3m) if grown on a
pillar. Plants grown as large shrubs need
regular pruning. The scented flowers
are like those of hybrid teas. They are
large and double, pink with darker
centres changing to a salmon-pink as
they age. The flowers are produced
freely, appearing throughout the season.
This cultivar derives its free-flowering
habit from 'New Dawn' which is one of
its parents. The stiff stems perfectly suit
its climbing habit.

'American Pillar' (*above*) z 4
A vigorous rambler, it should be pruned
by cutting the flowering shoots hard,
down to ground level, in late summer:
the new shoots are then tied in. Each
quite large, pinkish-blue single flower
has a white eye and is produced in a
large cluster. The flowers are unscented.
Plants bloom once in the summer but
are very floriferous; they are susceptible
to mildew. They reach a height of 15ft
(4.5m) and may be trained up arches
and pergolas as well as pillars.

'Blaze Improved' z 4
This American climber, introduced in
1932, is one of the most commonly
grown in the United States because of
its unfailing reliability. The large bright
scarlet flowers are 2-3in (5-8cm) across
and cover the plant in early summer and
again in early autumn with a spattering
in between. It grows quickly to 12-15ft
(3.6-4.5m), making it ideal for
trelliswork and pergolas. The dark
glossy green foliage complements the
flowers. Tolerant of most soils and
shade, it is an excellent, versatile garden
plant that well merits its popularity.

'Bobbie James' (*above*) z 2
One of the best ramblers, this vigorous
plant reaches 25ft (7.5m). It is related to
R. multiflora and was named in 1960
after the Hon. Robert James who
cultivated a beautiful garden in
Yorkshire. The fragrant flowers are
cream in bud, opening white with gold
stamens. Huge clusters are freely
produced in one flush in mid-summer.
The sturdy stems bear abundant glossy
green foliage. Ideal for a pergola or for
growing through a tree.

'Constance Spry' z 4
The large and extremely fragrant
flowers are produced in a single display
in mid-summer, to spectacular effect.
With its open, arching growth, this
plant is suited to growing either as a 6ft
(1.8m) shrub or as a climber, reaching
15ft (4.5m) with a 6ft (1.8m) spread.
The flowers are a glowing pink in the
centre, tending to be paler on the
outside. They are fully double, 4in
(10cm) across and held in groups of
three or four. The foliage is deep green.
Plants tend to throw up long vigorous
growths which need support. Effective
against a grey brick wall or on a pillar.

'Félicité et Perpétue' (*above*) z 4
To maximize flowering on this semi-evergreen rambler, leave the prickly overlapping growths unpruned, cutting out only dead, diseased or damaged wood. The long strong-growing shoots can reach 18ft (5.4m) in length, making it ideal for pergolas or for training into an old tree. The fragrant, small creamy-white flowers with a hint of pink are double and globular, held in large clusters. They appear from mid to late summer. Grows well even in light shade and has small, dark, shiny green leaves.

***Rosa filipes* 'Kiftsgate'** z 2
A vigorous Himalaya rambler clone, this plant was bred in the garden of the same name in Gloucestershire. It needs a large and robust pergola for support as it can reach 50ft (15m) and is capable of covering buildings and trees. In mid-summer the plant is spectacular, covered in sweetly scented, small, creamy white single flowers which cascade in corymbs over the grey-green foliage. Few roses can rival the huge cascades of flowers.

'Golden Showers' z 4
A very popular yellow rose which flowers continuously from early to late summer and is tolerant of wind, rain and some shade. This floribunda climber is ideal for trelliswork. It can reach 10ft (3m) in height with its stiff upright growth, carrying rich lemon-coloured flowers which are large, double, with a lemony fragrance and pointed when in bud. They fade in strong sunlight and should be regularly deadheaded. In winter cut out one older stem to ground level to promote new growth, as well as removing dead or diseased wood.

'Joseph's Coat' (*below*) z 4
Considered by different authorities to be either a tall floribunda or a large-flowered climber, this plant can be effectively trained as a pillar rose. Its growths reach 8ft (2.4m) high and it is repeat-flowering. The semi-double flowers are bright yellow with red and orange flushes, especially at the petal edges, and are produced in large trusses. They appear over a long period and well into autumn. The leaves are dark glossy green. Equally at home grown as a shrub or, with hard-pruning, as a bedding rose.

'Lawrence Johnston' z 4
A large-flowered climber growing to 10ft (3m), it produces bright yellow blooms in mid-summer, followed by a succession of smaller displays. The semi-double flowers are strongly scented and the leaves are a glossy rich green. The first specimen was bought by Major Lawrence Johnston and planted at Hidcote Manor in England. It was originally named 'Hidcote Yellow', although this name is no longer valid. Can also be grown as a shrub.

'Mermaid' z 4
Rarely happy in cold situations, where it may die back in severe winters, this modern climber is a vigorous grower which thrives in sun or in a north-facing position in a warm area. Growths reach up to 30ft (9m) and carry clusters of single sulphur-yellow blooms with amber stamens, the latter remaining for a few days after the petals have fallen. The flowers appear repeatedly through the summer, are slightly scented and do not require deadheading. Plants resent root disturbance and should be pruned only to remove dead, diseased or damaged wood.

'Souvenir de la Malmaison' (*above*) z 4
Named in memory of the Empress Josephine's private garden just to the south of Paris, this bourbon rose is suitable for growing on a pillar or as a shrub. It has vigorous shoots which can reach 10ft (3m) in length. The large flowers are pink fading to white, double, cup-shaped when opening, flattening as they mature. Each bloom is up to 5in (13cm) across and strongly scented. The flowers have two flushes, one in mid-summer and a second in late summer. They dislike wet weather, the rain spoiling the petals.

'Swan Lake' (*above*) z 4
This cultivar was introduced in 1968 and is also listed as 'Schwanensee'. It is one of the best white climbers available and is very resilient in poor weather, which is unusual for a white rose. 'Swan Lake' forms a strong free-growing plant which is well-suited to trelliswork, but can also be grown on pillars and arches. The large flowers are double, white with pinkish centres. They have little scent and appear throughout the season. The leaves are mid-green and are prone to the blemishes of blackspot.

FOR WALLS

Rosa banksiae banksiae   z 7

Plant this vigorous climbing species rose on a south-facing wall where it can grow to 30ft (9m). Several forms of the banksian rose exist, all being early and free-flowering with almost thornless stems. Young plants should be allowed to reach their desired height before any pruning starts. The white or pale yellow flowers appear in the second or third year on the older shoots, which tend to trail. Prune to ripen the wood. The leaves have a yellow tint.

'Climbing Iceberg' (*above*)   z 4

Discovered by B.R. Cant in 1968, this is a climbing sport of 'Iceberg' or 'Climbing Schneewittchen' (as it is also known) and is a spectacular sight when well trained. It will reach 12ft (3.6m) on a wall and carries a profusion of white flowers early in the season, with more flowers appearing throughout the season on mature plants. The flowers are lightly scented, opening flat to reveal a cluster of brownish stamens. Plants grow well in shade, but are prone to mild attacks of mildew and blackspot.

'Danse du Feu'   z 4

Also known as 'Spectacular' and well suited to both its names, this strong climber which will reach 10ft (3m) in rich, well-drained fertile soil which contains plenty of humus. In early summer this cultivar is massed with bright scarlet, slightly scented, semi-double flowers, with a few blooms appearing through the rest of the season. Young foliage is bronzed, ageing to dark glossy green. Suitable for a north-facing aspect, it will grow on a wall, pillar or pergola; benefits from light shade. Deadhead regularly.

'Desprez à Fleur Jaune'   z 6

Also known as 'Jaune Desprez', this cultivar was raised by Desprez in 1830 and is probably the earliest yellow climbing rose. Choose a high wall for this plant. Growths can reach up to 15ft (4.5m) and have few prickles. The flowers are held singly or in small clusters, and are beautifully fragrant, appearing from mid-summer through to autumn. They are double, rather flat, pale yellow with peach shades. Plants need some shelter and thrive in sun. Prune in late winter, removing old, weak or diseased wood.

'Dortmund' (*below*)   z 4

The bright flowers of this climbing *kordesii* hybrid are reddish-crimson with a white eye surrounding the central golden stamens. The single flowers appear in large clusters and will keep being produced with deadheading; this restricts the production of the large number of striking but energy-consuming hips. Good for the shaded wall, but also valuable for pillars and as a large shrub. The abundant foliage is a healthy, glossy, dark green. This is a very hardy rose with little scent.

'François Juranville'   z 4

When young the foliage of this vigorous rambler is bronzed, turning to a rich glossy green as it ages. The strong growths can reach 25ft (7.5m) and are ideal for a large shaded wall. Plants have a rather weeping habit. They flower only once with some later blooms after the main flush. The strongly scented flowers are salmon-pink, double, opening large and flat, with deeper-coloured centres, and are held singly or in clusters. They are paler in dry summers and on dryer soils. Also useful for a large pergola or tree.

'Gloire de Dijon' (*below*)   z 6

The double flowers of this hardy climber are up to 4in (10cm) across, of an apricot-orange colour with some darker and lighter petals, and strongly fragrant, especially in hot still weather. This cultivar is very popular and is often seen growing to 15ft (4.5m). It likes sun, but will also grow on north-facing walls and can be grown as a pillar. The bottom half of older plants tend to become bare and needs obscuring with other plants. Blooms appear continually from mid-summer onwards in great numbers.

'Handel'   z 4

The unusually coloured flowers of this climber make it popular: each flower is composed of petals which are creamy edged with pink, making an attractive combination, and are beautifully shaped. The flowers are carried on vigorous shoots capable of growing to 20ft (6m) in a hot sunny summer, about half this in cooler seasons, and are weather-resistant. They are only slightly scented and tend to fade in hot weather. The dark green leaves have coppery shades; they are prone to mildew. Blooms appear throughout the season.

'Hume's Blush'   z 6

This clone of the vigorous hybrid climber *R.* × *odorata* originated in China and was introduced to England from the East Indies by Sir A. Hume in 1809. It flowers on wood grown in the previous season so should only be pruned lightly. The flowers are a blushing pink, very strongly scented, large and double, and open from mid-summer onwards. It needs a sunny position to thrive. *R.* × *odorata* is an important cross in rose history, with *R. chinensis* and *R. gigantea* for parents.

'La Follette' z 4

Raised by Busby at Cannes around 1910, this half-hardy but vigorous climber is often grown into trees on the Italian and French Rivieras where it flowers early. It requires a sheltered wall (or in colder areas the protection of a cold greenhouse) and sun to achieve 20ft (6m). The huge, double, loose flowers appear in early summer in one main burst and are rose pink with shades of salmon and cream, especially towards the outside of the petals. The flower buds are long and pointed.

'Leverkusen' z 4

A useful plant which can be used either as a climber for a wall or pillar or grown as a shrub. Plants grow to 10ft (3m) in height and are very hardy with moderate vigour. The semi-double, pale creamy-yellow flowers with darker centres have their main display in mid-summer, followed by fewer recurrent blooms during the rest of the season. The smallish leaflets are a deep glossy green. An extremely useful rose for its abundant flowers.

'Madame Grégoire Staechelin' z 4
(*below*)

Thriving on shaded walls, this very vigorous climber can grow to 20ft (6m) in a sunny position. The thorny shoots need careful pruning to prevent flowers forming only at the top of the plant: cut some of the most vigorous shoots to the base in the winter after planting, and when mature remove one or two of the old woody stems completely each season. The pink flowers appear early in the season and are slightly pendent which is an advantage on taller plants. They have a fragrance not unlike sweet peas. In autumn the hips turn light orange, adding to the plant's interest.

'Maréchal Neil' (*above*) z 7

Popular in Victorian conservatories, this rather tender climber will grow better under glass in cold areas, with the roots planted outside the greenhouse. Elsewhere, train it against a warm sheltered wall in a sunny spot, where it can grow to 15ft (4.5m). Large tea-scented flowers are produced during summer. They are golden yellow and are held on weak flower stalks which give the plant a nodding habit. In Britain, this cultivar is only sufficiently hardy to be grown in the open in southern England.

'New Dawn' (*above*) z 4

This disease-resistant hardy rose is useful for shady pergolas, walls and fences. A vigorous lateral grower, given space the stems can exceed 15ft (4.5m). The medium-sized flowers are profuse during early summer, of apple-blossom pink with deeper pink centres and a very strong fragrance. A second flush of flowers appears in late summer. The flowers tend to fade to white during hot weather. The foliage is shiny light green. It also grows well into small open-canopied trees.

'Royal Gold' (*below*) z 7

Also suited to growing as a pillar, this climber is rather tender and will only succeed on a sheltered sunny wall in warmer areas. Die-back is common after a severe winter in colder regions: any dead shoots should be pruned out in the following spring. Deep yellow flowers appear from mid-summer onwards; they are large and double, scented and held singly or in clusters. Only moderately vigorous, this cultivar will give poor results unless planted on rich and fertile soil, where it can grow to 10ft (3m). The flowers resemble those of a hybrid tea.

'Veilchenblau' (*below*) z 4

A distinctive plant among ramblers because of its blue-purple flowers and sometimes listed as 'Violet Blue'. It is virtually thornless and has small semi-double flowers which open purplish, with white centres, maturing to dark blue-violet and finally greyish-mauve. They produce a scent of apples. The flowers appear in large clusters in mid- to late summer; there is no repeat flowering. Often called the "blue" rose due to the colour of its blooms, this plant is best grown in shade as the petals fade in direct sun.

HEDGES AND WINDBREAKS

The way in which a hedge is intended to be used in the garden, whether it be for its aesthetic qualities or for purely practical reasons or a combination of the two, influences the species chosen to make the hedge.

Aesthetically, hedges compartmentalize a garden creating a number of distinct areas that can each be given an individual style and character with a feeling of intimacy and seclusion from other parts of the garden. However, with a clever use of openings, either "windows" or "doors", an element of surprise and invitation is introduced which gives the illusion that the whole garden is larger than it really is. In addition, hedges form a valuable backdrop against which any

composition of other plants stands out and in a relatively short period of time they give the garden a satisfying air of maturity.

As windbreaks, hedges generate a precious microclimate which enables a wider range of plants to be grown. Often in an exposed new site it is necessary to use the fastest growing species. If there is the space, it may be a good idea to choose trees, such as poplars, alders or scots pines, that do not require any pruning and maintenance as this can make for heavy and time-consumming work. In the last 25 years or so the Leyland cypress has been used in many small gardens to create quick screens, but is invariably left to grow too

Right: Rhododendron ponticum is an evergreen that grows vigorously in cool shady conditions. It makes a tall, windproof, informal hedge that is a blaze of colour in late spring and early summer.

Left: A tightly clipped cypress hedge makes a fast-growing backdrop to a traditional herbaceous border, giving good protection from wind. Yew would be slower growing, requiring only one clip a year. Even when this border is dormant, the hedge remains interesting because of the way the top has been shaped.

Below: Privet is a semi-evergreen that is commonly used as a fast-growing hedge. To the right of the golden form shown here is a tiered topiary specimen of holly and, behind this, a formally trained beech hedge.

big before it is pruned severely and left looking like a skeleton. In many cases a good solid hedge of yew, for example, requiring only one cut a year, would have been achieved in less than eight years and is exceedingly long lived. If there is any risk of livestock eating any part of the hedge then use thuja instead of yew.

Yew and thuja make dense evergreen screens that are usually kept tightly trimmed, both responding to this treatment by generating plenty of new shoots after being cut back. The structural quality of a tightly clipped hedge gives a garden a strong form, whatever the season, and is best used in formal designs. A variety of textures and colours are available to the gardener through the choice of species. For example, a beech or hornbeam hedge offers a soft green colour which turns to russety brown in the autumn lasting through the winter and into spring, in contrast to the evergreen broadleaves of the Portugal laurel, *Prunus lusitanica*, or the English holly, *Ilex aquifolium*, which make a strong, glistening, dark green hedge all year round. For those who live in very cold climates, the choice of evergreens may be limited to the hardiest conifer, the western hemlock, *Tsuga heterophylla*, or a number of deciduous plants such as *Ilex verticillata* (z 3), which has rounded leaves that are smaller and less prickly than those of the English holly or sea buckthorn, *Hippophae rhamnoides*.

Left: The frost-hardy *Fuchsia magellanica* is deciduous but makes a good informal hedge, flowering over a long season in summer and autumn. The pendulous flowers are followed by black fruits. Pruning in early spring will help to keep plants strong and compact.

Below: Several spiraeas are good shrubs for informal hedges, the arching stems being wreathed in glorious white flowers in late spring or early summer.

Some plants that respond well to tight clipping, such as lime and hornbeam, can be used for pleaching, creating what is sometimes referred to as a hedge on stilts. This is a useful technique for making a boundary without reducing the sense of space. Others, such as the small-leaved box 'Suffruticosa' and wall germander (*Teucrium*), are small enough to use for edging and parterres. Box and yew are the best choice for topiary. They are slow-growing, with small, dense leaves, and respond well to very specific, intricate cutting. Patience is vital with topiary, and dedication to maintaining the chosen forms. It is important to select shapes and designs well within your capabilities.

A hedge can also be used informally, such as in a cottage or landscape garden, where it introduces a free-flowing line to the design. For example, *Rhododendron ponticum* makes a tall, windproof evergreen hedge, that is covered with purple blossoms in spring. Where space is at a premium compact forms need to be chosen. In most cases informal hedges are made of flowering and, in some instances, fruiting species giving them seasonal interest. Some, like the laurustinus, *Viburnum tinus*, combine glossy evergreen foliage with pink winter flowers that are followed by blue-black fruit. There are a number of flowering plants that flower on old wood, such as forsythia and *Cornus mas*, that can be lightly pruned to make an informal hedge. They can also be clipped hard back to make a formal hedge, although flowers will be lost.

Quick-growing

Alnus cordata   z 4
Italian alder
An extremely useful plant for wet
conditions, this quickly forms a barrier
against the wind and reaches 40ft (12m)
in twenty years with a narrowly conical
habit. In spring the crown is hung with
clusters of yellow, male catkins. The
tiny female flowers form small, round,
woody fruits which persist throughout
winter. The deciduous leaves are a shiny
dark green above, paler beneath and up
to 3in (8cm) long. Thrives in all moist
soils, acid or alkaline; dislikes dry
conditions. Needs sun or partial shade.

Chamaecyparis lawsoniana (*above*) z 4
Lawson cypress
One of the fastest-growing evergreen
conifers used in gardens, this can be
free-grown, reaching 60ft (18m), or
clipped for formal use. Drooping, deep
green leaves with greyish undersides set
off small pinkish-red male cones in
spring, then (on mature plants) woody
cones. Forms have blue, grey, green or
yellow foliage: 'Green Hedger' is ideal
for screens. Excellent for exposed,
windy sites and heavy soils; succeeds in
shade. Plant 2ft (60cm) apart. Trim in
late summer if used formally.

Crataegus monogyna   z 4
Common hawthorn
This deciduous shrub has extremely
spiny stems which act as a deterrent to
unwanted animals. If free-growing it
reaches 20ft (6m) in ten years and
produces large clusters of single white
flowers followed by red berries. For a
formal hedge, plant 1ft (30cm) apart and
clip monthly from late spring to late
summer. The small, lobed leaves turn
yellow in autumn. Useful for coastal
sites and all exposed, windy gardens;
excellent for heavy clay soils.

Cupressus macrocarpa   z 7
Monterey cypress
One of the best evergreen conifers to
grow for shelter in coastal areas, this
species has bright green foliage that
grows in upright, dense sprays. The
leaves smell of lemons when crushed.
Left unclipped, the Monterey cypress
makes a tree 25ft (7.5m) high in about
ten years. The conical habit broadens
with age. Yellow-foliaged forms such as
'Goldcrest' must be planted in full sun
or they fade to green. Older plants carry
clusters of small, shiny brown cones.
Plant 2ft (60cm) apart.

Elaeagnus × ebbingei (*below*)   z 6
A fast-growing evergreen that reaches
6ft (1.8m) in ten years. The large, oval
leaves are dark green above with round,
silvery scales beneath. Yellowish-silver,
fragrant flowers appear in autumn,
followed by orange, silver-specked fruits
in spring. 'Gilt Edge' has gold-margined
leaves that need protection from cold
winds. Plants dislike their roots being
disturbed, which leads to the sudden
death of entire limbs. Cut back long
shoots by two-thirds in spring to
promote bushiness.

Escallonia macrantha   z 8
Plant specimens of this evergreen shrub
2ft (60cm) apart for a semi-formal, 6ft
(1.8m)-tall hedge in five years. The
small, scented, sticky leaves have
indented margins. In summer it is
covered with masses of rose red flowers.
It thrives in most soils, resists drought
and tolerates alkalinity: a good choice
for exposed coastal gardens in warmer
regions. Cut out a third of the oldest
wood after flowering and trim back long
shoots. Overgrown plants can be cut
back to the ground and will take two to
three seasons to regrow.

Hippophae rhamnoides (*above*)   z 3
Sea buckthorn
This shrub is the perfect choice for a
coastal windbreak. The silvery, narrow
leaves are 2in (7cm) long and give good
yellow autumn colour. Male and female
plants must be grown together to ensure
fruiting; the orange-yellow berries last
into winter. Reaches 10ft (3m) in ten
years, spreading rapidly by seed and
suckers if well-established. Grow in full
sun and, ideally, in light, sandy soil.
Pruning is unnecessary but the plant
will regenerate if cut hard back to
ground level. It can become invasive.

Ligustrum ovalifolium (*below*)   z 5
Privet
This species grows quickly, is evergreen
or semi-evergreen, ideal for exposed
sites, and will tolerate alkaline soils as
well as atmospheric pollution. It reaches
8ft (2.4m) in eight years but is prone to
sudden die-back in patches. The roots
may deprive neighbouring plants of
nutrients and water. For a bright yellow
hedge grow 'Aureum'. Plant 1ft (30cm)
apart. Clip at least monthly from mid-
spring to late summer for a pleasing
formal appearance.

Formal

Populus alba 'Richardii' (*below*)   z 4

This form of the white poplar makes 33ft (10m) in ten years if free-growing. It has bright, golden yellow lobed leaves with white undersides and wavy margins. Trees make excellent windbreaks if pollarded; alternatively, grow the plants as large shrubs, cutting them back every two to three years. Valuable for exposed sites and for coastal areas, it tolerates some waterlogging but fails in dry soils. Grow in full sun to keep foliage colour. Plant well away from buildings and drains.

Thuja occidentalis (*below*)   z 3
American arborvitae

An evergreen conifer with a broad, conical habit and reddish-brown peeling bark, this species makes 10ft (3m) in ten years. The smaller 'Rheingold' has coppery-gold foliage that darkens to orange by winter. *T. plicata* 'Atrovirens' (z 5) has flat sprays of shiny foliage, and will tolerate shade and thin alkaline soil. The Chinese arborvitae, *T. orientalis*, has a formal habit, producing its foliage in vertical sprays. Plant 2ft (60cm) apart and trim during late summer. The foliage of the American arborvitae releases a fruity aroma when crushed.

Buxus sempervirens (*above*)   z 7
Common box

This slow-growing evergreen shrub makes only 4ft (1.2m) in ten years. It has small leaves and is able to withstand severe pruning, making it an ideal subject for a formal hedge; it is also used extensively for topiary. Mature, free-growing plants make small trees or large shrubs 8ft (2.4m) high. For a low edging along a path or for a knot garden or parterre, choose the dwarf form 'Suffruticosa'. Grows in most types of well-drained soil.

Carpinus betulus (*above*)   z 4
Common hornbeam

On heavy, damp soils, unsuitable for beech (*Fagus sylvatica*), hornbeam makes a good alternative. Bright green summer foliage turns yellow-brown in autumn. It retains its dead leaves during winter, providing an effective wind-filter throughout the year. As the new leaves unfold the old ones fall. Plant 18in (45cm) apart and trim frequently to form a dense hedge 8ft (2.4m) high in ten years. Hornbeam succeeds in sun or shade and makes a fine backcloth for the herbaceous or mixed border.

Fagus sylvatica (*below*)   z 4
Common beech

Beech grows best on well-drained, sandy or chalky soil and is intolerant of damp conditions which are better-suited to *Carpinus betulus*, the common hornbeam. Leaves open bright green but darken. The dead leaves are carried throughout winter. Susceptible to late spring frosts, it will only make 8ft (2.4m) in ten years in a sheltered spot; in the longer term, it is useful for windy sites. Plant 18in (45cm) apart and prune in late summer.

Ilex aquifolium (*below*)   z 4

Reaching only 5ft (1.5m) in ten years, this holly makes an excellent dense hedge with very prickly, dark green leaves. The leaves of 'Golden Queen' have yellow edges, while those of 'Silver Queen' are white-edged (both of these cultivars are male). 'J. C. Van Tol' has spineless leaves. The hardiest hollies are *I. × meserveae*, the blue holly, and the deciduous winterberry, *I. verticillata*. Plant 18in (45cm) apart in fertile soil; useful for heavy soils and coastal gardens. Trim plants in late summer. For berries, female forms need a pollinator to ensure setting.

Lavandula angustifolia (*above*)   z 7
A fine shrub for a low hedge, both the
mauve flowers and the silver-grey,
evergreen leaves are aromatic. 'Hidcote'
is dense with violet flowers. Thrives in
full sun, in well-drained soil and is
useful in coastal areas. Clip the plant
several times during the growing season
for a formal shape; this effectively stops
flowering. Unclipped plants reach 2ft
(60cm) with an equal spread. Discard
leggy plants and replant every five to six
years. Complements blue and grey
borders, rose gardens and stonework.

Lonicera nitida (*above*)   z 7
This evergreen shrubby honeysuckle
needs careful and regular clipping into a
wedge-shape to prevent bare patches
developing, particularly at the base of
the plant. The stiff, twiggy branches are
clothed with tiny, glossy green leaves
which are golden in 'Baggessen's Gold'.
Plants grow quickly to 5ft (1.5m). An
old or neglected hedge can be renovated
by being pruned hard back in early
spring to stimulate fresh growth. Grow
plants 1ft (30cm) apart, in any soil;
prune back to 1ft (30cm) immediately
after planting.

Prunus laurocerasus   z 7
Cherry laurel
This evergreen shrub quickly makes a
dense hedge 20ft (6m) high if free-
growing. It has large, dark-green, glossy
leaves. 'Rotundifolia' has leaves half as
broad as long. Succeeds best in acid soil
with some shelter; tolerates shade and
dripping water from overhanging trees.
Plant 2ft (60cm) apart and trim in
summer with secateurs: shears or hedge
trimmers cut through the leaves which
turn brown at the edges. Useful as a
dark backcloth for a border.

Rosmarinus officinalis (*above*)   z 6
Rosemary
A fast-growing evergreen shrub which
can be clipped into a low, formal hedge
or left as an informal hedge, making
5 × 5ft (1.5 × 1.5m) when mature. The
leaves are deep green, off-white below
and aromatic when rubbed. Flowers are
blue. 'Benenden Blue' is smaller-
growing with dark, very narrow leaves
and bright blue flowers. Plant 18in
(45cm) apart in a sunny, sheltered spot
in well-drained soil. Clip often when
young to induce bushiness. Rosemary is
useful in herb gardens, as an edging, or
in knot gardens.

Taxus baccata   z 6
Yew
This popular plant makes a dense hedge
if regularly clipped. The narrow, glossy,
evergreen leaves are poisonous, as are
the seeds (surrounded by a fleshy red
aril). *T. × media* 'Hicksii' is hardier,
with a broadly columnar habit. A fairly
rapid-grower if top-dressed annually
with fertilizer, it reaches 8ft (2.4m) in
ten years. Plant 2ft (60cm) apart:
tolerant of shade, exposed windy sites
and heavy or chalky soils. Trim in late
summer. Much-used for topiary.

Teucrium chamaedrys (*above*)   z 6
Wall germander
This shrub has a dwarf, bushy habit and
grows from a creeping rootstock. It has
dark grey-green, toothed leaves. Useful
for edging and in parterres where, with
regular clipping, a neat low hedge can
be produced. If plants are left
untrimmed they produce whorls of rose
pink flowers from mid-summer
onwards. Grow in sun in well-drained,
fertile soil. Can reach 3ft (90cm) if free-
grown. A good alternative to box, *Buxus
sempervirens*.

Tilia × euchlora (*below*)   z 5
Limes are tolerant of hard pruning and
are often seen as pleached specimens.
While free-growing trees can exceed
50ft (15m) in height, plants can be kept
to the required height with regular
clipping. The 4in (10cm)-long rounded
leaves are a shiny, dark green above and
pale and glaucous below, with brown
tufts between the veins. This form is
not susceptible to attack by aphids.
Grows well in full sun on all but the
poorest soils. Prune in spring before
growth begins. Plants can be trained to
form a tunnel or arbour.

Informal

Acer campestre (*below*)   z 5
Field maple
This deciduous plant is an excellent choice for a country or cottage garden. It is moderately fast-growing and reaches 35ft (10.5m) if left free-growing. The lobed leaves are green in summer and turn reddish-yellow in autumn. The trunk and stems of older plants develop corky, raised ridges. Plant 18in (45cm) apart in alkaline soil, in an open, sunny position, or in some shade. Prune to restrict growth in winter or, preferably, in summer.

Arbutus unedo (*below*)   z 8
Strawberry tree
An unusual ericaceous plant in that it is tolerant of alkaline soils. This species makes a shrub or small tree some 20 × 20ft (6 × 6m). It is often gnarled or twisted when mature, with deep brown, peeling bark. The evergreen leaves are narrow, dark and glossy. Panicles of white, pitcher-shaped flowers and edible fruits are carried together in autumn and winter. 'Rubra' has pink-flushed flowers. The strawberry tree is a good choice for exposed coastal gardens. Pruning is necessary only to keep the plant to the desired height.

Berberis thunbergii (*above*)   z4
This deciduous, spiny barberry reaches 5ft (1.5m) in ten years, 6ft (1.8m) when mature. It makes a dense hedge of small, bright green leaves with grey undersides. Red-tinged, yellow flowers open in spring, followed by bead-like, shiny red fruits. The reddish-brown bark is striking in winter. 'Rose Glow' is illustrated; *atropurpurea* also has reddish-purple leaves, which take on good colours in autumn. Plant 18in (45cm) apart. Grows in alkaline or clay soil, in sun or shade: suitable for an exposed position. Prune in winter.

Camellia × williamsii (*above*)   z 7
Camellias need shelter and are unsuitable for very cold and exposed positions; this is one of the best and hardiest. In winter and early spring velvet-petalled flowers in shades of pink, red and white are set off by the evergreen, dark, glossy leaves. Cultivars include 'Donation' (dark pink double flowers) and 'Francis Hanger' (white). Can grow to 10ft (3m) in ten years in humus-rich acid soil; will not tolerate a trace of lime. Plant in partial shade. Prune out long, leggy shoots.

Cornus mas (*below*)   z 4
Cornelian cherry
Usually seen as a free-growing large shrub or densely-branched small tree, this dogwood can be grown as a closely-pruned hedge if clipped in early summer. Clusters of small yellow flowers appear on bare branches in early spring. The dark green, oval leaves turn orange-red in autumn. After a warm summer, small, red, edible fruits form. Enliven with *Tropaeolum speciosum* or *Clematis* 'Perle d' Azur'. Grows in sun or partial shade in most fertile soils.

Forsythia × intermedia '**Spectabilis**'   z 5
(*below*)
The golden bell bush is covered with rich yellow flowers in spring. This vigorous deciduous hybrid is particularly floriferous. It has stout growths and can make a wide-spreading hedge 12ft (3.6m) tall by 10ft (3m) wide in ten years if left unpruned. The summer foliage is mid-green and sharply toothed, unfolding as the flowers fade. Other notable cultivars are 'Lynwood', 'Beatrix Farrand' and 'Spring Glory'. This bush tolerates most soils and is suited to exposed sites. Cut back after flowering if necessary.

Hibiscus syriacus (*above*)   z 5
This shrubby mallow carries large cup-shaped flowers from summer into autumn. The red, pink, purple, blue or white flowers last only a day before fading. Grey-green stems give winter colour; lobed leaves appear in late spring. 'Blue Bird' has dark-eyed, violet-blue flowers; 'Woodbridge' is the best large, single, pinkish-red form. Plants grow to 5 × 5ft (1.5 × 1.5m) in ten years, unless they are pruned in spring to keep them within bounds. Best in rich, well-drained soil in a sheltered, sunny position.

Hypericum 'Hidcote' (*above*)   z 5
One of the most popular flowering shrubs, this hardy, semi-evergreen has slender, low-growing, arching brown stems which can grow to 5 × 5ft (1.5 × 1.5m). The leaves are bright, apple green; the large yellow summer flowers are noted for their prominent golden stamens. This cultivar has the largest flowers. Grows equally well in dry or humus-rich soil, in full sun or semi-shade. Reduce plants if necessary by pruning hard back in late winter or early spring to the desired shape.

Osmanthus delavayi (*below*)   z 6
Grow this evergreen shrub for a wonderful fragrance in spring. The small, sweetly scented flowers are creamy-white and trumpet-shaped; they are held in plentiful clusters. The small, oval, dark green leathery leaves are fringed with minute teeth. It will grow to 5 × 4ft (1.5 × 1.2m) in ten years in well-drained soil, in sun or partial shade, with some shelter from other evergreens. Slower growth can be expected in cold areas. Any trimming should be carried out straight after flowering, using secateurs.

Potentilla fruticosa 'Goldfinger'   z 2
(*below*)
In ten years this shrubby cinquefoil can grow to 5ft (1.5m), forming a rounded bush with twiggy stems. The deciduous pinnate leaves are deep green and hairy. A profusion of large, deep yellow, five-petalled flowers appear from summer into autumn. Other forms include 'Katherine Dykes' (pale yellow flowers), 'Farrer's White' (white with yellow stamens) and 'Red Ace' (vermilion flowers with yellow centres). Plant 18in (45cm) apart in most soils. Prune in early spring to control growth.

Rhododendron ponticum (*above*)   z 6
This very resilient rhododendron will succeed in deep shade and is excellent for hedging. An evergreen shrub with large dark green ovate leaves, it grows to around 6ft (1.8m) in ten years. In late spring and early summer it is covered with tubular, lilac-pink flowers. 'Variegatum' has creamy-white margined leaves and is one of the few variegated rhododendrons. Needs a moist, acid soil and will benefit from a humus-rich mulch in summer. When the desired height has been reached, prune selected shoots after flowering.

Viburnum tinus (*above*)   z 7
Laurustinus
The stems of this adaptable plant carry dark, glossy, evergreen leaves and flat cymes of flowers at the tips. Pink in bud, these open white from late autumn to mid-spring. Shiny blue-black fruits often coincide with some flowers. Plants reach 10 × 10ft (3 × 3m) in ten years. 'Eve Price' is denser and smaller with pale pink flowers. Tolerates most soil conditions, shade, pollution and salt spray. Remove weak growth and prune lightly to maintain the shape.

GROUND COVER

For most people, the aim of ground cover in a garden is to minimize the number of weeds that seed themselves and grow rapidly, marring the appearance of the planting and competing with cultivated plants for moisture, nutrients and, in some cases, light. In the last 40 years or so, as labour has become more expensive, densely leaved low-growing plants have been widely used to accomplish this aim and the term "ground cover plants" has been applied to them.

They are comparatively cheap to buy, easy to plant and available in many different forms: quick or slow to increase; suitable for sun or shade; thriving in freely draining or moisture retentive soils; appropriate to formal or informal schemes, according to species or cultivar. Ground cover plants can be prostrate conifers, shrubs or herbaceous plants, evergreen or deciduous: something to satisfy every need, taste and planting plan.

Ground cover plants quickly colonize sizeable areas and build up a thick thatch of vegetation that suppresses most weeds. The one exception is woody weeds, but these usually appear singly and are easily removed. The perennial quality of most ground cover plants ensures that, with a minimum of pruning and splitting during the winter months, maintenance during the growing season is negligible. Once they are established, there is no longer any necessity to dig and hoe the areas of the garden that are planted with them. The chances of success are maximized if the ground is cleared of perennial weeds before planting. This can be a time-consuming task but it pays dividends.

The art of ground cover lies in spacing the plants correctly to ensure that the ground is covered quickly but without the plants competing for space or losing their characteristic habits from having to spread too far. The estimated spread of a plant can be used as a guide, taking into consideration the means by which it spreads. Those plants that spread by underground or overground runners are, as a rule, the most vigorous. They can be useful when a large area needs to be covered, but the larger plants, in particular, tend to suffocate and choke everything in sight. Clump forming plants are much more containable and there are a number that self-seed as well. These days, when a plant becomes a pest it is possible to eradicate it by painting it out with a glyphosate-based translocated herbicide that is deactivated as soon as it comes into contact with the ground; this should be used sparingly, over limited areas. However, most plants can be kept at bay by digging them up regularly.

The value of leaves cannot be overemphasized when looking at ground cover plants, the different textures and colours being so closely juxtaposed that they create an intricate tapestry. There are greens in every hue, yellow-flushed plants and white-variegated cultivars that prefer shade (for example, *Hosta fortunei* 'Aurea', *Lysimachia nummularia* 'Aurea' and *Lamium maculatum*); while silvery, yellow-variegated, purple and glaucous foliage perform best in sunshine (*Heuchera* 'Palace Purple', *Stachys byzantina*, *Ruta graveolens*). Flowers must be woven into the whole scheme, bringing seasonal interest to the composition (*Geranium endressii* 'Wargrave Pink', *Helleborus orientalis*, *Phlox subulata*).

Ground cover plants can be used in great informal drifts, covering large areas of the garden. A suitable scheme for a moist shady position would include hostas in variety, pulmonarias, hellebores, bergenias, solomon's seal and epimediums; in direct sunlight catmints, pinks, thrifts, snow-in-summer, jerusalem sage and thymes thrive. A steep bank, where it may be difficult to grow grass, can be successfully clothed in a thick mat of St John's wort (*Hypericum calycinum*) which carries bright yellow flowers throughout the summer, or periwinkle (*Vinca*) that raises starry blue eyes over a dense carpet of green leaves in spring – both require pruning in late winter.

In formal designs, where labour-intensive bedding plants might have been used in the past, it is possible to associate neatly clipped cotton lavenders, coloured leaved sages, blue leaved festuca, ivies and chamomile for a pleasing effect.

Left: A sunny well-drained sloping site is completely clothed with low-growing perennials, including *Convolvulus sabatius*, helianthemums, pinks and thrift. Dense planting suppresses weeds and creates a rich tapestry effect. The conifers introduce a discreet vertical element that emphasizes the flatness of the ground cover. This planting demonstrates the wealth of colour and texture provided by ground cover plants.

Below: Ivy is a thorough and accommodating ground cover in shady, cool conditions, creating a dense and weed-proof carpet.

For flowers

Arabis caucasica z 3

Often listed as *A. albida*, this useful plant forms loose mats of grey-green oblong leaves with bright white, slightly fragrant flowers carried in lax racemes 8in (20cm) tall in spring. It succeeds in dry situations and combines well with *Aubrieta* hybrids and *Alyssum saxatile*. The best forms are the double 'Flore-Pleno', 'Rosabelle' with its single, deep pink flowers, and the green-and-yellow leaved 'Variegata'. Propagate from cuttings taken in the summer or raise from seed sown during the autumn; plants may also be divided. Deadhead after the flowers have faded.

Asperula odorata z 4
Sweet woodruff

Also listed as *Galium odoratum*, the whole of this carpeting perennial is aromatic. It bears whorls of star-shaped white flowers during summer and reaches a height of 6in (15cm), with a spread of 12in (30cm). When in ideal conditions – partially shaded and in moist but well-drained soil – sweet woodruff needs to be kept in check as it tends to be invasive. Propagate either by softwood cuttings or raise from seed sown in early summer.

Cerastium tomentosum (above) z 6
Snow-in-summer

This widely-spreading, extremely vigorous perennial is an excellent for dry, sunny banks. It will become straggly if grown in the shade. From late spring the star-shaped white flowers are held above the foliage in a dense bright display. The spreading, prostrate stems are clothed in a mat of very small, grey shiny leaves. Plants reach a height of 6in (15cm) and tend to be rampant when established. Propagate by division or sowing seeds during spring.

Cotoneaster dammeri z 6

In well-drained soil, this low evergreen cotoneaster makes excellent ground cover, especially beneath other taller shrubs. It reaches 4in (10cm) in height, spreading to 2ft (60cm) or more, and needs hand weeding until a dense canopy is formed. The prostrate stems carry oval alternate leaves which are 1in (2.5cm) long, with small white flowers appearing in late spring and bright sealing-wax-red fruit in autumn. The deciduous *C. horizontalis* reaches 2ft (60cm); it has a variegated form.

Geranium endressii 'Wargrave Pink' (above) z 3

Originating from the Pyrenees, this geranium is ideal in a mixed border between large evergreen shrubs. 'Wargrave Pink' is a vigorous plant which produces flowers (bright salmon-pink with pale veins) throughout the summer and into the autumn, if cut back. The stems can reach 2ft (60cm) in height; the deeply divided leaves are 2-3in (5-8cm) across and form neat clumps. Plants will grow in most soils, in sun or light shade, and are useful as a weed-suppressant. Propagate by division in autumn or spring.

Helleborus orientalis z 3
Lenten rose

Choose a sheltered spot to grow this beautiful, evergreen hardy perennial. The flowers are extremely variable, ranging from creamy-white to deep-purple with yellow stamens, as plants readily cross-pollinate. They open from mid-winter onwards on stems 12-18in (30-45cm) high, above divided, mid-green leathery leaves. Plants self-seed very easily. Combines well with galanthus (snowdrop) and the perennial *Brunnera macrophylla*.

Iberis sempervirens (above) z 4
Candytuft

With its compact, cushion-like growth of dark green, evergreen leaves and dense smothering in late spring of white flowers, this sub-shrub makes ideal ground cover. It is also often grown as edging or in rock gardens. For best results plant in well-drained, slightly alkaline soil. Plants can reach 9in (23cm) in height and spread to 2ft (60cm). 'Snowflake' has larger-petalled, brighter flowers; the smaller 'Little Gem' has more erect growth. Propagate from softwood cuttings in mid-summer.

Hypericum calycinum (above) z 5
Rose of Sharon

The suckering habit of this dwarf evergreen shrub allows it to cover large areas quickly, even on poor and impoverished soils. The solitary flowers appear at the end of shoots up to 20in (50cm) tall. They are 4in (10cm) across and golden-yellow with a central boss of yellow stamens tipped by red anthers. Once established, cut hard back in spring to promote fresh growth, which is vital if plants have been affected by rust disease.

Lamium maculatum (*below*) z 3
Spotted deadnettle
In deep shade this rampant perennial will establish quickly where other plants might struggle. It has the characteristic "square" stems of the Labiate family, cream-striped, pungent leaves and mauve-pink flowers which appear in early summer. Plants can spread to 3ft (90cm), reaching a height of 8in (20cm). The cultivars tend to be less vigorous: 'Beacon Silver' has green-edged silver leaves and pink flowers; 'Aureum' has pale yellow leaves with pink flowers.

Lysimachia nummularia (*below*) z 3
Creeping Jenny
In moist, sunny conditions this plant is especially rampant and needs to be checked by regular pulling and thinning of wandering shoots. 'Aurea', which has yellow-green leaves, is less invasive and makes an excellent low-growing perennial ground cover; it is also used in hanging baskets, containers and for edging. The leaves are opposite on the prostrate stems, barely 1in (2.5cm) long and an ideal foil for the bright yellow flowers in summer. Plants reach only 1in (2.5cm) in height but can spread for 3-4ft (60-90cm).

Phlox subulata (*above*) z 2
Moss phlox
In spring, mats of bright flowers hide the narrow, spiky leaves of this evergreen, mound-forming perennial. Colour variations include the clear blue 'G.F. Wilson' and 'Scarlet Flame' with its deep red flowers. Plants need sun and fertile, well-drained soil. They reach 6in (15cm) in height and spread up to 20in (50cm). In early spring liven the flat mounds with underplantings of dwarf bulbs. Propagate by taking 2in (5cm) cuttings through the summer. 'Marjory' is illustrated.

Polygonum affine 'Donald Lowndes' z 3
This evergreen perennial is outstanding when planted in bold drifts on large banks. It produces small rose-red flowers in dense spikes in summer which fade and pale as they age. Plants grow to a height of 6in (15cm) and spread up to 6in (15cm). The narrow, pointed green leaves often take on attractive bronze tints in autumn and winter. For a larger plant grow *P. bistorta* 'Superbum' which has 2ft (60cm)-tall pokers of pink flowers in late summer. Grow both in sun or partial shade, where they will succeed in most fertile soils. Divide in autumn or spring.

Saxifraga umbrosa z 6
London pride
The dark green leaves of this saxifrage cover the ground throughout the year. In summer, small pink flowers are carried in delicate sprays 1ft (30cm) above the evergreen rosettes of leaves. Remove flowering stems as they fade. Plants need a moist soil and partial shade to grow well. Propagate in spring by dividing clumps. 'Variegata' has yellow-splashed leaves.

Vinca minor (*below*) z 4
A trailing evergreen perennial of use in shady positions and on inaccessible, steep banks. The bright bluey-mauve flowers appear from early spring to autumn, with the main flush in summer, among glossy, dark green, lanceolate leaves. To encourage a second flush, cut back after the main display. Plants need well-drained soil. The arching shoots can reach 8in (20cm) in height, spreading to 2ft (60cm). There are a number of cultivars; 'Variegata' has creamy-white splashed leaves and 'Multiplex' double plum-purple flowers.

Waldsteinia ternata (*below*) z 4
Also listed as *W. trifolia*, this semi-evergreen creeping perennial is notable for its trifoliate leaves and saucer-shaped, yellow flowers. In autumn, the leaves turn golden which is an added attraction. Plants grow to a height of 4in (10cm) forming loose spreading mats in well-drained soil in sun. Useful on banks where it soon spreads by fast-growing runners. Propagate by division in spring. Similar is *W. fragarioides* which has deeper toothed, strawberry-like leaves. Both are uncommon but well worth growing.

For foliage

Aegopodium podagraria 'Variegata' z 3
(*above*)
**Variegated bishop's weed, gout weed
or ground elder**
A variegated form of the weed ground
elder, this perennial has lobed pinnate
leaves, with creamy-white variegated
margins, which smother the ground.
Plants grow to a height of 4in (10cm). In
summer insignificant white flowers
appear which are best removed. A good
plant for a shady position, it will grow
equally well in full sun; prefers moist
soil. Propagate by division of the
rhizomes in spring. Fully hardy.

Arctostaphyllos uva-ursi z 2
Bearberry
This attractive and low-growing plant
barely reaches a height of 5in (13cm). It
succeeds best on well-drained acid soils,
in sun or light shade, and has a spread
of 2ft (60cm) after two years. The
leaves, which are small, shiny and
evergreen form a weed-suppressant mat.
In spring the plant is studded with pale
pink, bell-shaped flowers followed in
autumn by small bright red berries.
'Massachusetts' is lower-growing with
long-lasting flowers. Plants root readily
from stems touching the soil.

Asarum europeum z 4
The European ginger
A faint marbled effect is created by the
bright glossy-green and pale veined
leaves of this unusual perennial ground
cover plant. The leaves are evergreen
and grow on 6in (15cm)-long stalks
which hide the bell-shaped, maroon
flowers beneath. Individual plants
spread to 12in (30cm) and are best
grown in cool moist conditions. For
interest, plant in a drift with the mouse
plant *Arisarum proboscideum*.

Bergenia cordifolia (*below*) z 4
Elephant's ears
The large, leathery evergreen leaves of
this plant, from which its common
name derives, take on a range of reddish
and mauve tints in winter. From late
winter onwards pink or white flower
heads are carried on 18in (45cm)-tall
stalks. Individual plants spread to 24in
(60cm) and tolerate sun or shade. They
are excellent for planting as an edging to
a large shrub border, on most soils. *B.
purpurascens* and *B. p.* 'Ballawley', *B.*
'Abendglut', 'Silberlicht' and
'Morgenrote' are all worth growing.

Epimedium × rubrum (*below*) z 4
Barrenwort
An ideal choice for planting where dry
soil and shade are the main factors, such
as beneath trees. A relative of *Berberis*,
this low-growing plant has red or
bronze-tinted leaves during spring along
with crimson flowers with white spurs
which are carried on thin stems 9in
(23cm) tall. In summer the foliage is
pale green. In winter, cut away the old
leaves, taking care not to damage the
flower buds, to reveal the flowers.
Propagate by dividing the rootstock and
plant 9-12in (23-30cm) apart.

Euonymus fortunei 'Sparkle 'n' Gold'
(*above*) z 5
This popular, woody carpeting shrub
grows to 9in (23cm) high in sun or
shade. Its small, dark green leaves are
edged with bright yellow and form a
dense cover. Plants succeed on most
soils and should be planted up to 18in
(45cm) apart. In winter the leaves
assume pinkish tints as the temperature
falls. Useful for mass planting on banks
and other large areas. 'Emerald Gaiety'
has white-edged leaves, while
'Kewensis' grows to 4-6in (10-15cm)
with tiny leaves in dense mats.

Hedera helix cvs (*above*) z 5
English ivy
There are numerous forms of this plant,
all ideal for ground cover in a wide
range of conditions, including shade.
'Glacier' (*above*) has greyish-green
variegated, cream-edged leaves with
reddish stalks. The narrow lobes of
'Digitata' contrast well with those of
'Pedata'; 'Goldheart' is popular for its
bright yellow centred leaves; the dark
green 'Atropurpurea' turns deep purple
in winter. Plants grow 1in (2.5cm) high,
spreading to 18in (45cm).

Helxine soleirolii (*below*)　　z 8
Baby's tears or mother-of-thousands
Also listed as *Soleirolia soleirolii*, the common names of this plant come from its small rounded leaves and its capacity to grow from the tiniest fragments. This evergreen, prostrate-growing perennial forms a dense ground-hugging carpet which can choke other plants if not controlled. It will grow well beneath trees. At most it achieves a height of 2in (5cm). Plant in moist soil; divide in spring. The leaves may be burnt back by winter frosts.

Heuchera 'Palace Purple' (*below*)　z 4
Grown for its impressive foliage, which is purple-red, brighter red on the undersides, this clump-forming perennial remains evergreen only in mild winters. The leaves are heart-shaped with deep veins, above which in early summer are carried delicate sprays of small, bell-shaped white flowers. Plants grow to 18in (45cm) with equal spread, thriving best in a semi-shaded spot in moisture-retentive but well-drained soil. Divide in autumn or spring, using the young outer pieces of the woody crown. *H. sanguinea* has blood-red flowers and rounded leaves.

Juniperus horizontalis 'Grey Pearl'　z 3
(*above*)
With its pale grey-green foliage, this prostrate evergreen conifer grows to 8in (20cm) and spreads widely, up to 10ft (3m). It will thrive in sun or light shade. Other cultivars include 'Emerald Spreader', which barely reaches 4in (10cm) high, and the bluey leaved 'Glauca', 6in (15cm) high. *Juniperus × media* 'Pfitzeriana' is a vigorous hybrid which is capable of reaching 5ft (1.5m) in height after ten years. Plant junipers on well-drained soil.

Lonicera pileata (*above*)　　z 5
Evergreen in all but the coldest areas, this shrub is well-suited to planting in bold drifts. The stiff, spreading, almost horizontal branches fan out in layers, forming a dense canopy as adjoining plants knit together. The small glossy leaves are a fresh green, paler on the undersides. Small, fragrant white flowers appear on the undersides of the branches followed by beautiful translucent purple berries. Grows to 2ft (60cm) with a spread of 3ft (1m). The flat growth is a good base for a summer-flowering scrambling clematis.

Pachysandra terminalis (*below*)　z 4
Tolerant of deep shade and a tough grower, this plant has a place in all gardens. Growing to 10in (25cm) and quickly spreading to 3ft (90cm) due to its rhizomatous roots, it has leathery, shiny green leaves at the top of 6-8in (15-20cm)-tall stems. The small, scented flowers appear in spring and are creamy-white and rather insignificant. The plant will grow quickest in moist, acid conditions; it will grow equally well but slower on dry acid soils. 'Variegata' and 'Silveredge' are less vigorous with narrow white margins on their leaves.

Stachys byzantina (*below*)　　z 4
Bunnies' or lambs' ears
Also known as *S. lanata*, this low-growing evergreen perennial has silvery-woolly leaves. It is ideal for a hot, dry sunny position. The leaves are oval, up to 4in (10cm) long, forming a spreading, weed-smothering carpet, never reaching more than 6in (15cm) high, spreading to 18in (45cm). Flowers appear in grey-purple heads and are usually removed because they grow on 20in (50cm)-tall stems. 'Silver Carpet' is flowerless, making it particularly suitable as an effective ground cover.

BORDER PERENNIALS

The most successful borders are those that are designed with a balanced mixture of plants to produce a year-round display. The mainstay of the border is the perennials, while shrubs give a strong form to the composition and bulbs and annuals add seasonal interest. Many perennials are herbaceous (such as astrantia, peonies, dicentras, meconopsis and polygonatum), that is to say they die down in the autumn and overwinter under ground, and some are evergreen, including sub-shrubs (which are woody at the base and herbaceous at the tips) such as santolina, rue and sages.

Mixed borders are a rewarding form of gardening because a display can be produced in a short time and

then any errors can be corrected by moving plants about or by removing them, if they overstep their mark. Many perennials, given a good soil, spread quite rapidly. However, when selecting them care should be taken to match the plants to the climatic and soil conditions of a garden because in some cases, particularly with those perennials that spread by underground rhizomes, they can become rampant or self-seed with abandon.

Traditionally, in England, the border was set in a long, thin piece of ground – occasionally up to 300ft (90m) in length and at least 10ft (3m) wide – usually positioned in front of a wall or hedge and planted

Left: In early summer popular perennials for traditional borders include delphiniums, lady's mantle, lupins and poppies. A patch of the annual *Limnanthes douglasii* (with its unusual yellow and white flowers) fills a gap at the front of the border and will eventually be replaced by late-flowering annuals.

Right: In autumn the tall, creamy plumes of *Cortaderia selloana*, the pampas grass, are a perfect foil in a large border for the purples and mauves of asters and warm reds of *Dahlia* 'Bishop of Llandaff', and *Persicaria amplexicaulis*. Note the marked contrasts in forms and textures.

exclusively with herbaceous perennials. The plants were arranged according to height, with the tallest at the back and the shortest at the front, and usually in an almost random, polychromatic way. Borders were designed to be at their peak for two or three of the summer months, when the owners were most likely to visit their country residence, and as they were part of a sizeable garden they could easily be avoided during the rest of the year. As a consequence little attention was paid to spring and autumn colour or winter form.

In the early part of the twentieth century Gertrude Jekyll, the famous garden designer and author of many books, encouraged gardeners to think more carefully about selecting plants according to their colour, about extending the season by making use of foliage as well as flowers, and about planting late-flowering species beside earlier ones to hide these as they faded. For example, the frothiness of gypsophila will soon cover the fading crowns of poppies while the dark stems and star-like white daisy flowers of *Aster divaricatus* will arch nicely over the large glossy leaves of bergenias.

The variety of possible colour schemes for a border is enormous and in the end the choice is a personal one, but such books as Miss Jekyll's and, more recently, Penelope Hobhouse's on the subject of colour are classics and serve as good inspiration, as do other gardens – often as examples of what not to do. The important thing to remember is that once you choose a colour scheme it is essential to adhere to it if the border is to succeed. For example, the introduction of yellow tulips in a border of grey, whites, purples and mauves, pinks and maroons, spoils the whole effect even if they flower for only two or at most three weeks during the year.

If you wish to have several different schemes but the garden is too small to accommodate more than one border, it is possible to devise a graduated scheme.

The colours of the rainbow can serve as a good guide-line, starting with purples and deep blues at one end, progressing through lighter shades of blue to white and then introducing light yellows which increase in density through oranges to deep reds. If space allows, the colour can move back down the scale, creating an effective, definite rhythm.

An alternative is to introduce banks of neutral colours to separate successive schemes. In large gardens, dark green buttresses of yew against a wall or other hedge can be successful, while on a more modest scale patches of grey foliage (from such plants as santolina, artemisia or stachys) serve as a good foil to many colours and can link one scheme to another.

Not all borders need to be linear and backed by a wall or hedge. Much can be made of beds positioned in the centre of the garden that can be viewed from all sides. In recent years, island beds that fit into an informal garden plan – often irregularly shaped and surrounded by serpentine paths – have been made popular by the nursery, Blooms of Bressingham. Colours can be divided according to aspect, with warm reds, oranges and yellows on the sunniest sides and cooler pale blues, pinks and whites where it is shadier.

In a more formal setting, a central regularly-shaped bed, divided into four or more compartments depending on size with box edging and a pattern reminiscent of a parterre or knot garden, can equally well be planted with perennial plants. The rigidity of the design will hold together the essentially informal habit of the perennials.

It is possible to have a border in most situations, such is the diversity of perennial species. Whether the site is sun-baked and freely draining (in which case artemisia, sage, eryngium and phlomis are a good choice) or in the shade of trees and moisture retentive (where *Brunnera macrophylla*, astilbes and dicentras will thrive) it is possible to produce a successful border. If the conditions are particularly demanding then great drifts of a few suitable species can look just as spectacular as a large collection of different-coloured flowers in a kinder environment.

While there are a number of species that bloom for several months (for example penstemons, astrantias, erodium and *Sedum* 'Autumn Joy'), it is always important to include a good number of plants that are grown primarily for their foliage (such as artemisias, hostas, alchemilla, ferns and grasses) as the leaves will last for most of the season. With such foliage plants, flowers must be considered as extras that appear for a few weeks with continuity being achieved through the use of many species.

It is always a bonus to bring a little of the garden into the house to enjoy at close quarters. While most plants can be cut, it is useful to grow some that bear plenty of blossoms that last particularly well in water indoors – for example, coreopsis, astrantias and dianthus. In many cases cutting flower stems encourages more to grow and thereby lengthens the flowering time of the plant.

Perennial plants, like most others, should usually be planted out or moved when they are dormant, any time during autumn and winter when the conditions are suitable. Sometimes it is useful to do this while they are growing, between spring and autumn, when it is easier to evaluate their size and spread. In such circumstances, planting should be done with extreme care, speed and plenty of water to prevent the roots from dehydrating. If the plant is checked by being moved at this time it will usually have recovered by the following season.

Some staking is often required to prevent tall-stemmed plants from flopping over and swamping all around them. There are a number of different types of stakes available on the market, often in plastic-coated metal and in shades of green or in black; alternatively, tall hazel or beech twigs can be used and look a little more natural. However, on the whole it is best to avoid using stakes if at all possible and rely on the density of planting to ensure that most of the plants remain upright.

The permanent character of a border can make perennial weeds something of a problem, it is therefore important to ensure that the ground is clear before planting which usually means careful hand weeding. A generous layer of clean organic mulch (spent untreated mushroom compost, well-rotted manure or forest bark are among the best) applied in spring will help to prevent weed seeds from germinating; in addition it will improve the soil composition and nutrient levels and help to conserve moisture throughout the season.

Left: Crocosmia 'Lucifer' thrives in a hot sunny border, making a large clump of sword-like foliage, topped by brilliant, flame-red flowers. The sub-shrub cotton lavender (*Santolina chamaecyparissus*), with its grey, conifer-like foliage and small, yellow, pompon flowers, and the purple-blue spikes of *Salvia* × *superba* spill over the gravelly path, softening the edge of this striking border.

For cutting

Acanthus mollis   z 5
Bear's breeches
It is the architectural qualities of this perennial that make it such a dramatic addition to the garden and to any arrangement of cut plants. The large, oval semi-evergreen leaves are deeply cut and bright shiny green. During summer strong spikes of funnel-shaped white and mauve flowers appear, reaching up to 4ft (1.2m) in height. Plants spread to around 18in (45cm) and prefer a warm sunny spot in well-drained soil. They die back to a crown in autumn. Propagate by division when dormant or through root cuttings.

Anaphalis triplinervis   z 3
Pearly everlasting
Cut the heads of small papery flowers of this perennial during late summer and hang them upside down to dry out naturally. They are ideal for indoor winter decoration. Plants grow to 1ft (30cm) high with around a 6in (15cm) spread. The stems and lance-shaped leaves are silvery and woolly, and the flowers are whitish. Plants prefer full sun and well-drained soil, and can be divided in the spring.

Artemisia ludoviciana (*above*)   z 5
White sage
A lovely foliage plant for cutting. The aromatic, silvery-white lance-shaped leaves of this bushy perennial are woolly all over. In summer the narrow plumes of whitish-grey flowers appear when the plants reach about 4ft (1.2m) in height. They thrive in a hot dry border where the soil tends to dry out in summer, and go well in blue- and grey-themed plantings. Increase by softwood or semi-ripe cuttings in summer and trim plants lightly in spring before growth starts. White sage can be invasive.

Aster × frikartii '**Mönch**'   z 6
Encourage the production of blooms on this autumn-flowering perennial by pinching back the shoots in spring and early summer. The large, daisy-like, scented, clear bluey-mauve flowers appear from late summer to mid- or late autumn. They are carried on 3ft (90cm)-tall strong stems. The plants are easily grown in well-drained soil, and should be divided every three to four years, replanting with the outer sections of the crowns. Plants spread to 15in (40cm). The many forms of *A. novi-belgii* and *A. novae-angliae* are worth growing.

Astrantia major (*above*)   z 4
Masterwort
These beautiful flowers create interest in both the border and the vase. Each bloom resembles a small red pincushion stuck with green and white florets which are surrounded by a frill of papery bracts. The strong flowering stems emerge from a cluster of deeply divided, basal leaves which form good ground-covering mounds. For variegated foliage grow 'Sunningdale Variegated' and for plum-coloured flowers grow 'Rubra'. Plants need moist soil in sun or light shade, and reach about 2ft (60cm) in height. Divide them in spring.

Bupleurum angulosum   z 4
The most striking feature of this umbelliferous plant is the collar of large pale jade green bracts, ¾in (1 ½cm) wide, that back the clusters of tiny yellow flowers. The flowers are arranged in small umbels which are part of larger umbels and form dense clumps in summer. The flower heads are held high above the lanceolate leaves. Plants grow to 18in (45cm). They are slow to spread and need cool, well drained conditions in an open site. Evergreen in mild areas.

Coreopsis grandiflora (*above*)   z 3
Prized as a border perennial and for its strong upright stems which are ideal for cutting, the coreopsis has bright yellow flowers through the summer and into early autumn. They are carried on stems up to 3ft (90cm) tall on which the green narrow leaves grow. The petals or ray florets are split at their tips and have a small dark-maroon spot at their base. Several good forms exist: 'Goldfink', 'Mayfield Giant', 'Badengold' and 'Sunburst'. Grow plants in large clumps in moist rich soil in the sun. Divide in spring or take cuttings in summer.

Dianthus '**Doris**'   z 3
One of the most popular of all the pinks, this modern carnation has strongly fragrant flowers and strong stems suitable for cutting. The flowers are pale pink, semi-double with a reddish ring toward the centre. Plants grow compactly and produce a continuous flow of flowers through the summer months. They grow as evergreen clumps with numerous flowering shoots, 12-18in (30-45cm) tall. Plants need a sunny spot and fertile soil.

Gypsophila paniculata   z 3
Chalk plant or baby's breath
The flowers of gypsophila form delicate clouds of white during summer. They cut well and add great beauty to flower arrangements of any size. Plants grow to 3ft (90cm) in height with a similar spread, flourishing on alkaline soils in full sun. The grey-green foliage grows at the base of the plant. 'Bristol Fairy' is a double form with bright white flowers; 'Flamingo' is also double but pink. Plants tend to be short-lived and die away after a few years. New specimens are best obtained from a nursery.

For shade and dry soil

Scabiosa caucasica (*above*)   z 3
The flowers are like pincushions, 2in (5cm) or more across, and are a beautiful lavender-blue throughout the summer. Good cultivars include the creamy-white 'Miss Willmott', the pure white 'Bressingham White' and 'Clive Greaves' which is bluish-violet. The leaves are narrow, more deeply divided further up the stems and quite hairy. This perennial prefers alkaline soils and is ideal for a cottage-style border. Plant young plants in spring, dividing older clumps to increase stocks.

Thalictrum speciosissimum (*above*)   z 5
Meadow rue
This species of meadow rue is useful for cutting even when the flowers have faded, as its blue-grey divided foliage remains attractive for the entire summer. The small flowers are lemon-yellow in fluffy heads which fit well into a border where the colour theme is blue and yellow. An underplanting of lady's mantle, *Alchemilla mollis*, is recommended. Plants reach a height of up to 5ft (1.5m), forming good strong stems. Plant in fertile moist soil in full sun. Large plants can be divided.

Aruncus dioicus (*below*)   z 4
Goat's beard
Also listed as *A. sylvester* and *Spiraea aruncus*, the common name aptly describes the branching feathery plumes of small creamy-white flowers which grow on stems up to 6ft (2m) tall. The flowers appear in summer above an attractive mound of broad fern-shaped leaves. Plants grow well in dry or moist soil. 'Kneiffii' has finely divided foliage and creamy flowers growing to 3ft (90cm). Male plants tend to be the most floriferous, while the females have the seed heads which are used for drying. Divide plants in spring or autumn.

Aster macrophyllus   z 3
Grown for its ability to create good ground cover, this spreading aster reaches a height of 2ft (60cm), with equal spread, soon meshing together when planted in a group. The leaves are large and heart-shaped, and the main flush of pale lilac flowers is in autumn. It thrives in dry soil near to trees and shrubs, where its roots can be invasive, but should be avoided elsewhere. Lift and divide to propagate.

Dryopteris filix-mas   z 4
In even the most inhospitable places the male fern will produce its distinctive upright fronds which look like shuttlecocks. It adapts well to dry and shady conditions, staying evergreen in mild winters. Plants reach a height of 4ft (1.2m) with a spread of 3ft (90cm). The arching fronds are much-divided, lance-shaped and mid-green, unfurling from crowns coated in papery brown scales. The tough, rhizomatous brown roots form thick clumps. Divide mature plants by cutting younger crowns cleanly away from the older parent. 'Grandiceps' is a superior form.

Epimedium perralderianum (*above*)   z 5
The barrenworts are noted for their tough growth and tolerance of dry shaded sites, making resilient ground cover plants. This species is semi-evergreen, forming carpets of growth 1ft (30cm) high, which are studded in spring with clusters of bright yellow, pendent flowers with short spurs. The glossy deep green foliage can be clipped back to allow the flowers to be seen more easily. The new leaves which grow out in spring and summer are tinted with shades of red or bronze. To propagate, divide the woody rootstock during spring or autumn.

Filipendula hexapetala 'Flore Plena'   z 3
Dropwort
Also named *F. vulgaris* 'Flore Plena', this form has double white flowers which can be flushed pink, carried in large flat panicles above the finely divided carrot-like foliage during the summer. The plants are perennial with thick, fleshy swollen roots and reach a height of 2ft (60cm) with an 18in (45cm) spread. They succeed on dry chalky soils in shade. Division of the rootstock in winter and spring is essential because dropwort does not come true from seed.

Geranium endressii 'Wargrave Pink'   z 3
A reliable plant which is excellent for suppressing weeds and for colonizing virtually any garden situation. Its cup-shaped, bright salmon-pink flowers are carried above light green, delicately lobed basal leaves, on plants 18in (45cm) high with a spread of 2ft (60cm). This cultivar has particularly bright flowers which work well in a dry shaded position planted with purple-flowered irises. Divide in spring or autumn or take semi-ripe cuttings in summer.

For shade and moist soil

Helleborus foetidus z 3
Stinking hellebore

The common name should not deter the planting of this adaptable evergreen plant which can bring early colour to a shaded dry border. It associates well with early-flowering perennials: try its pale green, red-margined flowers next to those of honesty, *Lunaria rediviva*, or the spring pea, *Lathyrus vernus*. The flowers appear in large panicles from late winter onwards, held high above the leaves. Plants can be seen at their best when on a slope. Propagate by division, with minimal disturbance.

Iris foetidissima (above) z 5
Gladwyn iris

In the autumn the greenish-brown seed pods of this iris split open to reveal fiery orange seed. To view the heavy pendulous pods, plants are best placed on high banks or in raised beds. In summer the purple flowers are carried among the evergreen, dark green grassy leaves. 'Variegata' has cream variegation, but has few if any seeds. Plants thrive in poor dry soil in shade, growing to 18in (45cm) high. Lift and divide them in spring, keeping them well-watered until established.

Phyllitis scolopendrium z 5
Hart's tongue fern

Also known as *Asplenium scolopendrium*, the light green fronds of this fern brighten up shady dry corners during spring. When mature, the evergreen plants can be up to 2ft (60cm) in height. An added attraction is the rows of spore cases in a chevron-like pattern on the undersides of fertile fronds. Plants grow in any fertile, preferably alkaline soil. 'Undulatum' has fronds with ruffled margins, while 'Cristatum' has attractive crested leaf-tips.

Aconitum 'Bressingham Spire' z 3
(above)
Monkshood

A valuable plant for late summer and autumn flowers, the erect panicles of 'Bressingham Spire' are carried on 3ft (90cm)-tall stems which often need staking. The hooded helmet-shaped flowers are deep purple-blue. The foliage is deeply lobed. Plants thrive in moist cool soil which should be mulched with organic matter. Every three or four years lift and divide the tuberous roots in early winter. Monkshood is poisonous, most especially the roots.

Astilbe × arendsii z 4

In light shade and deep, rich, moist soil the astilbes provide a marvellous display of both foliage and flowers throughout the summer. They are beautiful delicate plants with deeply cut, dissected foliage in various shades of bronze and green. The foliage sets off perfectly the tiny flowers – dark crimson in 'Fanal', white in 'Bridal Veil' – which are carried in wispy plumes. Plants range in height from 18in-2ft (45-60cm) with similar spread. Lift and divide every three to four years, replanting young sections.

Brunnera macrophylla z 3

Of Russian origin, this spring-flowering perennial makes excellent ground cover beneath evergreen shrubs at the front of a border. Small, vivid blue flowers appear in spring on 1ft (30cm)-tall stems above mid-green heart-shaped leaves, which are bristly-hairy. Each plant can spread to 2ft (60cm) when growing in rich, moist fertile soil. Lift and divide the plants every three to four years, discarding the central piece of the clump. Brunnera is easy to grow and goes well with *Berberis darwinii*.

Cimicifuga ramosa (below) z 3
Bugbane

This fine perennial is happy in shade and will enliven the garden in late summer and early autumn with its sheer elegance. Its impressive, 1ft (30cm)-long pure white inflorescences are held on slender branching stems capable of reaching 7ft (2.1m) in height. After flowering, green seed pods remain on the plants well into winter. The foliage forms a mound of large divided leaves which takes on attractive yellow shades at the end of the season. Plants need cool, moist humus-rich soil. Divide them in autumn or spring.

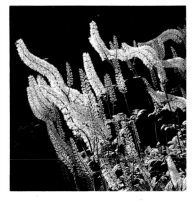

Claytonia virginica z 6
Spring beauty

An evergreen clump-forming perennial with flattish, black underground tubers which can be difficult to grow until it is established. It needs shade and moist but well-drained soil to succeed. The leaves are succulent, spoon-shaped, red-tinted when young turning green and glossy as they mature. In early spring the branched stems carry cup-shaped white to pink flowers which are striped with a deeper pink. Propagate by autumn division or from seed.

Corydalis ochroleuca z 5

Ideal for a shaded spot, this dainty corydalis looks superb spilling out of a north-facing wall or in a border. Plants form clumps with fleshy fibrous roots and finely-divided grey-green leaves. The dense spikes of creamy-white flowers tipped with yellow are carried above the foliage from late spring onwards, at a height of up to 1ft (30cm). Individual plants spread to about 1ft (30cm), forming low but effective ground cover. Plants self-seed profusely; divide larger specimens.

Dicentra spectabilis (*above*) z 3
Bleeding heart, lady's locket, lady-in-the-bath or Dutchman's breeches
To add a coolness to the garden in early spring, the delicate fern-like foliage and deep blue-pink flowers of this perennial are unsurpassed. The leaflets are of a blue-green glaucous hue and are followed by the heart-shaped flowers which hang from arching 2ft (60cm)-tall stems. For white flowers grow *D. alba*. Plants need cool moist soil and do well near water. They become dormant in hot summers. Divide in late winter.

Doronicum 'Miss Mason' z 4
Leopard's bane
This makes an ideal early spring partner for the perennial honesty, *Lunaria rediviva*. Plants form spreading clumps of growth, 2ft (60cm) across. Each of the bright yellow, daisy-like flowers is 3in (7cm) across and distinct for its thin narrow petals are all carried at the same level on 18in (45cm)-tall stems. The flowers last for several weeks. The heart-shaped leaves are strongly toothed. Plants need moisture-retentive soil and should be divided in autumn.

Gentiana asclepiadea z 5
Willow gentian
One of the tallest-growing of all the garden gentians, this evergreen perennial has narrow leaves and graceful arching stems. The rich blue trumpet-shaped flowers appear in pairs in late summer to autumn. Plants grow best in shade and must have deep, moist rich soil with humus added in. They can achieve 3ft (90cm) in height, but tend to be more lax in habit. A long-lived perennial which improves with age, the roots of which should not be disturbed. Lift and divide in early spring.

Geranium macrorrhizum 'Bevan's Variety' z 3
Use it to effect under a light canopy of overhanging trees or in a shaded courtyard border, where it will form a valuable ground-covering mat, 1ft (30cm) high. The aromatic leaves are pale green as they emerge, changing to russet shades in autumn, and are often retained through the winter in warm zones. During summer the long-lasting cerise flowers are carried in rounded heads on long stems. Divide plants in autumn or early spring.

Lysimachia punctata (*above*) z 3
Garden loosestrife
Rather prone to getting out of control if not checked, the garden loosestrife produces erect spikes of bright yellow flowers and mid-green bracts during the summer. It is ideal for a moist shaded corner. The brownish dead flowering shoots can be left through the winter to add some colour, before being cut back in spring. *L. clethroides* has white flower heads late in the season. Both grow to around 3ft (90cm). Divide large clumps in spring; burn discarded roots.

Meconopsis betonicifolia z 7
Blue poppy
Few plants can equal the eye-catching sky blue flowers of this poppy, carried on tall stems above pale green foliage in late spring and early summer. Plants form a basal rosette of leaves from which the stems emerge, reaching up to 4ft (1.2m) high, spreading 18in (45cm). They grow well among established rhododendrons if the summers are cool, thriving in moist, neutral or acid soil, but will not tolerate humidity or great heat. Divide plants in spring or raise from seed sown in late summer in moist acid compost.

Mertensia virginica z 3
Virginian cowslip or Virginia bluebell
For a cool border in a woodland garden, there is no finer choice than this elegant perennial with its hanging clusters of violet-blue tubular flowers during spring. The flowers appear at the top of stems up to 2ft (60cm) high, which die back later in the summer. The oval leaves are bluish-green, quite soft and bristly. Each plant spreads up to 18in (45cm) across. When they are dormant, protect the crowns of the plants from slugs. 'Rubra' has pink flowers. Divide plants in early spring before they flower.

Peltiphyllum peltatum z 6
Umbrella plant
The common name derives from the big (up to 1ft (30cm) across) umbrella-like leaves which are held on 3ft (90cm) stalks. They are preceded by quite spectacular flowers carried on tall, white-haired purple stems, rising straight up from the dark roaming rhizome. The pale pink to white flowers are held in clusters. The leaves take on shades of yellow, orange and red in autumn. Divide the rhizome to increase. Useful for stabilizing banks.

Polygonatum × hybridum (*above*) z 3
Solomon's seal
No moist and shaded part of the garden is complete without the arching 3ft (90cm)-tall stems of Solomon's seal, carrying translucent, opposite, green oval leaves 2-6in (5-15cm) long. Below the leaves hide the small, bell-shaped cream flowers, edged with green, which appear from spring to early summer. The giant *P. canaliculatum* (also listed as *P. commutatum* or *P. biflorum*) has leaves which take on yellow tints in autumn. Divide in early spring. Check every day for sawfly caterpillars.

For hot, dry places

Primula florindae (*above*)   z 6
Giant cowslip
Although this lovely Tibetan primula
will thrive in moist shade, it is quite at
home in wet soil next to water. Plants
form a clump of large rounded leaves
from which several flowering stems
emerge, carrying drooping heads of
scented, yellow bell-like flowers which
last for several weeks during the
summer. The stem and flowers are
powdered with a silvery-white mealy
bloom. Raise more plants from seed
sown as soon as it is ripe or preserved
and sown in spring.

Pulmonaria saccharata (*below*)   z 3
Lungwort
This rough-leaved member of the
borage family makes useful ground
cover. In hot and dry conditions it tends
to suffer from mildew. The flowers
appear in early spring in arching heads,
pink buds emerging from purplish
calyces and then turning blue. The dark
evergreen foliage is heavily spotted with
grey blotches, making some of the
leaves almost completely grey. Plants
grow to 1ft (30cm) tall when flowering.
Divide in spring.

Artemisia stelleriana (*below*)   z 4
Dusty miller
A rhizomatous perennial which becomes
woody at its base, forming a more or
less shrubby evergreen. Plants form
clumps or carpets of deeply lobed and
toothed greyish-white foliage. In
summer the small, yellow daisy-like
flowers appear in slender sprays borne
on grey stems. Dusty miller will grow
well near the coast and succeeds in cold
gardens. Plants grow to a height of 1-2ft
(30-60cm) with similar spread.
'Boughton Silver' is a vigorous, arching
cultivar. Divide in spring or autumn or
take stem cuttings in summer.

Ceratostigma plumbaginoides   z 5
Normally regarded as a shrub, this
lovely late summer flowerer is often cut
back to ground level by winter weather.
It loves a hot sunny position and rich
well-drained soil, growing to 1ft (30cm)
high. This species is ideal for the front
of a bed or border, but can be invasive.
At the end of summer each reddish leafy
shoot is tipped with a bristly head of
dark blue flowers, with new ones
opening every day. Cut back frost-
damaged shoots in spring before the
new growth emerges. Take cuttings in
summer or divide in spring.

Chrysanthemum haradjanii   z 8
Also listed as *Tanacetum haradjani*, this
evergreen mat-forming perennial tends
to become woody at its base and has a
deep tap root. The leaves are lance-
shaped, finely divided, silvery-grey and
the perfect foil for the clusters of yellow
flower heads which appear in summer.
Plants achieve a height and spread of up
to 15in (40cm) and should be divided in
spring if necessary. This species is a
useful border plant and at home in a
rock garden or alpine house.

Crambe cordifolia   z 5
The huge stately panicles of flowers
produced by this member of the
cabbage family demand ample space.
Numerous white flowers appear on
stems up to 7ft (2.1m) tall in early
summer. The large dark green leaves
can be 2ft (60cm) long and are hairy and
deeply-veined. The base of the plant has
a spread of 4ft (1.2m). Plants grow well
in slightly alkaline soil, so long as it is
well drained and in full sun. Suffers
badly from attack by caterpillars.
Divide in spring or sow seed. The
crambe is magnificent when seen against
a dark background such as a yew hedge.

Eriophyllum lanatum   z 6
This perennial produces delightful
sunny flowers. An abundance of eight-
petalled, bright yellow heads covers the
plant during summer. They are held on
grey stems which give the plant a height
of 12in (30cm). Clumps of divided
silvery leaves give it a similar spread. It
requires sun and well-drained soil but is
frost hardy. A very attractive plant for
the rock garden or the front of a border.
Propagate by division in spring or by
seed in autumn.

Eryngium × oliverianum (*above*)   z 5
This spiny upright perennial is prized in
the border for its large, thistle-like
rounded flower heads of bluish-lavender
which are at their peak in late summer.
Each head is subtended by a collar of
thorny bracts. The many flowers in each
head eventually open covering the entire
plant with blooms. The basal leaves are
mid-green with jagged edges. Plants
grow well even in the poorest soils, but
must have sun. They reach 2-3ft (60-
90cm) in height with a spread of up to
2ft (60cm). Propagate by division in
spring or by root cuttings in winter.

Liatris spicata (above)   z 3
Gayfeather
Also known as *L. callilepis*, this is
something of an oddity among flowering
border perennials in that its flower
spikes, which look like thick pinkish
bottlebrushes, open from the top
downwards. The spikes grow from
clumps of dark green grassy foliage.
Good forms include 'Kobold', with
rosy-purple spikes up to 18in (45cm)
high, and 'Alba' for white flowers. All
are easy to grow, needing full sun and
regular deadheading in summer.

Nepeta × faassenii   z 3
Catmint
Cats will roll in this wonderfully
aromatic herbaceous perennial – hence
its common name. The leaves are grey-
green, soft and downy. In late spring
and early summer blue-purple flower
spikes appear, with a second flush of
blooms in autumn if the plants are
sheared back after the first flowering.
Catmint will grow even in the poorest of
dry soils. Ideal for edging beds and
borders. Propagate by tip cuttings in
summer or division in spring.

Phlomis russeliana   z 4
An evergreen perennial which makes
excellent ground cover, growing to 3ft
(90cm) high when in flower. The strong
flower stems appear in summer carrying
several whorls of soft butter-yellow
hooded flowers above the foliage. The
large hairy leaves are heart-shaped. In
winter the dead flower heads add
interest. Plants can achieve a spread of
2ft (60cm). The leaves are aromatic if
rubbed. They need full sun and are
ideal for baked, dry positions. Divide
plants in spring or take softwood
cuttings during summer.

Ruta graveolens (below)   z 3
Rue
If not grown in full sun in an open spot,
rue tends to become drawn and floppy.
It is an excellent border plant and very
useful as edging. Clusters of mustard-
yellow flowers appear above the foliage
during early summer, at which time
plants can reach up to 3ft (90cm) in
height, with similar spread. 'Jackman's
Blue' is illustrated, with blue-grey fern-
like foliage. The leaves release a
pungent odour. Contact with the foliage
or sap can cause a skin rash. Clip back
shoots in spring; take semi-ripe cuttings
in summer.

Santolina chamaecyparissus 'Nana'   z 7
Cotton lavender
This dwarf and compact form has finely
toothed, narrow leaves which are
covered with a woolly white coating.
Plants form low mounds of silvery
fragrant foliage topped in summer by
small, yellow button-like flowers.
Blends well with the true English
lavender, *Lavandula officinalis*.
Deadhead in autumn and cut older
plants hard back in spring. Propagate
by semi-ripe cuttings in late summer.

Stachys byzantina   z 4
Bunnies' or lambs' ears
Also listed *S. lanata* and *S. byzantina*,
this popular evergreen perennial makes
good ground cover. It forms thick mats
of deeply felted, silver-grey leaves. In
summer the flower spikes, which are
also covered in silver hairs, grow
upright from the mats carrying clusters
of tiny pink-purple flowers. Lamb's ears
is at home in hot dry soils and loves to
be baked next to paving in full sun. It
goes well with old fashioned roses and
pinks and with *Sedum* 'Autumn Joy'.
Divide clumps in spring or autumn.

Achillea filipendulina 'Gold Plate'   z 3
(above)
Yarrow or milfoil
Thriving on dry, poor soils, this plant
flowers throughout the summer. The
bold flat heads of tiny, golden-yellow
daisy-like flowers face upwards on stiff
stems 4ft (1.2m) high. The foliage has
an elegant feathery nature and is
aromatic if rubbed or crushed. For paler
yellow flowers and grey foliage grow
A. 'Moonshine'. Plants can spread to 2ft
(60cm) across. Divide them in spring or
autumn, or take cuttings in summer.

Anemone × hybrida   z 5
'Honorine Jobert'
This Japanese anemone flowers for three
months from mid-summer to autumn,
producing saucer-shaped flowers with
clear white petals and yellow stamens.
Even though the branched flowering
stems are up to 3ft (90cm) tall, they do
not need staking. The deeply lobed
leaves form a neat mound, 2ft (60cm)
across, in heavy soil; in lighter soils
these anemones can be quite invasive.
Plants grow well in full sun or light
shade. Divide in spring or take root
cuttings in winter.

Bupthalmum salicifolium   z 6
Yellow ox-eye
While tending to be invasive in borders,
the yellow ox-eye is worth growing for
its deep yellow flower heads carried
singly on thin stems. Its vigorous nature
can be curbed somewhat by regular
division and by digging out unwanted
growth. Plants grow to a height of 2ft
(60cm) when flowering, and have dark
green, narrow leaves. They thrive on
slightly starved, infertile soil in full sun.
The flowers appear for many weeks.
Increase by division in spring.

Chrysanthemum maximum (*below*) z 4
Shasta daisy
Even after bad weather, the flowers of
the shasta daisy will show little sign of
damage. This old border favourite
grows 2-3ft (60cm-90cm) tall, the stems
being topped with large, white daisy-
like flowers with yellow button-like
centres. The dark bottle-green leaves
form a dense carpet in spring from
which the flowering stems emerge
throughout the summer if regularly
deadheaded. Fine cultivars include the
frilly-petalled 'Aglaya' and the pale
yellow 'Cobham Gold'. Plant in sun.
Divide clumps in spring or autumn.

Erodium manescavii (*below*) z 7
One of the most useful cranesbills for
the border, this species will flower for
several months during the summer. It
forms mounds of blue-green, divided
fern-like foliage topped by clusters of
single lilac-pink flowers. Plants need a
sunny position. They reach a height and
spread of 20in (50cm) and self-seed
quite readily, from which good forms
can often be selected if the seedling
plants are allowed to flower. As an
alternative, semi-ripe cuttings can be
taken in summer.

Patrinia gibbosa z 5
This unusual Japanese plant emits a
rather unpleasant smell. It produces
long-lasting flowers during late summer
each with one long greenish-yellow
petal. The flowers are small, appearing
in massed heads above a clump of broad
basal leaves, and are attractive even
when they have faded. The roots need
to be kept reasonably cool and moist.
Plants grow to 18in (45cm) tall and
spread to 1ft (30cm). Divide in spring or
grow-on self-sown seedlings.

Penstemon 'Alice Hindley' z 9
The greatest asset of the penstemons is
their long flowering season – from early
to late summer – which can be extended
through regular deadheading. They are
also available in a wide range of colours,
from white to deep red, with many
intermediate shades of blue and mauve.
Hardiness is also variable: it is often
said that the wider the leaf the more
tender the plant. This cultivar has the
characteristic tubular flowers which are
pale lilac, and is more or less evergreen
with rich green leaves. Plants can grow
to 4ft (1.2m) and may need staking.
Take cuttings in summer.

Sedum 'Autumn Joy' (*above*) z 3
This large stonecrop is prized not only
for its display of large, flat pink flower
heads in autumn, but also for its dried
seed heads in winter. The young leaves
are also attractive and grow to 2ft
(60cm) by late summer. In full flower
the plants attract clouds of bees,
butterflies and other insects. Plants will
soon form bold clumps 2ft (60cm)
across on fertile soil, and must be in a
warm sunny spot. As the flowers age
they turn to shades of coppery red. Cut
back the old flowering stems in late
winter. Divide the crowns in spring.

Spring flowering

Aquilegia vulgaris 'Nora Barlow' z 4
(*above*)
This unmistakable cultivar of granny's
bonnets is a spring favourite in the
border, noted for its double spurred
flowers with red petals which are pale
green at their tips. The grey-green
foliage is deeply divided and forms a
loose clump below the 2½ft (75cm)-long
flowering stems. Plants spread to 20in
(50cm). They need well-drained soil and
an open sunny position. Cultivars such
as this only occasionally come true from
seed. *A. vulgaris* has flowers of purple,
white, pink and crimson.

Convallaria majalis (*below*) z 3
Lily-of-the-valley
An old favourite of cottage gardens,
noted for its wonderfully scented
flowers. The white bell-like flowers
appear on arching stems during spring,
emerging from a pair of broad, mid-
green lance-shaped leaves. Plants grow
to around 8in (20cm) tall and spread
quickly. They prefer moist soil with
plenty of organic matter added, and are
ideal for carpeting a small bed or the
ground below shrubs. Increase by
replanting sections of the rhizome.

Euphorbia polychroma (*below*)   z 4
Dappled shade is perfect for this early-flowering spurge, which emerges in spring reaching a height of 18in (45cm). The sulphur-yellow flower heads are held above fresh green leaves, most of the colour being provided by the yellowish bracts. During summer the heads fade to green and finally to reddish-brown. This species associates well with *Brunnera macrophylla* or red tulips. Plant it in moist well-drained soil. Divide plants during autumn or take cuttings in summer. Avoid skin contact with the plant's white latex.

Geum 'Borisii'   z 5
The bright orange flowers of this avens have striking yellow stamens and add a touch of warmth to a border in spring. A clump-forming perennial, its leaves are broad and unevenly lobed, forming a loose clump at the base of the 1ft (30cm)-tall flowering stems. The stems are hairy and each one carries several single flowers. This perennial is at its best in full sun and needs moist but free-draining soil. Increase by seed sown during autumn or by division.

Heuchera sanguinea cvs   z 3
A number of fine cultivars have arisen from crossing this species with *H. americana*. 'Palace Purple' is an evergreen perennial hybrid with large clumps of deeply purple-bronze leaves, against which are set creamy flowers in spring and summer. 'Red Spangles' has silver-marbled leaves and spikes of bright crimson, bell-shaped flowers in summer. Both these make good ground cover and need moist soil, in sun or light shade. The flowering stems grow to 18in (45cm) tall and should be cut back as they fade. Divide the plants in spring or autumn.

Omphalodes verna   z 5
Verna means early, in this case the early-flowering of this semi-evergreen perennial which is decked in spring with sprays of white-eyed, bright blue flattish flowers. Plants form clumps of mid-green oval-shaped leaves and grow to 8in (20cm) high. They make good ground cover for a shaded or semi-shaded border and need well-drained but moist soil. Similar, but with heart-shaped deeply-veined leaves, is *O. cappadocica*, which carries clear blue flowers above its leaves during spring. Plants can be divided in spring or raised from seed.

Paeonia officinalis **'Rubra Plena'**   z 2
The deep velvety-red flowers of this old-fashioned, European herbaceous peony are fully double and are carried in great, sometimes unwieldy clusters. Plants form large 3ft (90cm)-wide clumps of glossy foliage which lasts for the entire season. This species does not like being moved, but will survive under adverse conditions for many years. Cultivars with single flowers include 'Phyllis Pritchard' and 'J.C.Weguelin'. Increase by root cuttings in winter or division in late autumn or early spring.

Papaver orientale (*above*)   z 3
Great oriental poppy
With its enormous papery-petalled flowers on gently curving 3ft (90cm)-tall stems, this poppy is a spectacular spring-flowering plant for the border. Plants form rather loose clumps of long basal leaves. They thrive in dryer borders and must have full sun. 'Marcus Perry' has red petals with a black blotch and those of 'Perry's Pink' are grey-white. Plants will self-seed, but cultivars must be increased by root cuttings during winter.

Symphytum × ***uplandicum***   z 3
Russian comfrey
A tough herbaceous perennial which grows to 3ft (90cm) in height and carries spectacular cymes of pinkish-blue flowers in late spring and early summer. Plants grow best in deep moist soil and go well with yellow-flowered azaleas and rhododendrons. 'Variegatum' has similar flowers plus grey-green leaves broadly margined with pale cream. Plants will self-seed, although 'Variegata' must be increased by division in spring. Because of their deep roots, they can be difficult to eradicate.

Trollius europaeus (*above*)   z 3
Globeflower
In spring this relative of the common buttercup produces large, globe-like lemon-yellow flowers on 2ft (60cm)-tall shoots. For best results grow it in moist soil next to a stream or pool, in sun or shade. Plants form clumps 18in (45cm) across of mid-green deeply-divided leaves. Hybrids are usually listed as cultivars of *T.* × *cultorum*, including the lovely 'Alabaster' with its yellowish-white blooms. Propagate cultivars by division in early autumn, and species from seed sown in summer or autumn.

Veronica gentianoides   z 4
A pretty and dainty perennial which forms mats of broad dark green leaves from which rise spikes of washed-out blue flowers in spring. It is ideal for the front of borders and for mixing in with red or orange companions such as *Geum* × *borisii*. On strong plants the flowering stems grow to 18in (45cm), less if grown on poor dry soils. 'Variegata' has the added interest of cream splashed leaves. Propagate by division or softwood summer cuttings. Plants love a sunny spot in well-drained light soil.

Summer flowering

Acanthus spinosus (*below*) z 7
This species of bear's breeches is very variable but tends to be somewhat smaller than the commonly grown *A. mollis*. Both are prized for their architectural qualities. The shiny dark green leaves achieve 2-3ft (60-90cm) in length and form spiky clumps at the base of the 4ft (1.2m) flowering stems. The stems are clothed almost to the top in hooded purple and white flowers in late summer. Plants grow best in full sun. They can become invasive. Divide plants in autumn or spring, or take winter root cuttings.

Campanula lactiflora (*below*) z 4
An easily grown perennial bellflower needing moist soil to succeed, this species produces 4ft (1.2m)-tall stems which are clothed in pointed leaves. Bell-shaped mauve flowers appear in large branching heads at the top of the stems. 'Loddon Anna' is taller with pale pink flowers. To extend the flowering season cut back some of the stems in late spring. Plants need sun or light shade. Propagate by division in late autumn or spring, or through softwood or basal cuttings during the growing season. Stake on windy sites.

Delphinium hybrids (*above*) z 3
Delphiniums form large and, if not supported, unwieldy clumps of growth up to 2ft (60cm) across, and tall flowering stems up to 6ft (1.8m) high. The flowers appear in narrow racemes, in vibrant tones of blue, white and purple, or now in reds in the University Hybrids. Plants need deep humus-rich soil, sun and shelter from wind for the taller types. Common hybrids are the Pacific Giants and Blue Fountains Series. Increase plants by division or by taking cuttings from young basal shoots during spring.

Digitalis × mertonensis (*above*) z 4
A clump-forming perennial, this attractive foxglove has 2½ft (75cm)-long spikes of nodding, tubular, rose-pink to coppery flowers, held all around the flowering stems. The basal rosette of soft, hairy oval leaves grows to 1ft (30cm) across. Plants should be divided after flowering in autumn. For best results plant in moist fertile soil in light shade. If seed sets this can be sown when it ripens in the autumn. *D. ferruginea* is best treated as a biennial and has pale orange-brown flowers.

Echinops ritro (*below*) z 3
Globe thistle
Any cottage-garden-style border is incomplete without the beautiful globe thistle. In summer its rounded bright blue flowers attract hordes of bees and butterflies. The flowers are held well above the jaggedly lobed leaves, which are fresh green on their upper sides and white-felted below. The flowers stay open for many weeks, while the seed heads carry interest into autumn. Strong plants reach 3-4ft (90-120cm). To propagate, sow seed in spring, or divide or take root cuttings in autumn.

Euphorbia griffithii 'Fireglow' z 5
The massed flower heads of this beautiful spurge look like glowing embers in a fire when seen against a dark green background. The lance-shaped leaves appear all along the length of the 2-3ft (60-90cm) flowering stems and have a prominent pinkish-red midrib. Plants spread to 20in (50cm). After autumn frosts the foliage takes on attractive tints. 'Dixter' is similar but more compact. Divide in spring or autumn. The white sap can cause skin irritation and can damage the eyes.

Geranium 'Johnson's Blue' z 3
A lovely hybrid cranesbill resulting from a cross between *G. pratense* and *G. himalayense*, which grows to a height of 1ft (30cm). The large flowers appear throughout the height of summer and are of a deep lavender-blue with distinct darker veining on the petals. The deeply lobed rounded leaves appear in spring before the blooms and will sometimes take on attractive reddish tints in autumn. Cut back in late summer for late flowers. Plants work well beneath pale yellow or apricot roses. Divide in spring or autumn.

Hemerocallis cvs z 3
Daylily
This robust border perennial can survive drought, large amounts of watering and being transplanted at any time of the year. Plants look good both in flower and foliage, and with careful choice of cultivars continuous flowering is possible throughout the summer. 'Pink Damask' has pinkish flowers; *H. flava* has fragrant yellow blooms; while those of *H. fulva* are tawny-orange. Both of these species can be invasive. Newer hybrids need only be split when flowering begins to diminish. Plants grow in sun or light shade, need feeding in spring and reach a height of 1-4ft (30-120cm) depending on cultivar.

Hibiscus moscheutos z 4
Swamp rose mallow
A native of the eastern United States, this lovely plant has spectacularly large, rounded satiny flowers of crimson, white or pink. It needs fertile moist soil in full sun for best results, although it will grow in dryer conditions. Plants reach 3ft (90cm) in height with a similar spread. Raise plants from seed sown during spring.

Inula magnifica (above) z 3
For a splash of late summer cheer in the border, this herbaceous perennial is an ideal choice. Huge 6ft (1.8m)-tall stems appear from a basal clump of oval leaves 1ft (30cm) long. They are crowned with large flower heads containing numerous bright yellow, narrow petals which give them a shaggy appearance. Where space is limited, the more modest *I. hookeri* can be grown. Plant both in well-drained moist soil and propagate by division in spring or autumn. They look really good when seen against a dark green backdrop such as a yew hedge.

Kniphofia 'Little Maid' (below) z 6
This is one of the more discreet and tasteful of the red hot pokers, providing colour in the late summertime. It has narrow bluey-green foliage and flowering stems 2ft (60cm) high, carrying spikes of pale lemon-yellow flowers which fade to cream from the base up as they age. Other cultivars have flowers ranging from deep red to bright yellow. Grow plants in free-draining soil in a warm sunny spot. During winter tie up the leaves to keep the crowns dry. Divide in spring.

Ligularia dentata 'Desdemona' z 4
A lightly shaded position at the back of a border, where the soil is cool and moist, is perfect for this majestic clump-forming perennial. It looks wonderful in front of *Gunnera manicata*. The large rounded kidney-shaped leaves are dark green on their upper sides and deep red-purple below. In late summer the foliage is topped by bunches of up to 12 large, daisy-like, bright orange flowers, carried on reddish-purple stems 3-4ft (1-1.2m) tall. 'The Rocket' has palmate, strongly dentate leaves and pale yellow flowers. Divide plants in spring.

Lychnis × arkwrightii z 6
The electric scarlet flowers of this hybrid maltese cross make it stand out in any border. A clump-forming perennial, it spreads to 18in (45cm) and has dark green oval leaves all the way up its quite weak, 18in (45cm)-tall stems. The stems carry clusters of brilliant orange-red, five-petalled flowers. *L. coronaria* has grey-furry leaves in great clumps, studded with bright purple-cerise flowers. Plants are often treated as biennials. They need sun and well-drained soil. Self-seeds freely; alternatively, divide plants.

Lythrum salicaria 'Firecandle' (above) z 3
Purple loosestrife
An adaptable plant which needs fertile, moist or dry soil to succeed. The oval 3in (8cm)-long leaves are held in opposite pairs all the way up the 3ft (90cm)-tall stems. The stems carry terminal spikes of deep rose-red flowers opening in mid-summer. For pink blooms lasting from early summer to early autumn, try 'Morden's Pink'. These plants thrive near to water, in full sun or semi-shade. Divide the crowns in spring before growth starts.

Monarda 'Cambridge Scarlet' (above) z 4
Bee balm, bergamot or oswego tea
The flowers are peculiar, borne in circular heads at the top of stiff erect stems, each being strangely hooded and of great attraction to hummingbirds and bees: deadhead regularly through the summer. The sharply-pointed oval leaves release a scent when rubbed or crushed. Other good cultivars include the compact 'Adam' with cerise flowers, 'Snow White', and the brownish-red 'Mahogany'. Grow in moist soil in sun. Divide every three to four years for the best results.

Oenothera tetragona   z 4
Evening primrose

Carried on stems 1-2ft (30-60cm) tall, the reddish fragrant flowers begin opening in the late afternoon and by the evening are fully open, only to fade the next day. The bright yellow, cup-shaped flowers are held well above the broadly oval, dark green leaves which are bluish on their undersides. 'Fireworks' ('Fyrverkeri') has deep red buds and greenish-purple young foliage. Best in light, well-drained soils and sun. Divide the clumps during early spring or in autumn.

Phlox paniculata cvs   z 3

A popular border plant which flowers over a long period in summer, and again in early autumn if the first display is cut back as it fades. Plant in deep, free-draining humus-rich soil and water throughout the growing season as necessary. Pinch back weak shoots in spring. Plants reach 2-4ft (60-120cm) in height and are best grown in bold drifts, in sun or light shade. Always choose mildew-resistant cultivars. 'Eva Cullum' has bright pink flowers with red eyes. Divide in autumn.

Physostegia virginiana   z 3
Obedient plant

If you bend the flowers of this plant to one side they will stay there. This late-flowering perennial adds interest to a summer border with its slender, pink snapdragon-like flowers arranged neatly on 2½ft (75cm)-tall stems. The lance-shaped mid-green leaves grow on the stems up to the first flowers. 'Vivid' has rich pink flowers; 'Alba' is white; 'Variegata' has white-edged foliage. Plant in a moist well-drained spot in full sun, but avoid highly alkaline soils. Divide in spring.

Platycodon grandiflorus   z 3
Balloon plant

The buds appear in summer and look like clusters of small blue-purple balloons. They open to become cup-shaped flowers with dark veins. This perennial grows up to 2ft (60cm) tall and spreads to 18in (45cm). The leaves are greenish-blue, forming a tuft at the base of the plant, and also clothing the stems. Grow plants on light sandy soil in full sun. To propagate, detach non-flowering basal shoots with a piece of root attached during the summer, or sow seed in autumn.

Polygonum bistorta 'Superbum'   z 3
(*above*)

One of the finest bistorts for the perennial border, this plant forms spreading clumps of leathery basal leaves. From these rise the 2½ft (75cm)-tall flowering stems which are topped with bottlebrush-like spikes of small pale pink flowers from early to late summer. Plant in sun or light shade, in moist conditions. *P. amplexicaule* 'Atrosanguineum' has rich crimson flowers. Divide in spring or autumn, watering them well until established.

Romneya coulteri (*above*)   z 8
Tree poppy

For the best results grow this plant in the shelter of a south- or west-facing wall. It detests being moved and must be planted in light, very free-draining soil to flourish, where it will produce a summer display of huge flowers, which have pure white, crinkled petals around a cluster of yellow stamens. The deeply-divided leaves are a beautiful bluish sea-green. Plants reach 6ft (1.8m) in height. Cut the stems to ground level in autumn and protect with mulch. To increase, cut away root pieces in spring.

Rudbeckia fulgida 'Goldsturm'   z 3
(*below*)
Coneflower or black-eyed susan

This easily grown perennial has distinctive cone-shaped flowers with black velvety centres in late summer. This cultivar's flowers are 3-4in (8-10cm) across with thin golden-yellow petals. The flowers are carried on 2ft (60cm)-tall stems which have numerous oval leaves at the base. These long-lived plants need moist soil in sun or light shade. Divide the spreading rhizomes in autumn or spring.

Salvia × *superba*   z 4

This herbaceous perennial can reach a height of 3ft (90cm) or more and is a relative of the culinary sage *S. officinalis*. It has the characteristic stiff, square stems and oval dull-green leaves with toothed margins. The stems branch out in summer to form numerous narrow spikes of ½in (1cm)-long flowers of a deep violet-blue, surrounded by red-purple bracts from the base up. Cut right back as the flowers fade for a second flush in early autumn; this also prevents legginess. Some staking is advisable. Well-drained soil and full sun are essential. Divide in spring or take summer cuttings.

Sidalcea hybrids   z 5

These plants, which make neat rounded clumps of long-stalked weed-smothering leaves, are like miniature versions of hollyhocks. The flowering stems are 3-4ft (90-120cm) tall, have deeply-lobed leaves, and end in elegant branching spikes of pink cup-shaped flowers. Flower colour ranges from the deep red of 'Croftway Red' to the pale pink in 'Elsie Heugh'. Grow in moisture-retentive but well-drained soil, in full sun or light shade. Divide in spring.

Autumn flowering

Winter flowering

Aster novi-belgii (*above*)   z 4

Michaelmas daisies are variable in both habit and colour but they are always invaluable additions to the autumn garden. Anything from 1-4ft (30-120cm) in height, flowers range from deep crimson to white through every shade of purple, mauve, pink, red and blue ('Sheena' is illustrated). Quickly spreads to 18in (45cm); benefits from frequent splitting – retain the outside and discard the centre. Thrives in moist fertile soil. Mildew can be a problem.

Catananche caerulea   z 4
Cupid's dart or blue cupidone

Once used in love potions, this plant produces crisp blue flowers in a papery calyx on wiry 2ft (60cm)-high stems. Its grass-like thin foliage is grey-green, forming a tufted crown 1ft (30cm) across. Plants withstand drought well. Superior cultivars are 'Major', 'Perry's White' and 'Bicolor'. Split the crown every few years, discarding the old centre and replanting the vigorous outer sections. Root cuttings can be taken in winter. The flowers can be dried.

Chelone obliqua   z 4
Turtle's head or shell flower

An intriguing plant on account of its deep-lilac flowers, which are curiously-shaped, hooded and weather-resistant. They stand out well against the dark green, clearly-veined lance-shaped leaves held in opposite pairs all along the 3ft (90cm)-tall stems. This upright perennial is occasionally found in its two rarer forms: *C. alba* with its white flowers and the dwarf clone 'Praecox Nana'. Plants need moist soil in light shade to do well. Propagation is through spring or autumn division, seed or soft tip cuttings taken during the summer.

Echinacea purpurea (*below*)   z 3
Purple or hedgehog coneflower

A native of the central and eastern United States, this sturdy plant has single daisy flowers with raised mahogany-coloured discs surrounded by purplish-pink to palest pink drooping rays. They can reach 6in (15cm) across on stems 2-5ft (60cm-1.5m) high. The best cultivars include 'Robert Bloom', with deep crimson rays and orange discs, and 'White Swan', with pure white rays. They are useful for flower arrangements and attractive to bees and butterflies. Need a sunny position.

Eupatorium purpureum   z 3
Joe Pye weed

Not the showiest of plants but useful for the back of a border or in a damp position where space is not restricted. The dark, dull green lanceolate leaves are up to 1ft (30cm) long and are held in whorls of three or five. The stiff stems stand 4-6ft (1.2-1.8m) and are topped by large panicles of pink to purple flowers that last from mid-summer well into autumn. Fertile, moist soil is most suitable although clumps can become very large in ideal conditions and need splitting regularly.

Tricyrtis hirta 'Variegata'   z 5
Hairy toad lily

The golden edged leaves of this plant make it attractive for much of the year but it is most striking in autumn when strange upright flowers appear in clusters in the axils of the top leaves. They are spotted and speckled with dark purple and last for up to three weeks. It reaches 1-3ft (30-90cm) with a spread of 18in (45cm). Grow in partial shade. Prefers moist, humus-rich deep soil on the acid side which never allows the rhizomatous roots to dry out.

Bergenia 'Abendglut'   z 4
Elephant's ears

Also known as 'Evening Glow', this hardy evergreen perennial will flower in late winter if the weather is mild. It makes good ground cover, forming rosettes of crinkly, shiny purple-tinted leaves, with the tinting becoming more pronounced during winter. This cultivar reaches a height of 9in (23cm) and spreads to 1ft (30cm). The deep crimson-magenta, semi-double flowers appear in dense heads on stout stalks. Plants will grow in sun or shade and can be divided in spring.

Erica carnea (*below*)   z 6

The winter-flowering heather is a woody evergreen perennial which can flower from early winter to spring. To achieve this choose reliable cultivars such as 'Springwood Pink' and 'Springwood White', both of which have large sweetly-scented flowers; for deeper red-mauve blooms grow 'Vivellii' and 'Ruby Glow'. Plants form dense mats of dark evergreen foliage which set off the bright papery flowers. They grow to 6-12in (15-30cm) high, spreading to 2ft (60cm); excellent for raised beds.

Erysimum 'Bowles' Mauve'   z 6

Also listed as *Cheiranthus* 'Bowles' Mauve', in a warm spot this bushy, evergreen perennial wallflower will flower from early spring to summer. It produces shoots up to 2½ft (75cm) high, which are topped with spikes of small deep-mauve flowers. The leaves are dark green, narrow and lance-shaped, some plants having a grey-green hue. Plants will not survive severe winters, so propagate by taking softwood cuttings in summer and overwintering them in a frame or cold greenhouse. They succeed best in alkaline soil.

For foliage

Helleborus niger z 3
Christmas rose
Protection from winter rains and wind is needed to get the best from this plant. It will flourish in a shaded position in moist soil which never dries out. Flowers appear in winter, if the weather is not too severe, but are easily spoilt by bad weather. Each one is creamy-white, made up of an intermediate whorl of petal-like tepals surrounding a central cluster of yellow stamens. They grow on 1ft (30cm)-tall stems above clumps of dark green, leathery evergreen leaves. Divide plants in spring or sow the seed.

Iris unguicularis (*above*) z 8
Winter iris
Also listed as *I. stylosa*, the winter iris will produce flowers continuously from late autumn until spring. The delicate flowers are lilac with yellow centres and smell of primroses. Plants form a dense carpet of grassy evergreen leaves. They grow best at the base of a south- or west-facing wall, forming quite large clumps, 8in (20cm) tall. Two good cultivars are 'Walter Butt' and 'Mary Barnard'. To propagate, lift and divide the rhizomes. Slow to establish.

Petasites fragrans z 5
Winter heliotrope
This is a truly mid-winter flower, with one of the sweetest scents imaginable. On a warm day the fragrance spreads across a large area. The flowers are small, pinkish-white and daisy-like. Dark green, heart-shaped leaves follow. It is a very easy plant to grow, tolerating even quite poor soils, and makes excellent ground cover. Indeed, it can become rampant so is best for a large garden. Reaching a height of 9-12in (23-30cm), plants can spread to about 4ft (1.2m). Propagate by division.

Acorus calamus 'Variegatus' z 7
Myrtle or sweet flag
The sword-like leaves of this marginal water plant smell like oranges when crushed. A semi-evergreen perennial, it forms thick clumps of tough leaves which are green with creamy-white margins. Early in the season the young leaves are often tinged with pink. Clumps grow to 2½ft (75cm) tall and spread to around 2ft (60cm). Plants need to be in 10in (25cm) or more of water, in sun. To prevent them becoming invasive, lift and divide them every three to four years in autumn.

Alchemilla mollis (*below*) z 3
Lady's mantle
Beaded with droplets of glistening water around their crinkled edges, the pale green leaves can be a beautiful sight early in the morning. This low-growing perennial makes good ground cover, reaching a height and spread of 20in (50cm), less on poor soils. In summer the plants are covered in a haze of tiny lime green flowers which have large conspicuous calyces. Plants grow well in all but the wettest soils. Trim after flowering; divide in spring or autumn.

Anthericum liliago z 3
Spider plant or St Bernard's lily
An upright-growing perennial with long, narrow greyish-green leaves in tight clumps. Plants grow to a height of around 2ft (60cm), spreading to 1ft (30cm). In early summer they produce tall racemes of white trumpet-shaped flowers like tiny lilies. The seed heads are attractive in autumn, while the foliage adds colour to a border through the entire season. Plants need full sun and moist fertile soil which does not dry out. Increase by transplanting self-sown seedlings or by division in spring.

Artemisia absinthium 'Lambrook Silver' (*below*) z 4
A lovely cultivar derived from *A. absinthium*, which has masses of finely dissected, aromatic silvery-grey leaves. Plants grow as bushy perennials, needing protection during winter in exposed gardens. Vigorous bushes can reach 2½ft (75cm) in height and spread to 2ft (60cm), making a bold silver statement in the summer border. The flowers are insignificant. Give these plants a warm sunny spot in fertile soil, trimming them to shape in early spring. To increase, take cuttings in summer.

Athyrium filix-femina z 3
Lady fern
Although this fern prefers moist soil, it will grow in dryer conditions. It dies back to a scaly crown during winter; new fresh green fronds unfold in spring and have a fine lacy appearance. Plants reach 3 × 2ft (90 × 60cm) and continue to look good until late summer when the foliage withers. Remove fronds as they die back. Increase by division of larger crowns in autumn and winter. Add humus-rich material before planting in a shady spot in a border.

Euphorbia characias wulfenii z 8
In their first season plants produce clusters of grey-green leaves, followed in their second season by enormous dense spikes of yellow-green flowers with collar-like, pale green bracts. These impressive heads are carried on 5ft (1.5m)-tall stems. Through winter the foliage takes on a bluish tinge. Best planted in full sun in moist but free-draining soil, plants will tolerate light shade. Take basal cuttings in summer, allowing the cut end to dry before insertion, or divide in spring or autumn. Avoid skin contact with the sap.

Foeniculum vulgare (*above*) z 4
Fennel
Fennel makes a fine border plant with its finely divided feathery leaves making a soft background to many other border plants. Plants can stand 6ft (1.8m) high in mid-summer, the branching stems being topped by flat umbels of yellowish-green flowers followed by yellow seed heads which self-seed prolifically. Remove unwanted seedlings soon after germination. 'Purpureum' has deep bronze foliage. Plants grow well in thin dry soil in sun.

Galax urceolata (*above*) z 3
Also listed as *G. aphylla*. Only where the soil is moist, rich in leaf mould and of a low pH, will this valuable ground-covering evergreen perennial thrive. The leathery mid-green leaves are large and rounded, taking on purplish-bronze tints in autumn and winter. Densely-packed 8in (20cm)-tall spikes of white flowers appear in late spring and early summer. Increase by separating sections of rooted runner in the spring. Plants can be underplanted with early spring bulbs such as *Narcissus cyclamineus* which push up through the leaves.

Hosta sieboldiana '**Elegans**' (*below*) z 3
The popular plantain lilies are available in a wide range of species and cultivars. The broad or narrow, lanceolate leaves vary in colour from deep blue to pale green, and may have gold, white or silver variegations. The purplish or mauve flowers are fairly insignificant. This cultivar forms large clumps of rounded glaucous leaves up to 3ft (90cm) high and spread to 5ft (1.5m). Plants must have rich, moist, cool well-drained soil in shade to do well. They are prone to attack by slugs and snails. Divide the crowns in early spring.

Houtuynia cordata '**Chamaeleon**' z 3
(*below*)
This herbaceous perennial spreads rapidly making useful, though invasive, ground cover. The leathery heart-shaped leaves are splashed with bright streaks of orange, yellow and red, mostly at their margins. Crushing the leaves releases a shocking strong aroma. *H. cordata* 'Variegata' is also recommended. In dryer borders plants tend to lack vigour. Full sun brings out the best colours. Sprays of white flowers appear in summer. Propagate by detaching rooted runners in spring.

Lamium galeobdolon '**Variegatum**' z 4
(*above*)
Also called *Galeobdolon argenteum* and *Lamiastrum galeobdolon* 'Variegatum'. This semi-evergreen perennial makes good ground cover for a border, some 1ft (30cm) tall with spreading runners which root readily at their nodes. The mid-green oval leaves are marked with splashes of silver, above which in summer appear racemes of yellow two-lipped flowers. Plants will tolerate shade and can become invasive. The soil should be well-drained. Divide well-rooted runners in late winter or spring.

Liriope muscari z 6
An odd plant whose tufts of grassy foliage seem quite dull until autumn when spikes of dense violet-blue flowers appear, giving a wonderful display especially when in large drifts. *L. spicata* is similar with flowers of pale lavender appearing from late summer onwards. Both species grow to 12in (30cm) in height, slowly spreading to 18in (45cm). Plants need sun and well-drained soil to do well. Divide the rhizomes in spring. Plants take a few seasons to produce a good display.

Macleaya cordata z 4
Plume poppy
Sometimes listed as *Bocconia cordata*, plume poppy flowers in late summer on shoots which can be more than 7ft (2.1m) tall, and is admired for both its flowers and foliage. The lobed leaves are grey-green above and downy-white on their undersides; the small petalless cream flowers are held in large terminal panicles. *M. microcarpa* is more invasive with rosy-buff flowers. Plants need full sun and well-drained fertile soil. Divide in spring or take root cuttings in winter.

Grasses and bamboos

Matteuccia struthiopteris (*below*)   z 3
Ostrich plume fern or ostrich fern
The fresh-green, lance-shaped sterile
fronds unfurl in spring and are deeply
divided along their length. They are
arranged in such a way as to resemble
shuttlecocks and are easily damaged by
drying winds and drought, so plant in a
sheltered spot preferably in wet soil in
semi-shade. In late summer the fronds
become ragged. Throughout winter the
stiff, spore-bearing fronds stand erect,
up to 2ft (60cm) tall on older plants.
Propagate by dividing dense clumps in
spring or autumn.

Ophiopogon planiscapus nigrescens   z 6
A highly distinctive evergreen with
grassy black leaves growing in dense
clumps. In summer racemes of lilac
flowers appear above the leaves,
themselves followed in some seasons by
shiny, jet black rounded fruits in sparse
clusters. Plants grow up to 9in (23cm)
with a 12in (30cm) spread, forming a
dense mat if planted together. Grow in
sun in well-drained soil. Similar, but
with green and white or yellow striped
foliage, is *O. jaburan* 'Variegatus'. To
increase, divide plants in spring.

Polystichum setiferum   z 5
Unlike many ferns, this species retains
its fresh green fronds from spring until
late winter. The fronds are beautiful as
they unfold in spring, being clothed
with papery scales of a pale brownish-
grey, which are retained along the
orange-brown midribs. A useful fern for
borders as it withstands fairly dry
conditions and grows virtually
anywhere, although it prefers semi-
shade. 'Divisilobum' is perhaps the best
cultivar. Plants grow to around 2ft
(60cm) tall and need soil rich in organic
matter. Divide in spring.

Salvia officinalis 'Purpurascens'   z 8
(*above*)
Common sage
The young stems and leaves are flushed
with purple, fading to darker green as
they mature. This form needs full sun,
fertile well-drained soil and plenty of
nutrients to succeed. It is a perennial
evergreen shrub and has purple flowers
in summer. Plants form well-rounded
2ft (60cm)-high bushes. Take softwood
cuttings in summer or semi-ripe
cuttings in autumn which are then
rooted in a cold frame over winter.

Veratrum nigrum (*above*)   z 3
Black false hellebore
The chocolate-purple coloured flower
spikes catch the eye in late summer and
early autumn. They appear on stiff 6ft
(2m)-tall upright stems, with several
shorter spikes forming a branched head.
Ribbed pale green leaves with
distinctive parallel veins clothe the
stems. The white false hellebore, *V.
album*, has panicles of yellowish-white
flowers. Both are well worth growing
and are ideal for a shaded woodland
border, needing moist humus-rich soil.
Divide plants in autumn.

Arundinaria variegata   z 7
White-stripe bamboo
Also listed as *A. fortunei* and *Pleioblastus
variegatus*, this dwarf bamboo has white
stripes in its narrow downy leaves. The
stems branch near their bases and reach
a height of 2½ft (75cm). Plants will
spread slowly over a large area if
unchecked, making good evergreen
ground cover. They grow easily in any
moist fertile soil. All tattered shoots
should be clipped back in spring.
Propagate by dividing the thick roots in
early spring. Cut right back occasionally
to promote new growth.

Arundo donax (*above*)   z 8
Giant reed
Grown for its dramatic foliage, this
herbaceous grass rarely if ever flowers in
cultivation. It has thick rhizomes which
form dense clumps, and can send its
vigorous shoots to a height of 20ft (6m).
The shoots are thick and sturdy,
carrying floppy, bluish-green broad
leaves. 'Versicolor' or 'Variegata' have
creamy-white striped leaves. Plants
thrive in dry or wet soil. Propagate by
rooting sections of stem or young side
shoots in wet sand in summer.

Carex pendula   z 5
Pendulous sedge
A graceful plant which has tufted
clumps of narrow, arching, glossy green
leaves, 18in (45cm) long, with sharp
margins. From these emerge tough 3ft
(90cm)-tall flowering stems. The brown-
green pendulous flower spikes are
produced freely throughout the
summer. Plants have a spread of 1ft
(30cm) and should be planted in cool
moist soil, preferably with some shade.
C. buchananii, the leatherleaf sedge, has
narrow coppery-bronze leaves. Divide
plants in spring.

Chusquea culeou (*above*) z 7
Chilean bamboo
A lovely bamboo which forms dense
evergreen clumps 15ft (4.5m) high,
which add an exotic feel to any garden.
The sheaths are clear white when young
and attached at swollen nodes. Clumps
spread to over 10ft (3m) and are very
difficult to dig out at this stage. The
narrow dark green leaves are carried in
whorls at each node. Thin out older
shoots each year to open up the centre.
To increase, hack away young pieces of
the clump using a sharp spade.

Cortaderia selloana (*above*) z 7
Giant pampas grass
Toward the end of summer this grass
begins to send its enormous plume-like
flower heads 8ft (2.4m) into the air,
rising from large clumps of narrow saw-
edged leaves. By late autumn the
feathery plumes are fully developed and
should be cut for drying or left to add
interest to the garden in winter.
'Rendatleri' has pink plumes and
'Pumila' reaches only 5-6ft (1.5-1.8m).
Plants need well-drained fertile soil and
can be split in spring. Wear gloves if
cutting out dead leaves or flower stems.

Erianthus ravennae (*below*) z 6
Ravenna grass
Even though this sun-loving grass will
only do well in a warm position during a
hot summer, it is well worth trying. Its
tall purplish stems can reach 6ft (1.8m)
and carry long spikes of greyish-purple
flower heads at their tips. Large leaves
form a greyish clump at the base. Some
discreet staking of the tall stems might
be necessary, particularly in windy
areas. Plants must have well-drained soil
and should be planted facing west or
south to take full advantage of the sun.
Divide in spring.

Festuca glauca (*below*) z 4
Blue fescue
One of the smallest and most beautiful
of the cultivated grasses, this makes
neat tussocks of thin, wiry blue-grey
leaves no more than 1ft (30cm) tall. As
the leaves age and die they turn to
shades of fawn. Plants can be divided
every two to three years in spring by
careful teasing. Cut back by two thirds
in late summer to promote fresh autumn
growth. Complements purple-leaved
plants like *Ajuga reptans* 'Atropurpurea'.
Useful for its evergreen nature, blue
fescue needs sun and well-drained soil.

Luzula maxima 'Variegata' (*above*) z 5
Woodrush
Also given as *L. sylvatica* 'Marginata'
and *L. s.* 'Aureomarginata', this dainty
plant is ideal for shady borders. It
makes excellent ground cover. Even
where the soil is dry, plants will soon
form solid mats of broad grassy foliage
with hairy white edges, reaching 1ft
(30cm) in height with sprays of
insignificant flowers in loose heads
during summer. Tolerant of a wide
range of soil conditions; at its best in
dry shade. Divide in spring or autumn.

Milium effusum aureum (*above*) z 4
Bowles' golden grass or wood millet
The flat golden-yellow leaves of this
form are spectacular in spring,
especially when seen in bold drifts. In
summer the flowers, which are
yellowish-green, appear in tiered
panicles above the leaves. Its colour is
best in partial shade. In moist humus-
rich soil plants can grow to 3ft (90cm) in
height and spread to 1ft (30cm). The
seeds are shiny and can be collected for
sowing the following spring, although
they will self-seed. Alternatively, divide
plants in early spring.

Miscanthus sinensis 'Zebrinus' (below)   z 4

Few grasses have as many uses in the garden as this large clump-forming perennial. 'Zebrinus' is noted for its green and yellow-banded leaves; in 'Variegatus' each leaf carries a whitish-silver stripe; for a display of large, pinkish silky flowers try 'Silver Feather'. Plants send up 5-7ft (1.5-2.1m)-tall shoots with narrow leaves which have hairy undersides. The foliage lasts well into winter and makes a lovely rustling sound in a breeze. In spring cut back dead shoots and divide.

Molinia caerulea (below)   z 4
Purple moor grass

Coming from quite inhospitable conditions in the wild, this grass can tolerate extreme cold and soil which is damp and acidic. The species has attractive purple flower heads in summer, but much more valuable in the garden are the cream-striped, arching leaves of 'Variegata'. Plants grow as dense tufts up to 2ft (60cm) tall and spread only slowly. In autumn the leaves fade to pale fawn and are very beautiful in winter sunshine. In spring divide and clip back old leaves.

Pennisetum alopecuroides (above)   z 5
Chinese fountain grass

A clump-forming herbaceous perennial that grows to 3ft (90cm) high with a spread of 2ft (60cm). The leaves are mid-green and narrow. In late summer or early autumn the bottlebrush-like flower spikes appear which can be 5in (13cm) long. They are a deep purple colour with terminal white tufts. Plants prefer a warm spot, in full sun, with light free-draining soil. The flowers retain their colour into winter. Lift and divide clumps in late spring.

Phalaris arundinacea picta (above)   z 3
Gardener's garters

In moist soil this grass can become invasive, but this can be avoided by placing it in a drier spot, such as near the roots of trees and shrubs. An evergreen perennial, its broad leaves are striped with white and in summer it produces narrow spikes of pale flowers on upright stems. Plants grow to 3ft (90cm), rapidly producing a bamboo-like thicket. They are set off by a dark green background, such as a hedge of *Taxus baccata*. Propagation, if found to be necessary, is by planting rooted tufts.

Phyllostachys nigra (below)   z 7

In their second season the olive-brown stems of this bamboo turn black, so that in established clumps there is a range of colours, from the light green of the young shoots to olive-brown and black. Plants are evergreen and form clumps 20ft (6m) high. The leaves are narrow, mid-green and arching. Clumps need thinning to prevent the centre becoming too cluttered. Considerable strength is needed to propagate the plants using a sharp spade to split the rootstock. If plants become too invasive, contain the roots to a depth of 3ft (90cm).

Stipa gigantea (below)   z 7

The flowers of this most beautiful grass are held on strong 8ft (2.4m)-tall stems. The narrow leaves make a ground-covering clump and are around 18in (45cm) long. When they open the flower heads are a shiny purple, changing to golden-yellow as they mature, with a silvery sheen. In full flower there are numerous pendulous yellow anthers. Stems can be cut and used in dried arrangements or left through the winter to add interest to the garden. In spring cut back dead stems and divide. Plant in sun in fertile soil.

ANNUALS AND BIENNIALS

Annuals and biennials are useful in the garden, whatever its style and stage of development. In the early years, their fast rate of growth is a great asset when furnishing large empty spaces, while their temporary nature allows experimentation in the use of colour and form before committing oneself to a more permanent and expensive scheme. As the garden matures they can be used to produce seasonal highlights either in beds of their own or mixed in with border perennials, shrubs or bulbs, in informal or formal designs.

Traditionally annuals and biennials were favourites with cottage gardeners. Self-sown hardy species such as cornflowers, pot marigolds, night-scented stock, sweet sultan (*Centaurea moschata*) foxgloves, eryngium and Queen Anne's thimble (*Gilia capitata*) give the garden a soft and natural appearance which is a trademark of the style. Once established, they find the spot best suited to their requirements, but where they are not wanted it is easy to weed them out.

The use of annuals and biennials in bedding schemes reached its peak in the late nineteenth century when plants were grown and planted out in their thousands, providing changing displays in gardens and parks throughout the year, each one more vivid than the

Far left: A stylish and colourful parterre of box, cotton lavender and lavender is brought to life in spring with plants grown as biennials. Daisies, forget-me-nots, pansies, polyanthus and wallflowers create a colourful display for several weeks.

Left: The nemesia is a half-hardy annual, usually raised from seed under cover in spring. This mixed strain will make an attractive and useful pattern of soft colours from early summer through to the first frosts.

Below: Ageratums, lobelias, petunias and small zinnias are among the summer-flowering annuals well suited to growing in containers alongside tender perennials, which should be raised from cuttings annually for the best effect.

last. Those most frequently used included wallflowers, forget-me-not and polyanthus in the spring, and salvias, cinerarias, pelargoniums and begonias in the summer. Often, so called "accent plants" were introduced to add height to the scheme; these included burning bush, love-lies-a-bleeding, castor oil plant, *Coleus blumei* and *Cordilyne* cultivars. Such carpet bedding schemes are very labour intensive, but in a small space, using a few trays of bought plantlets, a very pleasing effect can be quickly achieved and reward the effort involved.

Annuals are often grown exclusively for picking, either in rows or within a border. Continual cutting will encourage more flowers to form and lengthen the season. Particularly well suited to this use are the long-stemmed species such as bells of Ireland, cosmos, zinnias, sweet peas, love-in-a-mist, stocks and gypsophila; everlasting species should be cut on a dry day towards the end of the season and hung upside down to dry. Take these flowers in their prime.

Most annuals and biennials are adaptable to most soils, but the richer and more moisture-retentive the soil the lusher the growth and longer the flowering

period. In poor dry soil they will be thinner, flower more quickly and die off sooner. While the plants will survive dry periods, they do need adequate water, especially when they are getting established. Most, particularly summer-flowering species, need sun to flower well, but there are a number that will tolerate shade so most spaces can be filled. As ever with plants, it is a matter of careful selection.

Many people do not have the space to raise their own seedlings and need to buy strips of plants in the spring ready to plant out, but it is very rewarding to grow one's own. Annuals are usually divided into hardy and half-hardy categories; the category a plant belongs to will determine when it should be planted. Spring-flowering hardy annuals and biennials are sown in summer in a nursery bed in the garden and transplanted to where they are to flower in the autumn. Once establised they will self-seed, but highly bred annuals tend to degenerate and it is best, on the whole, to start with fresh plants each year. Summer-flowering hardy annuals can be sown in spring directly in their flowering position. Half-hardy summer-flowering annuals should be raised under heat in the spring and transplanted into the garden as soon as the last frost has passed.

Above: Delightful warm hues predominate in a planting that includes the bright yellow *Calceolaria* Sunshine, *Rudbeckia* Rustic Mixed Dwarf and *Salpiglossis* Splash.

Left: A cottage-garden effect is achieved by the apparently haphazard mingling of African marigolds, impatiens, nasturtiums and petunias.

Mixed border

IN SUN

Amaranthus caudatus
Love-lies-a-bleeding or tassel flower
This striking half-hardy annual has tight hanging tassels of crimson flowers which can be 18in (45cm) long, on plants 4ft (1.2m) tall with a spread of 18in (45cm). Ideal as the centrepiece in a formal bedding scheme or as a specimen plant in a container. Plants need rich, fertile well-drained soil and should be raised under glass or sown outdoors after the last of the spring frosts. For bright green flowers grow *A. viridis*.

Atriplex hortensis 'Rubra'
Red orache or red mountain spinach
The unmistakeable, triangular, deep red leaves of this fast-growing half-hardy annual can be up to 6in (15cm) long and are edible. Ideal for a coastal garden, plants need full sun and fertile well-drained soil. They grow to a height of 4ft (1.2m) or more. The flowers are insignificant and followed by small reddish fruits. Sow plants *in situ* in late spring and early summer. They require pinching regularly to keep them bushy. Propagation is not necessary as plants self-seed readily.

Calendula officinalis (*above*)
Pot marigold or English marigold
Used in the past as a culinary herb, this quick-growing bushy annual suits a cottage garden or annual border, where it can grow up to 2ft (60cm) tall. The narrow, pale green leaves are aromatic. The flowers are daisy-like, single or double, appearing from spring to autumn, in colours ranging from yellow to orange, cream and mahogany. Plants can be sown in autumn and over-wintered or in spring. Deadhead flowers and pinch regularly. Prone to mildew.

Campanula medium
Canterbury bell
A hardy biennial which is planted in autumn for flowering the following summer. It is a favourite in cottage gardens and widely used in beds and borders. Plants need well-drained soil and a sunny position. Tall cultivars can grow to 3ft (90cm) in height and need supporting. From the basal clump of bristly-hairy leaves appear spikes of single, semi-double or double flowers in pink, white, mauve or blue. Space plants 1ft (30cm) apart. 'Bells of Holland' has single bell-shaped flowers.

Centaurea cyanus (*above*)
Cornflower
Blue cultivars such as 'Blue Ball' and 'Blue Boy' grown among yellow- and bronze-flowered pot marigolds, *Calendula officinalis*, can produce a beautiful display in a bed or border. In other cultivars the flower colour ranges from white to pink: 'Frosty' has white-specked flowers. Plants will seed themselves freely. For an early spring display sow *in situ* in autumn and protect the plants with cloches during severe weather; alternatively sow outdoors in spring or earlier under glass and transplant. Deadhead to prolong flowering into late summer.

Clarkia elegans
Popular in cottage gardens and excellent as cut flowers, this plant is grown for its frilled flowers in upright spikes of pink, red and mauve. It is best grouped in a bed or border. Tall cultivars can grow to 2ft (60cm) in height and may need supporting. Sow plants *in situ* in slightly acid, fertile soil in spring and thin to around 9in (22cm) apart. They thrive in sun. The dwarf clarkia, *C. pulchella*, grows to 1ft (30cm).

Cleome spinosa (*above*)
Spider flower
Also listed as *C. hassleriana*, this half-hardy plant adds an exotic touch when grown as a dot plant in a bedding scheme or as a gap-filler in a mixed border. The pinkish-white rounded heads of flowers are ideal for cutting. Plant in fertile well-drained soil in sun and water well in dry weather. When mature, plants reach 4ft (1.2m) in height and spread to 18in (45cm). Both the flowers and leaves are aromatic. Raise under glass and plant out after frosts. Colour Fountain is a reliable mixture.

Eschscholzia californica (*above*)
California poppy
Ideal for infilling in a sunny border, preferably where there is poor well-drained soil, this species is easy to grow. With regular deadheading flowering will continue all through the summer and into autumn. Scatter the seed thinly over the ground and lightly rake in. Plants grow to a height of 6in (15cm) and carry their silky-petalled poppy-like flowers above finely divided blue-grey leaves. They are hardy and self-seed. Monarch Art Shades has frilled petals.

Godetia grandiflora

The godetia never fails to bring a bright splash of colour to a border in late summer. A hardy annual, it can be sown *in situ* in autumn or spring, and should be thinned in spring to 9in (22cm) apart. Each flower is up to 4in (10cm) across with four fluted petals of pink, orange, white or red, the colours being in stripes and picotees in some forms. The flower spikes are leafy and up to 2ft (60cm) in height. Water the plants well in dry weather, but avoid overfeeding. Best results are seen in light, slightly acid soil.

Lavatera trimestris (*above*)

This elegant and showy mallow is a hardy annual and goes well with striking perennials. The flowers, which are up to 4in (10cm) across and come in pink, rosy-red or white, are trumpet-shaped with a delicate sheen. Plants may be sown *in situ* in autumn or spring (preferably in a sheltered spot), or raised under glass in pots for planting out. Deadhead to maintain flowering. Plants often self-seed. They reach a height and spread of 2-4ft (60-120cm). 'Silver Cup' has pink blooms.

Matthiola bicornis
Night-scented stock

Plant the night-scented stock near the house: the flowers of this hardy annual are closed during the day, opening only at night to fill the air with a delicious fragrance which may waft into the house through an open window. Although not the most attractive of annuals, it can be worked in between other plants simply by sowing seed in small patches during spring. Plants reach 1ft (30cm) in height with equal spread. They become straggly after flowering. Sow in succession until early summer.

Nicotiana (*above*)
Tobacco plant

The modern hybrids are derived from *N. alata* and are less scented than older forms, but they do have flowers which stay open all day and face upwards rather than drooping. Raise this half-hardy annual under glass and plant it out after frosts have passed, in sun or part shade where the soil is fertile. Domino (*above*) grows to 1ft (30cm), Sensation to 2-3ft (60-100cm); 'Lime Green' has yellowish-green flowers. Space plants 1ft (30cm) apart, and deadhead regularly. Prone to aphids.

Onopordum acanthium (*above*)
Cotton thistle or scotch thistle

This dramatic hardy biennial spends its first season producing a rosette of leaves at ground level. In its second season tall flowering shoots appear which can reach 6ft (1.8m) or more if the soil is rich. The stems are clothed with silvery-grey thistle-like leaves and the tips of the shoots carry deep purple flower heads topping a very spiny receptacle. Plants spread to 3ft (90cm) when mature. Raise from seed sown in autumn or spring. Slugs may damage lower leaves.

Portulaca grandiflora (*below*)
Sun plant

A sunny position and well-drained, preferably sandy soil is essential if this half-hardy annual is to do well. This succulent grows close to the ground and dislikes overwatering; feeding is usually unnecessary. The flowers are 1in (2.5cm) across, semi-double with golden-yellow stamens and silky ruffled petals. They open fully only in sun. Raise plants under glass from seed, planting out after frosts. Mixed-coloured strains include Calypso and Sundance. Plants grow to 8in (20cm).

Salvia horminum (*below*)

Sow this unusual ornamental sage *in situ* in autumn or spring. A hardy annual, this beautiful plant is grown for both its colourful leaves and its bright pink or blue flower bracts. The bracts appear in dense spikes during summer, and can be cut and dried when mature for indoor decoration. 'Pink Lady' and 'Blue Beard' are reliable cultivars. Pinch young plants to keep them bushy. Plants grow up to 18in (45cm) tall and spread to 8in (20cm). This species is a good choice for grey, silver and blue borders as a gap-filler in summer.

Digitalis purpurea (*above*)
Wild foxglove
The foxglove relishes shade and moist, humus-rich lime-free soil. A hardy biennial, it flowers in the second season of growth. The tall spikes of tubular flowers can reach 3-5ft (90cm-1.5m) in height. The flowers are purple with darker spotting. *D.p.* f. *alba* has white flowers. Sow outdoors in summer and move plants to their flowering positions in autumn. The Excelsior hybrids have flowers of red, purple, pink, yellow or white, all with maroon spotting inside their throats.

Impatiens (*above*)
Busy lizzie
Modern strains, which are lower, more compact and hardier than older forms, come in a range of colours from pink, white and orange to salmon and purple. These half-hardy annuals are ideal for shaded corners of mixed beds or for under trees. Flowers open continuously, and have glistening petals. Good strains of *I. walleriana* include Super Elfin and Blitz. For foliage, grow the New Guinea hybrids. Plant after frosts into fertile soil. 'Novette Mixed' is shown.

Lunaria annua (*below*)
Honesty
This popular hardy perennial is prized for its large, flat silvery seed pods and early-scented four-petalled flowers of deep purple, white or pink. Plants self-seed in large numbers and need rigorous thinning. They grow in sun or shade and are at home growing around the base of evergreen shrubs. 'Variegata' has bright green leaves with white margins. Plants grow rapidly to 2½ft (75cm) tall with a 1ft (30cm) spread. Remove the seed heads as the seed pods begin to open.

Myosotis
Forget-me-not
Although it tends to become leggy in deep shade, the forget-me-not is ideal for creating a splash of blue among permanent plantings in borders. Seed of this hardy biennial is sown outdoors in summer and the young plants transplanted to their flowering positions in autumn. Plants are 1ft (30cm) tall when flowering, with similar spread. Most garden forms are hybrids of *M. alpestris* and *M. sylvestris*; cultivar names speak for themselves – 'Blue Ball', 'White Ball' and 'Pink Gem'.

Nemesia strumosa
A fast-growing, bushy half-hardy annual which tends to bloom very quickly if the summer is hot and dry. To avoid this, stagger sowing. Plants should be grown in fertile, well-drained lime-free soil in a cool position. Taller cultivars grow up to 18in (45cm). The lovely trumpet-shaped wide-lipped flowers come in shades of purple, white and yellow. Space plants 6-12in (15-30cm) apart and cut back after the first flowers have faded. Carnival and Funfair are good mixtures. Water well in dry weather.

Bedding plants

Ageratum houstonianum **cvs**
Floss flower
Often used as an edging plant in bedding schemes, this half-hardy annual has powderpuff-like clusters of flowers throughout the summer. The blue cultivars are still the most widely grown; white forms turn brown as they fade and the pink strains have yet to gain popularity. Plants form hummocks between 6-12in (15-30cm) tall with similar spread. Raise seed under glass and plant out after frosts. Deadheading keeps flowers coming. Plants grow in sun or part shade and should be well-watered in dry summers.

Antirrhinum majus **cvs**
Snapdragon
A huge range of cultivars and hybrids of this popular perennial exist. It is grown as a half-hardy annual and needs rich well-drained soil in full sun. The flowers are basically tubular or trumpet-shaped, and can be single, semi-double or double. Seed is sown under glass, the plants going out after frosts. Pinch the tips of young plants to make them bushy. Plants grow from 4in-3ft (10-90cm) tall depending on the strain. Use Monarch if rust disease is present.

Begonia semperflorens (*above*)
The introduction of this fibrous-rooted begonia has revolutionized bedding schemes. It flowers throughout the summer until the first frosts of autumn, is compact and available in a wide range of colours, and has attractive bright green or bronze foliage. Plants are best raised from plugs and moved to their flowering positions after frosts. They are happy in shade and need compost-enriched soil. Plants grow to 4-12in (10-30cm) depending on cultivar and can be potted up for winter flowers indoors.

319

Bellis perennis

For carpet bedding, edging, or for filling in gaps along borders the English daisy is ideal. Flowers appear from mid-spring onwards and can be rosy red, bright pink, white or crimson. Blooms last for many weeks. Plants are grown as hardy biennials, although they are actually perennial and can be replanted when taken from bedding displays. Sow seed in early summer outdoors and transplant to beds in autumn. Deadhead to maintain vigour. For large flowers grow 'Monstrosa' and 'Super Enorma', and for daintier plants 'Pomponette'.

Cheiranthus cheiri (above)
Wallflower

A wonderfully scented hardy biennial for a spring bedding scheme. The narrow, dark green leaves are topped by clusters of four-petalled flowers in shades of yellow, orange and red which open during spring into early summer. Raise plants from seed sown outdoors in summer and move to their flowering positions in autumn. They are susceptible to club root disease and should be grown in fertile well-limed soil. 'Orange Bedder' and 'Scarlet Bedder' are trusted cultivars.

Kochia scoparia tricophylla
Burning bush or summer cypress

Used widely as a dot plant for its striking summer foliage, the leaves of this half-hardy annual are feathery and mature plants resemble a conifer in shape. In autumn the foliage turns bronze-red. Plants can grow to 3ft (90cm) and need sun; well-drained sandy soil is best. They are rapid growers which can be clipped over if they become too large. Raise plants under glass planting out after spring frosts, 2ft (60cm) apart.

Mesembryanthemum criniflorum
(*above*)
Livingstone daisy

More correctly named *Dorotheanthus bellidiformis*, there are few summer-flowering bedding plants to rival the large, glistening daisy-like flowers of this half-hardy succulent annual. In addition, the narrow fleshy leaves and stems have an attractive sparkling coating. Seeds are usually bought as mixtures – red, white, yellow, orange and many intermediates. Plant after frosts, 8in (20cm) apart. Plants love dry, sunny positions.

Mimulus cvs (above)
Monkey flower

Its strength as a bedding plant is being able to provide red and yellow colour in shaded or dark spots such as on patios which face north; it also suits hanging baskets. Plants are raised under glass in spring and planted out after frosts. They will flower in as little as seven weeks from sowing, producing blotched and spotted trumpet-like flowers. Plants can be up to 1ft (30cm) tall and should be spaced around 9in (22cm) apart in damp soil. 'Yellow velvet' is illustrated.

Tagetes patula; T. erecta
French marigold; African marigold

T. patula carries a mass of single flowers on plants growing up to 9in (22cm) high, while *T. erecta* is a larger plant, up to 2ft (60cm) high, with fewer but much larger, usually double flowers. The flowers appear throughout the summer and are bright orange or yellow in colour. The mid-green pinnate leaves have a strong pungent aroma when rubbed. Plant in spring after frosts and remove all flower buds for a few weeks after that. *T. patula* 'Naughty Marietta' is an old trusted favourite.

Salvia splendens (above)
Scarlet sage

One of the most reliable summer bedding plants for red flowers. This tender perennial is grown as a half-hardy annual and is planted after frosts. The dense racemes of tubular scarlet flowers appear from mid-summer providing colour right into autumn. Plants grow to 1ft (30cm) in height and should be spaced 1-1½ft (30-45cm) apart. 'Blaze of Fire' is a popular scarlet cultivar, while 'Laser Purple' has mauve flowers. White strains are also available. Plants grow well in most soils in sun.

Viola × wittrockiana

With careful planning pansies can be in flower in every season. All the modern strains and hybrids come from this species. Universal, Multiflora and Floral Dance are the hardiest and most reliable strains. Plants are treated either as hardy annuals or biennials. Sow plants for winter and spring bedding displays in early summer and plant out in autumn. Colours include blue, purple, yellow, white, orange and red, with bicoloured and blotched forms. The petals are edible. Protect from slugs.

For cutting

Asperula azurea setosa

Most asperulas are perennial plants, this dainty hardy annual being a welcome exception. Seed is best sown where the plants are to flower, and the young seedlings not disturbed by transplanting. Autumn sowing is usual, for an early spring flowering. Plants grow to a height of 2in (5cm), and being quite small fit easily into any bare patches in borders or on rock gardens. The small green narrow leaves are studded with clusters of tiny four-petalled pale blue flowers which have the scent of new-mown hay.

Callistephus chinensis
Annual aster or China aster

This plant can provide a welcome crop of flowers for cutting in late summer. The flowers come in many forms; some are the typical daisy-type, others are double or have plumed petals, while still others resemble small chrysanthemums. Treat plants as half-hardy annuals, planting after the most severe frosts. They grow to ½-3ft (15-90cm) depending on cultivar. Never grow asters in the same spot year after year to avoid aster wilt, a soil disease.

Cosmos bipinnatus
Cosmos

With its large blooms and delicate feathery foliage, cosmos is an easy annual to grow, providing a useful supply of flowers for cutting through the summer. Plants will bloom until the first frosts if deadheaded regularly. Tall cultivars (up to 3ft (90cm) in height) may need staking, but all will grow well on poor but well-drained, preferably sandy soil. Seed is usually sold as mixtures; Sensation is a tall mixture with white, red and pink flowers.

Helichrysum bracteatum
Straw flower

This is one of the most popular "everlasting" flowers grown for its papery heads. What appear to be petals are in fact bracts which come in a range of colours including pinks, mauve, red, yellow and white. Cut the stems just before the flowers are fully open and hang to dry. Easy to grow, this hardy annual can be sown outdoors in spring or raised earlier under glass and planted out. Hot Bikini and Bright Bikini are good mixtures. Plants grow to 1-3ft (30-90cm) at a spacing of 1ft (30cm) apart.

Gilia capitata
Queen Anne's thimble

With its feathery leaves and rounded heads of pale lavender flowers, this branching hardy annual is ideal for cutting. Twiggy supports may help the more lax-growing plants on windy sites. Seed can be sown *in situ* in autumn or in spring, or under glass for planting out later into rich, fertile soil in full sun. Flowers will continue to be produced into early autumn on well-grown plants if cut regularly. Space or thin plants to 8in (20cm) apart. They will grow up to 18in (45cm) tall.

Moluccella laevis (*above*)
Bells of Ireland or shell flower

The most conspicuous part of this plant is the large, pale green, bell-like calyx surrounding the small white, tubular flowers. These cluster all the way up the attractive, erect stems along with the rounded leaves. As the flowers fade, interest is maintained by the green calyces, making this a much sought after cut flower for summer. Plants are half-hardy and fast-growing, needing rich soil and full sun. Sow seed under glass in early spring or *in situ* after frosts, planting 1ft (30cm) apart.

Nigella damascena
Love-in-a-mist

The flowers of this hardy annual emerge through its finely divided foliage. Most seed gives rise to plants with a mixture of pink, white, blue and lavender flowers, and sowing should be staggered because the flowering season is short. The stems are useful as a fresh cut flower in summer, and the seed heads can be used as dried flowers. Enrich the soil with compost before sowing, which can take place in autumn or spring. Plants grow up to 2ft (60cm) tall.

Ornamental Grasses

What they lack in colour, ornamental grasses make up for in fine textures and sounds. Quaking grass, *Briza maxima*, is perhaps the most popular with its papery lanterns rustling in the breeze; while the half-hardy Job's tears, *Coix lacryma-jobi*, has pearly seeds which appear among the reed-like foliage. Other species include hare's tail, *Lagurus ovatus*, and cloud grass, *Agrostis nebulosa*. Sow or plant in full sun in well-drained soil, with 1ft (30cm) between plants, or sow small patches to fill gaps. Plants self-seed freely.

Scabiosa
Sweet scabious or pincushion flower

Similar to the cornflower and useful as a summer cut flower, most modern strains of sweet scabious are derived from *S. atropurpurea* which is a hardy annual. Most flowers are double and available in pinks, reds, mauves and white. Plants suffer in prolonged wet weather. Sow the seed outdoors in autumn or spring, or raise under glass and plant out 1ft (30cm) apart. Plants reach up to 3ft (1m) in height if grown in slightly alkaline well-drained soil. Single colour varieties are avilable.

Zinnia (*above*)

The modern types of *Zinnia* have complex parentage giving rise to flowers which can be as large as dahlias or small and button-like (Lilliput miniatures are shown). The flowers are daisy-like, single, semi-double or double, and come in a huge range of colours. A compost-enriched soil and full sun are vital. Plants grow to ½-2ft (15-60cm). Space plants 1ft (30cm) apart when planting out the young plants raised in spring under glass. They will not stand frosts or prolonged, cool wet weather.

BULBS AND CORMS

Bulbs are often associated with the dramatic and vibrantly colourful displays seen in public open spaces, but they can also be enjoyed in the garden where they can be put to many different uses. Bulbs reliably come into flower within one season and associate well with bedding plants and in a mixed border, either in the bright sunshine or light shade, throughout much of the year.

All bulbs require an annual resting period. This may be during the summer, as is the case for the spring-flowering species which most commonly originate from areas with a Mediterranean climate. In the winter many tender summer-flowering species, which require hot- house conditions to grow out of their natural habitat (or must be lifted in the autumn before the frosts and kept in a cool, dark frost-free place throughout the winter), are dormant. Other bulbs, such as the sweetly scented *Acidanthera murielae*, are usually cheap enough to be able to be replanted annually, after the risk of frost has passed, as one would bedding plants from the garden centre.

Throughout the resting period the bulbs disappear under ground, leaving gaps which need to be furnished with other plants. This is most noticeable with

Left: The pink *Cyclamen hederifolium* and the white variety *album* do well in dry shade, as here at the base of a blue atlantic cedar. The cyclamen, which flowers in autumn and self-seeds readily, has the peculiarity of sending out roots from the top of the corm. It benefits from a mulch of leaf mould after flowering.

hardy late winter- and spring-flowering species. There are several different techniques of covering the spaces while allowing the bulbs to proceed through their cycle without damage and to increase steadily.

Many winter- and spring-flowering bulbs look at home in a border that is shaded by tall deciduous trees or shrubs, where they come into flower before the leaf canopy becomes too dense. Here, daffodils, winter aconites, snowdrops, cyclamen, bluebells and trilliums will thrive along with shade-loving herbaceous foliage plants such as hostas, geraniums and alchemilla which gradually cover the dying foliage, or ever-

green ground cover plants such as ivy, periwinkle and pachysandra. As a rule, in permanent bulb plantings it is useful to plant them very deep so that they are not damaged by any weeding or lifting of herbaceous plants that need dividing.

On a grander scale, all these plants can be naturalized in a woodland setting in great drifts. Alternatively it is possible to grow many species of daffodils, crocuses, the summer snowflake and snake's head fritillary in rough grass. The important thing to remember is that the flowers must rise above the grass to have any effect (so the later they bloom, the taller they

Left: Early-flowering narcissi and chionodoxas brighten an acid border that is suitably planted with heathers and rhododendrons.

Right: Bulbs are ideal for creating large drifts of colour in spring. These squills flourish in the shade of a winter-flowering cherry (*Prunus* × *subhirtella* 'Autumnalis'). Recommended precursors for them are winter aconites, snowdrops and *Arum italicum marmoratum.*

must be). They should be left in leaf and the grass un-cut for up to eight weeks to allow the next year's flowers to form in the bulbs.

In formal plantings, or where they have been grown with spring bedding plants, tulips, daffodils and hya-cinths can be lifted after flowering and replaced by a totally different scheme for the summer. Bulbs that are lifted in mid- to late spring should be heeled into another part of the garden or kept in boxes with moist peat, compost or soil around their roots until the foliage dies down. They then need to be dried, cleaned and stored in a well-ventilated place until autumn.

Where spring bulbs are used either on their own or in association with bedding plants it is important to think about the effect that is wanted when choosing colour combinations. Daffodils cover a broad range of yellows through creams and whites and some orange or pink cups, while hyacinths offer solid shades of blue, pink, white, peach and yellow and tulips range from black to white and red-striped. It may be that vibrant contrast is wanted in which case hyacinths are appropriate, but often the toning colours and refined forms of daffodils would have a more relaxing effect.

Above: The narcissus 'Thalia' and delicate grape hyacinths (muscari) crowd around the base of a large terracotta pot in which species tulips are coming into flower.

Left: Lilies are indispensable bulbs for summer borders. The species and hybrids include short-growing kinds as well as some of the tallest and most stately of bulbs. There is a wide colour range and many lilies are richly scented.

For shade

Anemone nemorosa   z 4
Wood anemone
This charming woodland plant, which is a rhizomatous perennial, thrives in shaded, moist, humus-rich but well-drained soil. Plants grow vigorously, forming a carpet 6in (15cm) high, which in spring is studded with star-shaped single flowers each with a central cluster of yellow stamens. 'Allenii' has blue-pink flowers and those of 'Vestal' are double. The foliage is a mid-green. Increase through self-seeding or by dividing the rhizomes, but undisturbed specimens flower best.

Arisaema triphyllum (above)   z 5
Jack-in-the-pulpit
The arisaemas are prized for their curious hooded flowers. In autumn, they have the added attraction of clusters of fleshy red fruits. Plants die away each winter to an underground tuber. They thrive in shade where the soil is moist and humus-enriched. The leaves are soft, three-lobed and remain through summer after the flowers have faded. Plants grow to 18in (45cm), spreading slowly to 1ft (30cm). Plant tubers 6in (15cm) deep.

Arisarum proboscideum   z 6
Mouse plant
Every garden should have a clump of this plant which succeeds in well-drained but moist humus-rich soil. The arrow-shaped, bright green, shiny leaves hide the shy flowers which emerge near soil level. Each flower is made up of a dark brown spathe wrapped around a central spadix. The tip of the spathe is drawn out into a 6in (15cm)-long "tail". This plant is easy to grow and reaches a height of only 4in (10cm). Propagate by splitting the tuberous root systems. Useful for ground cover.

Arum italicum marmoratum (above) z 7
This superior form of the cuckoo pint is prized for its bright green, shiny leaves which are beautifully veined with white or cream. They appear in autumn and so add some winter interest. The flowers appear in late spring and are green or creamy-white, followed in autumn by a spike of bright red berries. Plants reach a height of 6-10in (15-25cm) and a spread of 1ft (30cm). They need moist but well-drained soil and can be propagated by sowing ripe seed or by dividing the tubers in early autumn.

Cardiocrinum giganteum (above)   z 7
The flowering stems of this spectacular bulb grow up to 12ft (4m) high. Each of the tubular lily-like flowers are up to 6in (15cm) long, cream-coloured with purplish streaks inside the throat. After flowering, large green-brown seed pods form. The bulbs should be planted in autumn (in shade) just below the surface of humus-rich soil. The young shoots need protecting from frost and slugs. After flowering, the main bulb dies, leaving offsets which will flower when five years old, while seed-raised bulbs take seven years.

Cyclamen hederifolium (below)   z 6
Also known a C. neapolitanum, this low-growing tuberous perennial reaches only 4in (10cm) high and will add colour to a garden – anything from white through pale pink to mauve – in autumn when the flowers appear ahead of the leaves. It is impressive when seen as a mature clump at the base of a tree. The leaves are small and ivy-shaped, dark green patterned with shades of silver. They make good ground cover. The petals are sharply reflexed and slightly twisted. Plants need well-drained soil and are best raised from seed.

Erythronium dens-canis   z 6
Dogs'-tooth violet
An unmistakeable plant with its pair of purple-spotted basal leaves. From the centre of these emerge the nodding white, pink or purple flowers with brownish-yellow centres, to a height of up to 10in (25cm). This violet grows well when naturalized in thin grass where there is some shade. The tubers become dormant in summer and should not be planted where they will dry out. E. tuolumnense has deep yellow flowers. Plant both 6in (15cm) deep.

Hyacinthoides non-scripta   z 6
Bluebell
In spring, the tufts of strap-shaped leaves appear first followed by the flower buds which push up from within the leaves. The flower stems grow up to 16in (40cm) tall and arch at their tips. The bell-shaped flowers are fragrant, in shades of blue, pink or white, blue usually being predominant. This plant needs cool and shaded conditions to do well. Divide the clumps in late summer and replant only those bulbs that are 6in (15cm) or more across. Plants need moist soil.

Formal planting

Leucojum vernum z 6
Spring snowflake
Unlike its relative the snowdrop, this graceful plant has green tips to its six white petals. Each leafless stem grows up to 6in (15cm) tall and carries one to two pendent bell-shaped flowers. Plants grow best in moist soil. The leaves are quite erect and strap-like, rising from the base. *L. aestivum* (the summer snowflake) has smaller flowers in heads of three to seven and seed pods which float on water to spread the seeds. Divide in spring or early autumn.

Narcissus z 5
Several of the hardy species narcissi make excellent bulbs for planting in moist and shady spots. They are at their best when growing on the edge of a damp woodland. The delicate blooms of *N. cyclamineus* are characterized by their sharply reflexed petals and very narrow trumpets, which nod gracefully in spring. *N. pseudonarcissus*, often referred to as the wild daffodil, has flowers which range from white to deep golden yellow, and it naturalizes freely. It often hybridizes very successfully with *N. cyclamineus*.

Trillium grandiflorum (above) z 4
Wake robin, trinity flower or wood lily
On alkaline soils this species will form large clumps of whorled dark green leaves, above which are held the large white flowers from spring to early summer. The flowers take on tinges of pink as they age. Only one flower emerges from the centre of each leaf. Plants are 15in (38cm) tall when in flower, and spread to 1ft (30cm). The soil must be leafy and humus-rich for success. 'Flore Pleno' has double flowers. Propagate by division after the foliage has died away in summer.

Daffodils (*above*) z 5
This large and diverse group of bulbous plants work especially well in formal planting schemes, particularly when interplanted with lower-growing annuals or biennials in spring bedding displays. Choose the large-flowered cultivars of *Narcissus* for formal use. The golden-trumpeted types are the most popular and reach 1-2ft (30-60cm) in height. Plant the bulbs during late autumn. Deadheading the flowers retains energy in the plant. After flowering, the leaves should be left for at least six weeks.

Hyacinths z 6
The thick fragrant spikes of this plant are its major asset. The flowers are bell-shaped, fleshy and waxy, and come in varying shades of blue, pink, red or white. Hyacinths are ideal subjects for a formal spring display, especially if planted in quite narrow beds. For large groups, single-colour planting is most effective, perhaps interplanted with tulips or pansies. Popular cultivars are the yellow 'City of Haarlem', the pure white 'L'Innocence' and 'Delft Blue'. In autumn, plant fresh quality bulbs 6in (15cm) deep in moist well-drained soil.

Iris danfordiae z 6
In the first season after planting this charming miniature iris will produce a bright splash of golden colour with its sweet-scented flowers. After this, the bulbs divide naturally and take several years to flower again. Ideal for formal planters on a patio in spring or in bold drifts in a paved garden, this iris reaches only 4in (10cm) in height. The leaves die away in late spring and can be oversown with summer-flowering annuals. Choose a sunny position and well-drained fertile soil.

Iris reticulata (below) z 6
Many fine cultivars exist of this lovely blue miniature iris which is prized for its early flowers. In mild conditions the flowers can open from late winter onwards. This plant is well suited to containers and makes an excellent choice for edging along paths or for a bold dash of colour in a paved garden. Where possible work it in next to early yellow flowers, such as those of *Hamamelis mollis*. Hybrids include the pale blue 'Cantab', and the cream and azure 'Clairette'. Plant in free-draining soil 4in (10cm) deep in autumn.

Lilium (below) z 6
With their unmistakeable and elegant flower spikes, the lilies are naturals for use in formal planting. Most produce a flowering stem 2-6ft (60-180cm) tall and may require some staking. There are hundreds of species and cultivars to choose from and types to suit both acid and alkaline soil conditions. *L. regale* (*below*) has fragrant funnel-shaped flowers. The spring growth is attractive in its own right. Plant in autumn or spring into humus-rich soil which is in a shaded, cool position, but where the flowers can grow up into the sun.

Drifts of colour

Muscari armeniacum (*above*) z 5
Grape hyacinth
A tough plant which will grow well under shrubs and other plants. The flowers appear from mid-spring onwards and are a vivid blue, massed at the end of green stems like a tiny bunch of grapes. Two cultivars are commonly grown, the pale blue 'Cantab' and the darker 'Heavenly Blue'. Plants rarely grow to more than 9in (23cm) tall and make excellent ground cover, spreading rapidly when in well-drained soil in a sunny position.

Tulips (*above*) z 5
A huge range of cultivars of *Tulipa* exist. They are much used in spring bedding schemes, where their tall strong flower stems hold the blooms above lower-growing bedding plants. Flowers appear from mid-spring onwards, in colours ranging from pure white to the deepest purple, and can be single or double. Bulbs should be planted in autumn, 4-6in (10-15cm) deep. Lift cultivars after the leaves have died away and store in a dry place or replant each autumn. *T. kaufmanniana* has pink flowers with orange centres.

Camassia quamash z 4
Quamash
Group this plant in clumps in a border or near the edge of a pond. It loves heavy soil and partial shade. In summer, the star-shaped blue, violet or white flowers, 3in (8cm) across, are held in narrow spikes up to 32in (80cm) tall. At the base there are narrow, upright green leaves. Remove the faded flower stems. Divide clumps of bulbs in late summer and plant them during autumn 4in (10cm) deep. For dense spikes of white or bluish-violet flowers grow *C. leichtlinii* which can reach 5ft (1.5m).

Chionodoxa luciliae z 5
Glory of the snow
Often known as *C. gigantea*, these delightful, small spring-flowering bulbs are easy to grow. They are suited to a whole range of different situations, including the front of borders, rock gardens and in containers. The violet-blue star-like flowers have a white central zone, surrounding creamy filaments, and are carried on stems that grow to little more than 4in (10cm) high. There is a white form, 'Alba', and the pink 'Rosea'. Plants need well-drained humus-rich soil in full sun.

Colchicum autumnale (*below*) z 6
Meadow saffron or autumn crocus
Each corm of this plant can produce up to eight crocus-like flowers, in shades of purple, pink or in pure white. For a spectacular display in the autumn, plant corms in large groups, allowing for the foliage: the flowers are followed by large, glossy, deep green strap-shaped leaves which can grow to 6in (15cm) in length. 'Albo-Plenum' has double white flowers each with up to 30 petals. Plants naturalize well in grass in a sunny open position with well-drained soil.

Crocus tommasinianus z 5
One of the finest and earliest of the spring-flowering crocuses. It has narrow leaves and six-petalled purple flowers which have a white tubular throat. The stamens give the centre of the flower a deep orange splash. The colour of the flowers varies: shades of lilac and violet are also seen, while the petals are often dark-tipped and sometimes silvered on their outsides. Plants are 4in (10cm) tall when in flower, the flowers opening fully in bright sun. They are ideal for naturalizing in grass, eventually forming broad drifts. Plants succeed in alkaline soils, which must be well drained. Plant the corms 2in (6cm) deep in autumn.

Daffodils z 5
The most impressive massed displays are achieved when daffodil bulbs are planted informally whether in a natural or semi-natural setting. Both the large trumpet-flowered hybrids and the smaller and daintier species can be used to great effect in this way. Once naturalized, the plants should flower for several seasons. Use different cultivars to extend the display for up to two to three months during the spring.

Eranthis hyemalis (*above*) z 5
Winter aconite
This beautiful member of the buttercup family has bright yellow flowers which can peep through a blanket of snow during late winter. Plants are 4in (10cm) high when flowering, the base of each flower being subtended by a frilly green rosette of leaves. The flowers last for several weeks and are ideal as a winter underplanting, below *Rubus cockburnianus* or *Cornus alba* 'Sibirica'. The leaves are a useful ground cover. Plants self-seed regularly. Plant the tubers in autumn in moist soil.

Galanthus nivalis (*above*)   z 5
Common snowdrop
Along with *Eranthis hyemalis*, this early-flowering bulb signals the start of spring. The flowers hang like small white drops on green stalks. It is best seen in bold drifts and benefits from being in the shade cast by trees or shrubs, especially if they are deciduous. It can push up through low-growing ground cover plants. For unusual yellow and white colouring grow 'Lutescens'. Ideally, plant snowdrops in heavy soil straight after flowering.

Ipheion uniflorum 'Wisley Blue'   z 5
(*above*)
A South American bulb needing a sunny position and freely-draining soil: it does best at the base of a south- or west-facing wall, or at the front of a border. The soft blue flowers are star-shaped and face straight up to the sky, having a sweet soapy fragrance. The pale green grassy leaves flop loosely below the flowers and smell of garlic if rubbed. Plant bulbs 2in (5cm) deep in autumn or lift and divide large clumps. Plants reach a height of 5-8in (13-20cm) and make useful ground cover.

Ornithogalum nutans   z 6
Star of Bethlehem
This plant is grown for its white and green flowers, which are star-shaped and appear some time after the narrow basal leaves are formed. Each flower is translucent and up to 1¼in (3cm) long, held on spikes 6-14in (15-35cm) tall. Plants will form drifts when established in grassed areas so long as the soil is well drained. They prefer partial shade and the bulbs should be planted in autumn. For best effect grow on grassy slopes or banks where the flowers can be seen against a dark background.

Scilla peruviana (*above*)   z 7
This native of the Mediterranean needs a warm sunny spot and moist soil. The conical flowers heads appear in early summer, each with up to 50 flattish blue-violet flowers. Each head is ¾-1¼in (2-3cm) across on a stem 4-10in (10-25cm) tall. At the base are a cluster of narrow leaves. Propagate by division in late summer; plant bulbs shallowly in autumn or spring. *S. tubergeniana* flowers in early spring with pale blue, dark-veined flowers and *S. siberica* has bell-shaped, deep blue flowers.

Tulips   z 7
Apart from spring bedding displays, tulips can be put to good use in mixed borders, where they provide a bold splash of colour early in the season interplanted with other early perennials or spring-flowering shrubs. Many of the older types look good at the base of a stone wall and will blend in well in borders containing wall-trained fruit. For double flowers choose the yellow 'Monte Carlo' or for white, 'Snow Queen'; while for flowers with crested and ruffled petals 'Red Parrot' and 'Flaming Parrot' are ideal.

Acidanthera murielae   z 8
Also listed as *Gladiolus callianthus*, this beautiful plant adds a touch of elegance to any border. The exotic-looking flowers have six white petals with deep purple throats and are carried in groups of about ten on stems up to 3ft (90cm) tall. They appear in early autumn. Plant the corms in soil-based potting compost in autumn and keep in a cold frame, planting them out in a warm, sunny position the following spring. They must be lifted again before the first frosts in the autumn, or new bulbs must be bought in each year.

Allium giganteum   z 5
A member of the ornamental onion family, this plant will reach 4ft (1.2m) in height and has large rounded heads of densely packed lilac-pink flowers. The attractive grey-blue leaves are susceptible to damage by late spring frosts, so a warm sheltered spot is desirable. The large size of the flower heads makes a bold statement in a purple, blue or grey border. Plants need well-drained soil and the large bulbs need a handful of coarse grit scattered around them at planting time.

Crinum × powellii (*above*)   z 7
Although winter frosts will cut back the leaves of this South African native, the bulbs can be left planted outdoors year round in warm climates. Plant the bulbs with their necks just above soil level in a warm and sunny position, ideally at the base of a west- or south-facing wall. The strong, 3ft (90cm)-tall stems emerge in late summer with up to ten trumpet-shaped fragrant flowers. 'Roseum' has pink flowers, 'Album' white. Cover the leaves if late frosts are likely. Plants spread to 2ft (60cm). Plant fresh bulbs in spring in well-drained soil.

Crocosmia 'Lucifer' (below)   z 7
Montbretia

This hybrid will create an eye-catching display of large fire-red flowers during late summer and autumn. Other hybrids include 'Spitfire', with its large fiery orange flowers, and the darker orange 'Emberglow'. Plants grow to 1-3ft (60-90cm) high and have stiff sword-like leaves. Plant corms in spring in well-drained soil in an open sunny position. Divide large clumps every few years, just after flowering or in early spring. Plants go well with late-flowering perennials, such as *Helenium autumnale*.

Curtonus paniculatus   z 8

Also listed as *Antholyza paniculata* and *Cyrtonus paniculata*, this close relative of the crocosmias has been hybridized with *Crocosmia masonorum* to produce many fine cultivars which are usually listed under *Crocosmia*. However, it is a fine plant in its own right, reaching a height of 4ft (1.2m) with attractive zig-zagging sprays of tubular scarlet flowers. The leaves are erect, sword-shaped and pleated along their length. Plants need a well-drained soil and a sunny position.

Eremurus stenophyllus bungei   z 6
Foxtail lily or king's spear

Prized as a border plant for its elegant spikes of cup-shaped flowers held on a 5-6ft (1.5-1.8m)-tall flowering stem, this perennial needs a sunny growing position and well-drained soil to succeed. The flowers are yellow, turning darker at the base of the spike as they fade. The leaves are linear and form a loose basal rosette. The roots are fleshy and finger-like. It is necessary to protect early growth from frost with straw or sacking. In winter, the crown of the bulb should be mounded over with sharp sand or ash to keep it dry.

Fritillaria imperialis (above)   z 5
Crown imperial

A truly majestic spring-flowering bulb. The flowers appear on stems up to 3ft (90cm) tall and hang like bells below an apical tuft of green leafy bracts. 'Aurora' has orange flowers and 'Rubra' bronze-red. The stems are partly clothed with mid-green leaves. Plant the tubers on their sides in spring, 8in (20cm) deep, in humus-rich but well-drained soil. Propagate by division of clumps after the foliage has died away or by removal of offsets.

Gladiolus byzantinus (above)   z 7
Sword lily

This gladiolus is a native of the Mediterranean and has striking reddish-purple flowers carried on slightly arching stems which grow up to 3ft (90cm) tall. The flowers are set against bright green, narrow leaves. Plants rarely require staking and may even be naturalized in grass providing it is not too vigorous. Plant corms in autumn in fertile but well-drained soil. The sword lily never fails to look good when grown in the company of *Cistus* × *purpurea* or *Rosmarinus officinalis*.

Lilium candidum   z 6
Madonna lily

Succeeding on alkaline soil, this beautiful plant grows to 3ft (90cm) and has strongly fragrant, pure white flowers. It benefits from soil that has been enriched with compost or well rotted manure, the bulbs being planted shallowly and away from other lilies if possible. Growth begins in the autumn, the crown of basal leaves staying green through winter but then dying away as the flowering shoots emerge. The flowers are funnel-shaped, 2-3in (5-8cm) long, with five to twenty flowers on each stem in summer. The lance-shaped leaves are scattered along the stems.

Narcissus   z 5

These bulbous plants can be guaranteed to add early colour to a mixed border. While the smaller species narcissi tend to be lost in larger borders, many of the newer cultivars are perfectly suited to them. It is best to plant the bulbs in clumps, preferably in the spaces that will be covered by herbaceous plants later in the season. Underplanting of deciduous shrubs can also work well. 'February Gold' has large, slightly reflexed petals; those of 'Thalia' are creamy-white.

Triteleia laxa   z 8

Also known as *Brodiaea laxa*, this tender plant produces its funnel-shaped flowers in early summer. The flowers are carried in a large loose umbel, ranging from pale to deep purplish-blue, with each one being held erect and growing up to 2in (5cm) in length. The stem will reach a height of 20in (50cm) on a vigorous plant. Plant the corms during autumn in a sunny spot. The soil should be very well drained and dry out during summer. Propagate plants by seed or division. *T. hyacinthina* has white flowers which are sometimes tinged purple on thin stems.

Tulips   z 5

Like daffodils, tulips are very useful early-flowering bulbs. For bright bold patches of colour consider the larger flowered cultivars. However, there are several species of tulips which should not be overlooked because of their smaller size. For a clump of graceful flowers (red and white flushed with pink) grow the lady tulip, *Tulipa clusiana*. *T. tarda* has yellow and white flowers.

ROCK GARDEN PLANTS

The rock garden reached its apogee, in England, in the period spanning the latter part of the nineteenth century through to the First World War. At this time labour, in comparison to materials and transport, was inexpensive and large amounts of money were expended on creating monumental rock gardens. Rocks were imported from mountainous regions and as many gardeners as necessary were employed to carry out the weeding needed to prevent the establishment of perennial weeds which can be very difficult to remove from between the rocks. The subsequent demise of the monumental rock garden was due in large part to the increase in the cost of labour:

unkempt growth went against the spirit of precision and order inherent in rockery design.

The advent of the environment-friendly translocated herbicide, glyphosphate, that is deactivated as soon as it hits the ground, has made the control of weeds in a rock garden less of a problem. While taking extreme care not to touch the cultivated plants, weeds can be painted with a glyphosphate-based mix which kills them off *in situ* without running the risk of leaving bits of root behind or disturbing the root system of the rock plants. This should be done in conjuction with ensuring that the soil used is free from perennial

Right: A naturally sloping and open site is ideal for a rock garden. Dwarf shrubs, such as hebes and some willows, add weight to a planting of geraniums, hypericums, pinks, rock roses, saxifrages, sedums and other perennials that thrive in sunny and free-draining conditions.

Left: The cool, moist cracks at the base of a rockery have been colonized by a mauve campanula, creeping jenny, a lungwort and a pink sedum.

Below: On an impressive limestone rockery the pale yellow of a large broom blends with the vibrant, spring colours of alyssum, aubrieta and saxifrage.

weeds before planting and that it is covered with plants or mulch as quickly as possible to prevent new seeds from germinating.

Rock gardens are best suited to informally designed gardens and look most convincing on a large scale. Unfortunately the cost of construction and the lack of space in many modern gardens often leads to very awkward-looking mounds of inferior stones appearing in the middle of a carefully kept lawn. However, there are many ways of creating the right environment for growing rock garden plants, which are for the most part alpines, in a restricted space whether in a formal or informal setting.

In the smallest spaces sinks and troughs can be easily accommodated and are particularly well suited in areas devoid of soil such as patios. Small rocks can be incorporated to create a miniature landscape and dwarf conifers can be used to give structure to the composition while the rock garden plants spill over the edge of the container.

Raised beds are another possibility and can be constructed to any shape. Large numbers of plants can be grown, both in the soil within the bed and in the cracks of the walls around it. By including miniature bulbs in the planting schemes it is possible to have colour throughout most of the season. In addition,

cultivation and appreciation of the plants is possible
with a minimum of bending and backache.

Dry stone walls or the top of brick walls, whether
boundary or retaining walls, can also be the home for
many trailing rock garden plants, as can the interstices between paving slabs of patios and courtyards,
provided these have been laid on sand. In all these
situations the planting will be most effective if the
plants are allowed to find their own niche and self-
seed, colonizing the structure or surface.

All these growing environments have one characteristic in common. They all drain freely which is
essential to all plants that have their natural habitat in
mountainous regions. Whatever the situation it is
advisable to incorporate coarse drainage material in
the base of the container or rock garden, followed by a
layer of inverted turves and finally a mix of two parts
soil to one each of sharp sand and coarse peat. An
open site with plenty of light is also necessary for successful cultivation as is keeping the plants dry when
they are dormant, a period in nature when they are
either protected, in winter, by a layer of dry snow or,
in summer, baked by the sun. In the latter case it is
best to grow the most difficult and sensitive plants in a
scree or even under glass.

Above: A dicentra and a dwarf
geranium are among the plants
that have seeded themselves at
the base of these rocks. Great
patience is needed to get
plants to seed where they are
wanted as tiny plants are easily
washed away before they are
fully established. Often the
best strategy is to position the
first plants on flat ground
nearby and let them self-seed
naturally among the adjacent
cracks and crevices.

Left: Diascias, rock roses and
violas are among the plants
clothing the large blocks of
stone in this garden. Large
pieces of rock can be costly
and need to be positioned
carefully if they are to look
natural. A free-draining
compost needs to be
incorporated during building.

For flowers

Adonis amurensis   z 3

The flowers of this charming perennial open from late winter onwards: often the bronze-green shoots can be seen pushing through the snow. Each bloom resembles a buttercup and is borne singly at the end of a shoot. After flowering, the finely cut leaves expand, giving the plant an eventual height of 1ft (30cm), before it dies away at the end of summer. Plant in well-drained humus-rich soil in late summer away from baking sun. To avoid mud splash on the flowers, surround the plant with stone chippings. Very hardy.

Alyssum saxatile (*above*)   z 6
Gold dust

Sometimes known as *Aurinia saxatile*, this hardy evergreen perennial forms low mounds of growth with small, hairy grey-green leaves. In spring it is covered by bright golden-yellow flowers, and is the natural partner to *Aubrieta*. Plants reach a height of 8-12in (20-30cm) and should be clipped over after flowering to stop them becoming too large. They need full sun and well-drained soil. Increase by sowing seed in autumn or from softwood cuttings.

Androsace sempervivoides   z 5

A fully hardy, compact and cushion-forming evergreen perennial with leathery, oblong leaves. In spring smallish heads of four to ten flowers appear, which are flat, pinkish with yellow eyes turning red. The plants need sun and well-drained soil, and grow up to 3in (8cm) high with a spread of about 1ft (30cm). Propagate in summer by taking tip cuttings or by removing young stolons, or in autumn by sowing seed. *A. sarmentosa* (z 3) has bright pink flowers with yellow eyes and is good for all but the wettest areas.

Anthemis cupaniana (*above*)   z 8

With its finely cut, dense silvery foliage and small, daisy-like white flower heads with yellow centres, this evergreen perennial is an excellent choice in a warm climate. The flowers appear from early summer to autumn. The plants form spreading carpets, grow to a height of 1ft (30cm) with similar spread, and need clipping over after flowering. In winter the foliage turns green. Increase by taking basal cuttings from late summer through to spring. Plant in well-drained soil in full sun.

Arabis caucasica (*above*)   z 3

An ideal choice for sturdy ground cover in a large rock garden, this evergreen mat-forming perennial is very hardy. It has small, oval mid-green leaves and four-petalled white or pink fragrant flowers in late spring and summer. Plants reach a height of 6in (15cm) and are at home on dry banks in thin soil. They should be trimmed over after the flowers have faded. 'Variegata' has cream-splashed leaf margins; 'Plena' has double white flowers; 'Rosabella' is deep pink. Propagate by seed in autumn or by softwood cuttings in summer.

Armeria maritima (*below*)   z 3
Thrift, sea thrift or sea pink

In the wild, the evergreen hummocks (1ft (30cm) high) of this popular perennial cling to rocky outcrops along coastlines. In the rock garden, it should be sited in full sun, where the soil is very well drained. During spring and summer the hummocks are studded with globular flowers, ranging from lilac through pink to white: deadhead to prolong flowering. 'Vindictive' has rose-pink flowers. To propagate, divide plants in spring or take semi-hardwood cuttings in late summer.

Aubrieta deltoidea (*below*)   z 7
Purple rock cress

In spring the dense mats of this evergreen plant are smothered in flowers – of varying shades of blue, red, purple or pink – which look supurb next to those of *Alyssum saxatile*. Its spreading foliage makes excellent ground cover. Plants will flourish on dry chalky soils and in walls and other crevices, so long as the drainage is good. After flowering, cut hard back to maintain shape and vigour. Propagate by taking tip cuttings in spring, or by layering the plants during the summer.

Campanula carpatica
Bellflower
z 3

Ideal for the rock garden, this low-growing hardy perennial reaches a height of 3-4in (8-10cm) and spreads to 1ft (30cm). Its branching stems carry toothed, round-oval leaves, above which, during summer, the wide, bell-shaped, blue or white flowers appear. Named forms include the deep violet 'Jewel', 'Turbinata' which is lavender, and the pure white 'Bressingham White'. Plants need moist, well-drained soil, in sun or light shade. Divide in autumn or spring, or take softwood or basal cuttings in summer, or plant seed.

Chiastophyllum oppositifolium
z 6

Also called *Cotyledon simplicifolia*, this succulent trailing perennial has an evergreen spreading habit and large, oblong, serrated fleshy leaves. During spring and early summer small yellow flowers open on very distinctive, arching sprays 6-8in (15-20cm) tall. It is at home in the cracks and crevices between rocks, but needs some shade and moist soil to do well. Take cuttings during summer using side shoots.

Dryas octopetala
Mountain avens
z 1

The dark green, leathery leaves of this prostrate-growing evergreen perennial are held close to the ground. During late spring and early summer creamy-white, cup-shaped flowers appear just above the leaves, followed by attractive fluffy seed heads. Plants have a woody base, grow to only 2in (6cm) tall and make excellent ground cover, forming large patches in time. Choose a sunny spot and well-drained, gritty soil with some leaf mould added. Sow the seeds when fresh or take semi-ripe cuttings during the summer months. The fine *D. × suendermannii* is similar with pale cream flowers that open flat.

Erinus alpinus
Fairy foxglove
z 4

Sow this dainty semi-evergreen perennial in spring, after which it will self-seed readily without becoming a problem. The plants need light, well-drained soil and a sunny position. They grow to only 6in (15cm) tall when in flower; clusters of pink, starry flowers rising above the small mid-green leaves. 'Albus' has white flowers, while those of 'Mrs Charles Boyle' are large and pink.

Gentiana sino-ornata
z 6

A native of Tibet, the rich blue flowers of this hardy autumn-flowering gentian are a very impressive sight. They are borne singly above a cushion of fine grassy evergreen leaves, each 2in (5cm)-long trumpet having a green-striped throat. When in flower, the plants stand 2in (5cm) high and can spread to 1ft (30cm). Plant into moist, acid soil that is well charged with leaf mould, preferably in a spot that is shaded around midday. Propagate by dividing in spring every two to three years.

Helianthemum nummularium
(*above*)
z 4

Sun rose or rock rose

One of the most colourful and reliable of all rock garden plants, this evergreen sub-shrub forms a spreading prostrate mat of growth covered in small, single rose-like flowers throughout the summer. Plants grow to 6in (15cm) high and spread to 2ft (60cm). They need full sun and free-draining, gritty soil that is not too rich. In autumn cut back to a few inches from the ground. For grey foliage and large pink flowers grow 'Wisley Pink'; 'Beech Park Red' has crimson blooms; 'Wisley Primrose' has yellow flowers. Propagate from non-flowering shoots in late summer.

Hedyotis michauxii
z 3

Also listed as *Houstonia serpyllifolia*, this vigorous creeping perennial forms dense mats of spreading stems which root readily at the nodes. The mid-green foliage is dotted with violet-blue star-shaped flowers from spring to early summer. Plants reach a height of 3in (8cm), spreading to 1ft (30cm). Ideally, the soil should be sandy with added leaf mould, to hold moisture, and shaded. Divide in spring or sow seed in autumn.

Lewisia cotyledon (*above*)
z 6

A gem among rock garden plants, *Lewisia* needs the morning sun to show off its bright flowers that close soon after lunch, but must be shaded from the midday sun. The rosettes of evergreen spatulate leaves set off the 1ft (30cm)-tall panicles of pink to salmon flowers that age rose-red. It requires excellent drainage to thrive, particularly around the neck which is apt to wilt during the winter when growth stops, and even during wet periods in the summer; cracks in walls are ideal.

Saxifraga longifolia (*above*)
z 6

This hardy saxifrage is a rosette-forming perennial with long, narrow leaves encrusted with lime, which makes them especially attractive. When the rosettes reach three to four years old they produce long, arching flowering shoots smothered in panicles of white flowers. The flowers appear in spring and summer, and then the rosettes die without leaving any offspring. For this reason plants must be raised from seed, sown in spring or autumn. They are ideal for cracks and crevices, and need well-drained, alkaline soil and full sun.

For foliage

Asplenium trichomanes (*below*)   z 6
A dainty little fern suited to a limestone rock garden, where it will thrive in crannies, or planted in soil. It will tolerate full sun. It has slender tapering fronds (which should be removed once faded) with brown midribs carrying the bright green, rounded pinnae. The plant is semi-evergreen, often retaining most of its leaves through the winter. Plants grow to a height of 6in (15cm) spreading up to 1ft (30cm). Increase is by spores or more reliably by carefully dividing those clumps which have several crowns.

Bolax gummifera (*below*)   z 4
Prized for its hard cushions of foliage made up of evergreen blue-green leaves held in tight rosettes, this plant rarely produces its insignificant yellow flowers. Plants reach a height of only 1in (2.5cm), spread slowly to 6in (15cm) and need humus-rich but well-drained soil in full sun. They are very hardy and most at home in a gritty scree garden. Propagate by rooting rosettes during summer. Work plenty of sharp stone chippings in around the crown to prevent rotting. *Sagina boydii* is similar, growing to only ½in (1cm).

Dryopteris cristata (*above*)   z 5
Crested buckler fern
Moist conditions, such as are found next to a pond, suit this plant. It has light to mid-green fronds of two distinct types: sterile fronds which grow to 18in (45cm) in length and spread, and fertile spore-bearing fronds which can be 3ft (90cm) tall and stand fully erect. The latter, which have been likened to large shuttlecocks, give the fern a very distinctive appearance when planted in a group. Plants need some shade. Fading fronds should be removed regularly.

Sedum sieboldii ‘Variegatum’   z 5
(*above*)
Also called *S. sieboldii* ‘Foliis Medio-variegatis’, this tuberous perennial has rounded fleshy leaves in whorls of three. They are blue-green splashed with cream, sometimes with reddish edges. The flowers are pink and star-shaped, opening during late summer. Plants reach a height of 4in (10cm) and spread to 8in (20cm). It is also a useful plant for the front of a mixed border. Needs fertile well-drained soil and full sun. Propagate by division or through softwood cuttings in summer.

Sedum spathulifolium ‘Purpureum’   z 6
(*below*)
A purple-leaved form of the stonecrop, the leaves of this succulent perennial are spoon-shaped forming tight rosettes packed together on the plant. It produces mats or hummocks of growth to a height of 3in (8cm) and spreads up to 2ft (60cm). In summer, tiny yellow flowers appear in clusters: remove the flower heads in the following spring. Plants will tolerate some shade but prefer sun. Plant in well-drained soil and propagate by carefully detaching rooted rosettes.

Sempervivum tectorum (*below*)   z 4
Houseleek
Traditionally grown on the tiled roofs of houses to give protection from lightning and witchcraft, this plant grows as tight rosettes of succulent leaves, each rosette being anything from ½-8in (1-20cm) across. The leaves are normally green, but can be flushed with shades of red, pink and purple. Pinkish flowers appear in summer. Plants need good drainage and full sun to thrive. ‘Triste’ has green leaves tipped with reddish-brown. Increase plants by detaching rooted rosettes and replanting.

PAVED GARDEN PLANTS

In both large and small gardens it is often appropriate to have a paved area, such as a patio, terrace or flight of steps. Here, container-grown plants can contribute significantly to the success of the garden, introducing splashes of colour, architectural features, focal points and seasonal emphasis. They have the advantage that they can be moved around according to the mood and prevailing display of the moment.

There are also a number of plants that thrive in conditions where the soil is limited, poor and well drained, such as in the cracks between paving stones or in walls. For example, creeping thyme and chamomile can be used to soften the geometry of a paved area, as they will tolerate some walking on, while saxifrage and acaena are useful creeping around the edges. Erigeron and corydalis are suitable for colonizing cracks in walls and between steps, and tall plants such as verbascum make bold vertical statements.

Pots can be used to allow the inclusion of plants not suited to the soil in the garden (for example, camellias and rhododendrons in a garden where the soil is alkaline) or ones that have to be kept in frost-free conditions during the winter such as the sweetly-scented spidery-flowered bulbous hymenocallis.

Right: This decked courtyard contains numerous pot-grown, shade-tolerant plants, including impatiens, lamium and gardener's garters. Taller plants include a ginkgo, a willow (*Salix matsudana* 'Tortuosa') and a fig tree.

Left: Tender and hardy plants in carefully placed clusters of pots and individual containers do not obscure the decorative surface of bricks laid in a variety of patterns.

Below: Thymes and other tough, creeping plants occupy niches in the irregular paving of a sun-baked terrace on which a stone sink makes an attractive feature.

The importance of choosing the right container cannot be overstressed as it can make or break any aesthetic contribution the plant may bring to the garden. First, there is the style of the pot to consider, which should fit in with the chosen style of the garden. In a cottage garden, a mass of clay pots brimming over with flowering annuals and colourful bulbs will mingle happily with the exuberance of honeysuckles, roses, hollyhocks, phloxes and feverfew. In contrast, the recreation of a formal seventeenth-century garden will call for substantial containers of evergreen standards and topiary specimens displayed symmetrically about the main axes of the garden.

The containers may be of lead, stone or terracotta. There are many other materials available and much depends on the available resources, but it is better to have a few, well chosen containers than a host of second rate ones. Plastic pots may be light and cheap but should be hidden in wooden containers: marine ply stained dark green, black (which makes the vegetation stand out against it) or greeny-blue all work well. Alternatively, glazed containers created individually by potters that are in themselves pieces of art are an excellent choice as they would adorn the garden on their own or planted up.

The size of the container depends, within reason, on the size of the plant that is to be grown in it. It is

Left: Pansies and petunias form an underplanting beneath a mixture of shrubs – including trained cypresses, maples, pittosporums, roses and a yucca – grown in containers and raised beds that surround a small courtyard paved with York stone.

Below: Pot-grown plants, including elaborately trained ivy, have been used as accents and focal points within the formal geometry of this garden, in which the beds are divided by gravel paths.

important to remember that any container-grown plant requires sufficient nutrients to keep it growing healthily throughout the season without becoming so vigorous that it outgrows the container. Most good quality proprietary composts should contain enough nutrients, but at the height of the season it may be necessary to supplement this once a week with some liquid fertilizer. Watering is the single most important task when looking after pot-grown plants. During the main growing period, when evaporation is at its height, this usually needs doing twice a day.

Bearing these growing requirements in mind, it can be said that almost anything can be grown in a pot as long as it is accepted that it may not be as long-lived as normal, or, in time, will outgrow the container. So small trees (or larger ones grown as bonsai), shrubs, fruit trees and climbers can be included in a scheme of container-grown plants. Those that in their natural habitat tolerate drought are often best adapted to pot conditions; for example, many Mediterranean plants including bays, box, *Rhamnus alaternus* and pyracantha. Many species that need moist, shady conditions, such as rhododendrons and camellias, often fail through lack of watering. Usually, the most successful container displays are mixes of annuals and/or bulbs, newly planted as the seasons change.

Between the paving

Acaena microphylla z 7
This charming native of New Zealand is prized more for its soft, burr-like scarlet seed heads, which glisten in the sun, than for its flowers. The plants form spreading evergreen mats of bronzed leaves, 1-2in (2.5-5cm) high. They prefer light soils in sun, needing only a few rooted shoots to establish quick-growing colonies. 'Blue Haze' grows slightly taller, with wonderful blue-grey foliage and reddish seed heads. Underplant with dwarf spring bulbs.

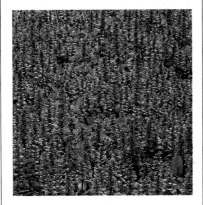

Ajuga reptans (*above*) z 4
Bugle
For paved areas in light shade where the soil is moist the bugle is perfect. Plants form an evergreen mat of dark green, glossy foliage with blue-purple flowers on elegant flower spikes in spring. In flower, the plants are up to 1ft (30cm) high and spread indefinitely unless checked. 'Burgundy Glow' has leaves variegated pink, purple, cream and green; 'Purpurea' has deep purple-bronze foliage. Bugles associate well with the small-flowered erigerons and blue-leaved grasses such as *Festuca glauca*. Remove rooted pieces of shoot to increase stocks.

Campanula portenschlagiana z 5
A vigorous bellflower which thrives in shade, needing moist soil. Plants produce a carpet of heart-shaped leaves covered from early summer to autumn with clusters of upright, open blue-violet flowers. At flowering the plants are 6in (15cm) tall, spreading up to 2ft (60cm). They are evergreen and hardy, but prone to slug damage in a wet spring. Plants self-seed and can become a pest in a sunny situation. Propagate by softwood cuttings of non-flowering shoots during summer.

***Chamaemelum nobile* 'Treneague'** z 6
A patch of this wonderfully fragrant, evergreen perennial releases the well-known "chamomile" scent when walked on or rubbed: a delight on warm summer evenings. It grows best on well-drained soils in full sun. Because the plant sets no seed it must be propagated by cuttings or division. The straight species is more vigorous and has white flowers with yellow centres; it grows to a height of 4in (10cm).

Corydalis lutea (*below*) z 5
The yellow corydalis produces its small, snapdragon-like yellow flowers nearly year-round above rounded mounds of finely divided, delicate grey-green leaves. The mounds grow to 1ft (30cm) high, with a similar spread, and are ideal between paving stones or spilling from crevices in walls. It self-seeds with ease, or the ripe seeds can be scattered by hand as required. A superb partner for early bulbs such as *Chionodoxa*. Plants do well on poor soils, especially in the sun. At the end of summer cut straggly plants to the ground.

Erigeron karvinskianus z 9/annual
A lovely fleabane with spreading loose stems carrying masses of daisy-like flower heads which open white, then turn pink, finally fading to purple. Flowers appear from summer through into autumn. The three-tone colour on established plants is quite eye-catching, especially when seen along the edge of garden steps. The stems also bear small, lance-shaped bristly leaves which are mid-green. Plants only grow 6in (15cm) tall, but spread widely, and should be clipped back in spring before new growth begins. Propagate by softwood cuttings in summer. Needs well-drained soil and full sun.

Helxine soleirolii z 8
Also listed as *Soleirolia soleirolii*, this plant can become a nuisance in the wrong place. It is very tolerant and will fill the gaps between paving slabs or stones, especially if laid on cool moist soil in a shaded spot; but it is too delicate to withstand constant treading. Normally an evergreen perennial, it forms a dense carpet of tiny rounded green leaves which can be burned off by severe winter frosts. Plants never exceed 2in (5cm) in height. To propagate tease away small clumps and replant. Makes a good pot or greenhouse plant.

Lobularia maritima (*above*) annual
Sweet alyssum
Formerly known as *Alyssum maritimum*. During spring, scatter the seeds of this quick-growing plant in the gaps between paving for a show of tiny white, scented flowers in small heads in the summer and autumn. Deadhead the flowers regularly to maintain the display. Plants have small, narrow greyish-green leaves, grow to a height of 6in (15cm) and spread to 1ft (30cm). They are hardy and need fertile soil and full sun to give of their best. 'Wonderland' has pink-purple blooms.

Mazus reptans z 5
With some shelter (from frosts), moist soil and full sun, this creeping perennial will produce an abundance of purple flowers in spring. The flowers have a large, three-lobed whitish lower lip, spotted with red and yellow, and a small, slightly hooded top lip. Plants grow to no more than 2in (5cm) high, spread to 12in (30cm), and have narrow toothed leaves held in pairs along the stems. Divide plants in spring and replant vigorous tufts; alternatively, collect seed and sow in autumn.

Container plants

Saxifraga moschata (*below*)   z 6
Plant this evergreen perennial where there is some shade from the midday sun and where the soil is constantly moist. It will form a tight hummock 4in (10cm) high, made up of rosettes of small, lance-shaped green leaves. From these grow thin stems during summer, each carrying up to five creamy-white or yellowish star-shaped flowers. 'Cloth of Gold' has bright golden-yellow leaves and is ideal for shade. 'Elf' is shown. Propagate by detaching and rooting vigorous rosettes.

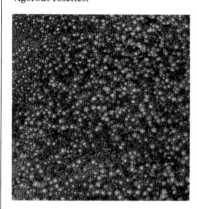

Thymus herba-barona   z 4
Caraway thyme
The common name of this evergreen sub-shrub comes from its small, dark green, caraway-scented leaves. The fragrance is released when the leaves are brushed against, but the plant will not tolerate trampling. Plants reach a height of 2-4in (5-10cm) and in summer are covered in small, lilac-pink flowers borne in clusters at the ends of the shoots. An ideal setting is among sand-coloured paving, especially if in tones of blue, grey and purple. Plants do best in full sun, where the soil is moist but free-draining. Take softwood or semi-ripe cuttings in summer.

Verbascum bombyciferum z 5/biennial
There are few more dramatic sights than this silver-leaved biennial mullein shooting up its tall racemes of densely-packed yellow flowers to a height of 4-6ft (1.2-1.8m). This it does in its second season, remaining evergreen through the previous winter. Both the large, oval basal leaves and the flower stems are covered in soft silvery hairs. Either allow to self-seed or scatter fresh seed, thinning in the following spring to produce strong plants.

Agapanthus Headbourne hybrids   z 7
(*above*)
Although the agapanthus is a native of South Africa, these hybrids originated in England and so tolerate cooler conditions. They are clump-forming perennials, evergreen in the mildest winters, with large, dark green strap-shaped leaves. In late summer the large, striking rounded heads of flowers rise to a height of up to 3ft (90cm). They range from deep blue to almost white. Plants need full sun, moist well-drained compost and protection during winter. Large plants can be divided.

Argyranthemum frutescens z 9/annual
Marguerite
Also known as *Chrysanthemum frutescens*, this tender bushy perennial is perfect for growing as a standard in containers. It has delicate, blue-grey leaves and numerous daisy-like flower heads – yellow, pink or white depending on the form grown – during summer. It may take several seasons to form a 3ft (90cm)-high standard but it is well worth the effort. Plants thrive in a sunny spot with fertile moist soil and can be moved indoors during winter for protection.

Ballota pseudodictamnus   z 8
For a hot and sunny spot, this mound-forming sub-shrub provides considerable interest. It has grey-green rounded leaves covered in woolly hairs. During summer, small pink flowers emerge which have large, pale green calyces. The calyces remain long after the flowers have faded. Plants reach 2ft (60cm) in height and can spread rapidly to 3ft (90cm). To check growth cut back in early spring. Semi-ripe cuttings can be taken during summer. Needs well drained compost.

Bidens ferulifolia   annual
A Mexican native, this attractive member of the daisy family is grown as a half hardy annual, being raised from seed under glass in spring. It makes an ideal plant for a container, such as a hanging basket, with its lax habit allowing it to spill over the edge. Choose a terracotta pot or tub to complement its yellow star-like flowers and finely dissected greeny-bronze foliage. It associates well with *Helichrysum petiolare*. Plant after the frosts in rich, moist compost in the sun.

Fuchsia (*above*)   z 10/annual
The range of cultivars available of this popular garden plant is staggering. Most are tender and need overwintering where the temperature does not drop below 6°C (43°F) for some or 1°C (34°F) for others. They are often grown in containers and put out after the last frosts. The flower is prized for its great beauty. All fuchsias grow with a shrubby habit, being easily trained into standards. They need good rich soil and a sunny position. For containers, bushy plants up to 2ft (60cm) tall are ideal. 'Morning Light' is shown.

Helichrysum petiolare z 8/annual
Grown primarily for its soft, silver-felted foliage, this rather tender sub-shrub is perfect for a mixed container planting. As the plant develops the shoots will trail and drape over the sides. It is best treated as an annual, young plants being overwintered from cuttings taken the previous season. Other cultivars well worth seeking are 'Limelight', with greenish-yellow leaves, and 'Variegata' which has cream variegation. Plants should be in sun and need well drained compost to produce their best displays.

Hydrangea macrophylla (*above*)   z 6
With care, hydrangeas will grow well in a good-sized container. Position them in a lightly shaded spot, as excessive sunlight will scorch the foliage, out of the path of strong cold winds. Use a free-draining humus-rich mixture when planting up. The flowers are produced either in large mop-like heads or in flattish clusters, known as lacecaps. 'Blue Wave' is a lacecap with blue-pink heads; the mophead 'Madame Emile Mouillière' has white flowers with pink or blue centres. The dead flower heads add interest in winter.

Lilium regale (*above*)   z 5
The regal lily
In summer, nothing can equal a grouping of weathered terracotta pots of this beautiful lily. The flowers appear on stems up to 6ft (2m) tall on really vigorous plants. Each stem can produce up to 25 funnel-shaped fragrant flowers, with petals that are whitish on the inside with a yellow base and tinted pink on the outside. The scaly bulbs can be repotted in fresh rich compost each spring. A few strong twigs are usually needed to support the flowers.

Lobelia erinus (*below*)   annual
Few containers would be complete without the annual lobelia. The plants are raised under glass and planted out after the last frosts. They grow as spreading or pendulous mats, reaching a height of 8in (20cm), forming large clumps which cascade over the edge of the container. The flowers are two-lipped, small, and appear throughout summer into early autumn. 'Red Cascade' and 'Cambridge Blue' are notable; a mixed display is shown.

Osteospermum ecklonis   z 9/annual
This evergreen semi-woody perennial must be planted in full sun in well-drained soil. It is ideal for pots or tubs as a central dot planting, reaching a height and spread of 18in (45cm). The main flush of the white daisy-like flowers with blue centres is in summer; they open to their maximum on sunny days. Take cuttings of non-flowering shoots in summer. Plants tend to become straggly and need some cutting back in late spring. In the ideal climate of subtropical areas they will flower almost all year round.

Pelargonium   z 10/annual
Ideal for summer containers, the best types of these perennials are the ivy-leaved, Swiss Balcony and zonals. All these have bright red to white flowers with numerous pink, mauve and salmon intermediates. Repot plants in late autumn and cut down by half before overwintering in a frost-free place. In spring cut back to healthy buds as growth starts. Alternatively, take cuttings in late summer and overwinter ready for spring planting. The zonals are usually raised as half-hardy annuals from seed, preferably in fairly poor and dry conditions.

Petunia   annual
The modern strains of this popular half-hardy summer bedding plant are available as grandifloras (with large, trumpet-shaped flowers) or multifloras (where the flowers are smaller and more numerous). Flower colour ranges from white, through red, pink, purple and yellow, and they can be double, striped or frilly. For best results plant in sheltered containers in full sun, where the plants will adopt a trailing habit. Allow 9in (23cm) between the plants, which can grow up to 16in (40cm) high. Wet summers tend to spoil the flowers. Raise from seed in early spring.

Tropaeolum majus (*below*)   annual
A very easy to grow hardy trailing annual. Sow the large seeds after the last frosts, choosing trailing varieties which soon produce vigorous, spreading shoots. During summer these are decked with large bright flowers in shades of red, orange and yellow. This plant will thrive in the poorest of soils and clamber through other container plants with ease, and off into nearby hedges and shrubs if allowed. Both the flowers and leaves can be used in salads.

Verbena   annual
Most forms of vervain are descended from *V.* × *hybrida*, which is grown as a half-hardy bushy annual reaching a height of 6-18in (15-45cm) with similar spread. The plants have oval, rough-haired leaves and bright flowers held in tight clusters of pink, red, mauve, salmon or white from early summer onwards. They need full sun and well-drained soil. Selected forms are raised from cuttings taken in late summer and overwintered, the mixed types (such as 'Showtime') from seed raised under glass in spring.

WATER PLANTS

Water in a garden is an undisputed asset to its design and attractiveness. The introduction of water plants not only helps to keep the water clean by natural means, but also helps to support a whole range of wildlife, including tadpoles and frogs, dragonflies, snails and fish. The position of a pond in the garden is important as most water plants require plenty of light to prosper. The shade cast by their leaves is welcomed by fish and other wildlife and reduces the growth rate of vigorous plants, such as duckweed and pondweed.

Regularly-shaped formal pools are well suited to the area adjacent to the house, where they will make an immediate impact and provide a focal point. In the smallest gardens they can be reduced to the size of a barrel (at least 1-2ft/30-60 cm deep), stone trough or tank, and planted with a single plant or two or three small-leaved species such as *Juncus effusus* 'Spiralis', frogbit (*Hydrocharis morsus-ranae*) and *Nymphaea tetragona* 'Alba'. The depth of the water and the vigour of plants can be regulated by planting each one in a basket that is supported by bricks so that it is immersed to the right depth. Larger pools call for simple treatments using only water lilies in a single striking colour or a subtle association of two colours.

Right: Astilbes, azaleas and ferns enjoy a cool, moist atmosphere, generated by a cascade and pool in a shady position. This well planned, established planting scheme looks completely natural.

Left: Yellow flags and arum lilies make a harmonious combination of white, cream and yellow that blends with the rockwork surrounding this sunny pool.

Below right: Although many waterside plants die down in winter, the foliage of some persists and can be very decorative. Here, the strap-shaped leaves of phormiums stand up stiffly behind irises and reeds.

An irregularly shaped informal pool looks most realistic if placed at the lowest point in a wild or informal garden, where water would naturally gather, and a path should lead the visitor down to discover it. A variety of plants will be appropriate here. The centre of the pool is suitable for deep-water plants, some of which root in the mud at the bottom of the pool or in specially designed baskets, while others, called floaters, are not rooted and have a tendency to spread very fast. Particularly fast-growing floaters are the oxygenators, which are essential to the ecology of the pool, but often need constant curbing. A common recommendation is that they should at the most take up a third of the pool's volume. Most frequently sold are the common duckweed, *Lemna minor*, and Canadian pondweed, *Elodea canadensis*, both of which can grow very quickly as the summer heat increases, choking all around them. They can only be recommended where it is easy to remove them regularly. *Myriophyllum spicatum*, the water milfoil, and *Cabomba caroliniana* are more desirable, being equally good purifiers and much less invasive.

For the edges of an informal pool, where the water is the shallowest, there is a wealth of "marginals" to choose from. With these, as with all other groups of plants, the art in designing is to select species of varying sizes and leaf shapes that harmonize and contrast with one another. In addition, they should complement the reflective quality of the water and the season, colour and habit of the flowers needs to be taken into account. These considerations should also be ex-

tended to the area immediately surrounding the pool, which can be made into a bog garden. For example, the upright heart-shaped leaves of *Peltandra virginica* and the diamond-shaped, serrated leaves of *Trapa natans* contrast well with the strap-like leaves of *Iris laevigata* and tall, leafless stems of the variegated sedge *Scirpus tabernaemontani* 'Zebrinus'. The shapes and habits of these marginals can then be echoed in the boggy surroundings of the pool with the tall leaves of the American skunk cabbage, *Lysichiton americanus*, the great clumps of *Hosta fortunei*, the straps of *Iris ensata* and ferny foliage of *Osmunda regalis*.

Water garden

Aponogeton distachyos (*below*)   z 9
Cape pondweed, water hawthorn
This deciduous perennial has floating, oblong, dark green leaves which are sometimes splashed purple. The attractive waxy-white flowers have a characteristic "forked" appearance, sweet scent and noticeable black stamens. They appear from early spring until autumn. At home in deep or shallow water, plants spread to 4ft (1.2m). The fading leaves need tidying up in autumn. Propagate in spring by division of the tubers or by sowing fresh seed: plants often self-seed.

Cabomba caroliniana   z 6
Fish grass, fanwort, Washington grass
A useful oxygenator for ponds, this deciduous or semi-evergreen submerged perennial is used by fish as a source of food and a suitable place to spawn. Plants form spreading hummocks of fan-shaped, coarsely divided leaves which are bright green. Tiny white flowers appear in summer. Propagate by taking stem cuttings in summer or by division when dormant. Tends to be cut back in severe winters.

Callitriche palustris   z 5
Water starwort
The bright green, oval-linear leaves of this plant are not only attractive but also help to aerate the water. At home submerged or part-submerged in deep water, plants will grow equally well rooted in wet mud. In mud they tend to grow as rosettes, while in deep water the stems can be 20in (50cm) long. The minute green flowers appear during spring and summer but are rather insignificant. Plants grow as annuals or perennials and can become a weed if not kept in check. Dredge the pond regularly leaving a few stems to re-grow.

Caltha palustris (*above*)   z 3
Marsh marigold or kingcup
In shallow water around the edge of a pond there is little to equal the spectacular spring display of this deciduous perennial. It is equally well suited to a bog garden, moist rock garden or herbaceous border. The rounded, dark green leaves set off the large, cup-shaped golden-yellow flowers. Plants can grow to 2ft (60cm) in height with a spread of 18in (45cm). The double-flowered cultivar 'Flore Plena' reaches only 10in (25cm). Sow seeds in an open sunny position.

Ceratophyllum demersum   z 4
Hornwort
An excellent choice for attractive, feathery submerged foliage, this deciduous perennial is easily controlled; its brittle nature makes thinning out a simple task. It will sometimes float and will spread over a large area given space. The hornwort is a good oxygenator and grows best in cool deep water. Plants are rootless. Divide the scaly winter buds or take stem cuttings during the growing season.

Cyperus longus   z 7
Galingale
This evergreen perennial sedge is fully hardy and can reach 5ft (1.5m) in height, and spreads slowly but strongly. For large ponds it is excellent for stabilizing banks, and will grow well in otherwise uninteresting ditches, where in summer the milk-chocolate coloured flowers appear in flattish umbels. Flowers appear above the dark green, glossy, rough-edged narrow leaves. They are long-lasting and useful for cutting. Plants will tolerate their roots being in water. Divide in spring.

Hottonia palustris (*below*)   z 5
Water violet
The dense whorls of finely pinnate leaves of this violet form a spreading pale green mass. In summer, flower spikes appear above the foliage carrying lilac or white yellow-eyed flowers in whorled clusters. This hardy, submerged deciduous water plant is a member of the primrose family. Plants should be thinned regularly as they mature to stop crowding. They need a sunny position and cool, clean, still, deep water. Propagate through stem cuttings during the growing season.

Hydrocharis morsus-ranae (*below*)   z 5
Frogbit
The kidney-shaped, olive green shining leaves and small white flowers of the frogbit are a delight in summer. This deciduous perennial can spread up to 4in (10cm), but groups of plants tend to grow together spreading to 3ft (90cm). The petals are distinctive, three-petalled with a central yellow eye and grow up to 1in (2.5cm) across. The leaves are often bronze-tinted. Plants grow in still, fresh deep water needing an open sunny spot. They are easily propagated by detaching young plantlets.

Iris laevigata (*above*)   z 4
One of the best of the hardy water irises for growing in shallow water. Plants form large spreading clumps to a height of 2-3ft (60-90cm). The flowering stems arise from the rhizomes, each carrying between two and four flowers of a brilliant blue. The beardless flowers appear in summer. Ideal for sun or part shade. Divide in late summer. 'Regal' has red flowers, those of 'Snowdrift' are double white, while 'Variegata', which flowers again in early autumn, has variegated foliage.

Juncus effusus 'Spiralis'   z 5
Corkscrew rush
A tufted evergreen perennial with mid-green leafless stems which are twisted and curled like a corkscrew. The stems often lie on the ground. The greenish-brown flowers appear in summer. Plants are best used at the edge of a pond, so that the stems can be seen against the reflective water surface. Strong plants can send up 3ft (90cm)-tall twisted shoots which are used in modern flower arranging. Divide clumps in spring.

Myriophyllum spp   z 4
The myriophyllums are a group of deciduous perennials with finely divided, spreading foliage which makes an ideal habitat for fish spawn. They need full sun and can spread widely if not checked. _M.proserpinacoides_ has blue-green leaves which take on red tints in autumn near the water surface, while _M.verticillatum_ has paler, olive-green foliage. Both can be fully or partially submerged, and look most attractive when spreading over the water surface. Insignificant greenish or creamy flowers appear in summer. Propagate by stem cuttings in summer.

Nuphar lutea   z 4
Yellow water lily or brandy bottle
The yellow flowers, which are quite small (2in (6cm) across), bottle-shaped and sickly-smelling, are held some way above a mat of broad, oval, mid-green leaves which are about 16in (40cm) wide, giving the plant a spread of up to 5ft (1.5m). The seed heads are rounded, warty and quite decorative. This hardy deciduous perennial thrives in deep water, in sun or shade, and is useful for a water-lily effect where _Nymphaea_ will not grow. To propagate, divide the thick crowns in spring.

Nymphaea 'Escarboucle' (*above*)   z 3
This water lily can achieve a spread of 10ft (3m) when given space. The floating leaves are dark green and in summer set off the semi-double, cup-shaped, deep crimson flowers. Each flower can be up to 6in (15cm) across and has a golden centre. Plants must have an open sunny position and still deep water. Dead leaves should be carefully removed as they fade. Propagate by lifting and dividing the thick tuber-like rhizomes in spring every few years or by using seed.

Nymphaea 'Marliacea' cvs   z 3
'Marliacea Chromatella' has olive green foliage, strikingly marked with deep bronze-maroon blotches, and canary yellow, semi-double, cup-shaped flowers. In summer, the flowers can reach 8in (20cm) across when fully open and have deep golden-yellow centres. 'Marliacea Albida' has pure white fragrant flowers and dark green leaves with red or purple undersides; 'Marliacea Carnea' has pink, semi-double, star-like flowers with gold centres. Propagate as for _N._ 'Escarboucle'. The attractive leaves are an excellent foil for the flowers.

Orontium aquaticum   z 6
Golden club
A favourite among water plants, the flowers of this aroid lack the typical spathe, leaving the central yellow and white spadix to provide colour. A deciduous perennial, the golden club grows equally well in shallow or deep water. In spring, the pencil-like flower spikes (spadices) emerge from among the floating mass of waxy leaves which are a bluish or greyish green. Plants grow to 10in (25cm) high spreading up to 2ft (60cm). Large seeds develop later in the summer and are used to propagate plants while they are still fresh, which is easier than trying to divide the tough rootstock.

Peltandra virginica (*below*)   z 5
Green arrow arum
This herbaceous perennial is grown for its bright green, distinctively veined, arrow shaped leaves, and its yellow to white spathes that enclose a short spadix and green berries in summer. It thrives in water up to 10in (25cm) deep, or in a bog garden. Plant in baskets of lime-free humus-rich soil in still or slow-moving water, in full sun.

Ranunculus aquatilis   z 3
Water crowfoot
A member of the buttercup family, this perennial has two leaf types: the submerged leaves are much-divided, while the floating leaves are solid and dark green. The flowers either float on the surface or protrude a little above the water. They are white, five-petalled with a yellow centre and appear during early summer. Plants grow in still or slow-moving water up to 3ft (90cm) deep. Thin plants occasionally, returning a few vigorous pieces to re-grow. This plant is poisonous if eaten.

Bog garden

Sagittaria sagittifolia — z 5
Common arrowhead
Ideally suited to shallow water conditions, this deciduous perennial grows to a height of 18in (45cm) with a spread of 1ft (30cm). It has upright mid-green leaves shaped like arrows and in summer flowers are borne in spikes, each with three white petals and a purple centre. In *S. latifolia* the flower centre is yellow. Plants need full sun. Propagate by dividing in spring or summer, or by detaching young scaly shoots known as turions.

Scirpus tabernaemontani 'Zebrinus'
(*above*) — z 5
Zebra rush
Also listed as *S. lacustris* subsp. *tabernaemontani* 'Zebrinus', this tall and handsome rush is useful in areas where the water is brackish. The leafless stems of this evergreen perennial sedge are striped markedly with white in horizontal bands. In summer, brown spikelets appear part way up the stems; these are the flowers. Remove any shoots that are all green to stop the plant reverting to the plain green form. Shoots reach a height of 5ft (1.5m) and spread indefinitely. Divide in spring.

Stratiotes aloides — z 5
Water soldier
Characterized by its rosettes of spiny, olive green leaves, this free-floating semi-evergreen perennial is commonly found in alkaline water. It spends most of its time submerged, rising up to 10in (25cm) above the surface during summer when the whitish-pink cup-shaped flowers appear. The leaves are sharp and edged with spines. Plants spread to 12in (30cm) in diameter and need deep water. Propagate by small buds which develop on the plants' base.

Trapa natans — z 6
Jesuit's nut or water chestnut
Grown primarily for its attractive foliage, the mid-green leaves are diamond-shaped with deeply toothed edges and grow in beautiful neat rosettes. The centre of each leaf is often marked with deep purple blotches. White flowers are produced in summer. Each floating plant can spread to 9in (23cm) and looks best if part of a group in shallow water. To propagate this annual, collect seed in autumn, overwinter in water or wet moss and plant in spring.

Typha latifolia variegata — z 3
Reed mace
The vigorous and invasive reed mace should be considered for planting only in larger ponds, in sun or shade. This deciduous perennial forms huge clumps of growth from which emerge green leathery leaves and spikes of brownish flowers in late summer. The flowers are followed by dark brown torpedo-shaped seed heads, which split open to release masses of fluffy airborne seeds and are very decorative through autumn and winter. Plants can reach 8ft (2.5m) in height. *T. minima* is more dainty. Propagate by seed or division in spring.

Utricularia vulgaris — z 4
Greater bladderwort
With tiny, bladder-like, bronze-green modified leaves on its submerged roots, this carnivorous perennial traps water-dwelling organisms. Only the flower stems rise above the surface to a height of 16in (40cm), carrying bright yellow flowers in summer. Plants spread to 12in (30cm), grow in deep water and are deciduous. They form large clumps which should be thinned when overcrowded. Propagate by division.

Zantedeschia aethiopica — z 8
Arum lily
This South African native grows well in shallow water. It flowers throughout the summer, with the erect funnel-shaped spathes being held well above the arrow-shaped glossy, deep green leaves. Each spathe surrounds a central yellow spadix. The leaves and flowering stems arise from a tuber. Plants can reach up to 3ft (90cm) in height, spreading to 18in (45cm). Ensure they are bedded deeply in the soil below water level. Propagate from seed or by division in spring.

Carex stricta 'Aurea' — z 5
Bowles' golden sedge
Also listed as *C. elata* 'Aurea', this evergreen hardy perennial has golden, lime-green striped leaves which create a splash of colour in summer, fading to greener shades later in the season. It grows equally well at the waters' edge as in a bog garden. Plants have a tufted habit, need moist soil and a sunny spot to colour well. They grow to 16in (40cm) in height and spread up to 6in (15cm). Dark brown flower spikes appear in summer. Propagate by division in spring.

Hosta fortunei (*above*) — z 3
Unlike many hostas, this species is prized more for its flowers than its foliage: tall mauve flower spikes appear around mid-summer, towering above the soft grey-green leaves. This hardy herbaceous perennial forms large clumps and grows to a height of 3ft (90cm) with an equal or greater spread. It needs a moist fertile soil and light shade. 'Albopicta' has yellow leaves edged with light green which become two-tone green in summer; 'Marginato-alba' has leaves margined with white and violet flowers. Protect against slugs and snails. Propagate by dividing the crowns in early spring.

Iris ensata — z 5
Japanese flag iris
Also listed as *I. kaempferi*. Plant this iris in partial shade, ensuring that the soil is rich in humus. Its flowering stems reach 2-3ft (60-90cm) in height and are branched, carrying up to 15 reddish-purple flowers, each up to 6in (15cm) across. There are many forms in a variety of colours. The rhizomes will spread indefinitely. To propagate divide them in late summer.

Kirengeshoma palmata   z 5

Even in the height of summer, this lovely herbaceous perennial exudes a coolness that is rarely matched by any other plants. An upright grower, it reaches a height of 3ft (90cm) with similar spread, and the stems carry lobed bright green leaves, topped by clusters of soft cream-yellow flowers from late summer to autumn. Prefers a lightly shaded position and moist, acid soil. Plants can be raised from seed or divided in autumn or spring.

Lysichiton americanus (below)   z 3
Yellow skunk cabbage

The large, bright yellow spathes emerge before the leaves, from early spring onwards, surrounding a central yellowish-green spadix which are the true flowers. Space must be made for the huge, fresh green leaves which can be up to 4ft (1.2m) long, 30in (75cm) in *L. camtschatcensis*, which has flowers with pure white spathes. These vigorous herbaceous perennials form large impressive clumps in full sun and will grow near still or running water, or in wet mud. Propagate through freshly collected seed or division in spring.

Mentha aquatica   z 3

A wonderfully aromatic bog plant which releases a cool peppermint-like fragrance when crushed. It grows as a hairy purplish perennial, the flowers appearing in rounded heads on 30in (75cm)-tall stems above oval toothed leaves. The pinkish-lilac flowers have hairy sepals. Divide plants using pieces of the creeping rootstock which can be invasive but is easily contained in a deep open-bottomed container sunk in the ground. One of the parents of the cultivated peppermint, *M.* × *piperata*, which is used as a culinary herb.

Mimulus guttatus   z 5
Monkey flower

With a height and spread of 2ft (60cm), this mat-forming perennial carries bright yellow snapdragon-like flowers which are spotted with brownish red. They appear throughout the summer until autumn. The mid-green leaves are oval. *M. luteus* (z 7) is similar but smaller and has large reddish blotches on the petals; rather more spectacular is *M. cardinalis* with its scarlet-orange flowers held on stems 2ft (60cm) tall. Propagate by division, through soft tip cuttings in summer, or by seed.

Osmunda regalis (above)   z 3
Royal fern

The thick mat of roots produced by this majestic fern is excellent at stabilizing the soil in very wet areas or near the edge of water. This deciduous perennial is tolerant of sun and can grow to 6ft (2m) in a season, with a spread of 3ft (1m). The young fronds are pinkish as they emerge in spring, turning a bright green as they mature. On established plants the ends of taller fronds terminate in a rusty-red, spore-bearing female spike, like a tassel. Propagate by division in autumn or winter.

Pontederia cordata   z 3
Pickerel weed

In late summer, blue flower spikes emerge from glossy, dark green leaves, which are narrow and lance-shaped. Plants form large clumps in time and grow best at the wet edges of a bog garden or in shallow water. They reach a height of 30in (75cm) and can spread to 18in (45cm). This deciduous perennial needs full sun to succeed and the flowers should be removed once they have faded. Increase in spring by seed or division.

Primula pulverulenta (above)   z 5
Candelabra primula

The common name derives from the appearance of the flower stems, which carry striking crimson-red flowers with deep purple eyes. The main flowering stem and the flower stalks are covered in beautiful white farina. Plants seed themselves readily, forming clumps of upright growth, 2-3ft (60-100cm) in height and 18in (45cm) across. 'Bartley' has pale-pink flowers with carmine eyes and mid-green, toothed lance-shaped leaves. Plants need moist fertile soil in sun or shade. Divide plants or lift self-sown seedlings to increase numbers.

Rheum palmatum 'Atrosanguineum'   z 6

Consider this large ornamental form of the rhubarb only where its height and spread of 6ft (2m) can be accommodated with ease. This herbaceous perennial has deeply cut, five-lobed leaves of reddish-purple, with darker veins. Each leaf can grow to 2ft (60cm) across. In early summer, upright panicles of crimson flowers rise above the leaves. Propagate by division of the thick rootstock with a spade in spring.

Rodgersia aesculifolia   z 5

Choose a spot away from strong winds to prevent damage to the large, crinkled bronze foliage (similar to that of the horse chestnut *Aesculus*), in sun or part-shade. Plants also grow well beside water. The rhizomes of this perennial form large clumps. Plants grow to 3ft (90cm) in height with similar spread. During mid-summer, plume-like, fragrant pink flowers appear from the foliage, held in rather flattish clusters. *R. pinnata* 'Superba' has bronze foliage, while 'Alba' has white flowers. Divide plants in spring.

Acid A term applied to soil or water with a pH value of below 7.

Aerial root A root growing above the soil from the stem of a plant.

Aggregate Small pebbles or gravel mixed with cement.

Alkaline A term applied to soil or water with a pH value of above 7.

Annual A plant that completes its life cycle within one growing season.

Anther The terminal part of a stamen that contains pollen.

Aril A covering on some seeds that is often brightly coloured and fleshy.

Batter The profile of a hedge or a dry-stone wall with sides that slope inwards towards the top, making the top narrower than the base.

Bent Any perennial grass which has spreading panicles of tiny flowers; ideal for garden lawns.

Bract A modified, usually reduced, leaf that grows just below the flower head.

Breastwood Shoots that grow outwards from a plant that is trained against a support such as a fence or wall.

Calcareous Containing, or resembling, carbonate of lime or limestone; chalky or limy in nature.

Calyx The outer whorl of a flower, consisting of sepals that may be free to the base or partially joined.

Catkin An inflorescence consisting of a hanging spike of much reduced flowers occurring in trees like hazel and birch.

Cement Fine grey powder, a mixture of limestone and clay, used with water and sand to make mortar, or with water, sand and aggregate to make concrete.

Chlorosis A condition in which leaves become unnaturally pallid, whitish or yellow. The disease is usually due to lack of essential minerals.

Compost (seed or potting) A mixture of materials consisting chiefly of loam, peat, sand and fertilizers. It is used as a medium for sowing seeds, planting on seedlings and potting plants.

Compound leaf A leaf composed of two or more similar parts.

Concrete Sand, cement and aggregate, mixed with water to form a hard building material for paving and foundations.

Coniferous Relating to the group of plants that typically bear cones. Most are evergreen with linear leaves.

Container-grown A plant in a container as opposed to a bare-rooted one that is lifted from the open ground.

Corymb An inflorescence with a flat-topped flower cluster.

Crown The basal part of a plant from which roots and shoots grow.

Cultivar A cultivated, as distinct from a botanical, variety.

Cutting A separated piece of stem, root or leaf taken from a plant in order to propagate a new plant.

Deadhead To remove the spent flowers or the unripe seed-pods from a plant.

Deciduous A plant that loses all its leaves at one time of the year, usually during late autumn.

Desiccating wind A wind that dries plants, soil and organic material.

Digitate Describes a compound leaf that resembles a spread hand.

Division Propagation by means of dividing a single plant into smaller portions; also a way of thinning plants.

Dormancy The resting period of a plant, usually in winter.

Double (flower head) A flower with a double or multiple rows of petals.

Dressing A top covering like pea gravel, applied to the surface of the soil.

English bond In brickwork, this consists of three or five courses of stretchers to one of headers.

Evergreen A plant that retains its leaves throughout the year.

Fescue Any grass of the genus *Festuca*; ideal for garden lawns.

Flemish bond In brickwork, this consists of three or five stretchers to one header per course.

Floret A small flower making up the head of a composite flower.

Former A wood or metal frame used to train in growth for topiary; also a guide for trimming a hedge or building a dry-stone wall with a batter.

Germination The development of a seed into a seedling.

Glaucous A bluish-white, bluish-green or bluish-grey waxy bloom.

Gravel board A piece of timber fiixed horizontally to the bottom of a fence to protect it from rot.

Grout A thin mortar for filling joints between tiles and masonry.

Habit The natural mode of growth and consequent shape of a plant.

Half-hardy A plant that is unable to survive the prevailing winter temparatures without some sort of protection but does not need to be kept in a greenhouse all the year round.

Hardcore Consists of materials such as small pieces of brick or stone, used as a foundation in construction.

Harden off To gradually acclimatize plants raised in warm conditions to cooler conditions.

Hardy A plant capable of surviving the winter in the open without protection.

Header A brick laid across a wall so that its ends are flush with the vertical surfaces.

Hoggin A mixture of sand and gravel used as a sub-base in construction.

Humus Fertile, partially decomposed organic matter in soil.

Hybrid A plant that is produced by the cross-fertilization of two species or variants of species.

Indumentum A hairy covering on leaves and other plant parts.

Inflorescence The flowering part of a plant.

Joist A beam made of timber, steel or reinforced concrete.

Lanceolate Describes the shape of a narrow, tapering leaf.

Lenticel One of many pores in the bark of woody plants through which gaseous exchange takes place.

Loam Any reasonably fertile soil that contains a free-draining mixture of clay, sand and organic material.

Microclimate A climate particular to a specific situation which differs from the overall climate of the garden or region.

Mortar A mixture of cement or lime or both with sand and water, used as a bond between bricks or stones or as a wall covering.

Mulch A soil covering that protects plants, reduces evaporation, suppresses weeds, prevents erosion and, in the case of organic mulch, enriches the soil.

Node The point on a plant stem from which the leaves or lateral branches grow.

Paling A fence made primarily of upright wooden posts.

Panicle A branched flower head, each branch having several stalked flowers.

Papery (petals) The term given to petals with a thin, paper-like texture.

Perennial A plant that lives for at least three seasons.

Petiole The stalk of a leaf.

pH The scale by which acidity or alkalinity is measured.

Pier A pillar, rectangular or otherwise, that bears heavy loads.

Plantlet A young plant produced naturally by the parent plant as a method of propagation.

Pleaching A technique for forming a dense hedge by interweaving the branches of well-spaced plants, usually trees such as limes or hornbeams, and often leaving bare trunks as stilts.

Plumb line A string with a metal weight attached, used to determine verticality.

Pointing The method of finishing joints in paving or brickwork with mortar.

Pricking out The transplanting of a seedling from a seed tray to a pot or another tray.

Propagation The production of a new plant from an existing one, either sexually by seed or asexually by cuttings.

Raceme An inflorescence in which the stalked flowers are borne along a stem.

Rhizome An underground stem, sometimes thick as in irises, other times thin as in grasses, and usually horizontal.

Riser The vertical part of a step or stair.

Rootstock The underground part of a plant from which roots and shoots grow.

Rosette A circular cluster of leaves growing from the base of a shoot.

Runner A trailing stem that grows along the surface, takes root and forms new growth at nodes or the tip.

Running bond In brickwork, this consists of stretcher courses with alternate rows staggered by half a brick.

Scarify To rub or scratch the surface of a seed to increase water absorption in order to speed up germination.

Seedling A very young plant with few leaves, raised from seed.

Semi-evergreen Describes a plant intermediate between evergreen and deciduous. It bears some foliage throughout the year, but also loses some leaves during winter.

Sepal The outermost, leaf-like structures of a flower.

Sessile A flower or leaf with no stalk, growing directly from the stem.

Shuttering (concrete) The timber frame into which concrete is poured.

Single (flower head) A flower with a single layer of petals.

Spacers small pieces of wood inserted between paving stones to ensure an even surface is laid.

Species A group of closely related organisms within a genus.

Spike (flower) An inflorescence consisting of stalkless flowers arranged along a stem.

Stamens The male reproductive organ of a flower.

Standard Any tree which has a main stem or trunk 4-6 ft (1.2-1.8m) in height with a large head; most commonly applied to fruit trees, roses and fuchsias.

Stigma The terminal part of the ovary, (the female reproductive organ of a flower) where pollen is deposited.

Stipule (leaf) Out-growths, usually paired, at the base of the leaf stalks in some plants that protect the young leaves.

Stooled Cut to the ground periodically and allowed to regrow, to encourage the growth of new whip-like stems.

Stretcher A brick that is laid horizontally so that its length is exposed.

Sub-shrub A plant with a woody base and herbaceous tips.

Subsoil The layer of soil below the topsoil. It is lighter in colour than the topsoil.

Tamp To firmly pack down a material such as soil or concrete.

Tender A plant unable to withstand the coldest prevailing weather conditions.

Tepal The outer part of a flower resembling a petal.

Thin To reduce the number of seedlings.

Tilth The fine crumbly surface layer of soil. The ideal tilth for a seedbed is about the consistency of coarse breadcrumbs.

Tomentum A felt-like covering of hairs on leaves and other parts of a plant.

Topsoil The upper layer of soil, the darkest and most fertile part, in which plants grow.

Tread The top surface of a step or stair.

Trifoliate Leaves that are divided into three, as in clover.

Umbel A flat-topped or dome-shaped flower head in which the flowers are borne on stalks arising from the top of the main stem.

Variegated Leaves with attractive coloured markings.

Variety A distinct variant of a species, either a cultivated form (a cultivar) or one that occurs naturally.

Watering in To water around the stem of a newly transplanted plant to settle soil around the roots.

Whorl Three or more flowers, buds, leaves or shoots arising from the same place on a plant stem.

GARDEN DESIGNERS LANDSCAPE ARCHITECTS

Acres Wild (Landscape and Garden Design)
45a High Street
Billingshurst
West Sussex
RH14 9PP

Argyll Landscapes
Drishaig
Inverary
Argyll
PA32 8XQ
Creative gardening and instant trees, all varieties supplied and planted anywhere.

Margaret Bestwick
12 Orchard Lane
Woodnewton
Peterborough
PE8 5EE
Exclusive formal or informal designs. Construction drawings and planting plans drawn up to suit customers' individual requirements.

Jean Bishop & Partner
Wood Farm
Dunston
Norwich
Norfolk
NR14 8QD

Alison Brett Garden Design
18 Dighton Road
Wandsworth
London
SW18 1AN

Chenies Landscape Design
Bramble Lane
London Road
East Amersham
Buckinghamshire
HP7 9DH
Landscape architects for all aspects of landscape design. Chelsea Flower Show gold medal winners.

Helen Clay Garden Design
Lings Cottage
Henson Lane
Cropwell Butler
Nottinghamshire
NG12 2JS

Alison Coleman
17 Kent Close
Bromborough
Wirral
L63 0EF
Trained in graphic design and horticulture, she combines her skills to offer a complete service of garden design, visualization and illustration.

Irene George BSc MA ALI
2 Pollicott Cottages
Ashenden
Buckinghamshire
HP18 0HH
Landscape architect with experience in design of town and country gardens.

Alexander Greenshields
Flat 2a
34 Boxridge Avenue
Purley
Surrey CR8 3AQ

Duncan Heather
34 Kings Road
Henley-on-Thames
Oxfordshire
RG9 2DG

The Julian Dowle Partnership
The Old Malt House
High Street
Newent
Gloucestershire
GL18 1AY

Landsberg & Newnham Garden Design
4 Campion Road
Putney
London
SW15 6NW
For romantic, zany or formal gardens in the town or country. Service ranges from consultation to full designs including site survey and complete working drawings for constructions and planting.

Landscape and Garden Design Consultants
4 Sandy Lodge Way
Northwood
Middlesex
Based in London and Gloucester, professionally qualified landscape architects who specialize in the design and building of town and country gardens; Garden planning, planting design, pools, ornamental features, and individual garden buildings using new or reclaimed materials.

Lees Associates
5 Dryden Street
Covent Garden
London
WC2E 9NW
Landscape architecture. Romantic and traditional garden design.

Frances Traylen Martin Dip. ISD
Saint's Hill House
Penshurst
Tonbridge
Kent
TN11 8EN
Garden designer professionally qualified, provides designs for traditional or modern, period or neglected gardens. Full working drawings and planting plans.

Graham A. Pavey & Associates
11 Runces Road
Bromham
Bedordshire
MK43 8QD

Roland Mayer-Jones BSc (Hons) Hort.
Merlindere
Old Monmouth Road
Longhope
Gloucestershire
GL17 0PD
A professional garden design/consultancy service covering Wales and England.

Hugh O'Connell MSGD
English Garden Designs
100 Yonder Street
Ottery St. Mary
Devon
EX11 1HH
Portfolio ranges from large country house commissions to city centre courtyards.

Plantation Group Ltd
Temple Gardens
Holloway Lane
Harmondsworth
West Drayton
Middlesex
UB7 0AD
Garden design and landscape gardening, also water features and fountains.

Plantech Garden Design
75 Curzon Street
Caln
Wiltshire
SN11 0DW
A comprehensive and professional design service offered. Re-establishment of old gardens and designs, plus consultancy service and soil testing.

Sue Prideaux Garden Design
Selehurst
Lower Beeding
Horsham
Sussex
RH13 6PR

Redman Garden Designs
51 Shandon Road
London SW4 9HS
Consultancy, garden design, planting and maintenance.

Sally Walker Garden Design
Bowling Alley Cottage
The Green
Horsted Keynes
West Sussex
RH17 7AP
Consultation through to construction and planting. London and the south of England.

Sheridans
37 Northcote Road
St. Margarets
Twickenham
Middlesex TW1 1PB
Garden design and construction; restoration and reclamation; year-round maintenance. Specialists in oriental gardens, herbaceous and uncommon plants.

Squies Landscapes
Holloway Hill
Chertsey
Surrey KT16 0AE

Andrew Stansfield
188 Station Road
Harpenden
Hertfordshire
AL5 4UL
Garden designer, landscape architect and horticulturist.

Joanna Stay
67 Dalton Street
St. Albans
Hertfordshire
AL3 5QH
Professionally qualified in garden design, horticulture and M.S.G.D. Advisory visits, designs and full working drawings.

Jacqui Stubbs Associates
24 Duncan Road
Richmond
Surrey
TW9 2JD
Design service for large and small gardens. Half day consultations to full design and planting plans. Brochure available.

Town and Country Gardens
8 Willow Walk
Petworth
Sussex
GU28 0EY
A well established garden construction company well known for its high-quality workmanship and individual design.

Stephen John White
12 Witt Road
Fair Oak
Eastleigh
Hampshire
SO5 7FR

SUPPLIERS OF MATERIALS

Countryside
PO Box 130
Swindon
Wiltshire
SN1 4LG
Garden planning and walling.

Dalestone
Unit 2a, Sandylands
Business Centre
Carlton New Road
Skipton
North Yorkshire
BD23 2AA
Paving and walling, fountains and stone garden ornaments.

Freshfield Lane Brickworks
Freshfield Lane
Danehill
Haywards Heath
Sussex
RH17 7HH
Independent brick-makers who still use traditional methods of production. A range of five types of clay pavers that look just like old bricks. Particularly suitable for gardens of traditional-style houses.

Holley, Hextall & Associates
Chittoe
Chippenham
Wiltshire
SN15 2EL
York, pennant and French lavantine stone flagstones and floor tiles. Cotswold and Purbeck walling stone, stone troughs etc.

Marshalls Mono
Southowram
Halifax
West Yorkshire
HX3 9SY
Garden paving, walling and garden furniture.

Minsterstone
Station Road
Ilminster
Somerset
TA19 9AS
Garden ornaments, balustrading, paving.

Stapeley Water Gardens
92 London Road
Stapeley
Nr. Nantwich
Cheshire CW5 7LH
Pumps, liners, fountains and quatic accessories.

Thames Valley Wirework
792/792A Weston
Road
Slough Trading
Estate
Slough
Berkshire
SL1 4HR
Plant supports and horticultural wirework.

Wessex Horticultural Products
South Newton
Salisbury
Wiltshire
SP2 0QW
Coco peat, composts and coco products.

SUPPLIERS OF GARDEN FEATURES

Agriframes Ltd
Charlwoods Road
East Grinstead
Sussex
RH19 2HG
Bowers, gazebos, walkways, arches, pergolas, obelisks, statues, benches, screens etc.

Annie Grant Garden Products
RGA Ltd
Cherrycourt Way
Leighton Buzzard
Bedfordshire
LU7 8UH
Many styles of planters with relief decoration.

Ann's Garden
10 Maunsel Street
London
SW1P 2QL
Terracotta pots.

Anthony Archer-Wills Ltd
West Chiltington
West Sussex
RH20 2LF
Specialists in the design, construction and maintenance of ponds, lakes and water gardens. Their work ranges from the creation of large butyl-lined lakes to the formal town garden. A wide range of large specimen bog plants grown.

Anthony de Grey Trellises
Broadhinton Yard
77a North Street
London
SW4 0HQ
Six ranges of architectural trellises, as well as trompe l'oeil, gazebos, arbour seats and columns all available in 30 shades.

Any Creations
"Birchwood"
Theobald Street
Radlett
Hertfordshire
WD7 7LT
Garden sculptures. Original one-off steel animal sculptures individually created. Commissions undertaken.

The Aquatic Habitat
Shurdington Road
Brockworth
Gloucester
GL3 4PU
Aquatic specialists. A large range of pond equipment, plants and fish.

Architectural Heritage
Taddington Manor
Taddington
Cutsdean
Nr. Cheltenham
Gloucestershire
GL54 5RY
Stone statuary and ornaments.

Armillary Sundials
Unit 1, White House Farm
New Hall Lane
Mundon
Essex
CM9 6PJ
Handmade dials in traditional designs.

Bel Mondo Garden Features
11 Tatnell Road
London
SE23 1JX
Cast iron and brass garden ornaments.

Boswell Roberts
46 Keyes Road
London
NW2 3XA
Oriental and Italian-style parasols.

The Bulbeck Foundry
Reach Road
Burwell
Cambridgeshire
CB5 0AH
English lead statuary, fountains, urns, planters and restoration work.

Cannock Gates
Martindale
Hawks Green
Industrial Estate
Cannock
Staffordshire
WS11 2XT
Mail order gate manufacturers offer a range of gates of any shape, size or design. Full colour brochure available.

Capital Garden Products
Hurst Green
Etchingham
East Sussex
TN19 7QU
Water tanks, urns, planters, edging tiles, steel furniture, fountains etc.

Chilstone
Sprivers Estate
Horsmonden
Kent
TN12 8DR
Classical garden ornaments handmade from reconstituted stone. Catalogue available.

Lloyd Christie
22 Doria Road
London
SW6
Trelliswork.

Classic Garden
Lower Puncheston
Pembrokeshire
SA62 5TG
Fine garden ornaments. Hardwood Versailles tubs, troughs, and window boxes, lattice pyramids, columns and wall panels, topiary, bronze and stone statuary and collectors' items.

The Classic Garden Company
PO Box 83
Pocklington
York YO4 2ZA
Make planters and obelisks and other decorative items.

Country Collections
Unit 9, Ditton Priors
Trading Estate
Bridgnorth
Shropshire
WV16 6SS
Traditional style sundials. Brochure available on request.

Courtyard Pottery
Groundwell Farm
Cricklade Road
Swindon
Wiltshire
SN2 5AU
Terracotta, terranigra and stoneware planters.

Crowther of Syon Lodge
Busch Corner
London Road
Isleworth
Middlesex
TW7 5BH
A renowned family-run antiques business with an extensive stock of antique garden ornaments and statuary including sundials, fountains, classical statues, animal figures,

temples, urns and vases, seats, benches, wrought iron gates and columns.

The David Sharp Studio
201a Nottingham Road
Somercotes
Derbyshire
Specialists in reconstructed stone. A fine selection of architectural ornamentation. Porticos, temples, columns, balustrading, urns, planters, fountains and ponds, statuary, entablatures etc.

Dibco
Unit D5, Chaucer Business Park
Watery Lane
Kemsing
Sevenoaks
Kent
TN15 6NR
Terracotta pots, weather vanes and sundials.

Drummond's of Bramley
Birtley Farm
Horsham Road
Bramley
Guildford
Surrey
Antique garden statuary.

R.C. Dummont-Aubrey
11 Clifton Park Avenue
SW20
A member of The Guild of Master Craftsmen. Specialists in handcrafted trelliswork, York stone, frescoes, terracotta tiling suitable for conservatories.

Erin Marketing
Astonia House
High Street
Baldock
Hertfordshire
SG7 6PP
Hanging baskets and patio planters.

Everton Water Gardens
Round Lodge
Newlands Manor Estate
Everton
Lymington
Bridges, water wheels, gazebos etc. Experienced in the design and construction of ponds and water gardens.

Frolics of Winchester
82 Canon Street
Winchester
Hants
SO23 9JQ

Designers and manufacturers of gazebos made in wood with cedar shingle roofs and side panels. Offer professional architectural advice and design service.

Garden Crafts
Sissinghurst Road
Biddenden
Kent
TN27 8EJ
Specialists in garden ornaments and garden furniture. The large selection includes statues, vases, busts, sundials, plaques, Victorian pattern benches, tables and chairs.

Garden Secrets
Dept 70
Charlwoods Road
East Grinstead
West Sussex
RH19 2HG
Stockists of a complete range of garden structures including pergolas, walkways, gazebos, arches, screens and obelisks. Measuring, design and construction service available in most parts of the country. Free colour brochure available.

Haddonstone Ltd
The Forge House
East Haddon
Northampton
NN6 8DB
Designers and manufacturers of garden ornaments, statuary and architectural stonework produced by highly skilled craftsmen. Can also produce architectural stonework to special designs.

Adrian Hall Ltd
The Garden Centre
Feltham Hill Road
Feltham
Middlesex
TW13 7NA
Stockists of reconstructed marble statuary and planting containers. Natural, new and reclaimed stone a speciality. Plus a range of plants and gardeners' requisites.

Richard Heanley Studio Forge
Offham
Nr. Lewes
East Sussex
BN7 3QD
Manufacturers of garden features including gazebos, arches, tables, obelisks, tree seats, chairs,

benches, gates, balustrading, wellheads, weathervanes, canopies and garden ornaments.

Holloways
Lower Court
Suckley
Worcestershire
WR6 5DE
Fine garden ornaments in lead, bronze, marble, stone and terracotta together with garden furniture in teak, cast and wrought iron. Stone troughs, saddle stones, cider mills and other interesting old farm artefacts.

Hozelock
Haddenham
Aylesbury
Buckinghamshire
HP17 8JD
Garden watering, lighting and spraying equipment.

Langdon (London)
Ickeford
Aylesbury
Buckinghamshire
HP18 9JJ
Garden arches and sundials.

Lightscape Projects
23 Jacob Street
London
SE1 2BG
Selection of lighting equipment.

Netlon
Kelly Street
Blackburn
Lancashire
BB2 4PJ
Garden nets, meshes and fenching.

New England Gardens Ltd
22 Middle Street
Ashcott
Somerset
TA7 9QB
Small buildings, fencing and furniture. Designs built by Walpole Woodworkers, Boston, Massachusetts, USA. Strongly constructed from cedar with a stained or natural finish.

Norfolk Garden Supplies
54B Yarmouth Road
Thorpe
Norwich
NR7 0HE
Italian statuary and fountains, classical English pots and urns, water garden products, lead fountains and statuary, specialists in old York stone flags and a full range of natural stone.

Ornate Products
Limecroft Road
Knaphill
Woking
Surrey
GU21 2TH
Manufacturers of garden ornaments including wall planters and plaques. Free brochure available.

Pots and Pithoi
Grange Farm
Turners Hill Road
Crawley Down
West Sussex
A large range of handmade Cretan terracotta pots and pithoi.

The Real Stone Company
The Forge
Penthouse Hill
Bath
Avon
BA1 7EL
Individually designed Bath stone summer houses and garden furniture.

Remanoid
Unit 44
Number One
Industrial Estate
Consett
Co Durham
DH8 6SZ
Pumps, pools, fountains, liners and outdoor lighting.

Rokes Ltd
Woodside Works
Stow Road
Andoversford
Cheltenham
Gloucestershire
GL54 5RJ
Garden stonework. Natural stone planters and ornaments.

Seagro
22 Pimlico Road
London
SW1W 8LJ
Period garden statuary, ornament and exterior design.

Stuart Garden Architecture
Burrow Hill Farm
Wiveliscombe
Taunton
Somerset
TA4 2RN
Specialists in the design and manufacture of quality treillage and trelliswork. A large range of architectural panels is available which can be combined to create a wide variety of designs and schemes. Also design and manufacture to individual requirements.

Traditional Gates and Railings

Cannon Steelworks
Pointbid Estate
Duck Lees Lane
Enfield
Middlesex
EN3 7SS
Manufacturers of traditional-style gates and railings either for self-fit or installation by their fitters.

Trident Gates & Railings
Islington Works
Railway Passage
Longton
Stoke-on-Trent
ST3 1BY
Design, manufacture and install gates and railings in a variety of traditional styles.

Walker's
101 High Street
Burford
Oxfordshire
OX18 4RG
A large range of garden statuary in bronze, lead or stone.

Whichford Pottery
Whichford
Shipston-on-Stour
Warwickshire
CV36 5PG
Specialists in producing high-quality terracotta using traditional methods.

GARDEN FURNITURE

Alford Artefacts
Alford
Lincolnshire
LN13 9PL
Bespoke ironwork for the garden or conservatory.

Andrew Grace Designs
10a Bourne Lane
Much Hadham
Hertfordshire
SG10 6ER
Traditional, comfortable and versatile wooden furniture, gazebos, pavilions, covered seats, oriental umbrellas, Versailles planters and pyramids. For use in the garden, conservatory or indoors

Barn Owl Woodcraft
Billingsley
Bridgnorth
Shropshire
WV16 6PF
Solid oak garden furniture. Brochure available on request.

Barnsley House GDF

Barnsley House
Nr. Cirencester
Gloucestershire
GL7 5EE
Classic teak and metal furniture for interior and exterior use.

Stephen Blake
199 Upper Allen Street
Sheffield
S3 7GW
Oak garden furniture, can be designed to fold for easy storage.

Branson Leisure
Roman House
Temple Bank
River Way
Harlow
Essex
CM20 2DY
Manufacturers of high-quality garden furniture in hardwoods.

Capricorn Architectural Ironwork Ltd
Tasso Forge
25 North End Parade
North End Road
London W14
Specialists in hand forged ironwork, traditional and avant-garde. Garden furniture, arbours, gates, railings and pergolas.

Dennis Cherry
Unit 2, Broadfields Farm
Great Somerford
Chippenham
Wiltshire
SN15 5BR
Lawn furniture built from fine hardwood, teak or pine in a range of colours.

D.J. Dynes
Hill Farm
Spooner Row
Wymondham
Norfolk
NR18 9LG
Handmade quality Victorian-style garden furniture.

Garsington Garden Furniture
'Farthings'
Southend
Garsington
Oxfordshire
OX9 9DJ
Metal garden furniture made to order in traditional styles.

Gatehouse Furniture
The Gatehouse
Wilsthorpe
Stamford
Lincolnshire
PE9 4PD
Turn-of-the-century design garden furniture. Brochure available.

Gloster Leisure Furniture Ltd

Universal House
Pennywell Road
Bristol
BS5 0TJ
English craftsmen-made furniture in solid teak. Complete range of chairs, benches, tables, loungers and planters ideal for garden, patio and in the conservatory.

Hammond Atkin Designs
Lower Ground Floor
54A High Pavement
The Lace Market
Nottingham
NG1 1HW
Garden furniture made from southern yellow pine in modern styles, also suitable for use in conservatories.

The Heveningham Collection
Peacock Cottage
Church Hill
Nether Wallop
Stockbridge
Hampshire
SO20 8EY
Wrought iron garden furniture.

Indian Ocean Trading Company
47 Rudloe Road
London
SW12 0DR
An extensive collection of English-crafted teak garden furniture and wooden sun shades.

Ironart of Bath
61 Walcot Street
Bath
BA1 5BN
Traditional makers of garden and conservatory furniture.

Ironbridge Gorge Museum
Mail Order Department
Ironbridge
Telford
Shropshire
TF8 7AW
Iron and wooden garden furniture.

Jardine
Rosemount Tower
Wallington Square
Wallington
Surrey
SM6 8RR
Designers and manufacturers of solid cast aluminium garden furniture for indoor and outdoor use reproduced from classic originals.

David Jones Designs

Erddig Hall
Wrexham
Clwyd
LL13 0YT
Hardwood garden furniture of high quality and design.

Julian Chichester Designs
202 Dawes Road
London SW6
A collection of English 18th and 19th century style garden furniture.

Lister by Geebro
Geebro Ltd
South Road
Hailsham
East Sussex
BN27 3DT
Manufacturers of high-quality garden furniture in teak using traditional mortice and tenon joinery, teak dowels and brass screws in its construction.

Oakcraft
Hammer Pond Road
Plummers Plain
West Sussex
RH13 6PE
Hand made solid oak garden furniture.

Ollerton Engineering
Samlesbury Mill
Goosefoot Lane
Samlesbury Bottoms
Preston
Lancashire
PR5 0RN
Garden furniture and gazebos.

Pageant Antiques
122 Dawes Road
Fulham
London
SW6 7EG
Dealers in 18th- and 19th-century garden furniture.

F. Peart & Co Ltd
Baltic Street
Hartlepool
Cleveland
TS25 1PW
Solid teak garden furniture seats, loungers, and tables in classic styles, hand crafted using traditional methods.

Pepe
The Somerford Log House Company
Somerford Lakes
Somerford Keynes
Cirencester
Gloucestershire
GL7 6ED
Garden furniture made using the traditional methods of Finnish craftsmen.

Philip St Piper Furniture Ltd

Washbrook Studio
Syde
Nr. Cheltenham
Gloucestershire
GL53 9PN
Designers and makers of commissioned garden furniture.

Roger Platts
Faircombe
Maresfield
East Sussex
TN22 2EH
Cast iron garden furniture and garden design.

Rusco
Little Farringdon Mill
Lechlade
Gloucestershire
GL7 3QQ
Wrought iron garden furniture, including garden umbrellas and hammocks.

Ruxley Manor Garden Centre
Maidstone Road
Sidcup
Kent
DA14 5BQ
A range of garden furniture.

South Western Supplies
52 Grange Road
Saltford
Bristol
BS18 3AG
Hardwood garden furniture including tables, loungers and sunbeds.

CONSERVATORIES AND GREENHOUSES

Abbeydale Conservatories
Hewell Road
Redditch
Worcester
B97 6AR
Individually designed hardwood conservatories, manufactured and constructed by skilled craftsmen. Finished in polished mahogany or white.

Abbey Glass (Derby) Ltd
Wetherby Road
Ascot Drive Estate
Derby
DE2 8HL
Conservatories manufactured to customers' individual requirements. Available in white or woodgrain PVC. A complete service including damp-proofed concrete base.

Alitex Ltd

Station Road
Alton
Hampshire
GU34 2PZ
Designers and manufacturers of high-quality garden greenhouses. The service ranges from replacing old greenhouses using an existing base to glasshouses specially designed and built for individual requirements.

Alton Conservatories
Fenny Compton
Leamington Spa
CV33 0BR
Greenhouses built from cedar with low-level ventilation, a choice of full length glazing panels or half-cladding to suit sun -and shade-loving plants.

Amdega
Faverdale
Darlington
Co Durham
DL3 0PW
Manufacturers and designers of period-style conservatories.

Ardep Ltd
7 Greenforge Way
Cwmbran
Gwent
Swimming pool conservatories.

Bartholomew Conservatories
277 Putney Bridge Road
London
SW15 2PT
Hardwood conservatories, glass pool houses and garden rooms.

Blackbird Conservatories
Merula Works
Kelsedge
Nr. Ashover
Derbyshire
S45 0DX
Comprehensive service offering groundworks through to installation of roof blinds and furnishings. Fully double glazed with a choice of roofing materials.

Cambridge Glass House Company
Comberton
Cambridge
CB3 7BY
Manufacturers of high-quality glass house which can be delivered for self assembly or built by one of their trained teams. Also a range of features and accessories.

Charterhouse Conservatories
42A High Street
Walton-on-Thames
Surrey
KT12 1BZ
Manufacturers of a wide range of double-glazed conservatories in traditional styles.

Churchill Conservatories Ltd
Unit 17
Park Street Industrial Estate
Aylesbury
Buckinghamshire
HP20 1EB
Conservatories, sun loungers and porches. Traditional and modern.

Clear Span Ltd
Greenfield
Oldham
Lancashire
OL3 7BR
Greenhouses.

Country Charm Conservatories
4 Coronet Close
Worthing
West Sussex
RH10 7GS
Specialists in the design and manufacture of quality hardwood conservatories, from the small Victorian style to the large orangerie or pool enclosure. All-inclusive service from planning through to construction, flooring and decoration.

Country Classics
Charlwoods Road
East Grinstead
West Sussex
RH19 2HZ
Manufacturers of high-quality mahogany conservatories. Styles include traditional Victorian white structures. Their specialist architectural building and design team take you from planning to completion.

Crown Conservatories UK Ltd
1 Dorset Road
New Road Industrial Estate
Sheerness
Kent
ME12 1LT
Conservatories in several styles. Brochure available.

Deane & Amos
South Portway Close
Round Spinney
Northampton
NN3 4RH
Hardwood

conservatories. Brochure available.

The Devizes Conservatory Company
3 Purley Knoll
Purley
Surrey
CR8 3AF
Fine hardwood conservatories, handbuilt by craftsmen. Brochure available.

Discover Enclosures
Chapel House
Mill Lane
Littlebury
Saffron Walden
Essex
CB11 4TR
Swimming pool enclosures.

Durabuild Conservatories Ltd
Wheler Road
Coventry
CV3 4LB
Individually designed and hand made to order using Canadian cedar wood.

Finch Conservatories Ltd
2-4 Parham Drive
Eastleigh
Hampshire
SO5 4NU
Manufacturers of conservatories in either PVC or Brazilian mahogany, with polycarbonate or glass roofs.

Glass Houses
53 Ellington Street
London
N7 8PN
Conservatories and orangeries. Brochure available.

Griffin Glasshouses Ltd
Boyneswood Lodge
Boyneswood Road
Four Marks
Alton
Hampshire
GU34 5DY
Glass houses, pool enclosures and conservatories.

Halls Traditional Conservatories
Church Road
Paddock Wood
Kent
TN12 6EU
Conservatories manufactured in cedar and mahogany.

Hasina Conservatories
Simmonds Road
Wincheap Industrial Estate

Canterbury
Kent
CT13RI
Conservatories individually designed and manufactured.

The Kent Conservatory Company
Woodford Coach House
Maidstone Road
Staplehurst
Kent
TN12 0RH
Traditional Victorian conservatories and garden rooms, barbecue lodges and landscaping.

Marston & Langinger Ltd
192 Ebury Street
London
SW1W 8UP
Suppliers of conservatories and swimming pool enclosures. Also, a range of willow and metal furniture, plants and accessories.

Oakleaf Conservatories Ltd
Clifton Common Industrial Park
Kettlestring Lane
York
YO3 8XF

Pound Garden Buildings
Dept. HG
Rock
Kidderminster
Worcestershire
DY14
Timber greenhouses, summerhouses, workshops and sheds.

Prylorn Ltd
Elmhurst (GD9)
High Street
Chatteris
Cambridgeshire
PE16 6NP
Greenhouses.

Room Outside Ltd
Goodwood Gardens
Goodwood
Chichester
West Sussex
PO18 0QB
Specialists in the design and supply of conservatories and garden accessories.

Town and Country Conservatories
Thumb Lane
Horningtroft
Dereham
Norfolk
NR20 5DY

Westbury Conservatories
Martels
High Easter Road

Barnston
Essex
CM6 1NA
Each conservatory is individually designed and hand crafted.

C.H. Whitehouse Ltd
Buckhurst Works
Bells Yew Green
Frant
Tunbridge Wells
Kent
TN3 9BN
Manufacturers of traditional quality cedar greenhouses. Each greenhouse individually built by craftsmen.

Wood Works
The Longbarn
Fox Lane
Elmhurst
Nr. Lichfield
Staffordshire
WS3 8HA
Bespoke summer houses, conservatories, log cabins, gazebos and pavilions.

PUBLICATIONS AND ORGANIZATIONS

Royal Horticultural Society
80 Vincent Square
London
SW1P 2PE

Botanic Gardens Conservation International
Descanso House
199 Kew Road
Richmond
Surrey
TW9 3BW
Wild species in danger of extinction.

British Association of Landscape Industries
Landscape House
Henry Street
Keighley
West Yorkshire
BD21 3DR
Advantages of domestic and industrial landscaping.

British Fuchsia Society
11 Hungerford Drive
Reading
Berkshire
RG1 6JA
Propagation and training of fuchsias.

British Pelargonium and Geranium Society
134 Montrose Avenue
Welling
Kent
DA16 2QY
Promotion of the popular pelargonium.

Gardening Which?
2 Marylebone Road
London
NW1 4DX
Choosing shrubs for your garden.

Institute of Groundsmanship
19/23 Church Street
The Agora
Wolverton
Milton Keynes
Buckinghamshire
MK12 5LG
Lawn problems and pesticide safety.

Ministry of Agriculture, Fisheries and Food
Whitehall Place
London SW1A 2HH
Plant health in the single market.

National Chrysanthemum Society
2 Lucas House
Craven Road
Rugby
Warwickshire
CV21 3HV
Promotion of chrysanthemums.

National Council for the Conservation of Plants and Gardens
Wisley Garden
Woking
Surrey GU23 6QB
Plants for alkaline and acid soils.

National Pelargonium Collection
Honeybourne Road
Pebworth
Nr. Stratford-on-Avon
Warwickshire
CV37 8XT
Pelargoniums.

Alpine Garden Society
AGS Centre
Avon Bank
Pershore
Worcestershire
WR10 3JP
Publications and publicity for the society.

Amateur Gardening
IPC Magazines
Westover House
West Quay Road
Poole
Dorset BH15 1JG

BBC *Gardeners' World* **Magazine**
Room 26, 35 Marylebone High Street
London W1

Garden News
EMAP, 13 Holkham Road
Orton
Southgate
Peterborough
PE2 0UF

Gardener Magazine
Greater London House
Hampstead Road
London
NW1 7QQ

Organic Gardening
PO Box 4
Wivelscombe
Taunton
Somerset
TA14 2QY

NURSERIES AND MAIL ORDER PLANT SUPPLIERS

African Violet Centre
Station Road
Terrington St Clement
King's Lynn
Norfolk
PE34 4PL
Saintpaulias

Allwood Bros
Mill Nursery
Hassocks
West Sussex
BN6 9NB
Carnations, pinks, dianthus and verichio-arctotis.

Jacques Amand Ltd
The Nurseries
115 Clamp Hill
Stanmore
Middlesex
HA7 3JS
Flowering bulbs including many rare and unusual spring flowering bulbs. Catalgoue available on request for mail order.

Apple Court
Hordle Lane
Lymington
Hampshire
SO41 0HU
Nursery specialising in hostas, grasses, ferns, day lilies, monocots and choice perennials.

Architectural Plants
Cooks Farm
Nuthurst
Horsham
West Sussex
RH13 6LH
Specialists in hardy evergreen trees and shrubs.

David Austin Roses
Albrighton
Wolverhampton
WV7 3HB

Fragrant old roses and their repeat flowering hybrids. Numerous climbing roses. 800 varieties.

Avon Bulbs (RHS)
Burnt House Farm
Mid Lambrook
South Petherton
TA13 5HE
Bulbs by mail order.

Barthelemy & Co
The Nursery, TG
262 Wimborne Road
West
Wimborne
Dorset
BH21 2DZ
Japanese maples and acer palmatum. Suitable for garden patio or bonsai. Catalogue and mail order service available.

Peter Beales Roses
London Road
Attleborough
Norfolk
NR17 1AY
More than 1000 varieties consisting mainly of old-fashioned shrub and climbing roses, many of which are rare and of historical interest. Catalogue available.

Blackmore and Langdon
Stanton Nursery
Pensford
Bristol
Avon

BS18 4JL
Begonias, delphiniums and phlox.

Walter Blom & Son Coombelands Nurseries
Thurleigh Road
Milton Ernest
Bedford
MK44 1RQ
Tulips.

Blooms of Bressingham
Bressingham
Diss
Norfolk
IP22 2AB
Hardy plants.

Bodwen Nursery
Little Ventowyn
Lodge
Hewas Water
Sticker
St Austell
Cornwall
PL26 7DW
Japanese maples.
Bonsai Kai
39 West Square
SE11 4SP
Bonsai.

J.W. Boyce
Bush Pasture
Lower Carter Street
Fordham
Ely
Cambridgeshire
CB7 5JU
Roots and beans.

Broadleigh Dwarf Bulbs
Broadleigh Gardens
G4
Bishops Hull
Taunton
Somerset
TA4 1AE
Over 300 varieties – many rare and unusual species, especially dwarf daffodils and tulips.

Buckingham Nurseries
28 Tingewick Road
Buckingham
MK18 4AE
Hedging and young trees, ornamental trees, fruit trees and ground cover.

Burncoose and Southdown Nurseries
Givennap
Redruth
Cornwall
TR16 6BJ
Trees, shrubs and ornamental plants, Liliums.

Burnham Nurseries
Forches Cross
Newton Abbot
Devon
TQ12 6P2
Orchids.

Caddick's Clematis Nursery
Lymm Road
Thelwall
Warrington
Retail, mail order and wholesale. Over 350 varieties grown. Catalogue available.

John Chambers' Wild Flower Seeds
15 Westleigh Road
Barton Seagrave
Kettering
Northants
NN15 5AT
Wild flower seeds, and other seeds.

Chessington Nurseries
Leatherhead Road
Chessington
Surrey
House, patio, garden and conservatory plants and all other garden requirements.

Chris Bowers & Sons Dept RH
Whispering Trees
Nursery

Wimbotsham
Norfolk
PE34 8QB
Specialists in fruit plants. Mail order service available.

Paul Christian
PO Box 468
Wrexham
Clwyd
North Wales
LL13 9XR
Rare fritillaries.

Colegrave Seeds
West Adderbury
Banbury
Oxfordshire
OX17 3EY
Multiflora petunias.

Cottage Herbery
Mill House
Boraston
Tenbury Wells
Worcestershire
WR15 8LZ
Herbs and cottage garden plants.

Cranborne Manor Garden Centre
Cranborne
Wimborne
Dorset
Specialising in old fashioned roses, Italian pots and statuary, rare and unusual plants. Box and yew hedging.

Deacons Nursery
Godshill
Isle of Wight
PO38 3HW
Family fruit trees.

Derek Lloyd Dean
8 Lynwood Close
South Harrow
Middlesex
HA2 9PR
Pelargoniums.

Donnington Plants
Main Road
Wrangle
Boston
Lincolnshire
PE22 9AT
Argyranthemums, primula sieboldii and auriculas.

Drysdale Nursery
Bowerwood Road
Fordingbridge
Hampshire
SP6 1BN
Specialist collection of bamboos and a wide range of unusual shrubs. Catalogue available.

Efenechtyd Nurseries
Llanelidan
Ruthin
North Wales
LL15 2LG
Streptocarpus, foliage and begonias.

Fibrex Nurseries
Honeybourne Road
Pebworth
Nr. Stratford-on-Avon
Warwickshire
CV37 8XT
Pelargoniums, hederas and hardy ferns.

Forest Lodge Garden Centre
Holt Pound
Farnham
Surrey
GU10 4LD
A wide range of quality plants and a display of their vast selection of specimen conifers, trees, shrubs, climbers and conservatory plants. All specimens are container grown.

Glantlees Trees & Hedging
Newton on the Moor
Felton
Northumberland
Trees and hedging plants including oak, lime, maple, beech and many more.

M. Gould
Stockerton Nursery
Kirkcudbright
Galloway
DG6 4XS
A large mail order selection of British wild plant species including shrubs, primulas and bulbs etc. Illustrated guide to Garden Use and price list available.

Growing Carpets
The Old Farmhouse
Steeple Morden
Royston
Hertfordshire
Specialists in plants for ground cover. Catalogue available.

Hannays of Bath
Sydney Wharf
Nursery
Bathwick
Bath
Avon BA2 4ES
Provide large size specimens of a wide range of uncommon species. Descriptive list available.

W. & L. Harley
Parham Nursery
The Sands
Market Lavington
Devizes
Wiltshire
SN10 4QA
Hardy perennials for the woodland and bog garden, herbaceous border and rock garden. Many rare varieties. Mail order catalogue available.

Heather and Brian Hiley
25 Little Woodcote
Estate
Wallington
Surrey
SM5 4AU
Tender and unusual perennials.

Hillier Nurseries (Winchester) Ltd
Ampfield House
Ampfield
Romsey
Hants
SO51 9PA
Catalogue available for mail order of over 4,000 trees, shrubs, climbers, conifers, roses and fruits.

Hostas
Sticklepath
Okehampton
Devon DX20 1RD
Specialists in hostas.

Hydon Nurseries Ltd
Clock Barn Lane
Hydon Heath
Godalming
Surrey
GU8 4AZ
Specialist growers of rhododendrons, azaleas, camellias and magnolias. A selection of new and unusual hybrids including the smaller Yakushimanum varieties.

Jarvis Brook Geranium Nursery
Tubwell Lane
Crowborough
East Sussex
TN6 3RH
Pelargoniums.

John Sanday (Roses) Ltd
Over Lane
Almondsbury
Bristol
Avon BS12 4DA
Rose specialists. Thousands of roses including beds of hybrid teas and floribundas, borders of climbers and ramblers.

P. de Jager & Sons The Nurseries
Marden
Kent
TN12 9BP
Fritillaries.

Langthorns Plantery
Little Canfield
Dunmour
Essex
Stockists of a comprehensive range of hardy trees, shrubs, herbaceous perennials and alpines, including many rare varieties.

Leonardslee Garden Nurseries
Lower Beeding
Horsham
West Sussex
RH13 6PX
Rhododendrons, rare and unusual varieties. Site visits and garden planning service available.

Lewdon Farm Alpine Nursery
Cheriton Bishop
Devon
EX6 6HF
Alpines, miniature shrubs and herbaceous plants. Mail order service available.

Lincluden Nursery
Bisley Green
Bisley
Woking
Surrey
GU24 9EN
Dwarf, slow growing and unusual conifers.

McBeans Orchids Ltd
Cooksbridge
Lewes
Sussex
BN8 4PR
Orchid hybrids.

Mallet Court Nursery
Curry Mallet
Taunton
Somerset
TA3 6SY
Rare trees and shrubs including an extensive range of acers, quercus and fagus. Catalogue available.

Maltocks Roses
The Rose Nurseries
Nuneham
Courtenay
Oxford
OX9 9PY
Roses.

S.E. Marshall
Regal Road
Wisbech
Cambridgeshire
PE1 32RF
Vegetable seeds.

J. & D. Marston Fern Specialists
"Culag"
Green Lane
Nofferton
East Yorkshire
YO25 0LF
Range of quality pot-grown ferns. Species for the greenhouse and outdoors. Catalogue available.

Meadowcraft Fuchsias
Church St Nurseries
Woodhurst
Huntingdon

Cambridgeshire
PE17 3BN
Fuchsias and pelargoniums.

Merlin Rooted Cuttings
Little Drym
Praze
Camborne
Cornwall
TR14 0NU
Specialist propagators of interesting and unusual garden plants. Mail order service available.

Millais Nurseries
Crosswater Lane
Churt
Farnham
Surrey
GU10 2JN
A unique collection of rare species and new hybrids, rhododendrons and azaleas.

Newington Nurseries
Newington
Wallingford
Oxon
OX10 7AW
Scented conservatory plants from around the world. Full advice service available.

Orchard Nurseries Foston
Tow Lane
Foston
Nr. Grantham
Lincolnshire
NG32 2LE
A wide range of herbaceous plants and clematis, including Euphorbia Red Dwarf. Catalogue available.

Pantiles Nurseries Ltd
Almners Road
Lyne Chertsey
Surrey
KT16 0BJ
Large and unusual conifers, trees and shrubs. A full planting and landscaping service, also a delivery service.

Priorswood Clematis
Priorswood
Widbury Hill Ware
Hertfordshire
SG12 7QH
Propagators and growers of quality clematis plants and other climbers and shrubs.

PW Plants "Sunnyside Nurseries"
Heath Road
Kenninghall
Norfolk
NR16 2DS

Grass, shrubs, climbers, perennials, bamboos, conifers, streptocarpus. Mail order service.

Read's Nursery,
Hales Hall
Loddon
Norfolk
NR14 6QW
Greenhouse and garden grapes.

The Romantic Garden Nursery
Swannington
Norwich
Norfolk
NR9 5NW
Specialist grower of topiary and ornamental standards, including plaitted stem oleanders, twisted stem bays, box spirals and animals, over 100 varieties of clematis, plus hardy and half hardy plants. Catalogue available.

Rougham Hall Nurseries
Ipswich Road
Rougham
Bury St Edmunds
Suffolk
IP30 9LY
Delphiniums, Iceland poppies and other hardy perennials.

Rushfields of Ledbury
Ross Road
Ledbury
Herefordshire
HR8 2LP
Herbaceous plants.

Southfields Nurseries
Lough Road
Holton-le-Clay
Grimsby
South Humberside
DN36 5HL
Cacti and succulents.

Southview Nurseries
Dept G
Chequers Lane
Eversley Cross
Hants
RG27 0NT
More than 200 choice perennials including old fashioned pinks, digitalis and penstemons. Catalogue for mail order service available.

Stems
Mountpleasant
Gressingham
Nr. Hornby
Lancaster
LA2 8LP
Argyranthemums plus a range of patio/bedding subjects including penstemons, gazania and others.

Suttons Seeds
Hele Road
Torquay
Devon
TQ2 7QJ
Vegetables and annuals.

Thompson & Morgan
Poplar Lane
Ipswich
IP8 3BU
Mail order seedsmen. Catalogue available upon request. An extensive range of annuals, perennials, alpines, house plants, cacti, trees and shrubs and vegetables.

Tilegates Garden
Little Common Lane
Bletchingley
Surrey
RH1 4QF
A vast collection of magnolias, rhododendrons, maples, birches, conifers and many more.

Philip Tivey & Sons
28 Wanlip Road
Syston
Nr. Leicester
Leicestershire
LE7 8PA
Dahlias and chrysanthemums.

Trehane Nurseries
Stapehill Road
Hampreston
Wimborne
Dorset
BH21 7NE
Camellias, azaleas, dwarf diamonds, glenn dales, satsukis and North Tisbury hybrids.

Tropical Rain Forest
66 Castle Grove
Avenue
Leeds
West Yorkshire
LS6 4BS
Bromeliads and exotic plants.

Unwins
Mail Order Dept. 529
Histon
Cambridge
CB4 4ZZ
A range of flower and vegetable seeds, including sweet peas, summer flowering bulbs, thornless bush roses, bedding plants and seedlings. Brochure available.

The Valley Clematis Nursery
Hainton
Lincoln
LN3 6LN
Mail order service – catalogue available.

The Vernon Geranium Nursery
Cuddington Way
Cheam
Sutton
Surrey
SM2 7JB
Large range of varieties including miniature geraniums. Mail order service available.

Water Garden Nursery
Wembworthy
Chulmleigh
Devon
EX18 7SG
Plants for all types of water gardening, sunny courtyards, shady moist woodlands, bog gardens and water meadows.

Woodfield Brothers
71 Townsend Road
Tiddington
Stratford-on-Avon
Warwickshire
CV37 7DF
Lupins.

Wyevale Gramphorn Garden Centres
Cressing Road
Braintree
Essex
CM7 8DL
A multiple retail garden centre group with 41 centres throughout the UK. Large range of plants includes over 2,500 varieties of shrubs and trees. Also offer an international plant finding service as well as their own Good Plant Guide.

MISCELLANEOUS

Boswell Roberts
Dept GA2
46 Keyes Road
London
NW2 3XA
Hand-painted garden umbrellas in a range of sizes and designs.

'Cons Co'
62 Askern Industrial Estate
Askern
Doncaster
DN6 0DD
Decorative, rust-free, cast aluminium brackets in high quality stoned enamel. Available in white or black.

Courtyard Pottery
Groundwell Road
Cricklade Road
Swindon
Wiltshire
Handmade, frost-proof terracotta pottery.

Dorset Weathervanes
284 Bournemouth Road
Charlton Marshall
Blandford Forum
Dorset
DT11 9NG
Over 30 different designs ranging from golfers to dragons. Making one-off designs a speciality.

Eastman Vaughan Wire Products Ltd
Stokes Croft
Bristol
BS1 3RD
Traditional Victorian rose garden arches. Made from woven wire mesh, weatherproof galvanized after manufacture.

English Basket and Hurdle Centre
Curload
Stoke St Gregory
Taunton
Somerset
TA3 6JD
Traditional wattle hurdles.

Good Directions Ltd
Sarum House
6 Winchester Street
Botley
Hampshire
SO32 3EE
Aged copper weathervanes and fibreglass cupolas.

J.E. Homewood & Son
20 Wey Hill
Haslemere
Surrey
GU27 1BX
Manufacturers of high-quality cleft chestnut fencing. Available in four different styles and six heights.

Paddock Fencing
French Drove
Thorney
Peterborough
PE6 0PQ
Ornamental Victorian-style tree fences. Wide enough to stake trees inside, even large specimens.

Pamel
The Cottage
Sproxton
Melton Mowbray
Leicestershire
LE14 4QS
Timber tubs produced in solid hardwood to a traditional design. Available in natural wood or white and three sizes. Alternative sizes and rectangular troughs made to order.

Roseney Farm Designs
Lanlivery
Bodmin
Cornwall
PL30 5DL
Makers of traditional style dovecotes, bird tables and planters. Several designs to choose from, kits also available.

Wells & Winter
Mereworth
Maidstone
Kent
ME18 5NB
Garden labels in zinc, copper, aluminium and also green plastic. Samples available.

West Meon Pottery
Church Lane
West Meon
Petersfield
Hants
GU32 1JW
Quality hand-thrown garden pots in all sizes.

The publishers would like to thank the following people for allowing Sue Atkinson and Paul Barker to photograph their gardens for the book:

Mr and Mrs Anderson, C.H. Bagot, Mr and Mrs B. Balmer, Lady Barbirolli, the Duke and Duchess of Beaufort, Mr and Mrs W.R. Benyon, Mr Bond, Dr and Mrs David Boyd, Roger Brook, Mr and Mrs C. Caplin, Mr Carver, Major and Mrs J.W. Chandos-Pole, Mr H.T.C Christie, Lady Clarissa Collin, Mr and Mrs N. Coote, Brigadier and Mrs C.F. Cox, Elizabeth Dorling, Mrs M. Dormer, Mr and Mrs P. Drysdale, Mr Honour, Mr and Mrs Denys Fraser, Lucy Gent, Dr. and Mrs F.W. Gifford, Mr and Mrs R. Goode, Mrs Grey, Joan and Robin Grout, Mrs Diana Guy, Mr and Mrs Handslip, Mr and Mrs David Hellewell, Paul and Kay Henderson, Mr and Mrs D.Heyward, Mr and Mrs John Heyward, Mrs Louise Hill, Adrian Hornsey, Mr R. Howard, John Hubbard, Dr. and Mrs Frank Hytten, Rosalind Ingrams, Mrs J. Joyce, Mr and Mrs E.C.B. Knight, Mr and Mrs C.R. Kruger, Mrs C.G. Lancaster, Dr. Sylvia Landsberg, Mrs M.D. Laverack, Mrs C. Lea, Mr and Mrs N. Lindsay-Fynn, Mrs C.M. Luke, Mrs McBurnie, Mr and Mrs R.R. Merton, Mrs Joan Moss, Mrs D.B. Nicholson, Mr and Mrs W.E. Ninniss, Mr and Mrs Norton, Paul O'Prey , Mr and Mrs A.J. Parsons, Mr Michael and the Hon. Mrs Payne, Mr and Mrs Alan Peck, M.R. Puddle, Mr and Mrs J. Pumfrey, Mr and Mrs P.A. Randall, Mr and Mrs Michael Redgrave, Mr and Mrs Simon Relph, Lord and Lady Remnant, Mr and Mrs W. Roxburgh, Mrs L. Rutherford, Colin Sanders, Mr and Mrs Ray Scott, Mr and Mrs C. Scroggs, Peter Sharp, Mrs Pauline Sheppey, Dr and Mrs Malcolm Slade, Mrs Betty Smith, Mrs Rosalind Squire, Mr and Mrs Michael Stanley, Miss Elizabeth Stephenson, Leonard Stocks, Dr. and Mrs Storrow, Arthur J. Thomas, Mr and Mrs Thomson, Mrs S. Tidd, Mr and Mrs Michael Todhunter, Mr and Mrs Derek Tolman, Lady Anne Tree, Mr and Mrs K. Wilkins.

The publishers would also like to thank the many organizations and individuals who allowed them to reproduce their photographs in this book. Page numbers are followed by codes denoting left (l), right (r), top (t), centre (c) and bottom (b); the location, owner and designer (D) of the garden are given in brackets where relevant.

Stephen Anderton: 83 r, 93 b; **Sue Atkinson/Mitchell Beazley**: 14, 28, 32, 34, 36 tl, tr, b, 40, 41 b, 43 b, 44 l, 45 bl, 47 br, 48 t, 49 t, 51 tr, 52 l, 54 l, 55 r, 57 b, 58, 59 tr, bl, br, 61 tr, 62 l, 63 r, 64 t, bl, br, 65 bl, 66-67, 68 tr, bl, 68-69 b, 70 l, 72 br, 73 tr, 78 l, 78-79, 82-3, 86 l, 90-91, 92 t, 93 t, 106 t, 109 cl, 111 r, 112 l, r, 113 bl, 114 r, 116 bc, 119 br, 121 t, 125 cl, b, 126, 128 r, 130 b, 131 l, 133 bl, 135, 136 l, 137 tl, 138 tl, tr, 141 t, 142 br, 143 l, 144 br, 145 tr, 146 t, bl, br, 147 r, 152 l, c, 156 r, 157 cr, 158, 159 cl, b, 160 r, 161 tr, b, 162 l, 163 t, 164 r, 165 tr, 167 tr, 169 bl, r, 173 t, 176 tl, r, 177 cl, bl, 184 t, bc, 185 l, r, 186 cl, bl, 190 t, bl, br, 191 cr, br, 193 cl, bl, br, 198 l, r, 200 r, 201 t, 202 l, tr, 204 t, c, bl, br, 205 c, 206 l, 210 t, 218 c, 219 tl, 221 t, bl, br, 224 tl, 227 cr, bl, 229 br, 230 br, 231 t, 232 bl, 236; **Paul Barker/Mitchell Beazley**: jacket insert, 6, 8-9, 13, 17, 30 tr, 35 t, c, b, 37 b, 41 tl, 42, 47 tl, bl, 48-49 b, 50 bl, 52-53 b, 54 t, 54-55 b, 55 tl, tr, 59 tl, 62-3, 65 t, 67 t, b, 69 br, 70-71, 71 r, 72 bl, 72-73 t, 73 cr, bl, br, 82 l, 91 r, 99 r, 104, 106 br, 107 t, b, 109 b, 115 t, 117 r, 119 c, bl, 123 tl, 125 t, c, 129 l, 130 tr, 134 l, r, 138 bl, 142 t, bl, 145 tl, 146 c, 147 l, 153 cl, br, 156 l, 157 bl, br, 159 cr, 160 l, 161 tl, 162 r, 163 cr, b, 165 tl, 167 c, 170 tl, 171 t, cr, br, 172 l, 177 cr, 178 t, 180 bl, 184 bl, 187 tl, br, 192 tl, tr, 195 bl, 197 tr, br, 199 br, 201 b, 207 tr, 208 tr, 214 tl, bl, 215 r, 216 tl, b, 217 tr, 219 tr, 220 r, 222, 223 tr, c, 224 br, 227 br, 229 bl, 230 t, 233 t, 237 b; **Tommy Candler**: 85 t, 116 c, 121 cl, 129 r, 130 tl, 131 r, 142 tr, 150 r, 166 r, 172 r, 173 cl, 180 tl, 186 br, 192 br, 197 bl, 199 bl, 205 b, 206 r, 208 bl, br, 210 c, 211 bl, br, 212 r, 214 br, 217 bl, 219 bl, 225 b, 231 b, 232 tr; **Eric Crichton**: jacket background, 38 l, r, 41 tr, 43 t, 45 t, br, 48 bl, 50-1 t, 53 r, 60 t, b, 68 tl, 80 t, bl, 81 c, 87 r, 88 b, 88-9, 89 t, 100 tr, 105 l, 108 l, 127 r, 157 cl, 163 cl, 171 bl, 180 br, 182 r, 183 t, b, 184 tr, 188 t, 191 tl, 194 r, 223 b, 225 t, 237 t, 238 b; **The Garden Picture Library: Jerry Pavia** 76 tl, b, 121 cr; **Brian Carter** 232 br; **Clay Perry** 232 tl, 233 b, **Ron Sutherland** 61 tl; **John Glover**: 128 l, 148 t, 216 tr, 217 c; **Jerry Harpur**: half title (D: Claus Scheinert, Alpes Maritimes), title (Heale House, Middle Woodford, Wilts), 4 (Arbigland, Kirkbean, Dumfries), 11 (Philip Watson, Fredericksburg, Virginia), 19 (D: Claus Scheinert, Alpes Maritimes), 26-27 (D: Claus Scheinert, Alpes Maritimes), 30 tl, b (D: Claus Scheinert, Alpes Maritimes), 31 (D: Claus Scheinert, Alpes Maritimes), 33 t, b (D: Claus Scheinert, Alpes Maritimes), 39 b (D: Claus Scheinert, Alpes Maritimes), 50-51 b (D: Susie Ranicar, Tasmania), 61 b (Meadowbrook Farm, Philadelphia), 74 l (Polly Park, Canberra, Australia), 74-75 (D: Patrick Miller, San Francisco), 75 r (D: Gary Orr, San Francisco), 76 tr (D: Keyes Landscape, Camden, London), 77 t (D: Garrett Eckbo, San Francisco), 81 t (D: Bruce Kelly, New York), 86-87 (Japanese Stroll Garden, Long Island), 88 tl (D: John Patrick, Melbourne, Victoria), 100 tl (D: Ann Alexander-Sinclair), 101 t, br (D: Edwina von Gal, New York), 102-3 (Wentworth, Sydney), 105 r (Dreamthorpe, Macedon, Victoria), 109 t (D: John Brooks, Denmans, Fontwell, Sussex), 110 (Hazelbury Manor, Box, Wilts.), cl (D: Mark Laurence), cr (Wycken Hall, Stanton, Suffolk) b (Stonecrop, Coldspring, New York State), 111 l (D: Patrick Miller, San Francisco), 113 top (D: Oehme & van Sweden, Washington DC), 114 l (Panmure, Stirling, Western Australia), 116 t (D: Oehme & van Sweden, Washington DC), 116 bl (D: Michael Balston, Patney, Wilts.) r (D: Christopher Masson, London), 117 l (D: Ron Simple, Philadelphia), 118 t, c (Contractor: Berry's Garden Construction Co.), 119 t (D: Ruth Shellhorn, Los Angeles), 120 l (D: Chris Rosmini, Los Angeles) r (D: Michael Branch, Wantage, Berks.), 122 l (D: Topher Delaney, San Francisco), 123 b (D: Claus Scheinert, Alpes Maritimes), 124 cl (D: Fred Watson, New Hampshire), 127 l (D: Edwina von Gal, New York), 132 l (D: Claus Scheinert, Alpes Maritimes), 133 t (Ladew Garden, Maryland) br (Dumbarton Oaks, Georgetown, Washington DC), 136 r (D: Gos Lieber), 137 bl (D: Ann Griot, Los Angeles) r (Mr. and Mrs. Klok, Hobart, Tasmania), 139 (Mr. and Mrs. Potts, Chiffchaffs Nursery, Bourton, Dorset), 140 l (Lower Hall, Worfield, Shropshire), r, 144 bl (D: Jan Martinez, Alkam, Kent), 145 cl (Bradenham Hall, Norfolk), cr (House of Pitmuies, Guthrie by Forfar, Tayside), 148 c, bl (D: Bruce Kelly, New York), br (D: Oehme & van Sweden, Washington DC), 149 t (D: Bruce Kelly, New York), cl (Dumbarton Oaks, Georgetown, Washington DC), cr (Williamsburg, Virginia), 150 l (House of Pitmuies, Guthrie by Forfar, Tayside), 151 tl (D: Peter Wooster, Roxbury, Connecticut), tr (Ballarat, Victoria), bl (Heale House, Middle Woodford, Wilts.), br (D: Anne Griot, Los Angeles), 153 tr (D: Bruce Kelly, New York), b (House of Pitmuies, Guthrie by Forfar, Tayside), 154-155 (D: Simon Fraser, Fulham, London), 157 tr (D: Fred Watson, New Hampshire), 159 t (Kay Purvis, Cairns, Queensland), 164 l (D: Keith Corlett, New York), 165 c (D: Edwina von Gal, New York), 166 l (D: Claus Scheinert, Alpes Maritimes), 167 tl (D: Ragna Goddard, Higganum, Connecticut), 171 cl (Dumbarton Oaks, Georgetown, Washington DC), 174 (Lower Hall, Worfield, Shropshire), 175 r (Hazleby House, North End, Newbury, Berks.), 176 br (D: Claus Scheinert, Alpes Maritimes), 178 b (D: Joe Eck and Wayne Winterrowd, Readsboro, Vermont), 179 l (Heale House, Middle Woodford, Wilts.), r (Arbigland, Kirkbean, Dumfries), 180 tr (Lower Hall, Worfield, Shropshire), 181 tr (Olivers, Colchester, Essex) and b (Heale House, Middle Woodford, Wilts.), 191 tr (King Henry's Hunting Lodge, Odiham, Hants.), 195 tl (Red Hill Farm, Deloraine, Tasmania), 196 tl (D: Claus Scheinert, Alpes Maritimes), bl (Jardin des Colombieres, Menton, Alpes Maritimes), 208 tl (D: Ragna Goddard, Higganum, Connecticut), 209 l (Ladew Garden, Maryland), 214 tr (Newry, Longford, Tasmania), 220 l (D: Keith Corlett, New York), 224 bl (D: Claus Scheinert, Alpes Maritimes), 226 b (D: Claus Scheinert, Alpes Maritimes), 227 tl (Ladew Garden, Maryland), 229 tl (D: Michael Wayman, Sydney, New South Wales), 230 cl (D: Bob Dash, Sagaponack, Long Island, NY), 231 c (D: Keith Corlett, New York); **John Heseltine**: 77 bl, 113 br, 124 br; **Marijke Heuff**: 65 bl (Mrs. M. van Bennekom-Scheffer), 69 tl(Mr. J. van den Brink), 81 b, 84 t (Mr. L.J.Ph Groeneveld) and b (Jaap Nieuwenhuis and Paula Thies), 88 tr, 115 c, 138 br, 141 cl, 210 b (Mr. J. van den Brink), 219 br (Mrs. M. van Bennekom-Scheffer), 224 tr (Mrs. M. van Bennekom-Scheffer), 226 tl (Mrs. L. Goossenaerts-Miedema), 227 tr (Jaap Nieuwenhuis and Paula Thies); **Hozelock Ltd.**: 221 c; **Andrew Lawson**: 44 r, 122 r, 124 bl, 141 cr, 173 br, 209 r; **James Merrell/Mitchell Beazley**: 213 b; **Clive Nichols**: 29 t, 46, 47 tr, 80 br, 85 b, 98 l, 100 b (D: Anthony Noel), 106 bl, 108 r, 109 cr, 123 tr, 138 cr (D: Anthony Noel), 143 r, 168 l, r, 169 c, 170 c, 175 l, 177 t, 178 c, 189 l, 194 l (D: Anthony Noel), 195 br (D: Anthony Noel), 200 l, 202 br, 205 tl, tr, 207 tl, 215 l, 217 br (D: Anthony Noel), 218 t, b (D: Anthony Noel), 223 tl, 226 tr (D: Anthony Noel), 238 t, 239; **Hugh Palmer**: 39 t, 52-53 b, 69 tr, 77 br, 79 r, 92 b, 98-9, 101 bl, 137 top r, 144 t, 153 tl, 170 tr, 182 l, 188, 189 r, 191 bl, 192 bl, 193 tl, tr, 196 tr, br, 199 tl, 207 b, 208 cr, 211 tl, 212 l, 213 tl, tr, 228, 229 tr, 234-235; **Photos Horticultural**: 51 br; **Reed Consumer Books Picture Library**: 29 b, 37 t, 49 br, 56, 90 l, 132 l, 181 tl.

From p. 240 to p.347 (Directory section) all photographs are by **Andrew Lawson**, with the following exceptions:
A-Z Botanical Collection 274 tr, 275 tc, cl, 276 cl, 278 tr, 279 bl, 285 tr, 286 bl, bl; **Sue Atkinson/ Mitchell Beazley** 257, 258 b, 343 b; **Paul Barker/Mitchell Beazley** 256, 268, 270, 331 t, 332 t, 343 t; **Eric Crichton** 254 tc, 255 b, 259 t, 261 bc, 264 tr, 272 cr, 274 b, 277 tl, 278 bc, 279 br, 283 cl, 284 tc, 285 tl, 287 bl, bc, 291 bl, 292 bc, 308 t, c, 309 tr, 310 tr, 312 tr, 313 bl, 318 tr, 319 tl, bl, 324 t, 325 cl, 331 b, 335 bc, 338 t, 340 l, 341 tl; **Garden Picture Library (Linda Burgess)** 314, **(John Glover)** 316 b; **John Glover** 250 c, 253 tc, 315 t, b, 316 t; **Derek Gould** 253 cr, 267 tl, 272 b, 275 bc; **Jerry Harpur** 259 b (Home Farm, Balscote, Oxfordshire), 269 b (Dreamthorpe, Macedon, Victoria), 288 ('Churchill', Campania, Tasmania), 324 b (D: Philip Watson, Fredericksburg, Virginia), 332 b (Royal Horticultural Society, Wisley, Surrey), 336 (D: Ann Griot, Los Angeles), 337 t (D: Victor Nelson, New York) and b, 338 b (Meadowbrook Farm, Philadelphia), 342 (D: Claus Scheinert, Alpes Maritimes); **Marijke Heuff** 258 t (Mrs. L. Goossenaerts-Miedema), 281 t (Mr. and Mrs. Bremmer-Smit), 282 t, b, 289 (Mr. and Mrs. Bremmer-Smit); **Clive Nichols** 269 t, 271 tl, 280, 294, 322, 323 t, b, 330; **Hugh Palmer** 296; **Photos Horticultural** 250 tl, 254 bl, 262 tc, 275 tl, 284 bl, 285 br, 291 cr, 292 tc, 293 bc, 298 tr, bl, 299 tc, 313 tc, tr, 318 tr, 334 tr, 335 tc, 339 r, 341 c; **Reed Consumer Books Picture Library**: 261 tc, 265 bl, 305 tl, tc, 340 tc; **Harry Smith Horticultural Collection** 275 cr, 279 tr, 293 tl, 303 bl, 312 tc, 335 bl, 346 br, 347 b.